The Legacy of Edith Kramer

The Legacy of Edith Kramer presents a unique exploration into the life and work of the groundbreaking artist and art therapist. This edited volume examines the artist's personal and cultural history prior to relocating to the United States, as well as the later years when she worked as an artist, art therapist, and teacher as she developed her theoretical understanding of art therapy. Kramer's solutions to creating a meaningful artist's life run throughout the chapters within this book, and provide the reader with a sense of what is possible. Written by an international group of contributors, this informative new text offers a multifaceted view of Edith Kramer that will be appreciated by current and future art therapists looking to better understand Kramer's exceptional mind and contributions to the field.

Lani Gerity is an author and art therapist with a master's and a doctorate from NYU. She studied with Edith Kramer and edited Edith's *Art as Therapy: Collected Papers*. She maintains a website, blogs, and online groups filled with encouragement and alternative arts for artists, art therapists, and art educators.

Susan Ainlay Anand is a graduate of the NYU art therapy program where she was trained by Edith Kramer. As an instructor in the Department of Psychiatry at the University of Mississippi Medical Center, Susan provides art therapy services and teaches psychiatry residents about the use of art therapy with medically ill and psychiatric patients.

The Legacy of Edith Kramer
A Multifaceted View

Edited by Lani Gerity and
Susan Ainlay Anand

NEW YORK AND LONDON

First edition published 2018
by Routledge
711 Third Avenue, New York, NY 10017

and by Routledge
2 Park Square, Milton Park, Abingdon, Oxon, OX14 4RN

Routledge is an imprint of the Taylor & Francis Group, an informa business

© 2018 Taylor & Francis

The right of the editors to be identified as the authors of the editorial material, and of the authors for their individual chapters, has been asserted in accordance with sections 77 and 78 of the Copyright, Designs and Patents Act 1988.

All rights reserved. No part of this book may be reprinted or reproduced or utilized in any form or by any electronic, mechanical, or other means, now known or hereafter invented, including photocopying and recording, or in any information storage or retrieval system, without permission in writing from the publishers.

Trademark notice: Product or corporate names may be trademarks or registered trademarks, and are used only for identification and explanation without intent to infringe.

Library of Congress Cataloging-in-Publication Data
Names: Gerity, Lani Alaine, 1953– editor. | Anand, Susan Ainlay, editor.
Title: The legacy of Edith Kramer : a multifaceted view / edited by
    Lani Gerity and Susan Ainlay Anand.
Description: First edition. | New York : Routledge, 2018. | Includes
    bibliographical references.
Identifiers: LCCN 2017027290 | ISBN 9781138681231 (hbk. : alk. paper) |
    ISBN 9781138681248 (pbk. : alk. paper) | ISBN 9781315545912 (ebk.)
Subjects: | MESH: Kramer, Edith, 1916–2014. | Art Therapy | Child |
    Paintings—psychology | Psychoanalytic Interpretation | Austria |
    United States | Biography
Classification: LCC RC489.A7 | NLM WZ 100 | DDC 616.89/1656—dc23
LC record available at https://lccn.loc.gov/2017027290

ISBN: 978-1-138-68123-1 (hbk)
ISBN: 978-1-138-68124-8 (pbk)
ISBN: 978-1-315-54591-2 (ebk)

Typeset in ITC Galliard
by Apex CoVantage, LLC

Visit the companion website: www.routledge.com/cw/gerity

For Edith
With love from all of us

Contents

List of Figures	xii
Foreword: A Fortunate Life	xvi
EDITH KRAMER	
Acknowledgments	xxiv
Notes on Contributors	xxv

**Introduction: A Generous and Challenging
Artist's Worldview** 1

LANI GERITY AND SUSAN AINLAY ANAND

History and Context 13

1 Feelings That Cannot Be Put into Words 15

DARCY MARLOW

2 Mumi Kramer, Grundlsee, and the Caring Net 23

JOHANNES REICHMAYR, CHARLOTTE ZWIAUER, LANI GERITY,
MARTHA HAESELER, AND EDITH KRAMER

3 Edith Kramer Remembered 33

ANNI BERGMAN

**4 Edith Kramer on Friedl Dicker-Brandeis,
Erna Furman, and Terezin** 38

INTERVIEWS WITH ELENA MAKAROVA

More Recent History 47

5 Edith Kramer: A Generous, Generative Genius 49

JUDITH A. RUBIN

viii *Contents*

6 **Importance of Cultural Roots** 56
IRENE ROSNER DAVID

7 **Edith Kramer at New York University: Recollections** 59
LAURIE WILSON

8 **Teaching with Edith** 67
IKUKO ACOSTA

9 **Art Therapy Experiences with Edith and a Group of Adults** 71
RAFFAELLA BORTINO, WILMA CIPRIANI, AND
RAFFAELA CAROLA LORIO

Artist Identity 81

10 **Edith Kramer's Artistic Legacy: Beyond the Studio** 83
GEOFFREY A. THOMPSON

11 **Remembering Edith Kramer** 91
KARL PALLAUF
(TRANSLATOR, MARTHA HAESELER)

12 **An Edith Collage** 93
KATHERINE WILLIAMS

13 **The Mosaic** 96
EDITH KRAMER

14 **Create Your Own: Kramer's Criteria for Quality
as Central to Art Therapy** 99
JORDAN S. POTASH

Edith Kramer's Theoretical Concepts 105

15 **Edith Kramer's Notion of "Quality"** 107
ELIZABETH STONE

16 **On Edith Kramer's Seminal Concept of Sublimation
in Art Therapy** 115
ELIZABETH STONE

Contents ix

17 **Sublimation Then and Now** 126
LAURIE WILSON

18 **The Building of an Artist's Identity** 133
KEVIN MAXWELL

19 **Edith Kramer's Third Hand: Intervention in Art Therapy** 141
KARIN DANNECKER

20 **Kramer's Sublimation: Creative Expansion or Limitation?** 148
DAVID HENLEY

Memories 157

21 **Panel Remarks: Edith Kramer** 159
DAVID HENLEY

22 **Gleaning the Pearls: Reflections of a Student** 162
KATHRYN E. BARD

23 **Tales of Edith** 166
PATTI GREENBERG

24 **Formed Expression** 171
DAVID HENLEY

Edith Kramer's Concepts Applied to Practice 183

25 **Edith's Legacy as Artist and Art Therapist in the Art Room** 185
MARTHA HAESELER

26 **Hector: A Case Study Illustrating Edith's Teachings** 195
MARTHA HAESELER

27 **Understanding Lineage, Difference, and the Contemplative Dimensions of Edith Kramer's Art as Therapy Model** 205
MICHAEL A. FRANKLIN

x *Contents*

28 Art and Cancer: Transference and Countertransference: Channeling Edith Kramer 214
ESTHER DREIFUSS-KATTAN

29 Edith Kramer's Influence on the Development of Medical Art Therapy 223
IRENE ROSNER DAVID

30 Experiences of Learning from Edith Kramer and Translating Her Book 228
SHYUEYING CHIANG

31 Edith, Puppets, and the Kindly Superego 236
LANI GERITY

Art, Art Therapy, and Culture 245

32 Quality and Inner Satisfaction: Re-Visiting the Importance of Quality in Art and Art Therapy 247
EDITH KRAMER, SUSAN AINLAY ANAND, AND LANI GERITY

33 Cultural Gifts of Wisdom, Hope, and Beauty 258
EDITH KRAMER, LANI GERITY, AND SUSAN AINLAY ANAND

34 Religion and Cultural Humility: Lessons Learned in Conversation and Practice 269
SUSAN AINLAY ANAND

35 Sense of Place: Edith Kramer's Wisdom for Times of Isolation and Dissociation 275
SUSAN AINLAY ANAND

Saying Goodbye 285

36 Do You Require Inspiration Just to Breathe? 287
ELENA MAKAROVA
(TRANSLATOR, TALI MAGIDSON)

37 Lyceum Art Therapy Training Program 297
MARGHERITA GANDINI
(TRANSLATOR, ELEONORA MARCHESI)

Contents xi

38 On Leaving and Preserving 305

DAVID HENLEY

**39 Creating a World of Possibility: Life Lessons
from Edith Kramer** 310

LANI GERITY

40 Conclusions: Is This the End or the Beginning? 317

SUSAN AINLAY ANAND AND LANI GERITY

Index 323

Figures

F.1 Edith painting after the Blitz. Photo contributed
by David Henley — xviii

F.2 A fair in the rubble of urban renewal. Oil painting
by Edith Kramer — xx

I.1 *In the Quietness of Her Studio*. Photograph taken
by Raffaela Carola Lorio — 3

I.2 *Her Teapot*. Photograph taken by Raffaela Carola Lorio — 4

I.3 *Her Braid*. Photograph taken by Raffaela Carola Lorio — 5

1.1 Etching by Edith Kramer. Christmas card from the
collection of Elena Makarova — 21

2.1 First set of film stills: Mädi's house, Pepa Kramer,
Mädi Olden, and Liesl Neumann on the balcony.
Mädi and, finally, Mädi with Pepa passing behind her. — 27

2.2 Second set of film stills: Siegfried "Brassi" Bernfeld
with Mumi, with an unidentified guest, being kissed
by Liesl, and Bernfeld wading. — 28

3.1 Edith Kramer sketching in Toronto, Canada. Photo by
Herschel J. Stroyman — 34

3.2 Edith and Anni — 36

6.1 *Beets and Onions*, 1988. Oil painting by Edith Kramer — 57

7.1 Edith teaching students at New York University.
Photo taken by Herschel J. Stroyman — 64

7.2 Retirement party for Laurie Wilson with Edith Kramer,
NYU faculty, and students — 66

8.1 Edith Kramer and Ikuko Acosta teaching together
at New York University — 69

9.1 Edith's painting of a mother and child — 75

9.2 Painting of a boat by Carlo — 76

9.3 Barbara's clay sculpture depicting a mother and her child — 78

10.1 Treasured objects in Edith Kramer's loft — 84

10.2 Gold still life with etching plates. Circa 2001. Oil, gold leaf,
and egg tempera on canvas by Edith Kramer — 88

10.3 *Landscape: The Alps*, circa 1935. Watercolor painting by
Edith Kramer — 89

Figures   xiii

12.1	Katherine Williams' granddaughters with the Edith Kramer subway mosaic at the Spring Street Station, New York City	94
13.1	Subway mosaic at Spring Street Subway Station. Photo by Herschel J. Stroyman	97
14.1	My sister's painting	100
15.1	Sitting clay figure	113
16.1	Reproduction of O'Keeffe's *Brooklyn Bridge* as Emma copies it	121
16.2	Large and small flowers, after Georgia O'Keeffe	122
16.3	Four flat clay heads	123
17.1	*Sky Presence I* (detail). Photograph taken by Laurie Wilson	130
18.1	*Broken Oven*. Tempera on paper	138
18.2	*Fixed Oven*. Tempera on paper	139
19.1	Edith Kramer and Karin Dannecker, 1990, Exhibit in der Galerie Taube, Berlin	142
20.1	Clay sculpture (unfinished) by Christopher	149
20.2	*Upon Leaving Chicago*. Graphite drawing by David Henley	151
20.3	*Uneasy Sleep*. Oil on sheet metal by Edith Kramer	154
22.1	*Alpine Wonders*. Oil on canvas by Kathryn E. Bard	165
23.1	Edith and Christmas tree. Photo from David Henley (no date)	169
24.1	*Six Persimmons*. Ink on paper by Mu Ch'i Fa-Ch'ang	172
24.2	Drawings by Edith Kramer (no date). Copy of oil painting by Velazquez. *Portrait of Sebastián de Morra* (1645).	176
24.3	Drawing by Edith Kramer (1930) of King Louis XVI and Marie Antoinette	180
25.1	Ceramic figures in subway. Clay and metal sculpture by Edith Kramer	187
26.1	*He Preyed at Dusk and Prayed at Dawn*. Painting by Hector	199
26.2	*Priests and Nuns in Catholic Heaven*. Painting by Hector	199
26.3	*Mother and Child*	203
28.1	*UCLA–SM, 2008, Salvage Chemo Ride*. Pen and markers on paper	217
28.2	*Untitled*, 2008. Pen and markers on paper	218
28.3	*Day after Chemo*. Pen and marker on paper	219
29.1	*Breast on Lawn*. Drawing by cancer patient	225
30.1	Cover of the Chinese version of *Art as Therapy with Children*	233
30.2	Edith with Shyueying Chiang	234
31.1	Edith Kramer and puppet. Photo by Edward Glanville	242
32.1	Photograph of fountain in Paris	249
32.2	Margaret at her home, Margaret's Grocery in Vicksburg, Mississippi, 2001	252
32.3	Mr George Berry in his home, Pearl, Mississippi, 2001	255
33.1	L.V. Hull in her home in Kosciusko, Mississippi, 2001	264
33.2	Young women being taught how to quilt at Cultural Crossroads, Port Gibson, Mississippi	265

xiv   *Figures*

33.3	Bottle Tree photo taken in Mississippi by photographer Eyd Kazery	267
34.1	Jane's puppet, "Lucifer"	272
35.1	Pastel drawing by a medical student showing him reaching out to a patient in distress	279
35.2	"Ganesha." Clay figure made by a resident raised in India	281
36.1	Edith Kramer's response to one of Friedl's exercises	291
36.2	Ruth Gutmann's response to Friedl's exercises in Terezin	292
36.3	Edith Kramer's response to one of Friedl's exercises	292
36.4	Charcoal study by Friedl Dicker-Brandeis from Bauhaus	293
37.1	E.Kr.A.M. logo	299
37.2	Portrait of Edith Kramer by female student in art therapy	302
37.3	"Thank you Edith." Collected papers placed on Edith Kramer's coffin	304
38.1	Painting by Edith Kramer. Photo courtesy of David Henley and New York University, Art Therapy Program	306
39.1	Juniper tree print by Edith Kramer. Contributed by Elena Makarova	313
39.2	*Don't Give Up*. Paper and digital collage by Lani Gerity	315
40.1	Laura McCann with a child's painting of a wedding. Photo by Susan Anand	319
40.2	Laura McCann with a child's painting, *Young Man with Switchblade*. Photo by Susan Anand	320

List of Center Figures

1   Herschel J. Stroyman – Edith Kramer at Wiltwyck School for Boys art show
2   Herschel J. Stroyman – Edith Kramer and Eleanor Roosevelt at Wiltwyck School for Boys art show
3   Herschel J. Stroyman – Edith Kramer
4   Herschel J. Stroyman – Edith Kramer's painting of "urban renewal"
5   Herschel J. Stroyman – Edith painting Herschel's children
6   Herschel J. Stroyman – Herschel's children supervising Edith
7   Herschel J. Stroyman – *Working in Stillness*
8   Herschel J. Stroyman – *The Loft 1*
9   Herschel J. Stroyman – Edith Kramer
10 Herschel J. Stroyman – *The Loft 2*
11 Herschel J. Stroyman – Edith Kramer with bas-relief subway study
12 Herschel J. Stroyman – Edith Kramer teaching at NYU
13 Herschel J. Stroyman – Edith Kramer studying drawings made with Friedl Dicker's techniques
14 Herschel J. Stroyman – *Objects in Window*
15 Herschel J. Stroyman – *Devil Puppet Obscured*

Figures xv

16 Herschel J. Stroyman – Edith Kramer
17 Herschel J. Stroyman – *Ladies and Bathtubs 1*
18 Herschel J. Stroyman – *Ladies and Bathtubs 2*
19 Herschel J. Stroyman – Edith and friends
20 Edith Kramer and Herschel J. Stroyman
21 Karin Dannecker – *Grundlsee*
22 Edith Kramer – *Child in Prague* (from Lani Gerity)
23 Edith Kramer – *Machinist during World War II* (from Lani Gerity)
24 Edith Kramer – *London after the Blitz* (from Martha Haeseler)
25 Edith Kramer – *Kostia Bergman* (from Lani Gerity)
26 Edith Kramer – *New York Subway* (from Kathryn Bard)
27 Edith Kramer – *Herschel J. Stroyman and Family*
   (from Herschel J. Stroyman)
28 Edith Kramer – *Still Life 1* (from Herschel J. Stroyman)
29 Edith Kramer – *Aunt Liesl* (from Kathryn Bard)
30 Edith Kramer – *Still Life 2* (from Herschel J. Stroyman)
31 Edith Kramer – *Juniper Tree* (from Susan Anand)
32 Edith Kramer – *Landscape* (from David Henley)
33 Edith Kramer – *Mountains* (from Martha Haeseler)
34 Edith Kramer – *New York Roof Top* (from Kathryn Bard)
35 Edith Kramer – *Still Life 3* (from Martha Haeseler)
36 Edith Kramer – *Vegetable Still Life* (from Martha Haeseler)
37 Edith Kramer – *Still Life in Window* (from Kathryn Bard)
38 Edith Kramer – *Potted Plants* (from Vinod Anand)
39 Edith Kramer – *Hay Stacks* (from Karin Dannecker)
40 Edith Kramer – *Telephone Book Page 1* (from Herschel J. Stroyman)
41 Edith Kramer – *Telephone Book Page 2* (from Herschel J. Stroyman)

Foreword
A Fortunate Life[1]

Edith Kramer

I'm going to tell you of my life in New York City, as it presented itself to me as an artist, later also as an art therapist, with brief excursions into other topics like nature, still life, and portraits and so forth (Kramer, 1994).

I have been a very fortunate person. Fortunate to have the chance to come to America, otherwise I would scarcely have survived the Nazi time in my native Austria. Fortunate in my upbringing, growing up in a bohemian environment, full of actors, psychoanalysts, artists, revolutionaries, where being an eccentric, where being stubborn and self-willed was quite normal. I did not have to fight to be myself. I was liberated from conventions; I did not have to liberate myself. I wasn't a part of this liberation movement because that was all prepared for me. This saved much energy that could be used for doing my work. I was fortunate to be in an environment during a time when I could learn my craft as a disciple from good artists for very little money, rather than as an art student. I think artists, even if they are competitive toward other well-known artists, are generous with young artists whom they like and respect. So I got my training without having to go into debt.

I worked with Friedl Dicker, a student of Johannes Itten, who was in Vienna before going to Bauhaus. Friedl also worked at the Bauhaus so this also was certainly part of my background. I worked with Fritz Wotruba, as a stone carving sculptor, as well as a few other sculptors. I was also fortunate to live in Vienna during a time when I could be acquainted with Freudian psychoanalysis (in its revolutionary days not its stodgy days) and with progressive art education theories. Viktor Lowenfeld was working with the blind in Vienna at that time, and that was the foundation of his theories of teaching art to children, which culminated in his book, *Creative and Mental Growth* (1947).

I was fortunate that when I came to this country, I was sufficiently formed as an artist and able to continue on my own. I was 22 years old, healthy, and educated; I could read with comprehension and knew where to find any information that I might need. I was at an age when it was natural to embark on a new career or adventure, live in a new environment, and begin a new life. I didn't have to suffer as many older people did when they were uprooted. It was the right time for me to come to the United States.

Foreword: A Fortunate Life xvii

Looking back at the art I did prior to coming to the United States I see there were certain interests that began even then and have continued. I began to study art exclusively from age 18 when I finished high school. I was interested in industrial landscapes, ordinary people doing ordinary things together, and in children doing art. All this was there, even then.

When I came to New York, it was my good fortune that the Little Red School House needed a shop teacher but couldn't afford the salary of one. They hoped to find among all the refugees coming over from Europe, a sculptor who would be more pliable and inventive than a carpenter who would be too rigid to work with children. This person turned out to be me. Elisabeth Irwin, an independent spirit and founder of the Little Red School House, sensed that same spirit in me. She allowed me to live in a little room that was in the school building. I could get my food from the leftovers in the kitchen, and was given some pocket money. They had hoped for a man in this position, but were reconciled with me. I worked as their shop teacher for three years.

Again, I was very lucky to fall into this bohemian environment, much like the environment that I came from. The bohemian environment of Vienna and Prague in 1938 was not so different from Greenwich Village in 1938, so it was not such a terrible culture shock when I moved here.

When the United States entered WWII, I became a machinist in a little shop on Grant Street. Grant Street at that time was one machine shop after another, a whole row of machine shops. If you wanted to be a toolmaker, you could start at one end of Grant Street and work your way to the other end, and you would be fully trained by the end. I worked there and enjoyed it. I had an agreement with the boss that after doing my shift, I could punch out and stay on and do drawings. I drew every night and enjoyed it very much. The greatest compliment I received from the other machinists was that if I had started young enough I could have been a toolmaker. Some of this work I enjoyed as an artist because you must be good with your hands and as a sculptor, you must do a bit of carpentry, a bit of this and that. It came easy to me. I had an offer at that time to be a shop teacher at City and Country, a good progressive school, because their shop teacher was drafted in the army. I decided to stay on as a machinist because I knew I would never have that kind of chance again, to do that kind of work.

When the war was over, I decided to go back to Europe because I had come to the US under duress. I figured I should find out if I really wanted to stay here, or go back home, or live in Paris. Somehow I found a way to do that and stayed in Europe for a year and a half and was able to paint.

I did some paintings of London following the Blitz, always painting on the spot. The ruins with weeds growing among them, was a very interesting sight to me.

Another interesting place to paint was the Amiens Cathedral, situated on a ridge overlooking the River Somme in Amiens. It was standing in a wilderness. Amiens had been bombed and most of the other buildings had collapsed, but

Figure F.1 Edith painting after the Blitz. Photo contributed by David Henley

the cathedral was built on arches and withstood the bombing. The windows of the cathedral had been removed to save them, which resulted in a strange appearance, so I did paintings there.

I decided to come back to the United States for several reasons. I had considered living in France, which I loved, but there was an unbroken line of visual artists and styles developing from the Romans on to the present. Because it was a mecca, receptive to artists from the whole world throughout history, I felt "so who needs one more artist in Paris?" America, on the other hand, was new territory with the beginnings of local schools – the Hudson River School, paintings of the West, paintings of the City, and of the industrial landscapes in America. However, this was swept away by abstract art and a kind of international style of a horrible, terrible sameness. I felt I could do something in America that would be new. Another reason for coming back was more practical in that it is easier to live on part-time work in the States than in Europe; at that time, it was possible to be poor without being destitute in New York. I returned in 1950 and even found a livelihood that I could pursue in good conscience without

Foreword: A Fortunate Life xix

selling my soul; I became an art therapist. The suggestion came from outside. People said, "You have been analyzed, you know a lot about psychoanalysis. You are a good teacher and you get along with difficult children. Put all this together and make something of it." There was one psychoanalyst who knew me, Viola Wertheim Bernard, who was on the professional advisory board of Wiltwyck School for Boys, where she suggested me for a position. In 1936, the school had been set up as an experimental summer camp for African-American juvenile delinquents and potential juvenile delinquents. Later, it became a year-round residential school, and in 1942 Judge Justine Wise Polier, Eleanor Roosevelt, and other interested judges were able to incorporate Wiltwyck as an interracial and non-sectarian institution. These judges wanted to create a place in New York City for children who needed treatment outside their homes, so they founded this school, which remained open until 1981.

I worked at Wiltwyck for seven years. When I first started there, Viola Bernard felt they needed an art teacher, an art therapist, because everything in this place had to be named "therapy," so I agreed to call what I did art therapy. There were some that felt they needed another counselor, but even they got used to me, and I was able to do a good job.

Art is something that is external to us. The children I worked with didn't have a set idea about what art was. It seemed amoral; it could do wild, crazy, and aggressive things without destroying them or anyone else. Childhood is a time when we have to live symbolically, we don't live quite in the real world entirely all the time; we prepare ourselves for adult life by living symbolically. Art is natural with children.

After five years of working at Wiltwyck, I felt that a book could be written about this work, and the board provided the financial backing to do so. In 1958, my first book, *Art Therapy in a Children's Community*, was published, and with that I was established as one of the pioneers of this new profession that kept me in bread and butter.

The first place I taught art therapy was at the New School for Social Research, a haven for people with new ideas. It was my luck that I did not have to go to school to be a teacher of art therapy, to be a professor, and I never had to take out a loan. I lived in New York City during this time on Orchard Street, in a rent-controlled apartment. I could draw on the street, even at night, which would not be as easy to do today. I had a little Volkswagen that I could sit in and paint. It worked okay. I'd paint the Sara Delano Roosevelt Park between Forsyth and Chrystie Street. After doing some paintings there I decided to do a collage.

I usually made a collage when I got stuck with a color or when something wasn't working in my painting. I would then embark on this terrible process of collage, where my whole apartment was turned into a pallette, paper all over, and I would stand on a chair or a ladder and look down on my work. I was busy for months, caught in the paper. But it was worth it, because I could find colors that I could never invent, and I came out of it with a new sense of color and structure that was very helpful for my painting. Another good thing about collage was that you could always glue over something. In oil painting, you have the liberty to go over it, but you mustn't abuse that liberty, or you get sticky, horrible paintings. However, in collage one can indeed glue a new piece of paper over an old one, and the old one does not make it lifeless. It can stay alive. I used acrylic medium as glue and protection. Collage is a fragile thing. I think it was kind of fun to reuse horrible advertising and all that junk and make something good of it. Use just the colors and make something new of it that has nothing to do with all those lies that are put in all those glossy, ugly pictures. I enjoy making all that disappear. It's an added pleasure to doing collage.

We had urban renewal then. Urban renewal can be fun, sometimes, for an artist. Near the river on Delancey Street, they were tearing down good neighborhoods and building brick beehives where people go crazy. But before the new things came up they had a Fair there that was fun to paint.

There was a park on Allen Street, now narrowed but still there with some trees. But for a while, during this urban renewal, everything was dilapidated. They had chopped down and dug up all the old trees and people sat there on pilings and stumps, sadly, waiting for it to be renewed a bit, waiting for new trees to be planted.

I also enjoyed painting the urban renewal projects on 9th Avenue between 22nd and 25th Street. This area had been a very nice neighborhood, a living

Figure F.2 A fair in the rubble of urban renewal. Oil painting by Edith Kramer

Foreword: A Fortunate Life xxi

neighborhood, which became a very sterile place. It was hard to paint there in the daytime, but I could paint at night from my car – those big excavators, bulldozers, and devouring machines. One night a policeman came by and saw my car with the light on inside. It was kind of drizzling, and as he looked inside he said, "At this time of the night, in this weather, I don't believe it." He went away saying he would come back in a little while to see that I was safe, which he did and so he kept me safe.

It seemed that I would always paint in series – usually a long series of urban renewal paintings. I also liked painting people who had survived. There was a park on Houston Street, called Green Guerillas Park, where I could paint the survivors, the homeless people that were sitting there even in the '60s. I had to paint from my car because you couldn't paint homeless people standing near, as they wouldn't leave you alone. I have always been very interested in the world as I see it. I have lived in the city most of my life. I've also lived in the very real wilderness. I like both, the *real city* or *totally real country*, but not suburban life. There it is, and I couldn't turn away from it.

Then there was the wilderness around New York. New York has its own wild places, particularly on the Belt Parkway in Brooklyn. I used to paint there quite a lot. There were areas that were not built up – marsh grasses, people fishing and swimming, and doing nice things there. It was filthy but very much alive, wilderness right there in the middle of the city. You could find cars there going back to the earth, in the spring, with all kinds of new growth coming out of them. I found this interesting, and I would paint there during all seasons except in the summer when I'd leave the city.

Sometimes it's good to change your environment. I used to go to New England a good deal in the summer. For the last several years, I've gone back to Austria for the summer, where my Aunt Liesl has a house near a lake that's very nice. I also have a little cabin in the mountains where nobody lives. It doesn't belong to me, but is owned by the farmers who have grazing rights in the mountains. They let me use this extra cabin that they were using for storage and I was able to fix it up a bit. There's no running water, just a stream that flows by. It's real wilderness, where I can paint mountains and things like that.

After the summers in Austria, I would return to the city and paint all the things that the city has to give – objects, people, urban renewal, renovation, plants on Wards Island, objects we collect if we live a long time in a place, industrial scenes which are always fascinating, strange growth under the Pulaski Highway in that bit of wilderness, and people. Now I'm painting my helper, who is cutting up marble for a mosaic of the subway that I am working on. I've painted myself every once in a while, but I think we paint ourselves when we are at a loss for what to do next. You always have yourself to come back to. Otherwise, the rest of the world has interested me more than myself.

I'd like to say something about psychoanalysis and art. I was in psycho-analysis, not for my art but for my personal life. It helped me in many ways and certainly didn't interfere with what I was doing as an artist. Perhaps for some people whose production is fueled by a lot of anguish, more anguish

xxii *Edith Kramer*

than they can otherwise bear, maybe for them, it isn't good. I know when I was a child, Siegfried Bernfeld, an early analyst and husband of my Aunt Liesl, said that something could be destroyed in a creative child, that "she should do analysis when she's an adult and knows what she is doing." And when I was an adult and did it, I think it was very helpful, and it really did not touch the art. If you are a human being, you experience conflict and are troubled. What you want to do in analysis is get rid of those conflicts that are ego alien that you don't approve of . . . Why is this in me? But I liked myself as a painter so why shouldn't I continue to be a painter?

Finally, I should say a little about my credo in art. I really do feel that today we have a new task, to celebrate that which is perishable and endangered and nourish and cultivate our capacity for experiencing our lives in this world. We live today, bombarded by so many completely chaotic kinds of perceptions that don't make sense, which is difficult because our perceptual apparatus is programed to distill meaning from complexity. The natural environment is complex, and we distill meaning from it. But we can't distill meaning from the cacophony of sounds, the noises in the streets, from the many things going on. We have to cut ourselves off from it. I think the danger is that we lose the capacity for experiencing it, from experiencing anything. We dull ourselves, we shut ourselves off; we learn to disregard stimuli. We work in windowless rooms, where temperature, light, and air are controlled beyond our reach. We kind of school ourselves in stoic resignation and endurance. This protection from overstimulation leaves an increasing incapacity for an emotional response to perception, and that's a kind of living death.

So as not to fall into this trap, we must brave the chaos, with its noise, with its craziness. If we do, we find it begins to make sense, and we come alive again. As artists, we have this task, to make this possible for people to perceive their world again and to make some sense of it. Today's artists must again become respectful and modest. The sovereignty that was natural to the artists from the beginning to the middle of the 20th century, like Picasso, Matisse, Kokoschka, Brock, or Klee, is no longer at our command. We have lost touch with the accumulated craftsmanship and wisdom of the past, and must begin anew and modestly. Rather than strive to astonish and shock, we must subordinate the personal experience to the task of interpreting the subject with respectful comprehension.

That's what I have been trying to do. We need to look again at what is really there; look at it respectfully, not with shock or hate. You can't protect anything through hating its enemies. You can only protect something well by loving it well, and then you might also go to battle for it or protect it. I think there must be an understanding of the intricacy and the intrinsic interest that there is in things that we tend to overlook. That's what I have been trying to do.

Art is so absent from our time now. The hunger for art therapy is partly the absence of art as a natural element in daily living. We are surrounded by objects that are machine-made, that don't tell us anything about the maker,

Foreword: A Fortunate Life xxiii

or anything about the *Weltanschauung* or worldview of that person. There is a hunger and really a lack that permeates all of our lives that then makes people search for art, or for an experience where they can do a little of that sort of thing – which might not have been necessary at the time when we made our own furniture. If we made a wardrobe, we might paint something on it, or if we embroidered things, or if we made a handle of a pitchfork, it got something of ourselves in the handle. All that is missing today. In part, I believe this absence has given rise to art therapy as a profession.

Another thing I had good fortune with is what you might call my "meshugge." I have a little neurosis about taking art around to the galleries, but I think in part it saved me. We have to be meshugge somewhere as artists and I think it's much better to be meshugge in the area of distributing my art than in the area of making the art. I never had a block in the area of making things. But I had tremendous blocks in the area of going out and begging people to show it. And maybe it was good because I've seen so many good artists really destroyed by being typecast or otherwise becoming successful and then being caught in this success. So maybe it was good having just a tiny bit of recognition, just a tiny bit coming to me at age 77 when it couldn't destroy me anymore. And also I was lucky that I did have recognition as an art therapist, so I didn't have to become bitter because I had one area where I was recognized as an authority. I didn't become the bitter misunderstood artist whom I might otherwise have become. So that was good fortune again. Lots of luck.

Note

1 The content of this foreword was transcribed from an audio recording of a lecture given by Edith Kramer at the New York Transit Museum in 1994.

References

Kramer, E. (1994). The CD recording New York Transit Museum Lecture [CD recording]. *Edith Kramer Papers*, MC 215, Access 10:26. New York University Archives, New York University Libraries, New York.

Lowenfeld, V. (1947). *Creative and mental growth*. New York: Macmillan.

Acknowledgments

We are deeply grateful for the support, enthusiasm, and generosity of each person who contributed to the writing of this collaborative book. Martha Haeseler provided translation from the German text into English, and because of her expertise, we could include some of Edith's typed and handwritten material that we found in the *Edith Kramer Papers* housed at the New York University Archives. In addition to the chapter authors, we appreciate the contributions made toward preparation of this book by: NYU Archivists and staff, Janet M. Bunde, Laura McCann, and Katie M. Ehrlich; Gretchen Miller for her answers to our questions about preparing the manuscript; and David Henley for his assistance in providing us with writing and additional information about Edith that was needed to complete the book.

The support and encouragement received from our spouses, Edward Glanville and Vinod Anand, and family members increased the joy and strength we received in working on this project together. Finally, we wish to acknowledge the wonderful example Edith was for us, showing us what is possible with a fair amount of determination, humor, curiosity, and generosity.

Contributors

Ikuko Acosta has been an art therapist and art educator for more than 35 years, and has directed the Graduate Art Therapy Program at New York University for the past 15 years. In addition to devoting herself to training art therapy students she has been introducing the field of art therapy internationally for the past 25 years.

Kathryn E. Bard worked and taught in medical/psychiatric hospitals in New York for 15 years following her education and training at New York University in the late '70s and early '80s. Kathryn relocated to Zurich, Switzerland with her family and heads "MultiArt STUDIO," which offers art therapy, the art studio, and art services/consulting to the international community. She is the author of several articles and exhibits artwork regularly. More information about MultiArt STUDIO can be found on her website: www.artmultifacet.com

Anni Bergman was born in Vienna and immigrated to the United States in 1939. She graduated with a degree in music from the University of California and eventually settled in New York City with her husband – writer and publisher Peter Bergman – with whom she had two sons. While in California, she met the psychoanalyst Christine Olden, who became a close friend and important influence. In 1959, Dr Bergman began to work with Margaret Mahler on the observational study of the separation–individuation process. She is co-author with Margaret Mahler and Fred Pine of *The Psychological Birth of the Human Infant*. Following her work with Dr Mahler, Dr Bergman continued to practice and teach dyadic work with autistic children and their primary caretakers. Some of this work has been published in her collected papers, *Ours, Yours, Mine: Mutuality and the Emergence of the Separate Self*, which was written in collaboration with Maria F. Fahey.

Raffaella Bortino is a psychotherapist and art therapist, sociologist, and Freudian psychoanalyst who has worked for years engaged in the practice and dissemination of art therapy. In 1983, Dr Bortino founded the

xxvi   *Contributors*

Psychotherapeutic Community "Il Porto" and the "Bus Stop Onlus Association" in 1998. She is the founder and teacher of the non-verbal school of psychotherapy, "Il Porto-ADEG," that was formed in collaboration with New York University in 1983.

Shyueying Chiang is an art therapist and counseling psychologist. She graduated from the Graduate Art Therapy Program at New York University in 1997. Dr Chiang has a master's degree in Children's Literature from the National Taitung University, a master's degree in art therapy from NYU, and a PhD in Art Education from the National Taiwan Normal University. She is currently an assistant professor in the Counseling Psychology Program at the Chinese Cultural University.

Wilma Cipriani is a philosopher and art therapist. In 1952, she graduated with a degree in Aesthetic Philosophy in Padova, Italy. Wilma has been a teacher for 50 years in high schools for state Italian literature and history. At the age of 52, she met Raffaella Bortino and Edith Kramer, and has been passionate about art therapy ever since. Following her training in Turin, she worked as an art therapist at the neuropsychiatric garrison Fatebenefratelli of San Maurizio Canavese for 12 years. Currently, Wilma is in private practice and under the supervision of Elizabeth Stone.

Karin Dannecker is the director of the Art Therapy Program at Weissensee Art School in Berlin, Germany. Dr Dannecker studied art, art education, and special education at Johann Wolfgang Goethe University in Frankfurt/M., Germany. From 1983 to 1985 she studied art therapy at New York University. On her return to Germany, she first worked at the university in Cologne. She then went to Berlin to design an art therapy program and teach in the field. In 2000, her program started as the first MA Art Therapy training course in Germany at the Weissensee Art School. She has published several books and numerous articles, and does research. In addition to working at the University, she works with psychiatric and psychosomatic patients in a clinic.

Irene Rosner David is the director of Therapeutic Arts at Bellevue Hospital in New York. She has been a medical art therapist since 1973 focusing on the contributory role of artistic expression in coping with physical illness and disability. Patient populations have included trauma, brain injury, stroke, paralysis, chronic illness, oncology, and palliative care. Dr David has presented and published on medical art therapy, served in various capacities of the American Art Therapy Association, and is recipient of awards for her clinical work and advocacy for the profession.

Esther Dreifuss-Kattan is a senior faculty member of the New Center of Psychoanalysis in Los Angeles, psychoanalyst, art therapist, and psychooncologist in private practice in Beverly Hills. She is an art therapist at Simms/Mann UCLA Center for Integrative Oncology, and a practicing artist. Dr Dreifuss-Kattan received her PhD in Psychoanalysis from the New Center for Psychoanalysis in LA in 1995; PhD in Art Therapy/Psychooncology at the Union Institute in 1989; MA in Art Therapy at Goddard College in 1976; and a Diploma in Fashion Design/Art in 1971 in Zurich, Switzerland. Her books include: *Practice of Clinical Art Therapy* (German); *Cancer Stories: Creativity and Self-Repair; Art and Mourning: The Role of Creativity in Healing Trauma and Loss; Creativity and Cancer: A Guide to Therapeutic Transformation* (Ed.), 2018. Chapters and publications can be found on her website: www.dreifusskattan.com.

Michael A. Franklin is the chair of the art therapy program at Naropa University and has practiced and taught in various academic and clinical settings since 1981. Michael is the founder of the Naropa Community Art Studio, a long-term research project training socially engaged artists and serving marginalized community members through the art community. He is the author of numerous publications including *Art as Contemplative Practice: Expressive Pathways to the Self* (SUNY Press, 2017).

Margherita Gandini is the teaching director, supervisor, and professor of the three-year training program in clinical art therapy at Lyceum, Milan, Italy. She is a graduate of the four-year training program in art therapy, Porto-ADEG, in Turin under the supervision of Elizabeth Stone. She became a registered art therapist in 2012 through the Professional Board of Art Therapists in Italy (APIART). She founded the "Edith Kramer Association" of Turin for which she conducted supervision, conferences, and seminars for art therapists. Margherita has enjoyed teaching "Reading in Art Therapy," "Methodology," "Experimental Paths," and supervising internships. She also enjoys giving presentations and conferences, and writing about art therapy.

Patti Greenberg is a writer living in Brooklyn and a member of Brooklyn Poets. She became Edith's student in 1979 when she entered the Graduate Art Therapy Program at New York University. They remained colleagues, fellow painters, and friends for as long as time allowed. She is indebted to Edith and all her teachers at the NYU Art Therapy Graduate Program for all they taught her about mothering and children, which proved invaluable in mothering her own children.

Martha Haeseler, painter and fiber artist, has been a student and friend of Edith Kramer since 1972. Martha has worked as an art therapist with children, adolescents, adults, and US veterans. Retired adjunct assistant professor at NYU, she has published and presented widely about her work with a variety of populations, as well as about ethics, PTSD, outsider art, resilience, and positive psychology.

David Henley is a renowned child art therapist, professor emeritus, and distinguished author, including three books, the latest titled *Creative Response Activities for Children on the Spectrum* (Routledge, 2017). He is also a practicing mixed media artist, working and living near Boulder, Colorado.

xxviii *Contributors*

Raffaela Carola Lorio, art therapist and photo-art therapist, is specialized in the Michael Sapir Method. She became a registered art therapist in 2007 through the Professional Board of Art Therapists in Italy (APIART). In the same year, Carola became a member of the American Art Therapy Association. She began teaching at the Lyceum School in Milan, Italy in 2015. Since 2002, Carola has been working as an art therapist and photo-art therapist in the therapeutic community of Bus Stop and Bluish Strawberries in Italy for dual diagnosed patients, where she specializes in trauma and abuse. In 2014, she became responsible for the exhibition *Abuse: Witnesses from a Therapeutic Community,* which has grown each year with new artwork from the patients of Bus Stop and Bluish Strawberries. A catalog of the exhibit was published in 2016.

Elena Makarova is a freelance writer, art therapist, historian, and exhibit curator specializing in Jewish spiritual resistance in the Terezin (Theresienstadt) concentration camp in 1941–1945. She received her master's from Moscow University and has written more than 40 books and numerous articles in 11 languages, and directed a large number of international exhibitions. Her book on Friedl Dicker-Brandeis (Vienna 1898–Auschwitz 1944) was translated into five languages. She resides in Haifa, Israel.

Darcy Marlow is an affiliate faculty member of Antioch University in Seattle. Darcy received a BA in art from the University of San Diego, an MEd with an emphasis on gifted education from Seattle University, and an MA in Art Therapy and Mental Health Counseling from Antioch University Seattle. Marlow has presented at both regional and national art therapy conferences on subjects including self-care and art therapy, strengths-based art therapy, and the influences of Edith Kramer on the field of art therapy.

Kevin Maxwell is a senior activity therapist and works with inpatients and outpatients at Maimonides Medical Center in Brooklyn, New York. Originally from Salt Lake City, Utah, he received a BFA at the University of Utah. Kevin studied under Edith Kramer at New York University where he received his MA in Art Therapy. Kevin is an exhibiting figurative and landscape artist in New York City.

Karl Pallauf was born in 1954 in Lower Austria as the sixth of a total of 13 children. In 1974, he immigrated to New York. Apart from his profession as a kitchen chef, later as a private cook with a high-ranking personality in the print media area, he was interested in art early on and acquired the first painting by Josef Floch in the autumn of 1975. Subsequently, he has worked intensively on promoting the works of painter Edith Kramer, and many other artists of Classical Modernism. He lives in New York, with occasional stays in Vienna.

Jordan S. Potash is a registered, board-certified, and licensed art therapist, and a registered expressive arts therapist. He is Assistant Professor in the Art

Therapy Graduate Program at The George Washington University. Jordan is primarily interested in the applications of art and art therapy in the service of community development and social change.

Johannes Reichmayr is affiliated with the Sigmund Freud University. Dr Reichmayr studied psychology at the University of Salzburg. He has been a deputy director of the Magisterium and head of the Department for Transcultural and Historical Research in Psychotherapy at the Sigmund Freud University (SFU) in Vienna. Since November 2009, he has also been the Dean for the foreign-language and foreign programs. Dr Reichmayr is doing research on the history of the psychoanalytic movement and ethno-psychology. He has worked in collaboration with Paul Parin, the Swiss psychoanalyst, ethnologist, and writer, and currently maintains and manages the archive and estate of Paul Parin.

Judith A. Rubin is a licensed psychologist, child and adult psychoanalyst, and board-certified art therapist. A past President and Honorary Life Member of the American Art Therapy Association, she has written seven books and created 13 films. President and co-founder of Expressive Media, she is currently working on the creation and dissemination of an online Training Film Library.

Elizabeth Stone is a New York State-licensed psychoanalyst and art therapist in private practice in Grenoble, France. She has been a faculty member of the Ecole de Psychologues Praticiens of the Catholic University in Lyon, NYU's Graduate Art Therapy Program, and has supervised the training of art therapists in Italy, Switzerland, and France.

Herschel J. Stroyman is an artist, art therapist/educator, and photographer residing in Toronto, Canada. Herschel met Edith in 1959, after walking into a storefront art exhibition in New York City, attracted by the obviously hand-lettered sign which read: "Exhibit: Art and the Troubled Child." The sign also indicated that Ms Kramer could be contacted at the Turtle Bay Music School. Wanting to know more, he called Turtle Bay, went for an interview, and ended up studying with her. That began his life-long mentorship and friendship with Edith. http://herschelstroyman.zenfolio.com/p1024744045

Geoffrey A. Thompson is an artist, creative art therapist, and assistant professor at Eastern Virginia Medical School. Dr Thompson has transdisciplinary research interests in art, aesthetics, art therapy, psychotherapy, and philosophy, and serves on the editorial board of the American Art Therapy journal, *Art Therapy*. He is also Editor-in-Chief of *Human Science Perspectives*, the journal of the Human Science Institute.

Katherine Williams is Associate Professor Emerita and former Director of the Art Therapy Program at The George Washington University. Currently, Katherine is an art therapist and clinical psychologist in private practice.

xxx   *Contributors*

She teaches at the Washington School of Psychiatry and the Institute of Contemporary Psychotherapy and Psychoanalysis.

Laurie Wilson is an art therapist, an art historian, and a psychoanalyst. She directed the Graduate Art Therapy Program at New York University for 23 years and is Professor Emerita there. In 2008, she was awarded the Honorary Life Membership in AATA in recognition of her "Distinguished Contributions to the Education of Art Therapists and to the Interdisciplinary Recognition of Art Therapy." She practices in New York City. Her book *Alberto Giacometti: Myth, Magic and the Man* was published by Yale University Press in 2003, and her biography, *Louise Nevelson: Light and Shadow,* was published by Thames & Hudson in Fall 2016.

Charlotte Zwiauer is affiliated with the University of Vienna. She has completed diploma studies in sociology as well as doctoral studies in philosophy at Freie Universität Berlin and at the University of Vienna.

Introduction
A Generous and Challenging Artist's Worldview

Lani Gerity and Susan Ainlay Anand

Have you ever noticed that there are times in life when synchronicity seems to be at play? For example, we may find ourselves in extremely challenging circumstances, in a cultural shift toward fear and aggression, when social unrest and injustice make the future seem uncertain and bleak. It is exactly these times when we yearn for voices of gentle wisdom. As we worked on editing this book, we found ourselves in that very position. Fortunately, we were working with a lot of material on resilience, strength, perseverance, and wisdom. Immersing ourselves daily in these varied impressions and stories of the life, wisdom, and generosity of Edith Kramer, was heartening during our troubled times.

Consequently, it is with great pleasure that we introduce *The Legacy of Edith Kramer: A Multifaceted View*. Many of you know Edith from studying her theories in graduate school. However, we are very interested in sharing with you much more than the theory itself. In the chapters that follow, you will find stories and illustrations of Edith's amazing strength and courage, out of which her theories emerged.

Following a plenary presentation devoted to Edith's life at the 2015 American Art Therapy Association conference, art therapist Lisa Furman thanked us and said, "I had no idea Edith was so 'bad-assed!'" and she seemed quite happy to have her view of Edith broadened. And, we were happy to broaden it. What Lisa was pointing out to us, the thing that we didn't realize very clearly, was that if you are only studying Edith's theories, you might not realize how much grit and determination she had. It is *that* Edith Kramer that we are confident you will find within these pages.

Not only will you read some of Edith's previously unpublished material, but you will also find an array of impressions and memories from various corners of the world. You will read summaries and applications of important ideas that Edith taught, but also some of the historical and cultural context behind these ideas. When looking at Edith's legacy in this way, you can see the antecedents, the things that gave Edith her strength and ideas. The contributors have connected the antecedents with Edith's concepts, so the book as a whole is a collection of what she gave us, and continues to give us. You will discover a rich tapestry of thought and art, and possibly see your own place in this tapestry – this is her legacy, and you are a part of it.

2 *Lani Gerity and Susan Ainlay Anand*

For the editors, working on the material submitted by each contributor has taught us so much. We knew our views were necessarily limited, but what we failed to realize was how much we would learn about Edith from working on this book. Working with all the chapters, like pieces of very tough, homespun fabric, was a comfort, and a joy. The tapestry for us, as a whole, is inspiring and full of stories of resilience, strength, and generosity; brilliant flashes of light and color come from the various jewels sewn into the fabric.

While attending the memorials for Edith at New York University and in Vienna, it became evident to us that if we could persuade our fellow presenters to contribute to this book, we would all benefit by having a multifaceted view of Edith, her life, and her legacy. We were eager for others to see this wider view, so we created a collaborative presentation for the American Art Therapy Association and informed contributors that we hoped their contributions to this plenary would be developed into the book you now hold.

Because Edith emphasized quality and art, we felt it essential to include both her paintings and the exquisite photography of Edith's dear friend Herschel J. Stroyman, who captured much of her day-to-day life, from when she worked at Wiltwyck School for Boys through the years of teaching at NYU. Our publishing editor at Routledge agreed, so in the book you will find Herschel's photography along with paintings from an exhibit in Austria, which Martha Haeseler, Kathryn Bard, and Lani Gerity documented. Edward Glanville, Susan and Vinod Anand, Karin Dannecker, David Henley, and the New York University Archives provided artwork and photos as well. So, please enjoy the images, quality, and memories that you will find in the book. (For more on New York University Archives, please see David Henley's "On Leaving and Preserving" and our "Conclusions" chapters.)

Although you will read various points of view throughout this book, you will find commonalities. There are many examples of Edith Kramer's inclusive, perhaps even what might be called "decolonizing," way of working, first noticed by Dr Venture, a Black art therapist from Maryland. She had written the first doctoral dissertation in the US on art therapy, "The Black Beat in Art Therapy Experiences" (Venture, 1977). Venture wanted to create an art therapy program that would benefit communities, that, in her observation, traditional forms of psychoanalytic art therapy did not reach. She felt the traditional models perpetuated exclusivity, while Edith Kramer's *art as therapy* model worked well with varied populations, including the poor, minorities, and oppressed. Venture felt that Kramer offered a way to build on strengths from within that would lead to growth and new possibilities. You will find in the various chapters aspects of Edith's life and identity, which contributed to her flexibility, strength, and belief that change and growth can and should come from within.

In considering Edith's strength and flexibility, we'd like to look at her identity as an artist and how her studio supported her. In the Foreword, "A Fortunate Life," Edith spoke to this identity in great detail, and in the "Artist Identity" section you will discover how Geoffrey Thompson came to curate an exhibition of Edith's works for the annual conference of the American Art Therapy Association in 2009 in Dallas, Texas. You will find Karl Pallauf, an Austrian art collector, writing about his views as a collector, curator, and friend. Katherine Williams writes passionately about various memories around Edith's subway mosaic, and to complement that, we included Edith's own description of creating that same mosaic. Jordan Potash's chapter, "Kramer's Criteria for Quality as Central to Art Therapy," is included in this section and expands upon the concept of the artist's identity.

When the authors wrote about Edith's studio, they often mentioned that it was a quiet place, a haven from the chaos of New York City, a place where one could hear oneself think. We wondered if this quiet haven might be what was central to her productive mind and life. Geoffrey Thompson, in his chapter, "Edith Kramer's Artistic Legacy: Beyond the Studio," described this stillness as he explored her studio space looking for artwork for the 2009 exhibit. Although she had left for Austria and wasn't likely to return, he felt her presence in the stillness of the space. And as photo-art therapist, art therapist Raffaela Carola Lorio said, "Nella quiete del suo studio, non potevo non posare lo sguardo sulle sue sue sculture, la sua treccia e la sua teiera." (In the quietness of her studio, I could not merely glance at her sculptures, her braid, and her teapot.)

Figure I.1 In the Quietness of Her Studio. Photograph taken by Raffaela Carola Lorio

4 *Lani Gerity and Susan Ainlay Anand*

Figure I.2 Her Teapot. Photograph taken by Raffaela Carola Lorio

Edith always emphasized the importance of stillness for her creativity, even when attending someone else's workshop. She would let it be known that silence was preferable to any music the facilitator might have brought. She wanted to be able to access what she called the "inner life." If she came up against a problem in an art piece as she was working on it, she wanted to be able to find the solution for herself, from within herself, rather than listen to external, cultural dictates. She wanted this for the children she worked with as well; she wanted them to have the freedom to explore their internal worlds. For more on the inner life, please visit Michael Franklin's chapter, "Understanding Lineage, Difference, and the Contemplative Dimensions of Edith Kramer's Art as Therapy Model."

Part of the artist identity for Edith, was her understanding about the things that helped her best work emerge; for her, these things revolved around intrinsic motivations or inner satisfaction. She observed from personal experience and from the children she worked with that when we create from an internal prompting, we are rewarded through inner satisfaction, which produces resilience

Figure I.3 Her Braid. Photograph taken by Raffaela Carola Lorio

and inner strength. No amount of external reward can give us this inner shift, this growth. To explore more of these ideas, please see the chapters, "Quality and Inner Satisfaction: Re-Visiting the Importance of Quality in Art and Art Therapy" and "Creating a World of Possibility: Life Lessons from Edith Kramer."

Edith would draw everywhere, even in her own workshops, or when she was with patients. As you will read, she felt the act of perceiving is a slow process. It cannot be hurried. She felt that photography doesn't replace the integration of messages that occurs when we observe the world through our eyes, with an active and receptive mind. As Elena Makarova recalls from a conversation with Edith in her captivating chapter "Do You Require Inspiration Just to Breathe?" Edith said, "A photograph – a historic document; a painting – an enigma with no age. It is no slave to time." Drawing was her way of interacting with the world, a way of slowing things down so that they could be understood and integrated. Her dear friend Anni Bergman explores this idea in her chapter, "Edith Kramer Remembered." She saw the need to

6 Lani Gerity and Susan Ainlay Anand

create as a part of Edith's being. She felt that Edith was not motivated to accomplish something, as much as she had a need and ability to turn her perceptions into works of art.

In the book's Foreword, in Edith's own words, we can imagine what New York was like through the eyes of a young refugee from Europe. Among Edith's first American experiences when she arrived in New York, was a ride on the subway. Because of her training as an artist, she saw the chaos and noise, the huge numbers of people all around her, as an excellent subject for her art, rather than something to be overwhelmed by or to hide from. Later, the subway became the inspiration and installation site for a large mosaic Edith made when she was 77 years old, which you can read more about in Katherine Williams' and Edith's short chapters.

Laurie Wilson includes in her chapter on recollections of Edith Kramer at New York University a quintessential Edith story about her studio, and her way of working with obstacles, which epitomized her approach to almost everything. At the time, when Edith was moving into her loft, she was planning to share it with Laurie and Jill Schehr. Although it had windows across the front that faced Vandam Street, Edith wanted more light and a view of the Hudson River. So, she persuaded Laurie and Jill to start chipping away at the solid brick wall facing west. After weeks, they finally broke through to the outside and Edith could have a window installed exactly where she wanted it.

This story clearly shows us another one of Edith's strengths, her willingness to create new points of view. She knew how to adapt to the hard facts of reality, but if she could create a way to break through them to a better reality, she would. In Ikuko Acosta's chapter on her experiences teaching alongside Edith, there are wonderful examples of how Edith helped students to open up and move beyond their habitual patterns of responding to the world and others, and to discover a "creative solution" or creative "genuineness." In Shyueying Chiang's chapter "Experiences of Learning from Edith Kramer and Translating Her Book," we see these same experiences, but from the student's point of view. Shyueying explains very clearly how the emphasis on art was so helpful in negotiating a new culture as well as a new profession.

Edith's studio became a generous meeting place to discuss ideas while sharing tea, often a mix of lapsang souchong and Earl Grey (Elinor Ulman's favorite), and bread and cheese from the Lower East Side. She believed the essence of art and of psychotherapy is flexibility and openness, and we observed the essence of her enjoyment of life was found in that same flexibility and openness. Edith never found life monotonous or mundane, and we could always expect the unexpected when in her presence. If she thought she needed a wider view on life, she would make it happen, quite literally. She actively sought out ways to feed her intellectual curiosity, new subjects for artistic exploration, and new media to work with. Readers can expect the unexpected as they delve into chapters by David Henley, Judith Rubin, Kathryn Bard, Irene Rosner David, and Patti Greenberg. In their descriptions of Edith's life and studio, we find diversity of experiences, flexibility, generosity, and openness.

Introduction 7

Martha Haeseler, Anni Bergman, Charlotte Zwiauer, Johannes Reichmayr, Elena Makarova, Karin Dannecker, Darcy Marlow, and Edith herself helped us develop a deeper appreciation for the cultural and historical influences of Edith's life. Within the chapters in the section on history and context, you will find a rich, in-depth account of Edith's life. Karin Dannecker generously provided us with additional information regarding Edith's background and history whenever it was needed.

Edith was born in Vienna, Austria on August 26, 1916 and her childhood was informed by a world that had recently experienced the "Great War." Johannes Reichmayr (contributor to the Mumi chapter) told us Edith's parents and the generation of men and women that had just come through the war were very concerned about the generations that followed them. They worked hard to provide the children with stimulating, meaning-filled lives, within a supportive "caring net," as Professor Reichmayr called it. Her summers in Grundlsee were very important for Edith's development. Her inner strength, her internalized good objects, her generosity of spirit, and her love of intellectual stimulation were all fostered here. For more on Edith's childhood and her Grundlsee experiences, please see "Mumi Kramer, Grundlsee, and the Caring Net."

When Edith was 17 years old and in the midst of her final exams, her mother gave her Freud's *Introductory Lectures on Psychoanalysis*. Edith said that this book changed her in ways that art had not and that psychoanalysis somehow provided exercise for the part of her brain that loved intellectual pursuits and conceptual thinking. In research for her chapter on Edith Kramer, Darcy Marlow uncovered information that was new to her about the relationship Edith had with her mother, which helped us gain some sense of the loss Edith must have experienced when her mother died, when she left Europe for the first time, and when she discovered her mentor, Friedl, was murdered in Auschwitz.

We discovered, while working with the chapters related to history and context, a deeper appreciation for Edith's life and that being a part of a lineage creates a sense of community. Lani observed that sense of community and lineage when visiting Edith in Austria in the late '90s. The sense of a history going back generations and the sense of a strong, living, generous, caring community was so very alive in Grundlsee. Edith wasn't just Edith Kramer, artist/art therapist in Grundlsee; she was called "our Kramer," in a way held by the community, as if they had created a supportive transitional space with this feeling of history and community.

The land itself around Grundlsee reflects this holding environment – mountains holding the lake and the community. This community held the property for Edith's family until they could return after the war, not a common circumstance. Grundlsee was very important to Edith's survival, both as a community and as an amazingly beautiful natural environment. She returned each summer to paint while she lived and taught in New York. She could internalize this holding environment and carry it with her. By doing that, Edith

8   *Lani Gerity and Susan Ainlay Anand*

could help her students and the children she worked with to do the same. Just knowing such communities can be possible creates a sense of hope and is deeply comforting.

Edith believed and taught us that mentors are very important. For her, having mentors in the fine arts and being a "disciple" of several master artists rather than an art student at a university was most beneficial. Friedl Dicker-Brandeis was central to Edith's development of her ideas of art as therapy, and she felt art therapists ought to know something about Friedl – her ideas and her fate.

Many of the chapters discuss this relationship of Edith and Friedl, but Elena Makarova's chapter, "Edith Kramer on Friedl Dicker-Brandeis, Erna Furman, and Terezin. Interviews with Elena Makarova" and Margherita Gandini's chapter, "Lyceum Art Therapy Training Program," go into the most depth, giving North Americans a much clearer understanding of the relationship between a mentor and a mentee.

In looking through images of Edith's work, her home in Austria, and photos from her family, we realized that Edith valued history very much, as well as the idea of being a part of a generous lineage. We learned the things that Edith learned from Friedl, and of course you will discover them now, as well. Lineages are a very good thing to be a part of – we aren't as isolated and separate as we might imagine.

Edith joined Friedl in Prague from 1934 to 1938, to study with her and to help her work with refugee children and families who were fleeing Germany. She learned much from Friedl, and one of the best things she taught us – that we don't have to wait to do good things in the world – came from Friedl's life experience.

Friedl told Edith that she thought something was wrong with her for feeling very alive when she was locked up for communist activity and that this must be masochism, so she should be analyzed immediately. However, her ability to remain fully alive under extreme adversity served her and the children she taught in Terezin very well. This is comforting because if Friedl could do so much good without achieving perfection and under such impossible conditions, then surely we can also do some good, wherever we find ourselves.

During the Prague years, both Edith and Friedl were in psychoanalysis with Annie Reich (married to Wilhelm Reich). Analysis and attending lectures on child development were extremely helpful in understanding some of the art work they were seeing from the refugee children and was later beneficial to Friedl's continued work in Terezin. The children's work in Prague showed a willingness to identify with their persecutors. When the children were helped to break free from identification with the aggressor and able to recognize their own very real inner strengths through their art, the result would be powerful and empowering. This, we believe, is the core of Edith's decolonizing art as therapy method.

Edith felt that much of her sense of heritage was bound up in art, art education, and psychoanalytically informed psychotherapy. Her Freudian

Introduction 9

psychoanalysis with Dr Annie Reich was also important in enabling her to practice art therapy. Edith used her art making for her reparation and understanding of psychodynamics, which we will see in the chapter written by Raffaella Bortino, Wilma Cipriani, and Carola Lorio. In this chapter, Edith described her painting of a mother and child, and how in the process of painting this pair, she could explore the very complex relationship and conflicts that coexist within it. She felt that she would not have arrived at or been able to communicate this same level of complexity if she were using words alone.

Edith fled to the US in 1938 on the last ship out of Poland, as the Germans were ordering the ship to turn around, which the captain refused to do. Aunt Liesl was waiting for her at the docks in New York City. Within a week, she had a job as a shop teacher at The Little Red School House. Then from 1943 to 1945, she worked as a machinist as part of the "war effort." She would often stay after work to create sketches and drawings of people at work. After the war, she traveled through Europe, using her painting to help her integrate everything she saw around her – the rubble, destruction, and new life returning. Finally, she decided to return to New York for reasons Edith describes in the Foreword in this book.

Edith experienced much pain, loss, and heartbreak in her life. Even so, rather than spend effort avoiding this kind of experience, she used her art making and these life events to explore and grow. She helped many turn hardships and trauma into personal growth; helped many find appreciation of life, personal strength, and new possibilities (as Friedl did before her). We discovered that she continues to help us find our strength and new possibilities as we revisited her life stories. We, too, can use life events to explore and grow, and as art therapists, we can help others with this task. To this end, the section on Edith Kramer's concepts applied to practice offers many examples of how art therapists using art as therapy are helping others. Martha Haeseler, Michael A. Franklin, Esther Dreifuss-Kattan, Irene Rosner David, Shyueying Chiang, and Lani Gerity offer a revisiting of theory, descriptions of art therapy programs, case illustrations, and narratives of resilience.

After her return from Europe in 1949, Edith began working at Wiltwyck School for Boys, one of Eleanor Roosevelt's pet projects, which served predominantly African American boys. Much like the refugee children she had worked with in Prague, these children were living under very stressful conditions, and their artwork showed quite a bit of identification with the aggressor.

In her work at Wiltwyck, Edith used all of her strengths – her knowledge of fairy tales, her memories of the generous, caring adults in her life, the internalized good objects, the kindly ego ideals, her artist identity and her psychoanalytic understanding – to create a wonderfully inclusive, supportive, and generous art room for the boys. She believed and observed that children love art, that to have a place where they can communicate with themselves, recognize their inner thoughts, is very important. Her experience was that children create a lot of commotion, but that peace is very welcome, very important. She

10 *Lani Gerity and Susan Ainlay Anand*

would foster a stillness, a concentration where everyone was absorbed in their art. She would use fairy tales to engage the verbal part of the children's minds so that "they forget to fight or they forget to curse at each other."

Edith also observed that the boys would censor each other's work, demanding an identification with the dominant culture, painting White presidents and other "important" White people. She encouraged exploration of mixing paint to help the boys create ego ideals of their own ethnicity and cultural background, rather than the icons of the dominant culture. When the boys started painting "Indian Chiefs" and "Arabian Princesses" Edith felt hopeful. But it was only after Haile Selassie, King of Ethiopia, visited New York City, that the children allowed themselves to paint people of their own ethnicity. With Haile Selassie's assistance and a little decolonizing experience with mixing paint, the boy Edith referred to as Martin was finally able to paint his mother (the cover art for *Art as Therapy: Collected Papers*, see Kramer & Gerity, 2000).

Elizabeth Stone and Martha Haeseler, in their chapters on quality and Edith's legacy in the art room respectively, describe how Edith understood when a child painted a human being, it was often a disguised self-portrait. Edith was very sensitive about finding the exact color of the skin that the child wished to paint. Even though a child would often begin by not knowing, once the mixing began, and more often than not, he would arrive at the color of his own skin. This way of working was a paradigm of art as therapy. The child's connection with the symbolic meaning in the artwork served to strengthen the ego in ways that did not necessarily need verbalization.

For more of Edith's concepts we would suggest the section "Edith Kramer's Theoretical Concepts." Here you will discover Elizabeth Stone's important chapters on "Edith Kramer's Notion of 'Quality'" and "On Edith Kramer's Seminal Concept of Sublimation in Art Therapy." There is also Laurie Wilson's fascinating discussion of "Sublimation Then and Now."

Kevin Maxwell illustrates the use of quality of materials, the third hand, and sublimation in his highly informative chapter on working with inpatient adults in art therapy groups, "The Building of an Artist's Identity." Karin Dannecker explores the theoretical underpinnings of the third hand, as well as other key concepts, in her chapter, "Edith Kramer's Third Hand: Intervention in Art Therapy." David Henley ends this section with a fascinating examination of memories mixed with theory in "Kramer's Sublimation: Creative Expansion or Limitation."

Edith's Legacy

In the Foreword, you will find Edith's ideas on the possibility of art and art therapy serving a social function. She found that in our everyday lives, there is an absence of art, but that humans still have longings for art experiences, now mostly unfulfilled, which she believed contributed to the rise of the profession of art therapy.

Introduction 11

Like Martin Luther King Jr, Edith advised us to maintain ourselves as maladapted to all in our culture that was not just, that would stifle independence of thought and action. If we don't want our cultures to die, we have to allow for (even encourage) diversity of expression. Edith taught us that as artists, we are good at that very thing, allowing or appreciating diversity of expression, so we need to practice helping our cultures and institutions grow and expand in this area. In the section on art and culture, you will find examples of Edith's thoughts on this in chapters written by Susan Anand, Edith Kramer, and Lani Gerity: How her wisdom is being used to build community, recognize and honor diversity, and create safe environments in which an egalitarian learning from each other is possible, and where inner satisfaction from making art is explored and realized.

On bestowing Edith with an honorary doctorate from Vermont College in 1996, Gladys Agell, former director of the art therapy program, said, "Ms Kramer has been the champion of people in need as well as a vocal critic of everything shoddy. Thus she is a hero and celebrated leader whose contributions to life on this planet have been exemplary" (1996).

Katherine Williams talked to us about being filled with memories of Edith's fortitude. She said surely this was part of the reason Edith could lead us in exploration, in staking out new territory, and building a "cabin" of art therapy in the "wilderness of mental health treatment." And with that fortitude internalized, Shyueying Chiang could translate Edith's *Art as Therapy with Children* and make the "cabin" of art as therapy available in Taiwan, which you can read about in "Experiences of Learning from Edith Kramer and Translating Her Book."

Karin Dannecker described in her chapter the huge pleasure it was to sit down and have a conversation with Edith. Her wisdom, her unconventional thinking, and her enormous knowledge about what moves the world inside and outside was profoundly inspiring and enriching. We agreed wholeheartedly, and we are glad she, as well as David Henley and Elena Makarova, wrote about these conversations with Edith.

One place where Edith's international legacy is felt very strongly is in the Italian school, Lyceum Art Therapy Training Program (formerly called the Fomazione Training Course), which you can read about in the chapter by Bortino, Cipriani, and Lorio, and in another chapter by Gandini. Margherita Gandini wrote in her chapter about how the students in the training program kept art journals, and many wrote journal entries to "Dear Edith," creating a very real, internalized good, caring ego ideal, an inner-Edith. When the school heard of Edith's passing, they created art making experiences that included thank you notes to "Dear Edith."

As you read the chapters that follow, give some thought to this inclusive, curious art therapy legacy. Remember that you are a part of this wonderful community, a part of the net, and most definitely a part of this legacy.

As Judith Rubin said, "Edith helped bring out the best in us. And of course that's what we should all be doing."

References

Agell, G. (1996). Citation awarding the honorary degree of doctor of art therapy to Edith Kramer. *American Journal of Art Therapy, 35*(2), 38.

Kramer, E., & Gerity, L. (2000). *Art as Therapy: Collected Papers.* London: Jessica Kingsley Publishers.

Venture, L. (1977). *The Black beat in art therapy experiences.* Unpublished dissertation. Union Institute (formerly Union Graduate School), Cincinnati, OH.

History and Context

1 Feelings That Cannot Be Put into Words

Darcy Marlow

My fascination with Edith Kramer started with a standard writing assignment given to many art therapy students in their first or second quarter: Compare and contrast Edith Kramer and Margaret Naumburg. I had an awareness of the differing theories of the women but little understanding of how they evolved. Curiosity sparked my fascination with Kramer and the influence of her personal and cultural history on her theoretical development. As I continued to learn about Kramer, it became more and more evident that her theory, *art as therapy,* could have been a direct response to her experiences growing up in Austria during the evolution of the Nazi Party.

One of the first things that impressed me about Kramer was her commitment to telling the truth in life and in her art making. She was described in her later years by Laurie Wilson (1997) as having the "courage to think and speak for herself no matter the consequences and to keep doing so until she has put her convictions and observations into words and into the public domain for all of us to think about" (p. 102). I was so curious as to how she could maintain this commitment when she had grown up in a time of monumental adversity and danger.

With further investigation, I learned that truth became important to Kramer because it was strongly emphasized by her mother and by her beloved mentor, Friedl Dicker. Kramer stated:

> I don't take certain things lightly or easily. For example, . . . the artistic morality is that you cannot be a fake. It is a cardinal sin to lie in art – to be a fake. You have to be genuine. That means to work, you have to be free to work. You have to be free to shout and scream – to rant and rave.
> (Miller & Cook-Greuter, 2000, p. 116)

My question became: How does one adhere to a commitment to truth telling during a time when freedom to speak was being systematically eliminated and contradictory opinions could result in punishment or death? This became the topic of my master's project and my endless commitment to a better understanding of this mysterious, strong, and courageous woman.

16 *Darcy Marlow*

I began my research by looking at the world into which Kramer was born. I felt that the significance of her cultural experience and her family dynamics could help me understand Kramer better, and then subsequently understand her theory development. Kramer was born in Vienna, Austria on August 26, 1916 to Josephine Kramer (Neumann) and Richard Kramer in the midst of World War I. She was the only child of Josefine and Richard. Both of her parents had Jewish lineage. Her father had connections to the Communist Party. The world around her was precarious. Franz Josef, the ruler of the Hapsburg Dynasty, died leaving Austria void of a monarchy that had ruled their country for hundreds of years. Though not everyone agreed with the governing system, most people felt the uncertainty of change. Shortly thereafter, Austria lost World War I, leaving many people without food, work, or stable living conditions. Jewish people were being blamed. Although Kramer's family was not directly affected, she was part of a demographic that was being vilified. Kramer stated their family was not Jewish by religion, but that was of no consequence. People of Jewish heritage were beginning to be targeted. Stern (2001) comments on the end of World War I, "Truth, we know, is the first victim of war and in their war, the public lie was elevated into a weapon. Censorship was ubiquitous" (p. 3). My question remained: As truth was becoming dangerous, and Kramer was in a targeted demographic, how could she sustain her values?

Kramer discusses her childhood fondly in her writings, indicating no fear or concern about the changing world and emerging dangers. Kramer (2006) claimed her family to be "bohemian in the truest sense, with artists, actors, communist sympathizers, many of whom moved in Viennese psychoanalytical circles. Ever since I can remember the center of my life was making of art: drawing, painting, sculpting" (p. 11). Her mother encouraged her artistic development from an early age. Kramer stated:

> It all started as soon as I could take something in my hand and draw with it. I always knew I wanted to be an artist. There was never any doubt in my mind. I was always interested in making things. I always knew that I was gifted in art.
>
> (Miller & Cook-Greuter, 2000, p. 103)

At this point, I felt a more personal connection with Kramer, relating to the childhood love of art that would become an essential piece of my very being. I, like Kramer, understand the use of art as a means of understanding and living in the world.

When Kramer was seven, she left Austria to live with her Aunt Liesl in Berlin. It is important to note that antisemitism was rising, and more and more people were finding themselves to be in danger. The time in Berlin was particularly significant to Kramer's development because the three aspects of art therapy – teaching, psychoanalysis, and art – were enriched there. Kramer credits this experience as an essential contribution to her development as an art therapist.

Feelings That Cannot Be Put into Words 17

Her Aunt Liesl, an emerging actress who would later appear in the American classic *Cabaret*, modeled a creative and theatrical style that helped Kramer develop an ability to speak in front of groups, lead workshops, and teach (Miller & Cook-Greuter, 2000). Kramer credits her interest in psychoanalysis partially to Liesl's partner and future husband, Siegfried Bernfeld. He engaged Kramer in conversations that challenged her academically and offered a psychoanalytic perspective. He was an advocate for questioning authority, intellectual conversation, and the rights of women. Miller and Cook-Greuter (2000) quote Edith describing Bernfeld as "an important influence on me during these years – he taught me how to think. . . . I learned about the unconscious . . . and its power – from this man" (p. 104).

At this point, an interesting thing happened. It was one of three times in my research when a discovery about Edith caused an intense emotional reaction, almost bringing me to tears. Although I was reading extensively about the rise of Nazi power and the consequences, three completely separate events stunned me. I think this was because they were quite unexpected. The first was the discovery that while in Berlin, Kramer also spent time with her mother's lover, Hans Bellmer. In an interview with Miller and Cook-Greuter (2000), Kramer described Bellmer as someone she felt fondly toward and "remains appreciative of his benevolence and generosity to this day," as "he provided . . . brushes, paints, and other art materials" encouraging her to create art (p. 103). Years after knowing Kramer, Bellmer created extremely controversial art representing prepubescent girls in a variety of mutilated and distorted images. Bellmer claimed his artwork was created as a response to the rise of Hitler. I believe my reaction was twofold: one was my concern for the young Edith who spent time with this man. While there was no evidence or talk of any wrongdoing, I believe it was more that it highlighted vulnerability during that time and the emergence of danger that all of society was about to face. Second, the graphic illustrations by the man Kramer knew gave me pause to think of the terrible impact Hitler had on society in a very visual and graphic way. It appears to coincide with Kramer's developing belief that art can be used as a means of expression and potentially led to her theory of sublimation. Kramer later described sublimation as a vehicle through which her patients

> can derive pleasure from them [the artwork] without fear that such adventures might impair their adjustment in reality. . . . Indeed the burden of repressions and renunciations is made easier by such artistic expressions. . . . In this respect works of art resemble dreams and day-dreams. Dreams and fantasies can often be enjoyed with a minimum of guilt. . . .
> (Kramer & Gerity, 2000, p. 39)

Did she recognize this in Bellmer, in responses to Hitler, and in herself?

Kramer spent most of her youth living in different places with her mother. According to Kramer, their relationship was complex, as she found her mother

18   *Darcy Marlow*

to be creative, interesting, and perplexing in her actions. Miller and Cook-Greuter (2000) state that Kramer "seemed to both love and admire her mother greatly, and, at the same time, be troubled by her seductiveness" (p. 102). Their primary connection revolved around creative expression. In an interview with Kramer, Miller and Cook-Greuter (2000) quote Edith's response to her maternal relationship by stating, "art was very important between us – as if art were a kind of language or currency mother and daughter could share and understand" (p. 102). As her primary relationship, it seems the complexity of her relationship with her mother could potentially have led Edith to her philosophy about art as well as to her feelings about dedication to others and loyalty. In a time when national loyalty was being both tested and skewed, her mother's affairs could have distorted Edith's trust and informed her theory about truth in art as well as her own perception about life. Because this is complex and confusing, she might have recognized expression through art as the best way to explore those feelings.

In 1929, Kramer and her mother returned to Vienna. Shortly after, Friedl Dicker, a friend of her mother's and student of the Bauhaus, invited Kramer to become her mentee. Kramer attributes Dicker with her development as an artist and considered Dicker to be the "first art therapist." Their relationship continued to grow through Kramer's teenage years during which Kramer became further committed to her development as an artist. Meanwhile, Hitler continued to rise in power. When Kramer was eighteen, Dicker was arrested for being a Communist. Upon release, Dicker decided to leave for Czechoslovakia, and Edith Kramer followed. In Prague, Dicker and Kramer spent time working with German-speaking children, many of whom were offspring of political refugees who had fled Hitler's Germany and found temporary haven in Czechoslovakia. Through this work with Dicker, Kramer witnessed the dichotomy of being able to tell truth in art when times dictated a need for silence. This experience aided in the integration of art as therapy with Kramer's personal emergence as an artist herself. Knowing the importance of creative expression, she saw the opportunity made available for people in the most compromised of positions. According to Miller and Cook-Greuter (2000) "Friedl's requirement for precision and truthful expression, it appears, cultivated Kramer's own desire for truth, honesty, and exactness in artistic expression. Under Friedl's tutelage, Kramer became an arch enemy of all kitsch, imitation, and intellectual and artistic dishonesty" (p. 105). Dicker modeled this theory in her artwork and in her life choices.

Shortly after the move to Prague, two significant events occurred in Kramer's life. The first one shocked me because it took two years of research before I uncovered the fact that while Edith was away, her mother committed suicide. This revelation brought me to tears for the second time. I wondered about the pain the suicide would have caused Kramer during that time of fear and danger, if her response to the suicide involved a feeling of abandonment, and how she was able to process it. It occurred to me again that she adhered to her theory of art as therapy, processing her grief presumably through art and not discussion, as evidenced by the fact it took me so long to uncover this information.

Feelings That Cannot Be Put into Words 19

This was poignant to me because it proved again that she adhered to her theory, used it for her own healing, and truly believed in the power of art itself in a time of pain and sorrow. Kramer and Wilson later issued an interesting statement about the mother figure in general:

> This bond, particularly the one to the mother or the mothering person or persons, cannot be broken without the gravest of consequences. To survive as human beings children must manage to love those to whom they belong and feel themselves loved by them.
>
> (Kramer & Wilson, 1998, p. 8)

The second event was Friedl Dicker's detention. At this point in history, the Nazi Party was systematically arresting people of Jewish heritage. Although Friedl was Jewish, she held valid documentation that would allow her to emigrate. Her husband, however, did not have the paperwork that would allow him to leave. Dicker and her husband were sent to Terezin, a concentration camp with a specific purpose.[1] This was a unique facility designed to create the facade that the incarcerated children were being provided not only with the necessary care to survive, but with tutelage from skilled artists and performers to satisfy requirements of the Red Cross (Rubin, 2009). It has been said that instead of bringing personal effects, Dicker packed art supplies. She maintained her integrity during this experience through her extensive efforts to bring art and creative expression to the children while they were detained. Friedl Dicker was later transferred to Auschwitz where she perished with most of the children. It amazed me to discover that Dicker proved her unending hope for humanity in her actions of hiding the artwork of the children in the mattresses at Terezin before she left (Pariser, 2008).

Kramer held everlasting gratitude to Dicker for her support of Kramer's art education and for her contributions to Kramer's understanding of the use of art as therapy. After Dicker's death, Kramer clearly felt the absence of her beloved mentor. I have wondered if this experience contributed to the development of Kramer's theory. Could the pain of this experience have informed Kramer's need for expression without verbalization because she elected to attempt to flee Europe rather than follow Dicker to Terezin? It seems most likely that the loss of Dicker and the harrowing decision to leave must have been both haunting and extremely difficult for Kramer to discuss, yet troubling and requiring some sort of processing.

It became extremely challenging to get passage out of Europe to safety. Kramer (1994) states:

> Everyone knew our time was limited. . . . Everyone started writing letters, writing letters to see how we could get out. I was very lucky because one of my letters landed in an organization where there was a young woman helping, an American photographer, who was helping there . . . she had a sister, both had studied in Vienna. Her sister studied Montessori and she had studied . . . photography, and my mother had sewn clothes for both

those girls . . . so she knew me as a teenager painting, already painting all the time. So, she wrote to me and said she was sure she could find an affidavit because it is much easier to find an affidavit, first of all, for a young and healthy person, and secondly . . . for one who one knew and could vouch for. And sure enough, the affidavit arrived and I left Prague over Poland, which then still existed and got on a boat . . . and it was the last boat. I mean, while we were on the ship, the Nazis walked into Poland, but the ship did not turn around.

It did not go unnoticed that the act of art making potentially saved Kramer.

Edith Kramer arrived in New York on September 26, 1938 (ancestry. com, 2013). Upon seeing her name on the registry in Ellis Island, I cried for the third time, feeling unbelievable relief and gratitude that she made it to safety. The magnitude of her experiences, the good fortune that she survived, and how this affected my beloved profession was emotionally overwhelming.

Upon Kramer's arrival in New York, she worked with children with a variety of needs, developed her theory, and balanced her identity as a survivor, artist, and art therapist. In spite of the reality of the Holocaust with all of the losses entailed, Kramer did not become self-defeated or depressed. Instead, she utilized her experiences and created a theory and approach for art therapy. The approach that Edith created and that we use today allows for a patient or client in art therapy to access intense emotions without being forced to relive trauma through words. I can't help but wonder if this is how she herself survived. Did she utilize art as a means of processing things that for Kramer "could not and should not be put into words" (Kramer & Wilson, 1998, p. 10)? Did she use this subsequently to identify and help others who needed the same opportunity for processing their trauma?

Kramer escaped Nazi occupation, but she still carried the traumatic and complex story with her to America. It is impossible for me to understand fully the consequences and resulting emotions, belief systems, and feelings that would have resulted from living in occupied Europe, from losing a beloved mentor to the horrors of Auschwitz, and from losing a mother to suicide. Haaken (1990) states, "the horrifying realities left behind made them [Central European psychoanalysts] grateful for the haven they had found in America, but it was a haven that demanded silence about the past" (p. 289). It is no wonder to me then that Kramer's brilliant development of art as therapy was vital, not only from the aspect of having lived in a fear-based and oppressive society, but also from the perspective of the self-reproach of someone who survived it while leaving loved ones behind. I simply cannot imagine enduring that trauma, yet she did, and subsequently she successfully designed a theory for others. Kramer describes in a film by Makarova and Kuchuk (2012):

> In art you tell the truth. . . . You very often find the strength, rather than the pathology. Pathology is easy to find, but how to overcome pathology with what strength there is? That is what art therapy can . . . show and sustain, support – the strengths.

She summarizes beautifully her belief that people are not their diagnoses, but complex and interesting, deserving of an opportunity to explore their story in a private and meaningful way.

Kramer practiced her theory in America. It seemed she related to her patients potentially because they were troubled, labeled as difficult, and challenged. Perhaps, in the boys with whom she worked, she recognized and related to the need for truth telling but also feeling the lack of freedom to do so. Like Kramer, perhaps their experiences were too painful, too hard to reveal, or too implicating to share with words. She developed the concept of sublimation through art, offering a container for which to hold the experience and to discuss at one's own pace with personal control. She also experienced aggression on a national level, which she used to inform her understanding of that behavior. She realized she could foster the sublimation of feelings that could otherwise be harmful or damaging to the patient. She recognized the opportunity for truth telling within her work, and she maintained it was beneficial to others.

Kramer did not waver in her beliefs. She modeled integrity and strength not only in her work but also with her ongoing commitment to herself. She advocated strongly for art therapists to create art, showing her understanding

Figure 1.1 Etching by Edith Kramer. Christmas card from the collection of Elena Makarova

22   Darcy Marlow

that we need to take care of ourselves to be compassionate and capable healers. As art therapists, we can learn from Kramer. We can define for ourselves an approach to art therapy that supports our clients in healing, maintains personal integrity, and adheres to a commitment to the truth. We can look for strengths in times of weakness, hope in times of adversity, and creative opportunities when it feels as if silence is the only option. I have eternal gratitude to Kramer for her confidence in the power of art making, her fierce belief in the strength of creative expression, and her unending determination to experience life on its own scary, messy, amazing, beautiful terms.

Note

1 For more on the experiences of Friedl Dicker-Brandeis and Terezin, please see the chapter by Elena Makarova, "Edith Kramer on Friedl Dicker-Brandeis, Erna Furman, and Terezin."

References

ancestry.com (2013). www.ancestry.com. Accessed December 6, 2016.

Haaken, J. (1990). The Siegfried Bernfeld conference: Uncovering the psycho-analytic political unconscious. *The American Journal of Psychoanalysis, 50*(4), 289–304.

Kramer, E. (1994). *A portrait of artist/art therapist Edith Kramer*. Sacramento, Calif: Chuck Conners Productions.

Kramer, E. (2006). Edith Kramer, art as therapy. In M.B. Junge & H. Wadeson (Eds.), *Architects of art therapy: Memoirs and life stories* (pp. 11–30). Springfield, IL: Charles C. Thomas.

Kramer, E., & Gerity, L.A. (2000). *Art as therapy: Collected papers*. London: Jessica Kingsley Publishers.

Kramer, E., & Wilson, L. (1998). *Childhood and art therapy: Notes on therapy and application* (2nd ed.). Chicago, IL: Magnolia Street Publishers.

Makarova, E., & Kuchuk, H. (Directors). (2012). *Edith Kramer, Art Tells the Truth*. [Video file]. Israel: LenFim Studio. Retrieved from https://vimeo.com/33476299 Accessed 19 September 2017.

Miller, M., & Cook-Greuter, S. (2000). Edith Kramer – Artist and art therapist: A search for integrity and truth. In M. Miller & S. Cook-Greuter (Eds.), *Creativity, spirituality, and transcendence: Paths to integrity and wisdom in the mature self* (pp. 99–124). Stanford, CT: Ablex Publishing Corporation.

Pariser, D. (2008). A woman of valor: Friedl Dicker-Brandeis, art teacher in Theresienstadt concentration camp. *Art Education, 61*(4), 6–12.

Rubin, J. A. (2009). *Introduction to art therapy: Sources and resources*. London, UK: Routledge.

Stern, F. (2001). Subtle silence and its consequences. In H. Tewes & J. Wright (Eds.), *Liberalism, anti-semitism, and democracy: Essays in honor of Peter Pulzer* (pp. 1–10). London, UK: Oxford University Press.

Wilson, L. (1997). Edith Kramer honored at AATA conference. *American Journal of Art Therapy, 4*(35), 102–105.

2 Mumi Kramer, Grundlsee, and the Caring Net

Johannes Reichmayr, Charlotte Zwiauer, Lani Gerity, Martha Haeseler, and Edith Kramer

> I have been a very fortunate person . . . in my upbringing, growing up in a bohemian environment, full of actors, psychoanalysts, artists, revolutionaries, where being an eccentric . . . and self-willed was quite normal. I did not have to fight to be myself. I was liberated from conventions . . .
>
> (Edith Kramer, Foreword, this volume)

The idea behind this chapter began in 2014, when Martha and Lani presented at a Symposium honoring Edith Kramer in Vienna, Austria. One of the other presentations was a fascinating, old, silent film that psychoanalyst and historian Professor Johannes Reichmayr had found while researching material about psychoanalyst Siegfried Bernfeld. This lovely, grainy home movie showed our Edith at the age of 12, a happy playful child known by the endearing nickname of Mumi. We saw her in loving interaction with family and friends at a lake house belonging to analyst and children's magazine publisher Christine (Mädi) Olden, in Grundlsee, Austria, where she spent her summers for most of her life. Professor Reichmayr showed the movie and explained in German who the various people were as well as the stimulating, creative social climate the adults were providing for each other and for the children. We realized that this presentation needed a wider audience. Could it somehow be a part of this book? With that in mind, we had coffee and cakes with Professor Reichmayr in one of the old cafes that are so much a part of Viennese life. Professor Reichmayr explained to us (in English) what we had seen in the short piece of film, and it brought to life that period of history and the remarkable circle of adults who surrounded Edith when she was growing up. After our lovely coffee and cakes and a stroll through an older section of Vienna, we promised to keep in touch. Professor Reichmayr sent us stills from the film clip, which we have included below along with a written description of the activities and people in the film.

In this chapter, most of the information about Edith's childhood and family comes from a book we discovered in Vienna: Charlotte Zwiauer's *Edith Kramer: Malerin und Kunsttherapeutin zwischen den Welten/Edith Kramer, Painter and Art Therapist Between Worlds*. When invited to participate in this

24 *Johannes Reichmayr et al.*

book, Charlotte Zwiauer suggested that rather than write anything new, we could use her material for this chapter, which Martha translated.[1]

Edith's mother, Josephine (Pepa) Neumann, was a rebellious child of a middle-class Jewish family in Vienna. Against her parents' wishes, Pepa left home when she was barely 17, to marry Richard Kramer. Edith was born two years later, in the middle of WWI. The Kramers lived in a circle of artists, Marxists, intellectuals, and psychoanalysts, described by a contemporary as a "leftist, avant-garde, progressive, psychoanalytically-oriented social utopia with sexual freedom" and described by Edith as "bohemian." Pepa designed clothes and was friends with contemporary artists; Richard was artistic and had a degree in chemical engineering, but chose to become an activist and organizer in the newly founded Austrian Communist Party. Since they had little money and did not live together (they had an open marriage), Edith spent most of her early childhood being cared for by her maternal grandparents. She was an only child. When she was eight, she and Pepa went to Berlin to live with Pepa's sister Elisabeth Neumann and her lover, later husband, Siegfried Bernfeld. Aunt Liesl was an actress and an important role model and support for Edith throughout her life. Bernfeld (Brassi) was a psychoanalyst, educator, and founder of the new Jewish Youth Movement, and became a formative father figure to Edith.

On Bernfeld's recommendation, Edith attended progressive schools, first in Berlin, then in Vienna, to which she returned when she was 13. In conversation with David Henley, Edith told David of the transition between the school in Berlin and the one in Vienna. As she described it, her parents had moved back to Vienna and left her in the progressive school in Berlin. Not liking the school's dependence on corporal punishment, Edith made the train trip back to Vienna on her own.

For her whole life, Edith was never without sketching materials, and, at an early age, she attracted the attention of artist and art educator Friedl Dicker (later Dicker-Brandeis), who promised to teach her when she got older. In high school, she took private lessons with both Dicker and sculptor Fritz Wotruba.

Peter Heller, author and educator, who was analyzed by Anna Freud as a child, met Edith when she was 11 and became a lifelong friend. He wrote that she was always so unmistakable and unique and true to her own nature (something we continue to admire her for even today). He described the young Edith as shy, ever unruly, and opposed to the Austrian tone of polite clichés. She seemed to be a real recluse, but was precocious, and made up witty caricatures and posters for the exuberant vacation festivals at Grundlsee. Heller also wrote that as a young girl, Edith believed in Marxism, which Bernfeld tried to reconcile with psychoanalysis, but distanced herself from the erotic fast living of the adults of the Grundlsee circle, with their avant-garde manners. She adopted an ascetic attitude.

An indication of the creative richness in Edith's upbringing can be found in the Knurrland Game, invented by Pepa as a child, which she and her sister Liesl played throughout their lives. In the imaginary world of Knurrland [possible translations: Grumbleland, or Snarlland], Liesl was Kaiser, and Pepa was Grand Vizier. Knurrland had its own language in which 14 newspapers were published, and Pepa created props and sewed costumes. The game was so complex that a contemporary published an analysis of it in a psychoanalytic journal and wrote that Pepa was the one who made up the language, and that the different lands, spirits, and objects originated in her imagination. She slaved away, ever and ever harder, making new parts of the game or new games (Fuchs, 1922, p. 147).

Edith remembered her mother and Aunt Liesl playing the game with her when she was a child, and she could still recite a monologue from it by heart. Edith's observations of the game were often analytic, seeing it as an ironic commentary on and way of dealing with the concerns over which children (and adults) have no power. For example, Aunt Liesl gave her first husband, Bernfeld, a role that helped deal with the fear and worry about his delicate health. When Edith described the play world of Liesl and Pepa, in a personal communication, she said that she herself could not play creatively the way they could; she could only play the role of an artist. Although she certainly appreciated their creativity, she could only be herself. This wanting to stay with reality may be related to her enjoyment of painting what she saw, rather than what she imagined. We can surmise that the child Edith, in a social circle that was breaking every convention, where the line between reality and imagination was permeable, set very firm boundaries for herself. However, in later years, she did occasionally engage in imaginative puppet play with us (Lani and Martha).

When Edith graduated from high school, she decided to pursue a career in the arts and to intensify her lessons with Friedl Dicker. When Dicker moved to Prague for political reasons, Edith, at 18, followed her and worked alongside her with children of families fleeing from Hitler. Edith later wrote about the child refugees:

> They were still the uprooted, traumatized children of uprooted, traumatized parents. I learned from it the various effects such experiences of war can have on children. Getting stuck in schematic repetition, compulsive smearing, fragments that don't hang together, identification with the aggressor, regression. Especially impressive was the identification with the all-powerful Hitler, he who had put them through suffering, his power manifested. I further encountered the same phenomenon later in my work with neglected and disturbed children. Friedl found ways to bring these children to creative work and thereby to also help their souls.
>
> (Kramer, 1988, p. 2)

In the Grundlsee film, there is much playful and loving interaction, which shows that Edith grew up in the sheltering arms of a caring as well as a creatively and intellectually stimulating group of people, as seen in Professor Johannes Reichmayr's description, as follows:

> In this 1.5 minute long film we see the house of Christine "Mädi" Olden in Grundlsee. First, a view of the house from the lake will be shown, then people on the veranda on the first floor, then scenes from the terrace, and

26   Johannes Reichmayr et al.

in the end, the lakeshore in front of the house. In the summer months, visitors from Vienna, Prague, Berlin and other places met here, mostly friends and acquaintances of Mädi Olden, who was a renowned publisher, actress, and psychoanalyst. Siegfried Bernfeld, Liesl Neumann, and her sister Pepa Kramer with her daughter Edith "Mumi" Kramer were regular visitors. We see Mumi in the film at 12 years of age with her Aunt Liesl and Siegfried Bernfeld.

In the course of the film the following people step before the camera: Pepa Kramer, Mädi Olden and Liesl Neumann on the veranda; Mädi Olden with her German Shepherd dog on the terrace; behind her back Pepa Kramer passes by; Sergei Feitelberg and Liesl Neumann are following; afterwards the dancing Liesl warmly kisses Mumi; Feitelberg appears in the doorway; the visitor on the lounge chair is possibly the chemist Harry Sobotka, who in his mid-twenties emigrated from Vienna to the USA, and made his career in Beth Israel Hospital in New York; next Siegfried "Brassi" Bernfeld with his short lederhosen (his summer wear for the Ausseer region), next with Mumi, afterwards Liesl kisses her, in the background Feitelberg; next, Pepa wades in the lake next to a child from the neighborhood; the smoking "Brassi" Bernfeld stalks through the water, after him an unknown guest; the next scene again films Liesl and Siegfried, followed by Mumi and Liesl and finally Mumi is swimming between the legs of Brassi; the child does the same with Pepa; at the end Liesl and Mumi storm into the water and at the very end we see a portrait of Liesl.

The Ausseerland region was and is a popular vacation place. In 1930, Sigmund Freud vacationed here with his daughter Anna; writers like Hugo von Hofmannsthal, Arthur Schnitzler and Friedrich Torberg treasured this landscape; and Grundlsee was beloved by the younger psychoanalysts, artists, and intellectuals. Ever more friends came to vacation there, including Wilhelm and Annie Reich, Otto Fenichel, Karl Frank, Richard Kramer, Josi and Fredi Mayer, Hanns Sachs, Clara Happel and many others. Many of them were already friends, dating back to before the First World War, when they were Jewish high-school students in the Vienna Youth Movement, protesting against outdated moral standards in society, school, and the home. Siegfried Bernfeld was the intellectual protagonist of the movement, and Mumi Kramer was included in the circle of friends. Most of the visitors to Grundlsee were connected, either directly or indirectly, to this former peer group. Some of these friendships began even in childhood, and adolescence – the Fenichel and Neumann families knew each other well and lived in Vienna in the same neighborhood; Otto Fenichel's first love was directed towards Pepa Neumann; Friedl Dicker, Mumi's art teacher, was also active in the Youth Movement with Harry Sobotka and belonged even more closely to the circle of friends with Otto Fenichel. Siegfried Bernfeld was the mate of Mumi's Aunt Liesl, and lived with her together with Pepa and Mumi in Berlin until 1929. From 1934 to 1938, Mumi lived in Prague and was cared for also by Otto Fenichel,

Annie Reich, Steff Bornstein, Fredi Mayer and others whom she had known from Grundlsee. In Prague Otto Fenichel took care of getting an affidavit for Mumi. Mumi was held in this net, which held her lifelong, in Vienna, Grundlsee, Berlin, Prague and later also in New York.

(J. Reichmayr, Personal Communication, June 11, 2015)

Figure 2.1 First set of film stills: Mädi's house, Pepa Kramer, Mädi Olden, and Liesl Neumann on the balcony. Mädi and, finally, Mädi with Pepa passing behind her.

28 *Johannes Reichmayr et al.*

Figure 2.2 Second set of film stills: Siegfried "Brassi" Bernfeld with Mumi, with an unidentified guest, being kissed by Liesl, and Bernfeld wading.

If we look at Edith's parents' lives (living through WWI, engaging in various social justice activities, never having enough money to create a permanent home), we sense a great deal of instability. But thankfully for Mumi, the circle of caring adults of Grundlsee formed a profoundly supportive social net for her.

These adults cared deeply about the next generation. Mumi internalized that caring and expressed it throughout her life.

While exploring the NYU Archives we discovered a remembrance of Mädi (Christine Olden) that Edith had written. It describes Mädi in such a way that we realized she was very central in Edith's caring net, if not the center of it. What follows is the remembrance of Mädi. What will strike the reader is that the person being described could easily have been Edith.

Edith Kramer on Mädi (Christine Olden)

My earliest recollections of Mädi go back more than 30 years. I was, at the time, a little younger than Kostia (Anni Bergman's son) is today, and in many ways my feelings were akin to the feelings that he expressed in his story.

We met Mädi in Grundlsee. We had arrived by rowboat, after a long stretch of rowing. We saw her house first, set against the dark green pines and grey rock of the Backenstein. As we entered the house, it was full of treasures, it was beautiful, and the mistress, too, was beautiful – at that time, beautiful as only a young woman can be beautiful. There was an enchanting harmony between the house, its mistress and the landscape outside, and there was a most graceful hospitality. I was enchanted, and have remained enchanted from then on.

The first meeting marked the beginning of many summers, which we spent as Mädi's close neighbors. Within the next ten years, we participated in many changes, many ups and downs. Always there were many guests, people coming and going. Mädi was a passionate woman and a complex human being. There was conflict and struggle. From a young woman interested in writing and education, who edited a children's magazine, Mädi changed into an analyst. She acquired the methods and the knowledge to follow her interests in a much more profound way.

Certain qualities remained constant always. When later I met Mädi in many different settings not as ideally fitting as Grundlsee – in Berlin, in Prague, finally in New York – there was always the same enchantment. The qualities, which Mädi created, did not depend on a specific place or on certain objects; they belonged to her wherever she was.

Always there were beautiful things; always there was harmony and unity. Mädi acquired new treasures, and their number grew, but there was never an accumulation of objects, never a collection. Mädi's treasures were an organic whole that was more than the sum of its parts – because Mädi's relationship to her treasures was not the collector's pride in possessions, it was never a superficial one.

Nor were her pleasures limited to the enjoyment of works of art. Rather, the capacity for profound enjoyment was one of her greatest gifts. She could gain the same pleasure from nature, from ideas, books, music, and above all, from relationships. If she loved things, it was because she had the power to communicate with the stored-up life which resides in all things made by man, be it a peasant wardrobe, a piece of embroidery, beautiful china, or a painting.

With her enjoyment went the capacity for taking infinite pains in the care of everything she loved, be it an object that needed repair and maintenance, a flower that needed water or a human being that needed help. Sometimes Mädi complained about her many obligations and the time they took. But it was unthinkable that anything that had to be done for somebody would not be done and done in time.

Mädi was very Viennese. She had strong roots in the past. For those of us who had experienced discontinuity, a break of tradition, she was a link with the past. She embodied our culture and gave us a feeling of continuity. Yet Mädi transcended her past. The qualities she embodied could be felt and understood by Europeans or Americans, by children or adults. They had become timeless.

This timeless quality made it possible for her to live with people much younger than herself, without strain. There was respect, veneration; yet there was also an easy giving and taking between her and us.

Mädi accepted limitations in the people she loved. At times, she overestimated them. Yet she never accepted the mediocre or the superficial. She set standards for us in our actions and in our production. She was a wonderful partner in any creative endeavor. Here I have to speak of my own experiences, but I know that many others have had the same kind of experiences in their fields.

No painting is complete without an audience, someone who vicariously re-creates – shares the creative process. Mädi was the ideal audience. She was deeply interested in the process of creation and sublimation. She could sense it in a delinquent little boy or in an old master.

She had an insatiable desire to understand this process better – not because she thought it possible fully to understand one of the great mysteries of life, but because she knew that the never-ending attempt at understanding is one of the great tasks and the great pleasures of life.

When I began to write about art therapy, Mädi read each chapter as it was written. She contributed her judgment, her vast experience. More important still was her belief in the importance of my attempt. And it was evident that the participation gave her pleasure, so that there was a mutual interchange. Again, this is not just my experience. Mädi loved to participate in any creative effort.

Mädi's great interest was the problem of empathy – her great gift was the gift of empathy.

. . . Mädi's creative work went beyond her own direct production. To her, writing was never as important as living. But her life was itself a creative act. The beauty and quality of her person, the atmosphere she

Mädi, as a unique person, will live in our memories. Her humanity and strength will find new forms in the life and work of those who loved her.

created, were a source of pleasure and inspiration to those who knew her. It has become part of our lives and will continue as a living force. In this process, there will be change and transformation. Mädi, as a unique person, will live in our memories. Her humanity and strength will find new forms in the life and work of those who loved her.

(*The Edith Kramer Papers*, New York University; Kramer, n.d.)

Conclusion

Edith often spoke of the kindly care taking part of the superego or ego ideal that she felt was a part of the European experience. She thought this ego ideal should always be someone that a person could grow into, often a grandparent figure. In reading her description of Mädi, we realized that Edith did indeed grow into her ego ideal, becoming so very like Mädi. In our discussion with Professor Reichmayr, however, it emerged that perhaps not all Europeans experienced or internalized this warm, caring net of remarkable adults, that Edith's situation was perhaps more unique than she realized. Edith considered herself fortunate in so many ways. Growing up within this caring net, and then internalizing these wonderful caring adults, she was able to provide a similar net for everyone she worked with and everyone she taught. And all of us – art therapists, teachers, and students of art therapy – are part of her legacy. We are able to carry on this generous tradition.

Note

1 From the book *Edith Kramer, Malerin und Kunsttherapeutin zwischen den Welten/Edith Kramer, Painter and Art Therapist Between Worlds*, most of the quotes for this chapter are taken from pp. 16–84. Actual quotes can be found on pp. 18–20, 21, 30, 33, 35, 38, and 55. Additional material came from reminiscences written by Peter Heller, p. 13.

References

Fuchs, G. (1922). Knurrland. Versuch der Analyse eines Kinderspieles [Knurrland. An attempt to analyze a child's play]. In Bernfeld, S. *Vom Gemeinschaftleben der Jugend* [From the community life of youth]. Leipzig UA. Cited in Zwiauer, C. (1997). *Edith Kramer: Malerin und Kunsttherapeutin zwischen den Welten* [Edith Kramer: Painter and art therapist between worlds]. Vienna: Picus Verlag.

Kramer, E. (1988). *Erinnerungen an Friedl Dicker-Brandeis* [Memories of Friedl Dicker-Brandeis]. In Mit der Ziehharmonika [With the accordion]. *Journal of the Theodor Kramer Society/Zeitschrift der Theodor-Kramer-Gesellschaft*, 5. Jg. Nr.3.

32 Johannes Reichmayr et al.

Kramer, E. (n.d.). Mädi. [Handwritten comments for Christine Olden's memorial service]. *The Edith Kramer Papers* (MC215_box3_Folder 12). New York University Archives, Bobst Library, New York, NY.

Zwiauer, C. (1997). *Edith Kramer: Malerin und Kunsttherapeutin zwischen den Welten* [Edith Kramer: Painter and art therapist between worlds]. Vienna: Picus Verlag.

3 Edith Kramer Remembered

Anni Bergman

Christine Olden, a psychoanalyst, with whom I had a long-lasting and deep connection, introduced me to Edith. Both Edith and Christine Olden were representatives of the world of Viennese culture. When I first met Edith, she was a young artist living by herself in New York. I think my initial relationship to Edith was one in which I admired her for her painting and her general talents as an artist, but also her whole background and connections to the Viennese intelligentsia. We shared a background in Vienna as it had been, but no longer was. Edith remained very connected to the intellectual world of Vienna in New York, and psychoanalysis was part of this world.

I like to think Edith invented art therapy while working with my older son Kostia. Christine Olden suggested that Edith teach Kostia, who was a little shy, about art and carpentry. Edith soon became my closest friend and the admired friend of my whole family. Edith was a magician. She could do anything. She could paint and draw and sculpt and carve. She could tell dozens of fairy tales and recite volumes of German poetry. At the dinner table, she created families from molded bread and tea sets from foil candy wrappers. She could do anything.

Edith became part of my family when she joined us on our summer vacations. She had always been an inveterate companion for adventures, especially hiking in the mountains, and finding treasures in antique stores. We spent our summers together in the White Mountains of New Hampshire. We shared a summerhouse in New Hampshire, and I remember her going out every morning to spend the day painting in nature. At the end of the day my children would rush to meet her and ask her, what did you paint today?

Edith was always painting. But she was not only an artist who could draw and paint – she was also an artist in the way she could tell stories, particularly the stories of her life. And she wanted these stories to be part of her art, as well. Through our relationship, her paintings became part of my family's life and part of my house. I owe my first interest in psychoanalysis in part to Edith, who told me the intimate and exciting stories of her life in the intellectual circles of Vienna. The stories included her analysis with Annie Reich, another participant in Christine Olden's circle.

Sometimes the conversations at our dinner table with Edith would get heated. Edith was passionate, and she could have her strong opinions. Someone once told Edith about her own paintings which she created from photographs. Edith was dismissive: "It can't be art." Tact was not Edith's forte. Someone would arrive with a newborn baby, possibly my own grandson. "We don't need more babies. We have too many already. Where will we put them all?" Edith was very concerned about overpopulation of our planet; yet, whenever a baby was actually near her, she would draw a beautiful portrait of it, showing her love in her own, special way.

For years, she and I would set out a few days before Christmas to find the perfect presents for everyone, and the perfect Christmas tree for my house. Sometimes we drove to faraway places to find them. Sometimes we wandered through the freezing and windy streets of New York City. Getting really cold and exhausted was always a part of the "Christmas tree and present search" adventure. Once we'd found a tree and got it home, then we'd decorate it, and many of the ornaments were handmade by Edith. Christmas Eve in my house was the time for memories of Vienna. We would have a goose dinner and decorate the tree. We used Edith's ornaments, real Viennese cookies, and real candles. Edith would arrive with a huge backpack full of handmade gifts

Figure 3.1 Edith Kramer sketching in Toronto, Canada. Photo by Herschel J. Stroyman

Edith Kramer Remembered 35

for everyone but especially for the children. There were tiny pick-up stick sets and miniature carpenters' tools. There were carved sculptures of boys with axes. There were endless, marzipan painted sculptures of every possible animal and fairy-tale character, and Edith would insist they be eaten. Although Edith could not carry a tune, the singing of Christmas carols was always very important to her. Christmas Eve without Edith was quite unthinkable.

Edith lived in New York for most of her life. She used to have a walk-up apartment on the Lower East Side, which she kept for many years – even after she bought her beautiful studio – but she also had a home in the countryside of Austria where she spent many months every year. The people of the village were devoted to her. Edith loved to visit friends in different parts of Europe, and spent many months traveling and visiting every year. It was always exciting to see the work she had painted while on her many travels.

As a painter, Edith's work was remarkable in its versatility of subject matter. She painted industrial scenery as much as scenery of nature. She painted portraits, especially of families, and children and pregnant women. She also created exquisite still life pictures of flowers and beautiful objects. She found beauty in many different settings, including both urban and country environments. All her paintings were inspired by passion for the beauty of the real world. The need to create seemed to be a part of her. It is not something she tried to accomplish, but rather it seemed to be a need and ability to turn her perceptions of the world into works of art. Sometimes there seemed to be a fine line between play and work or maybe between intention and need. I never tire of looking at her paintings in my own home, which I had bought or she had given to me.

Even before Edith became an art therapist she was already deeply involved in psychoanalysis. Her analyst was Annie Reich. She was not just in analysis; she was also serious about her knowledge of psychoanalysis. I think she believed that without having her own analysis, she could not have fulfilled herself as an artist and as a teacher of art. And her experience as an analytic patient significantly informed her work as an art therapist. Edith understood that psychoanalysis could meaningfully contribute to therapeutic work with children.

Eventually, Edith became an art therapist. She was dedicated not only to art, but also to the people she helped as an art therapist. Edith understood how to work with the most disturbed children. I think she was interested in children who were confronted with difficulties in their upbringing. By bringing together art and play as a therapist, I believe that she fulfilled a very deep yearning of her own, which was to be creatively available to children.

She knew about the healing properties of creativity. She could inspire creativity in others by her profound knowledge, but also by her profound conviction about the essentialness of it for a life worth living. It is this deep knowledge that provided her with the ability to inspire others to find within themselves the ability to create, at whatever level, and in whatever way they could.

Edith worked as an art therapist with a very gifted, interesting patient of mine. She fully appreciated my patient's creative talent as an artist, but she also understood when the time had come to allow this talented young woman to work on her own. Edith respected genuine creativity in any medium, be it art or writing or living. She certainly inspired and always appreciated my efforts to live a genuinely creative life.

Our closeness, our friendship, is difficult to describe. Even though we were very different in our talents, there were important things that we shared, such as love of nature and hiking. Hiking had something to do with conquering anxieties connected to nature, such as anxiety of being alone, anxiety of being in danger with nobody there to help, anxiety related to being away from home, anxiety about finding one's way in life, and one's solution to the meaning of life.

Let me end by saying how important Edith was to both my personal and professional development. I think that her relationship to me brought together her love of art and her love of family. She loved painting portraits of families, which was important because she did not have her own family. Maybe this was a way that she compensated for not having a family of her own, which she decided not to have because she felt that if she did, then she could not be dedicated to working with children.

Figure 3.2 Edith and Anni

On one level, Edith's life was simple. It reminds me of an old Austrian folk song, "Cuckoo." In it the singer imagines if he marries his maiden fair, he would have no more desires. He sings that there would be a home for her to care for and some wood for the fire, what more could they want. The content is simple, but the circumstances are complex because they deal with the wish to fulfill one's desires that should be simple, but in fact, are always complex. Edith might have lived in a very simple house, but it was filled with beautiful objects, both made by her and by others. It was also filled by desires and by memories and thoughts about those she loved; in particular, her mother, her Aunt Liesl, and some special friends.

The loss of Edith is hard to bear because it is the loss of somebody unique, irreplaceable, often plain on the outside, but filled with intense feelings of love, desire, and longing.

4 Edith Kramer on Friedl Dicker-Brandeis, Erna Furman, and Terezin[1]

Interviews with Elena Makarova

Erna Furman (1926–2002)

My friendship with Erna Furman began when she found out that I had been a disciple of Friedl Dicker-Brandeis. She and Friedl had been close friends when they were both interned in the concentration camp of Terezin during the Second World War. Furman had always hoped to find someone who knew Friedl so she could share remembrances.

In 1972, Erna Furman was asked to review my book *Art as Therapy with Children* for the *Psychoanalytic Quarterly*. The spirit of the book seemed familiar to her. It reminded her of Friedl Dicker's way of teaching art to the children of Terezin. When Furman learned that I had known Friedl from 1932 to 1938, she was "overjoyed" to have found someone who knew Friedl as well. She was interested in getting to know me and invited me to Cleveland, Ohio, to give lectures at the Hanna Perkins Center for Child Development. We have been in touch from then on.

Terezin was the ghetto where prominent Jews were interned before transport to Auschwitz and other extermination centers where they were murdered. It was a showcase – a kind of Potemkin's Village – where a façade of peaceful living could hide the reality of the continuous transports.[2] At Terezin, supreme power resided in the SS (Schutzstaffel). However, the Jewish community was responsible for the management of the camp, distribution of food, fuel, and shelter, as well as for "leisure time" activities or "freizeitgestaltung."

The Jewish community allotted preferential care for the children. Throughout her time at Terezin (1942–1944), Erna Furman functioned as a childcare worker in a girls' home. There she met Friedl Dicker-Brandeis, who was giving art lessons to the children. The two women became friends. Furman assisted Friedl's teaching and helped to keep the children's work signed, dated, and preserved. Friedl helped sustain Erna's will to live, encouraging her to pursue her own art. Furman felt that her memories from that time with Friedl were among the fondest memories of her life. The fact that it was in Terezin made it more poignant, but she felt it would have been the same anywhere in the world. Furman preserved her sketchbook from Terezin all her life. It clearly showed Erna's undeniable artistic talent, particularly for portraiture, and testified to Friedl's exquisite teaching.

My relationship with Friedl Dicker began when she saw my drawings in a friend's house in Vienna when I was 12 years old. Friedl liked my work and said she would teach me when I was a little older. When I was just 15 years old, Friedl permitted me to attend art courses she conducted for Nursery School Teachers who worked for the city of Vienna.

When a reactionary government gained power in Austria in 1934, Friedl, an ardent communist, was apprehended for harboring false passports for the Party. She was confined in an Austrian prison. She immigrated to Prague, Czechoslovakia, after she had served her time.

After graduating high school (Gymnasium) in 1934, I followed Friedl to Prague. I became her disciple, performing various duties at her studio while I learned from her. My duties included assisting her when she conducted art classes for German-speaking children. A number of them were the offspring of political refugees – workers who had fled Hitler's Germany and found temporary haven in the then still democratic Czechoslovakia. They lived in camps maintained by the city of Prague awaiting admission to South-American countries.

As I observed the art of these uprooted, traumatized children, I began to recognize the various manifestations of emotional disturbance, chaotic imagery, distorted body image, sterile repetition, and above all, the ominous defense of identification with the aggressor. I also learned how work with art materials could help these children gain emotional equilibrium.

In 1938, I immigrated to the United States, while Friedl and her husband remained in Czechoslovakia. In 1942, they were confined in Terezin, where Friedl lived, painted, and taught art to children until her death at Auschwitz; her husband, Pavel, survived.

When I began to work as an art therapist in 1950 with underprivileged, traumatized children of greater New York, I applied what I had learned as an assistant to Friedl in her work with children in Prague; that was how Erna Furman recognized Friedl's spirit in my book, *Art as Therapy with Children*. From then on, Erna Furman read all my papers on art therapy. Her constructive criticism was invaluable. I am greatly indebted to her for the help she gave me.

Like many survivors, Erna Furman was a very private person. When I read at her memorial service in Cleveland, it was apparent that her colleagues knew next to nothing about Erna Furman's past as a survivor of Hitler's Czechoslovakia or of Terezin. In her conversation with Elena Makarova, Furman explained that she had decided to work through her horrendous experiences alone so as not to handicap her marriage and relationship to her children and with her co-workers. She also knew that most Americans were either unable to hear the refugee's experiences, or those that did listen would enter a state of heightened sadistic excitement about Nazis, the SS, and Hitler.

Erna's conversations with Elena Makarova were different, however. As a Russian who had lived through Stalin's regime, Elena could comprehend and even appreciate what it took to survive Hitler's Czechoslovakia and Terezin. Through these conversations with Elena, Furman's indomitable will to survive became apparent along with her inexhaustible energy, her presence of mind, and her

40 *Elena Makarova*

brilliant intellect. Furman said that to survive, one had to give up the primitive idea that "it cannot happen to me. Only then could we summon up the faculties it took to get by; only by facing reality could we find our will to live."

The hardship that Furman endured helped her see the power of sadistic rage that helplessness brings out. Yet, she believed it could be tamed. She felt one must immediately establish human connections. She shared two examples how giving up the "it can't happen to me" fantasy and establishing human connections saved her life. First, in Terezin she was put on a list for deportation. She went to Rahm, the SS Obersturmführer. He spoke to her with a noticeable Viennese accent. She answered in an equally strong Viennese accent. This commonality between them saved her life. The second incident was when the Russians took over Terezin. Furman was asleep in a bunker, nude, under a blanket. She woke up when a Russian soldier, dead drunk, sat on her bed, a pistol against her neck. She could speak Russian to him, telling him that she was alone, without her family, that he was probably also far from home. They talked about their parents. In the end, he wished her the best, and she wished him the best. I believe the saving grace for Erna was that she had been given sufficient love in her early life to possess a store of humanity to meet and tame sadistic rage.

Friedl Dicker-Brandeis (1898–1944)

Masters and Students

I was an apprentice with Friedl. She was my master and I was her student. It is a very old tradition. Friedl demanded a lot of me. I did my best, and sometimes I would rebel. That was the tradition. If one had a good master, but was not particularly talented oneself, one would work in the style of one's master and achieve good results. If one had an independent talent, one could continue to develop and create new things. But whatever was new was based on the foundation. One did not strive to be original only in order to distinguish oneself from others, back then.

I believe that when one has many teachers who all teach something different, no structure comes out of it. No personal relationship develops with the teacher, and respect is lacking. I had respect for Friedl, although sometimes I was also afraid of her. I believe that this is very good for art. One remains modest and does not develop delusions of grandeur. Naturally, everything depends on what kind of master one has; one who uses the students or one who helps them grow. Many masters exploit their students. She was a woman who did not use people, thankfully. However, she could be a harsh critic. It is good that she was. It has always been hard for me to find people who were good critics of art. I still dream of her – I dream that she is continuing to work, is finishing her pictures, that she shows me her pictures, and I show her mine. I would still be happy to show her my work.

Friedl's teacher, Itten, was an outstanding teacher, but a mediocre artist. That is where the difference lies. Friedl was also a great artist. She understood

Itten's method. She softened everything that was inflexible, and did away with all the mysticism. Everything was brought closer to reality. She went beyond Itten's concepts, but she respected and preserved what was valuable in his method and applied it with her own passionate temperament.

Friedl was versatile. She embroidered, wove, painted, designed furniture and costumes, and taught. She was not an intellectual – she did not have the same high level of formal education as most of her friends. She only graduated from the public technical school, or Bürgerschule. I think she always felt a little inferior because of it. There was a great deal that belonged to our general education that she did not know. She read a lot, but unsystematically.

Some of Friedl's Lessons

Dictation

She liked to dictate pictures to us. For example, she would say: "Here we have a heavy, smooth rolling pin and there a pair of rough, heavy bricks. Thin blades of grass are growing between them." Conversely, "A string shopping bag and a piece of planed wood." She would name different things, and one had to draw very quickly. No attention was paid to the composition. Then she might say: "There goes a fox with a long, bushy tail." Next would come something that did not fit at all, for example, something knitted: "Imagine how the thread slips in and out of the loop, so that you can see how the piece of knitting is made, and not just what it looks like." In this way one gets a feeling for how something comes into being, how a basket is woven or how bamboo grows: it sprouts a piece, stops for a moment, sprouts again, until finally it fans out. One perceives the movement. The dictations were funny. One never knew what was coming. She had a lot of imagination. One had to put completely different things together, for example, steps going up or down, and then a person who was climbing the steps or descending them. In this way, we were able to develop an understanding of what art is about.

Using Rhythm

One had to give a graphic translation of the tone of her voice, for example one – one and two – two. She set the rhythm, and one had to follow her voice very carefully and draw the rhythm very precisely, so that it could be read from the paper. That was a very good, simple exercise, because everyone has a feeling for rhythm. Even if one did not have any experience with drawing, beautiful graphic shapes appeared on the paper.

Wire Figures

She would say, "Imagine a figure in motion. This figure is made entirely of spiral-shaped wire, so that you can see through it. Then you will understand

42   Elena Makarova

how body parts come toward you, or move to the back or to the side. This does not result in correct nude drawings. One sees what is happening instead of copying something down. And when one copies a figure later, one draws better and more convincingly, because one understands what is happening."

Reportage

Friedl was passionate and temperamental. When she noticed that someone had "cheated" or done what she called "reportage," she would say: "I know that you can see. I know that you can draw an eye, but that is not enough. You have to represent the composition of the eye convincingly." She called it reportage when a drawing conveyed only a recognizable description and not the representation of the essence of a thing. That was not enough for her. She did not accept anything that was not done without absolute concentration. She demanded full concentration.

Friedl's General Suggestions

Sometimes she would say: "Try to paint a picture where you start from the top left and finish at the bottom right." Or she would ask that one begin a drawing of a standing man, by starting with the feet instead of the head. She also said, "If you paint a portrait and do not know where the person's backside is sitting, it is not a good portrait."

When I had developed a good command of drawing with charcoal, she told me I should stop: "It is too easy for you." I was supposed to draw with a pencil or a brush with India ink or with a pen – something that demands more discipline.

She liked making collages, because one can find colors and combine them instead of mixing them and creating a dirty mish-mash. With a collage, every-thing remains fresh. One's palette does not become messy, and that is a big help. I made collages in Friedl's class; she also made wonderful collages with the children in Theresienstadt. Whenever I get stuck in my painting, whenever my colors become lifeless, I help myself by doing a collage, so that color and structure complement each other.

I remember different things she said, for example: "If a picture is bad, it seems as small as a postage stamp. If a picture is good, it seems big. That is independent of its measurable size." Certain of her observations are so correct that I return to them again and again. If one of my pictures seems small, there is something wrong with the composition.

She believed that one should observe every object from different points of view in order to understand each element individually – the rhythm, the linear composition, the spatial arrangement, the structure, the color composition. One acknowledges the individual elements in order to prevent confusion. Then one consciously combines the individual elements again. This is true for abstract as well as representational art. In her courses, there was a kind of system – rhythm, structure, and dictations. We did not necessarily work according to a fixed schedule. Sometimes we would begin with a still life, and then the picture would require that we go outside, or do something completely different. She let us work from models and many other things as well. It was not a completely systematic class. She also said, "I know you are talented, but what are you going to do with your talent? That is what matters!"

Naturally, she was completely different with children. One can only make such stringent demands of adults or adolescents. Children need to be praised. One must accept them and expect nothing from them but enthusiasm. One must meet children at their particular level of development, and not push them to skip any developmental levels. One cannot teach children anything beyond their developmental capacity to learn. One can only help them to recognize what they already know. Then they say, "Aha!"

Friedl's Art Ethic

The artistic morality that Friedl embodied was part of my entire upbringing. The mortal sin in art for Friedl was fraud. It was not just Friedl's influence. Not only Friedl said this, but also Franz Singer, my mother, and the whole circle in which I grew up. I believe it to this day. And that is something else I adopted from her: I never compromise; I never bow to the fashions of my time. I consistently went my own way. I enjoy simple or unpretentious people. I believe that everyone can easily understand my work.

The Children in Prague

In Prague, Friedl taught children. Among them were the children of Prague's German-speaking intelligentsia, as well as proletarian children who had come to Prague with their parents as political refugees from Nazi Germany. I helped her. Her idea of art lessons for children was influenced by Viktor Lowenfeld's work with the blind. She did not come up with it on her own.

Friedl in Theresienstadt

The fact that Friedl remained in Czechoslovakia became a tragedy for her. But for the children of Theresienstadt, it was a piece of good fortune. I believe that Friedl became less aggressive in Theresienstadt. Friedl was always open-handed, always generous; nothing changed with regard to that, but she seemed to have been less aggressive than the Friedl I knew. Maybe she no longer needed to fan the flames of any conflicts, since life there was so hard. I believe that she really did change, a change for the better. In a certain sense, her destiny was fulfilled. But we do not know what would have happened if she had immigrated to Palestine, succeeded in getting her husband permission to join her there, and developed further as a painter.

44 *Elena Makarova*

The Children in Theresienstadt

What Friedl did in Theresienstadt was art education with therapeutic elements. Most of the children still had inner resources. So, she embedded some therapy into art education. I work with people whom no one wanted from the day they were born. They had a much harder, more destructive childhood.

It was very interesting for me when the first pictures came out of Theresienstadt: How strong and undamaged these children were, despite everything they had been through! One could help them in Theresienstadt, by making them aware of the beautiful experiences from their lives since there was no future. In a certain way, it resembles work with old people whose lives are deteriorating and whose wealth lies in the past: what they became, what they still are, what they carry within themselves. In the lives of these children, there had been butterflies, and they were present internally. In this sense, the work was unusual.

She would create exercises. And pictures by old masters would be analyzed. There were color rows and the systematic mixing of colors. She gave a lot to the children, helped them acquire the means of expression to work creatively. She did many rhythmic exercises with them so that their hands could become free for drawing and would not be used in the same way as for writing.

The pictures from Theresienstadt are full of life. One can see the personality of each child. The enthusiasm of the children is clearly visible and one senses how they defended themselves against their inhuman environment. These pictures represent very good children's art. One doesn't get that result by handing out paper and pencils and saying: "Now draw." Wherever one finds good children's art, there must have been someone present who helped the children be productive, someone who inspired them and for whom it was not a tiresome duty. Friedl achieved something wonderful, and probably helped the children develop and remain full of life until their deaths.

What Remains of Her?

There are the drawings by the children of Theresienstadt, there is her own work, and there is the influence she had on many people. That is all any of us can hope for after we die: That which one has made, what one has been, remains alive in one's fellow men.

One recognizes that good things have the ability to survive, because otherwise mankind would have perished long ago. It is unfortunate that many more of her works were not preserved, but what has survived is beautiful. It will speak to people, for as long as there is still paper and pastel chalk. Friedl's personality played a significant role in the life of Erna Furman, her friends, and the people who knew her. She was even important to many people who didn't know her, like Elena Makarova. There are many forms of survival.

Notes

1 For more information related to this subject, please see Makarova (1995, 1999, 2007) and Makarova, Makarov, and Kuperman (2000).
2 About 144,000 Jewish men, women, and children were sent to Terezin (Theresienstadt, T.), an 18th-century fortress town near Prague, from Czechoslovakia, Germany, Austria, Denmark, and Holland (via the transit camp Westerbork). About a quarter of them (33,000) died in Terezin, mostly because of the appalling circumstances there. About 88,000 were deported to Auschwitz and other extermination camps. When the war finished, there were a mere 19,000 survivors.

References

Makarova, E. (1995). *Therezienstadt: Kultur och Barari* [Culture and barbarism]. Stockholm: Carlsson Bökforlag.
Makarova, E. (1999). *Friedl Dicker-Brandeis, Vienna 1898–Auschwitz 1944.* Beverley Hills, CA: Tallfellow Press.
Makarova, E. (2007). *Erna Furman/Elena Makarova: Ways of growing up.* Rotterdam: Veeman Publishers.
Makarova, E., Makarov, S., & Kuperman, V. (2000). *University over the abyss. The story behind 489 lecturers and 2309 lectures in KZ Theresienstadt, 1942–1944* (2nd extended ed., 2004). Jerusalem: Verba Publishers.

More Recent History

5 Edith Kramer

A Generous, Generative Genius

Judith A. Rubin

Revisiting anything initially discovered in your youth can be risky. Memories often glow brighter with distance, and first love always feels and seems special. While you hope that the thrill of the original encounter will still be present, you also fear that the once wonderful will look drab and disappointing when viewed with older, more experienced eyes. Before I go on any further here, I shall first put my experiences with Edith Kramer into a personal historical context.

When I was in college, my child psychology professor was doing a study about the relationship of child-rearing practices to children's behavior with finger paint (Alper, Blane, & Abrams, 1955). I'll never forget Mrs Alper's excitement as she held up paintings in front of the class that vividly illustrated the differences in work by youngsters from various socio-economic groups. I was thrilled to discover that making art – my favorite pastime since early childhood – was related to how a person felt. This was something I "knew" from personal experience, but having it validated was deeply affirming. Later that semester, Mrs Alper allowed me to focus the required observation of children in the Wellesley nursery school on their behavior with art materials, and it was illuminating.

She also gave us a choice of supplemental readings for the course, which included a study of normal preschool children called *Painting and Personality* (Alschuler & Hattwick, 1947). Although I found the general chapters interesting, the case studies of individual youngsters – the connections between who they were and their painting, clay, and block play – were even more intriguing.

Investigating the field of art education for an assignment in another course at Wellesley, I discovered three books about work with children that resonated with my own previous experience as an arts and crafts counselor. The first was *The Nature of Creative Activity* (1939), and the second was *Creative and Mental Growth* (1947), both by a man named Viktor Lowenfeld, who had worked with blind and partially sighted children as well as those with normal vision. The third was *The Artist in Each of Us* (1951) by a woman named Florence Cane, who had taught gifted youngsters. All three stressed the power of creative activity to promote healthy emotional development, and to tap the unique resources inside each and every one of us.

50 *Judith A. Rubin*

While studying to be an art teacher in graduate school, I took a seminar in advanced child development where each of us was encouraged to present a class session on a topic of his or her choice. By then, intrigued by how much could be expressed in drawing and painting, I chose to study *The Psychology of Children's Art*. In the well-stocked Harvard library, I read the writings of child analysts like Madeleine Rambert (1949) and child psychologists like Dorothy Baruch (1952). Like Alschuler and Hattwick, they were attuned to the messages and meanings of children's work in crayons, paint, and clay. For the therapists, the artwork played a critical role in their efforts to help.

I also found a number of articles by an educator named Margaret Naumburg, who called what she did *art therapy*, a term that was then new to me. Naumburg's early papers were collected into a monograph in 1947 (Naumburg, 1947). Although its title was a bit off-putting, the case studies were fascinating. Naumburg (1950, 1953) also published two book-length case studies of art therapy – with an adolescent and a young adult – both of which I read with interest.

Just before my turn at leading the seminar, a new book came out entitled *Art Therapy in a Children's Community* (1958) by a woman named Edith Kramer, who had developed her own definition of art therapy while working with troubled boys at the Wiltwyck School. Like the others, it struck a resonant chord, reminding me of Lowenfeld (1939, 1947) and of Cane (1951). It further illuminated my practice teaching in Newton and Brookline, where I was being taught by master art educators to help children actualize themselves by creating.

All the chapters in Kramer's first book were inspiring for a beginning art teacher in the late fifties. They were even more useful when I had the opportunity to offer art to hospitalized children at the Western Psychiatric Institute and Clinic in 1963. Working with schizophrenic children in a psychiatric hospital I was, as I told Erik Erikson to whom I presented a case in 1964, "flying by the seat of my pants."

My supervisor was a wonderful child psychologist, Margaret McFarland, who had been one of the preschool teachers in the 1947 Alschuler and Hattwick study reported in *Painting and Personality,* and she even knew Mrs Alper, my college child psychology teacher. Dr McFarland, who was also Fred Rogers' mentor, was an excellent supervisor. However, although she was the first person to recommend the inspiring *On Not Being Able to Paint* by psychoanalyst Marion Milner (1950), she was not an art therapist.

Fortunately, my parents lived in New York, so for advice about how to meet the challenge of becoming an art therapist in the pre-training program era, I contacted the two US authors that had named this developing profession. Margaret Naumburg had retired by then, and our meetings were in her apartment, where she advised me about what to read and what to do, and told me about the *Bulletin of Art Therapy* that Elinor Ulman had founded in 1961. I eagerly and immediately subscribed, purchasing all the back issues, and discovering some very thoughtful articles by Edith Kramer.

Kramer: A Generous, Generative Genius 51

Fortunately, Kramer was still practicing her trade in the early sixties, and was also extremely gracious when I asked for her advice (which was, incidentally, almost identical to Naumburg's despite their different ideas about *art therapy*). Not only did she meet with me as often as I requested, she also invited me to attend her classes at the New School, coming for lunch afterwards at my parents' apartment across the street. Most generously, she allowed me to observe her at work – at the Jewish Guild for the Blind and at Jacobi Hospital. I loved being able to sit and watch this amazing woman doing *in vivo* some of what I had read about in her writing. I felt incredibly privileged.

When the Home for Crippled Children, a residential institution for children with disabilities, invited me to create a therapeutic art program in 1967, Edith's program at Wiltwyck was my model. Based on what she had so lucidly described, I could proceed with confidence having a clear image of what was possible, despite the differences in the two institutions. From what happened in the studio to what was exhibited in display cases and on bulletin boards, *Art Therapy in a Children's Community* (1958) provided me with guidance on how best to proceed in the then rather uncharted territory where I was myself learning in nontraditional ways.

Edith's first book and the papers she published in the interim in the *Bulletin of Art Therapy* (later the *American Journal of Art Therapy*) were also vital references when I was invited to initiate art therapy at the Pittsburgh Child Guidance Center in 1969. The Center was the outpatient clinic for child psychiatry and had a sophisticated and skeptical staff, many of whom were already using art in their work. I was challenged to prove the usefulness of this as yet unknown approach in a setting where there was a fair amount of suspicion. Not only did Kramer's writings offer invaluable guidance; they also served to legitimize art therapy for my clinic colleagues in related fields. And Edith herself was a major source of support, especially during the first months and years as I and my psychiatrist supervisor endeavored to convince the others that art therapy offered a unique and valuable contribution to our collective mission.

It may be hard to believe, but until the seventies, except for two books on art in hospitals by an Englishman named Adrian Hill (1945, 1951), Naumburg and Kramer were the only sources of information for someone wanting to pursue art therapy, for there were as yet no training programs and few classes, certainly none where I lived.

Fortunately for the field of art therapy, Edith Kramer did not stop with her first book, but went on to publish two more: *Art as Therapy with Children* in 1971 and *Childhood and Art Therapy* in 1979. Throughout her career, she continued to write articles and book reviews and to present at American Art Therapy Association conferences. Although many of the articles were collected into two volumes edited by her friend and colleague Elinor Ulman (Ulman & Dachinger, 1975; Ulman & Levy, 1980), both – like her first book – are no longer in print.

Luckily for art therapists of the 21st century, Kramer put together a book in 2000 – *Art as Therapy: Collected Papers* – consisting of selections from her

52   *Judith A. Rubin*

1958 classic, articles, and presentations, all of them revised and edited by herself and her colleague, Lani Gerity. Before I go into detail about the book's contents, let me say that rereading Edith Kramer is similar to rereading other seminal thinkers, such as Sigmund Freud or Donald W. Winnicott, an experience of both *déjà vu* and new discovery. Most chapters are not simply reprints of earlier publications, but are often thoughtful revisions, with occasional additions that serve to sharpen and bring them up to date.

As one who relishes any writing that illuminates the work of the art therapist, I found reading this book to be a veritable feast. Because Kramer pays as much attention to style as to substance, the meal is beautifully presented as well as delicious. That is not to say that all of it is sweet or easy to swallow. Indeed, because of her lucid and always honest prose, some of the book's statements are difficult to chew and take time to digest. Nevertheless, like an excellent meal, it is well worth it. Here are some especially tasty nuggets.

The book begins with Kramer's "Credo, as an Artist and an Art Therapist," two roles she kept separate throughout her career – each invested with profound meaning. The first section also includes "A History and Lineage of Art Therapy as Practiced by Edith Kramer," which, although I heard her deliver it as a commencement address, contains more nuggets of wisdom than my ears could process. In the second chapter of Part 1, she reminds us of the importance of unpretentious language, a cause her friend Elinor Ulman also championed throughout her long and articulate editorial career.

Part 2, "The Profession of Art Therapy," contains three seminal papers – "Exploration of Definition," "The Unity of Process and Product," and "Art Therapy and Sublimation" – her earliest and, in my opinion, best statement about her approach. Chapter 7 is a revision of another classic paper, "The Art Therapist's Third Hand: Reflections on Art, Art Therapy and Society at Large." Kramer's ideas about the importance of the *third eye*, as well as the use of the *third hand*, remain both practical and provocative, and in my opinion should be required reading for all art therapists.

Part 3, "Clinical Work," contains the case study of a gifted boy named Angel, which includes not only Kramer's early work with him, but later contacts as well. The next chapter is *"Art and the Blind Child,"* as well as a case study of a blind boy named Christopher. Both offer really useful ways of thinking about work with the visually impaired, something few art therapists have written about. These chapters are excerpted and revised from Kramer's 1958 book, and I for one am delighted that this generation of art therapists now has access to them.

Part 4 contains Kramer's writings on "Art Therapy, Ethology and Society." "The Etiology of Human Aggression" has always mattered for those who work with troubled people and since September 11, 2001, it seems particularly appropriate for an era in which sadistic, unmodulated aggression can suddenly wreak havoc on the civilized world. It also speaks volumes at a time when raw anger, so easily unleashed in those who are anxious, needs to be sublimated, not invited.

Part 4 contains two panel discussions presented at conferences of the American Art Therapy Association, which were subsequently published in the *American Journal of Art Therapy*. The panel on "Inner Satisfaction and External Success" was a follow-up to one on "Art Therapy and the Seductive Environment." In her contribution to the latter, Kramer notes the stern punitiveness of the American superego, and the rarity of an *approving inner voice* (or ego ideal). Her seven-page argument is rich with ideas, and is especially important for art therapists in regard to the enhancement of self-esteem.

Edith Kramer has long been "generative," not only by articulating her ideas for several generations, but in her energetic support of other art therapists. As one who greatly benefited from her generosity throughout my career, and especially at the beginning, I am deeply grateful for her willingness to mentor others.

As Kramer told the graduates on the day she received an honorary degree from Vermont College of Norwich University, she is "an old lady who has been comfortably maladapted all her life, and yet, because she has been so maladapted, is now being honored with a doctorate" (2000, p. 24). How vital for all of us – that we remain "maladapted" enough to stick to our principles, in spite of whatever pressures may be brought to bear upon us. In this regard, as in the clarity and consistency of her thinking, Edith Kramer is an excellent role model for art therapists of any age. What has been less visible for many is her extraordinary generosity.

A personal example: When my publisher requested that I revise my first book, *Child Art Therapy* (Rubin, 1978), I asked Edith if she were willing to help me out. She had reviewed it for the *Journal*, and had a number of thoughtful criticisms. Although initially a bit wounded, I soon realized the value of her critique. And I was delighted that she was not only agreeable, but that she handled my book revision with her usual attention to detail. Indeed, she went over the entire manuscript with her pencil, making suggestions that greatly improved the original. We spent long hours in her studio going over the book together page by page. What a gracious gift!

And it was given, like all the classes and clinical work she invited me to observe in the sixties, and all the advice she offered over many years, without any expectation of payment of any kind. Edith's generosity continued even when she fully expected that I would leave art therapy for child analysis while I was studying at an analytic institute. Though her fears were unfounded, her support was steady.

Finally, in addition to being generative and generous, Edith Kramer was, in my opinion, a true genius. Like Anna Freud and Erik Erikson, she did not attend college, where her original and brilliant mind might have been muted in some way. Instead, she was free to think creatively about her work, incorporating what she had learned from her voracious reading and discussions with colleagues like Elinor Ulman. As a result, Edith Kramer made major contributions to the field to which she devoted her energies. Although library shelves are now bulging with art therapy books in a way that was unimaginable when *Art*

54 *Judith A. Rubin*

Therapy in a Children's Community was published in 1958, few have attained the integration of form and content visible in Kramer's first book – as well as in everything she wrote afterwards. The field of art therapy is fortunate that the author, whose personal integrity was as clear as her writing, decided to invest so much libido not only in its early years, but in its maturation as well.

I remain grateful for her generosity throughout my own development as an art therapist, especially for letting me shadow her as she worked with children in the sixties. As I said to Lani Gerity during a conversation about Edith, she helped each person whose life she touched to bring out what was best in us, just as she did with the children and students she taught. Having recently learned more about her mentor, Friedl Dicker-Brandeis (Makarova, 2001), I realized Edith had a wonderful model who did just that for her, and who later helped the children through art in the concentration camp at Terezin. Fortunately for the field of art therapy, Edith escaped concentration camps, and was able to convey Friedl's optimism about bringing out the creativity in everyone to her own work and writing about art therapy. Edith often said how lucky she was to escape on the last boat in 1938; for myself, and for the profession I love, we too are lucky that she did.

References

Alper, T. G., Blane, H. T., & Abrams, B. K. (1955). Reactions of middle and lower class children to finger paints as a function of class differences in child-training practices. *Journal of Abnormal and Social Psychology, 51*(3), 439–448.

Alschuler, R., & Hattwick, L. W. (1947). *Painting and personality* (2 Vols.) Chicago, IL: University of Chicago Press.

Baruch, D. W. (1952). Developmental needs and conflicts revealed in children's art. *American Journal of Orthopsychiatry, 22*, 186–203.

Cane, F. (1951). *The artist in each of us.* New York: Pantheon Books.

Hill, A. (1945). *Art versus illness.* London: George Allen & Unwin.

Hill, A. (1951). *Painting out illness.* London: Williams & Northgate.

Kramer, E. (1958). *Art therapy in a children's community: A study of the function of art therapy in the treatment program of Wiltwyck School for Boys.* Springfield, IL: Charles C. Thomas.

Kramer, E. (1971). *Art as therapy with children.* New York: Schocken Books.

Kramer, E., & Wilson, L. (1979) *Childhood and art therapy: Notes on theory and application.* New York: Schocken Books.

Kramer, E., & Gerity, L. A. (2000). *Art as therapy: Collected papers.* London: Jessica Kingsley Publishers.

Lowenfeld, V. (1939). *The nature of creative activity.* New York: Harcourt Brace.

Lowenfeld, V. (1947). *Creative and mental growth.* New York: Macmillan.

Makarova, E. (2001). *Friedl Dicker-Brandeis, Vienna 1898–Auschwitz 1944.* Los Angeles, CA: Tallfellow/Every Picture Press.

Milner, M. (1950). *On not being able to paint.* Madison, CT: International Universities Press.

Naumburg, M. (1947). Studies of the "free" art expression of behavior problem children and adolescents as a means of diagnosis and therapy. *Nervous & Mental Disease Monograph, 71*.

Naumburg, M. (1950). *Schizophrenic art: Its meaning in psychotherapy*. New York: Grune and Stratton.

Naumburg, M. (1953). *Psychoneurotic art: Its function in psychotherapy*. New York: Grune & Stratton.

Rambert, M. (1949). *Children in conflict*. New York: International Universities Press.

Rubin, J.A. (1978). *Child art therapy: Understanding and helping children through art* (2nd ed.). New York: Van Nostrand Reinhold.

Ulman, E., & Dachinger, P. (Eds.) (1975). *Art therapy in theory and practice*. New York: Schocken Books.

Ulman, E., & Levy, C. (Eds.) (1980). *Art therapy viewpoints*. New York: Schocken Books.

6 Importance of Cultural Roots

Irene Rosner David

I was a student of Edith Kramer's in the mid–late 1970s among the first crop of students at the newly formed New York University program. I felt privileged and a bit intimidated to be studying with the Grande Dame of the profession, but over time, our relationship became more collegial as the dynamic of student and mentor changed. I feel even more privileged to have experienced a series of personal exchanges, now cherished memories that speak to her ethnicity and cultural roots. Edith seldom mentioned her own Jewish Austrian background, but several conversations revealed the depth and importance of context for her, and it was also a domain where we bonded beyond clinical interests.

A memory from the 1980s was the first to do with food. I spent an evening at Edith's loft having been invited while Elinor Ulman was visiting. Elinor had given a talk at NYU and had previously been editing my first paper for the *American Journal of Art Therapy*. Before we proceeded to work, much to my surprise, Edith said, "We must eat first," and she bounded to the stove to deftly prepare chicken paprikash. As I watched it became apparent she was as adept at the stove as she was at the easel – as I marveled, she said, "just sauté the chicken pieces, add a lot of paprika, then the sour cream" – and what a dollop of sour cream it was! Ethnic roots guided her in a very natural way – it was, in fact, a Hungarian dish which spoke to my paternal roots, which made me much more relaxed for an evening of dining with two greats – Edith and Elinor. Conversation ensued about ethnic origins and the appeal of associated reminiscences about one's beginnings. There was also a psychoanalytic aspect to the conversation in response to my comment that I loved good food but was not a very good cook – "ah, were there good cooks in your family as you were growing up?" Of course, the analysis should have been obvious, but it was fascinating to hear Edith say as she stirred, "One either becomes like them, or goes in the other direction." This was quite a mouthful of ideas and quite a delicious and memorable meal.

In the early 1990s at the American Art Therapy Association conference in Chicago, we stole away from the Palmer House for a quick lunch. Although I had enjoyed numerous social interactions at her infamous holiday parties, we had never had a one-to-one encounter, so I was delighted and curious as to what sides of Edith might be revealed. She suggested we get away from the hotel premises – I was aware of her dislike of these impersonal edifices. I suggested a Russian cafeteria that I had been to a couple of blocks away; she responded affirmatively with an enthusiastic lilt in her voice, and we energetically made our way. Once settled I ordered borscht, and she ordered matzo ball soup, then when the bowls were presented, she declared, "The food of our roots!" That one phrase made it clear that 1) the food of one's childhood makes for a significant component of cultural identity, 2) the food of *her* roots and *her* cultural identity meant a lot to her, and 3) sharing the food of one's childhood with someone of similar cultural roots made for a comfort zone of familiarity. Indeed, we went on to taste each other's soups with the pleasure of two children, complete with giggling.

An anecdote that embodies cultural meaning with Edith's brilliance as a therapist is what I call "The Onion Family." I was impressed by one of her paintings displayed along with others on the windowsills of her studio. This configuration of root vegetables was typical of her characteristic way of making the ordinary look extraordinary – a roll of paper towels or a bottle of *Mr Clean* was rendered aesthetically, enriching a mundane snippet of life. There were always countless paintings and sculptures around, but this small, white-framed grouping of beets, onions, and garlic pulled me in. I sat with Edith at her wooden pedestal table and talked about it – how I loved the way they leaned toward one another; how they differed in size and prominence; how they were each settled into the counter independently, yet seemingly talked to each other. As I freely associated she listened attentively and noted that I was personifying the vegetables. Voila! It became a personal projective as I delineated every member of my family and declared in Yiddish "the tzibele mishpocha." With her distinctive laugh, Edith repeated, "tzibele mishpocha"

Figure 6.1 Beets and Onions, 1988. Oil painting by Edith Kramer

as if punctuating it and added, "in our native language." She was at once the brilliant art therapist who listened and allowed the process to lead to revelation, and a down-to-earth, jovial, kindred woman. I told her I had to have the painting – the painting of what for me represented my family. I still have it prominently displayed, along with other pieces by Edith.

These seemingly mundane references to ethnic soups, chicken preparation, root vegetables, and a nearly defunct language illustrate the importance of cultural roots and identity for Edith. I hope these anecdotes provide *food* for thought – heightening awareness of origins, personal context, and ethnicity as realms for deeper understanding and cross-cultural bridging in our work and in our lives. In her teaching, Edith emphasized that we try to understand our clients in the context of their ethnic origins. Her own personal associations and reminiscences about her cultural roots poignantly underscored this lesson.

7 Edith Kramer at New York University

Recollections

Laurie Wilson

I met Edith Kramer in 1972 when she was giving classes on Art Therapy at the New School for Social Research in New York. I was working as an artist for a few years, scraping together a living by teaching art and selling a few pieces of sculpture at a time. When I met Edith Kramer, I was painting apartments to make enough money to cast my one-of-a-kind jewelry into gold. Through artist friends, I had heard about the new field of art therapy and decided to explore it for myself by taking whatever classes were available on the subject. I had taught art to children and adolescents for five years by that time and was looking for a way to concentrate the beneficial effects of art making on fewer than 30 children at a time, which was then the standard class size for art teachers. Art therapy sounded like it might be a good route.

In the early 1970s Margaret Naumburg was also teaching in New York at Columbia University, and I took one of her classes as well. Then, to see whether I liked doing the actual clinical work, I volunteered at Mount Sinai Hospital on the children's unit and found out how powerful the approach could be with individual children. I asked Edith for supervision of my work, but she demurred, and when I asked Naumburg, she tried to turn the supervision into therapy, which wasn't my idea of what I needed at all. In the meantime, I was earning a doctoral degree in art history so that I could eventually learn more about psychoanalysis. In those days, to study psychoanalytic theory at a reputable training center, one had to have either an MD or PhD degree. With art as my core interest, the art history degree seemed more appropriate.

I expected that I would look for full-time clinical work once I completed my doctorate, but Edith's call to help out at New York University (NYU) intervened. She was asked by the Art and Art Education Department at NYU to start a graduate program in art therapy. Many eager would-be art therapy students in New York City were showing up at the doors of NYU's Art Department with an interest in studying the new field. Years earlier, Margaret Naumburg had taught classes in art therapy in the art department, but the time was not right and nothing developed at NYU from those early classes.

By the 1970s the chair of the art department, Angiola Churchill, researched the new field and began looking for a person to teach it in a way that would be consonant with the department. In other words, she was looking for an

60 *Laurie Wilson*

art therapist who would keep art at the center of art therapy. Churchill was an art educator, and she had noted that Naumburg's focus was on the verbal component of art therapy. When she met and interviewed Edith, she knew she had found the right person for the department. And once the prospective students heard that Edith Kramer had started teaching at NYU they flocked in to take courses with her. For several years, they were studying with Edith Kramer but had no guidance or possibilities of practicing what they learned from her.

Edith had been teaching in the Art Therapy Graduate Program at George Washington University in DC for a few years. As a New Yorker, she didn't mind teaching in Washington, but she was interested in having a high-quality graduate program in New York. She thoroughly enjoyed teaching, but was absolutely adamant about not doing administrative work. Since we had met a few years earlier she recommended me for the full-time position of establishing and running the program. I turned down the job three times because I had not quite finished my doctorate but finally by the end of 1975, I had run out of money and grants so the offer of a full-time teaching position by New York University was both appealing and necessary. I worked with Edith at NYU from 1976 to 2000, when I retired. Edith went on teaching in the program until the spring of 2006.

My job as the new full-time director of art therapy meant not only teaching but also doing all the administrative work to set up the program, get it approved by New York State, and keep it running smoothly. Within the first two weeks on the job, I found myself on a train to Albany, the state capitol, with the Dean of the school and the goal of getting The New York State Education Department to approve of the new graduate programs in art therapy at New York University. Some enthusiastic bureaucrat at the university had the idea that there should be an undergraduate and a graduate program as well as a doctoral program. Edith and I agreed that the only viable program would be a Master's Degree in Art Therapy.

Students were already taking art therapy classes without an organized curriculum or internships. There weren't even any application procedures established. The moment I was hired, Edith and I worked together to design the entire program. New York University was already famous for starting courses in a new field and only later getting state approval for a program in that field. Our work involved long days and nights writing, planning, and rewriting every necessary piece of the program. Edith would often supply her homemade spinach soup and delicious dark bread from her neighborhood in the city's Lower East Side where she lived in a fifth-floor walk-up apartment on Delancey Street.

We quickly found that we worked well together and had similar high standards for all that we were organizing. It was going to be an *ideal* training for graduate students in New York City. I had become an art therapist in the only way possible before training programs had begun. Volunteering at clinical settings, finding someone to supervise the work, taking whatever classes on or

Kramer at NYU: Recollections 61

near the subject that could be found, and reading everything in or near the subject. My clinical supervisors had been psychoanalytically-oriented psychiatrists and psychologists at Mount Sinai Hospital since there were very few art therapists working in New York at the time. My new NYU job involved visiting all the art therapists working in the New York metropolitan area, which included New Jersey and Connecticut as well as Long Island. Edith knew most of them and in some cases had taught them. On those visits, I had to assess the work of these remarkably diverse and talented art therapists, and then set up internships with them for future NYU students.

Edith and I had to invent almost everything, borrowing some of what had been developed at George Washington University in DC but mostly designing our own program. It was a huge amount of work, but highly gratifying. Every step of the way allowed us to focus on *art as therapy*. We both had a psychoanalytic perspective on the human condition – Edith, because she had grown up in Austria surrounded by some of the founders of the field, including Siegfried Bernfeld, and I because when I started my clinical work at Mount Sinai Hospital, it was a prime setting for the psychoanalytic approach. All my "training" had been by psychoanalysts, and by the time I started working at NYU, I had experienced my own personal analysis. Because she knew all the European psychoanalysts in New York through the ones she had known in Europe, she of course knew Kurt Eissler, my first analyst, as well as almost every other analyst I met in the course of learning more about the field.

It was deeply gratifying to talk with Edith about any and every subject from a psychoanalytic perspective. I am sure that my later career as a psychoanalyst and author of books on applied psychoanalysis owes much to my years of talking with Edith Kramer. Conversations with her became the normal way to think about the world and especially the way to think about art and artists. We both enjoyed introducing students to this remarkably deep and complex way of thinking about the human condition.

We talked at length about the difference between art therapy art (art made in an art therapy session with the goal of a conversation about it), and art made for itself. Edith continued to work as an artist throughout her long life. I had spent ten years as a working artist but eventually turned to writing about artists as an art historian, art therapist, and psychoanalyst. We both felt very strongly that art therapists should offer a genuine experience of art making to their patients and had less respect for the clinicians who sacrificed the amount of time needed for patients to make art in order to get them to talk about their work, which did not mean that we thought talking to patients about their art and their problems was unimportant.

The prime focus on art making was also part of the reason we wanted to be sure that applicants to the graduate program in art therapy had had their own full experience of art making – something we felt we could see by asking for a portfolio of work as part of the admissions process. Another revealing part of the admissions process involved making art in response to certain questions or

62 *Laurie Wilson*

experiences. Once students were accepted in the program, they learned that there was a studio component for almost every class, and even a class Edith designed that was entirely based upon studio work. An example of an effective exercise in that class was to ask students to create a sculpture while blindfolded in order to replicate the experience of a blind patient. It worked and as a result students could much better empathize with patients who could only feel but not see.

Edith had strong ideas about patients needing the time to get a second wind for their work. She knew from much personal experience how much time it took to complete a work and aimed to have art therapy sessions last as long as possible within a clinical setting. She learned that longer sessions allowed patients to refocus their energies and return to the artwork they thought they had finished with a new perspective and carry that work to another level.

Edith and I found that we worked well together, especially on designing the program and writing about it. I had an unexpected knack for administrative work and plenty of experience teaching. I thoroughly enjoyed the process of creating something new that would eventually benefit many people. No slave to conventional wisdom, Edith was usually in favor of trying something that had not been tried before if she thought it would help educate future art therapists. She was a talented educator whose combination of brilliance and earthiness both dazzled and charmed students, though some were intimidated by her capacity for completely candid criticism.

We gradually hired faculty and established clinical placements for students to practice what they were learning. At the beginning of our work together, though Edith knew many of the art therapists in the New York area, I was the one who went to visit the settings and observe the students at their work. The few occasions when Edith made such visits, she almost invariably surprised people by letting them see how active she was during the sessions. Frequently, unlike the depiction of her work in the books she wrote, she would jump in and start making art with a young child or adolescent and tell wonderful folk tales and stories about people and animals that inspired children to relax and make art. She had come to see how a student was doing and then demonstrated how she thought they could do better. Her instant bonding with children in an art room brought to life her easy way of interacting with them – talking about the story that went with the figures or animals they had made of clay, or showing them some new ways of making the figures more lifelike.

Edith had a marvelously useful "philosophy" she called selective incompetence. Thus, she never had to run a slide projector claiming that she couldn't understand how they worked. She got someone else to do it. Similarly, our experience with her reluctance to supervise students – even when the program was in dire need of sophisticated supervisors – proved to us why we should not push her to do something she really did not want to do. During class supervision, she would fall asleep in the middle of a student's presentation. After one semester, we never asked her to supervise again.

Because I was relatively unknown in the field at the time we started working together, Edith urged me to write an article about my experience working with the mentally retarded – at present called developmentally disabled. Naturally, she edited my article and encouraged me to do even more writing, which was the beginning of an activity I now greatly enjoy. Much to my surprise, at the next American Art Therapy Association Annual Conference I became known as Edith's protégé and the person who had written a well-received article that had needed almost no editing by Elinor Ulman, the astute editor and founder of the *American Journal of Art Therapy*. Working closely with Edith opened many doors for me to art therapists who had already long established themselves in the field, such as Elinor Ulman, Bernard Levy, Judy Rubin, Gladys Agell, and all the faculty at George Washington University with whom I was fortunate to establish long-lasting friendships.

During that very full-time first year at New York University, I was still working on my dissertation. I had chosen for my topic Louise Nevelson, the well-known American sculptor who lived and worked in New York. Because I had studied art and made sculpture in the sixties in New York, it felt like a manageable project. I only had to travel to Maine where Nevelson grew up, and Washington, DC where she had deposited her archival material at the Archives of American Art. I interviewed Nevelson, many members of her family, lovers, friends, enemies, and colleagues in the process of gathering material for the first biographical and iconographic portrait of the artist.

Edith respected Nevelson's work but she also had a contact with someone who had been one of Nevelson's lovers in the 1940s – Richard Kramer, Edith's father – whom I could interview thanks entirely to Edith. It was fascinating to hear about how Nevelson urged Edith's father to write poetry in addition to selling underwear on the streets of New York. Like many of her admirers, he was dazzled by her charismatic presence and total devotion to creativity – everyone's creativity. Introducing me to her father, with whom she was on friendly terms but not so close, was a typical act of generosity on Edith's part.

We had what felt like a fair deal; she was hugely relieved that I was making her life easy at NYU, and she clearly respected my various talents. Over the course of the 24 years we worked together at NYU, a rich complex friendship developed. We wrote together – at first it was largely her writing that I helped augment or edit, and eventually we reversed roles. She was brilliant and almost always had original and strikingly unconventional approaches to world events and especially to the visual surround and contemporary art scene. She saw herself as an artist who found clinical work interesting, and theory building fascinating. Writing about her work and the ideas behind it along with training future art therapists were responsibilities she took very seriously.

We enjoyed designing new courses together and even designed a graduate-level art therapy training program in Turin, Italy, where we both subsequently taught. It seemed like a surefire way (or should I say, excuse) to go

Figure 7.1 Edith teaching students at New York University. Photo taken by Herschel J. Stroyman

often to Italy. As a result, we could engage in training a number of European art therapists.

Edith continued to teach at George Washington University, and her regular course there was Psychodynamically Oriented Art Therapy. It was a semester-long course and always included a few weekends of lectures by me. Since staying with Elinor Ulman was part of the experience of teaching in DC, I came to know and deeply appreciate Elinor, who had long been one of Edith's best friends.

Both of us attended the annual art therapy conferences where Edith would inevitably inveigh against the ugliness of the hotel in which the conference was held and often against the logo that AATA had selected for the conference. She was afraid of no one and suffered no fools. Most of her clinical work had been with children and adolescents to whom she responded with remarkable tact and good humor. That was not always true when she interacted with adults. She was famous for her occasional untactful remarks to adults about their appearance, conversation, or artwork. She once met a somewhat overweight but not pregnant woman who was running for political office. She turned to the unfortunate woman and asked her when the baby was due. I considered myself rather lucky that she rarely criticized my various efforts in any direction.

Another collaboration with Edith was the loft/studio we shared. When Edith was moving into a new studio on Vandam Street, she was planning to share it with Jill Schehr and me. Jill was a painter and former art therapy student. I was a sculptor and her colleague at NYU. It was a large loft with windows across the front that faced Vandam Street. Edith wanted more light in the loft and a view of the Hudson River. So Jill and I started chipping away at the solid brick wall facing west. After weeks of hammering and many trips to a dump to get rid of the broken bricks (at night so the landlord wouldn't know about this highly irregular activity), we finally broke through to the outside and Edith could have a window installed exactly where she wanted it. In retrospect, this anecdote about Edith, her studio, and her way of dealing with obstacles epitomizes her original approach to almost everything. The loft was filled with light, plants, paintings, and sculpture – all in all, a beautiful place to work. It was also the scene of the annual holiday party for NYU students. Since Edith had grown up in Austria where Christmas trees were lit by real candles she insisted on continuing the tradition in New York. The students were always amazed and a little frightened seeing a large tree lit with many candles burning in the room where they were congregating. Fortunately, there were never any accidental fires. All students who had attended them remembered her holiday parties with great warmth.

I was frequently surprised and always impressed with Edith's unique way of seeing world events, literature, art, and various truths about the human condition. She grew up around artists, actors, and writers at a very juicy time in Vienna. It was expected among her parents' friends that each person would think for her- or himself. And so Edith always did. Nothing conventional would do if she had a better idea. Not to say that she was out of touch with external reality. Edith knew very well how to adapt to the hard facts. But, if she could break through them, just as she had persuaded Jill and me to break through the solid brick wall to a better reality, she would.

Edith's friendships enhanced the art therapy program in many different ways. She could, for example, invite Elinor Ulman to come up from Washington, DC, to give a talk to NYU students. She could persuade Vera Zilzer to teach courses that perforce introduced students to a kind of flexibility of clinical approaches beyond anyone's expectation. Vera became a staple faculty member at NYU, if one can call such an original clinician a staple. Vera and Edith were close friends – both artists, both originals, both in their own ways outrageous. Edith cared little about how she looked, took her backpack everywhere, and not infrequently wore paint-spattered clothing. Vera cared little about how unusual her way of working with patients or teaching students might seem to outsiders. Her art therapy room in the hospital seemed less like a clinical setting and more like a comfortable, plant-filled lounge with music constantly playing, and patients reading, talking, or painting depending on their inclination at the moment. Yet, the artwork her patients made and the clinical progress that accompanied it surprised many. She knew how to create a setting that allowed for and encouraged growth. Edith's respect for Vera's originality and artistic talent was profound and lasting.

Figure 7.2 Retirement party for Laurie Wilson with Edith Kramer, NYU faculty, and students

In sum, Edith Kramer was an original that tolerated fellow originals and encouraged others to think for themselves, which made her a supremely talented clinician and teacher. She epitomized the meaning of art as therapy with her artwork, her daily life, and her unique form of teaching. We were very lucky to have her at New York University for so many years.

8 Teaching with Edith

Ikuko Acosta

The rare opportunity to co-teach with Edith came to me in the late 1990s and lasted over five years. The site was New York University's Graduate Art Therapy Program, which Edith founded in the 1970s. The course was Art for Art Therapists – the only studio arts-based course offered by the program. When Edith took me on board as a co-teacher, she was over eighty years old, and naturally needed an assistant. Edith directed the class art projects with her usual authority, and I took care of tasks related to art materials, while providing individualized assistance to each student. We worked as a team until she retired, after which I inherited the course.

Edith was a tiny woman with a single gray braid and rosy cheeks, yet when she lectured, she emanated power and wisdom. If you didn't know the soft and playful side of her, she could be intimidating, at least in a classroom setting. But in the context of her clinical work, especially her work with children, she radiated pure compassion, and her wisdom came through as strength, commitment, and dedication. In our long collaboration, I was very fortunate to see all sides of her, and to benefit from her tremendous breadth of knowledge, as well as her unique character, full of brilliance and eccentricities.

In the classroom, Edith was generous in offering her guidance with patience and honesty when students struggled with the creative process. What she was intolerant of was kitsch art or any expression that appeared superficial and disengaged with the wellspring of human emotion. Edith had a keen eye for true creative engagement, regardless of artistic skills.

It is an understatement to say that Edith possessed a strong independent mind and uncompromising sense of aesthetics. She advocated the importance of providing optimal expressive materials, such as paint, pastel, and clay, and detested materials like magic markers. If she were alive today, I could only imagine her reaction to the use of digital media and other unconventional studio materials, which have been developing in recent years.

Edith was a prolific artist until she was no longer able to make art physically. Thus, one of her mottos that she delivered to the students was "make art, make art. . . ." She proclaimed that an art therapist should only hold a part-time job to ensure plenty of time to make art. Edith believed that the creative process has a life of its own, and when the process is uninterrupted

68   Ikuko Acosta

and uncompromised, it will lead the artist to authentic work. She was an inspiration to all art therapists in her unwavering commitment to authentic arts practice.

A central mission of her teaching was to help students understand their preconceived notions of the visual world, and to facilitate fresh and novel ways of seeing. Her focus on intuition, along with art exercises to make the familiar world strange, pushed students to the outer reaches of the cultural comfort zone. She also had a habit of stirring up emotion by commentary that was itself more intuitive and metaphorical than literal, and more free-floating than outlined and sequenced. But disorientation eventually gave way to expanded insight as the class progressed. Students learned to write down Edith's comments in the class, as though they were collected notes of wisdom.

Edith's goal for the class, Art for Art Therapists, was to promote the development of student creativity, insight, and sensitivity in the dual roles of artist/clinician. Through the art exercises she developed, students evolved in their capacity to share internal processes in a group setting, maximizing mutual trust, reciprocal feedback, and insight.

Examples of Edith's Art Exercises

Organic/Inorganic: Here, students created two pieces of art, depicting an organic and an inorganic object. Edith would comment about the relation between the two, in content and form, and the class would discuss individual differences in choice of subjects.

Fairy Tale: Draw the same archetypal fairy-tale scene three times, from the perspective of children of three age groups (ages 3–4, 7–9, and 14–16). Here, students reencountered the feeling of the different developmental stages in artist development (perceptual, motor-coordination, and emotional stages, and other psychological aspects). This exercise tended to elicit intense emotional responses related to regression and forgotten memories.

Cross-Sensory Feelings: Students were encouraged to create a visual depiction of a taste and a sound.

The Clay Head: Here, students were given clay and asked to create a head self-portrait, in the dark, using only their hands to feel and map out their own faces. This was the exercise Edith spent the most time on. She chose the clay carefully – it had an earthy color with a sandy texture, and was not smooth white clay. Immediately after the lights were off, you would hear some exasperated sighs and murmurs, but gradually the room became very quiet except for the sounds of clay being manipulated. The silence in the room was comfortable and peaceful, with a meditative quality. Edith offered ongoing commentary such as "trust your hands and let the clay guide you" and "let your fingers touch the plane of your face and transfer that feeling onto your clay." The touching, feeling, and molding continued for some time, and then Edith would turn on the lights. Usually, students would protest, having somehow gotten used to working in the dark. It was quite interesting to observe student reactions to their art when the lights were back on, such as "wow, this looks nothing like me" or "this doesn't look like a human face." A student once commented that the head looked more like her grandfather than herself. After the initial remarks of amazement subsided, Edith would discuss the exercise: "This is not about creating a head that looks like what you think your head looks like . . . rather, you are using different sensory modalities to discover what your head might look like in the absence of your preconceived mental picture of yourself, and your habitual style of artistic representation." With her affirmations, students would continue the process. The end product of this project was a collection of bizarre yet amazingly expressive clay heads, all placed in one central table for group discussion. Some looked androgynous, some looked half animal and half human, and some looked like grandfathers, and so on. Students who were initially disturbed by the distortion of their heads ended up loving them, and in a sense, owning them, in contrast to distancing themselves from their creation.

These art experientials that Edith gave to students may sound simple, but the subjective experience for the students was very complex. Edith challenged students to open up their habitual ways of perceiving and responding to the visual world, encouraging them to find creative "genuineness," as she liked to put it. In Edith's view, this is the essence of what art therapists need to achieve in working with clients; namely, the facilitation of a creative solution to a habitual, often trapped life.

Figure 8.1 Edith Kramer and Ikuko Acosta teaching together at New York University

70   Ikuko Acosta

In her later years of teaching Edith began to lose her hearing, and it became increasingly difficult for her to communicate with our students. I would sit near her to repeat student questions in her ear. In spite of this obstacle, her mind and her eyes remained as sharp as ever.

It was one of the most unique and unforgettable experiences I have had in my teaching career, and I am grateful to have had this opportunity to teach alongside Edith. I have inherited her course, which I enjoy sharing with students. Like the hundreds of students of my generation who learned from Edith, we will always remember her with a mixture of awe, respect, and genuine warmth.

9 Art Therapy Experiences with Edith and a Group of Adults

Raffaella Bortino, Wilma Cipriani, and Raffaela Carola Lorio

Edith Kramer arrived in Turin, Italy, on May 25, 1984 to lead an art therapy experience with a group of people gathered at the psychotherapeutic community "Il Porto," founded in Turin the previous year. The founder, Dr Raffaella Bortino, sociologist and Freudian psychoanalyst, who had worked for years as an art therapist engaged in the practice and dissemination of art therapy, had invited her. Art therapy was established as a discipline in Europe in the years 1950–1980 in conjunction with the abolition of psychiatric hospitals, which raised a number of concerns. This closing of psychiatric hospitals coincided with a growing interest in the psychopathology of art, as well as the psycho-analytic study of art. The result was a humanizing of mental patients who were now being seen as people deserving of any form of care that would reconstruct or safeguard their personalities.

Art was ubiquitous in many institutions, even the most isolated. It was used as a means of expression, as well as a means of rewarding patients. The use of creative materials was encouraged with the many artists who were confined in psychiatric facilities, like Vincent Van Gogh. Art was simply waiting to be released and rediscovered in order to acquire the consideration that it deserved in the field of care.

Art as Therapy

On that day in Turin, Edith held an opening lecture on the topic of art's therapeutic value, as discussed in depth in her book *Art as Therapy with Children* (1977), which was already well known to her audience in its Italian edition. The lecture had a powerful impact, particularly because Edith did not hesitate to formulate and develop her conviction that art was the expression of the "inner experience." She told us that an inner life couldn't be achieved by means of discursive thought because its forms cannot be grasped using language structures. She said the word "form" is essential. Form is the order and structure with which artistic expression turns experience into something concrete. It gives us the opportunity to recognize, identify, and master our inner experience. As she said, "It is therefore art that brings out the inner life, making it something we can see and touch" (1985, Turin, Italy).

72   Bortino, Cipriani, and Lorio

It should be said that this conviction marked all the developments of our group (of which one of the authors of this paper had the opportunity to be a part). The group consisted of people who, for various reasons ranging from personal interest to work, were familiar with psychic suffering in the context of cooperatives, communities, and hospitals. Furthermore, the others attending that conference were already aware of the important book mentioned above, *Art as Therapy with Children*, which was experiencing huge success in Europe and had been translated into many languages.

The group consisted of a patient from the community, a group recorder (Raffaella Bortino), and four other participants from the outside, who met the next day in the basement of the Community Il Porto. Expectations were high, because the director and founder of the community, Raffaella Bortino, had previously been invited to New York where, as an art therapist, she had worked in close contact with Edith at New York University. In a workshop that was held there, she had presented some important aspects of the European art therapy method, including, for example, the practice of Psychoanalytic Relaxation, useful to free up creativity. Thanks to her, an art therapy training school had been set up by the community and after this second encounter, Edith contributed significantly to its program of activities, both in terms of its structure and of theoretical, practical, and didactic innovation.

The Group

The group was co-facilitated by Raffaella and Edith, and was lucky enough to spend a whole week, from morning to evening each day, working with Edith as teacher and co-leader. There were six participants in the group. First of all, Edith asked each participant to provide a brief introduction, to get to know each other better. We thus realized that the group was made up of people from different work and cultural backgrounds. The group consisted of the following members:

Anna – 31-year-old pediatric nurse who worked with children in hospitals – some so sick that they never left their beds.

Carlo – a young intellectual who was a patient currently living in this community.

Barbara – a 22-year-old woman who worked as a social worker in a former psychiatric hospital.

Luisa – a 54-year-old who taught Italian literature and history in a secondary school. She volunteered in the community because she was interested in the treatment of drug addiction.

Laura – a 29-year-old architect and teacher of art history to teenagers.

Marta – a middle school teacher, who also worked with teenagers.

In her presentations, Edith shared some seemingly generic information that was, in fact, very profound and introduced the quality of the work which

Art Therapy Experiences with Edith 73

she was preparing for the group. For example, when Anna said that her children were hospitalized for long-term care and bedridden, Edith quickly added the following consideration:

> In New York, we [art therapists] see them one week before they are hospitalized. We let them walk around the hospital and play with medical instruments: stethoscopes, syringes, etc. They can play with colored liquid and the syringes, so they can later receive shots without being afraid. It's important to be reassured in this kind of environment in a big city, because life in New York is really a battle, a jungle.
>
> (Kramer, 1987, p. 61)

In this way, Edith presented her teaching concerning the recognition of emotions in children, in a colloquial form that the group members could relate to, and hence, feel empathically at ease. She also made an important decision for the group when she said: "Since none of you makes art or is an artist, it may be best to start practicing from today" (Bortino, Cipriani, Gamna, & Gilardi, 1987, p. 61).

Now, the art studio was waiting for us. This was the beginning of the expressive activities that would bring a group of strangers together and, in five days of work and study, teach them that they could be united by mutual empathy and solidarity.

Edith's Commentary

Before we discuss the exercises, it should be mentioned that because of the work done, the therapeutic experiences that took place touched Edith so much she offered to write up a detailed report (Kramer, 1987). The report, accompanied by her commentary, was drawn up by Edith in the days following the group work, and dictated to Luisa, the community manager. We will provide some useful excerpts in the following section as we continue our narration.

Group Work Begins

As we resume the story, we should note from the very beginning, Edith Kramer always referred back to her belief that "art . . . brings out the inner life, making it something we can see and touch." The following will illustrate how this theoretical statement was tested throughout the experience of the group work. Perhaps the best way to illustrate the learning process of the participants is to choose some key examples from Edith's commentary.

Let us begin with the first example in which Edith assigned an exercise to the group. Each participant was asked to describe an image that came to mind and share it with the others. Among all the images proposed, we were to choose the one to which we felt more attracted. The image that was chosen was that of "Motherhood" (mother with child), and one in which the mother and the

74 Bortino, Cipriani, and Lorio

child would have to represent both the union and the separation. Everybody got to work, each finding their own way to achieve the figure. There were those who opted for a realistic representation, like Laura, who drew the act of childbirth (very brave!), or Anna who made the symbol of the sun on water, explaining: "The sun is warmth, energy, transformation, and birth" (Bortino et al., 1987, p. 64).

Edith made a sketch of her own, which she illustrated in the group when they talked about their experience. The teaching that ensued was surprising and enlightening. As you can see in Figure 9.1, she painted a mother sitting and holding her knitting on her lap, while her baby is near the half-open door to the room with a toy in his hand. At the mother's side, there is a closed window where a countryside landscape is visible, with a long road that disappears in the distance. Edith wanted to teach us how we could portray a complex situation through art, without using words. She explained how motherhood, in its great beauty, has its implicit conflicts, like union and separation – two needs that the mother has to reconcile, sacrificing her freedom for the child's growth. In this regard, Edith told us:

> There are different ways, depending on age, to experience a union and a separation. At the age of three, the child walks away from his mother to go to another room or out on the lawn near the bench where she is sitting: he feels already very distant, but he moves away because he knows that she is always there. At ten, the child gets away but also needs to know that his mother is always there. The teenager makes autonomous choices in life, but he too needs the historical memory of his mother to feel safe. In the small child there is no historical memory. He is familiar with the image of the mother, but is not yet able to internalize it enough to be able to move away from her for an extended period of time, without physically turning towards her.
>
> (Bortino et al., 1987, p. 63)

At this point, the whole group looked at Edith's painting and followed the explanation that she was sharing:

> He goes to the door, which needs to remain open at all times because if it closes, it will be a catastrophe for him. In this way, he can go away if he wants to and his mom lets him go without closing the door; he knows he is in this relationship with his mom. What is difficult for her is to let him go and to give him what she herself cannot have: *freedom*. For her, as for him, there is the difficulty of being free. She has to be there for the child, but, looking out the window, she feels the desire to not be there. It is a conflict between two different things that have to coexist.
>
> (Bortino et al., 1987, pp. 63–64)

Figure 9.1 Edith's painting of a mother and child

The group was surprised that such a simple image could contain such complex dynamics! Edith explained that the art therapist's task is to make it easier for people to draw and paint to help them realize they can express themselves creatively.

Some Theoretical Insights

Perhaps the time has come in this chapter to mention the ideas of Sigmund Freud and John Bowlby, the two theoretical bases upon which Edith Kramer's teachings rest. When dealing with the child moving away and his need to return immediately to his mother, Edith first referred to Freud where he spoke of conscious and unconscious emotions (like fear and joy), which are the inheritance of the human psyche, and the harmonization of which is very important for the stability of the personality. When Edith focused on how this harmony of emotions depended on how one experienced the primary attachment of the child with his mother, she pointed to the issue of the loss of a loved one, which was the main theme of John Bowlby's thought, one of the most important scholars in the field of attachment theory. In Edith's image, this psychological scenario is entrusted to art, where the latent conflicts in the individual's inner life (for both mother and child) take shape, and become "something we can see and touch."

Concrete Creative Practice

Very often, Edith provided concrete support to the participants, so that they would feel able to express their inner world through their artwork. There are many examples of the support she gave, and it is difficult to choose one to share here. In one instance, the support could be seen while handing someone a particular color or helping him to create a color by combining different colors, or showing him how to use the charcoal, or even as she approached someone who was struggling to complete a form; she spoke very few words. In practice, she provided support by reassuring him about his abilities, but she never influenced him with any judgment. This is particularly evident in the example that we take from Carlo, who painted a boat at sea (see Figure 9.2).

Case Vignette: Carlo

The group was now in the last day of the workshop, when Carlo, who in the earlier days had produced interesting works that also included the human figure, asked Edith to find a nice color to paint his final picture: a vast sea with

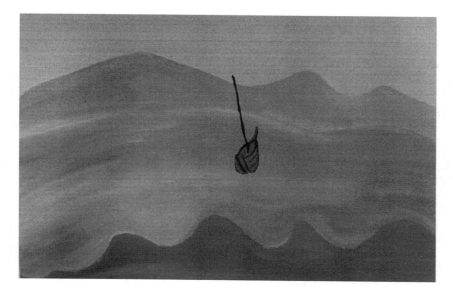

Figure 9.2 Painting of a boat by Carlo

Art Therapy Experiences with Edith 77

one single boat. Let us look at this image and read Edith's analysis of Carlo. Edith wrote:

> A real surprise came from Carlo, who since the beginning . . . had proven that he knew how to draw the human figure. . . . His portrait of Anna is powerful, although a little exaggerated, too emphatic. . . . Until that point, I had not understood his suffering until the end. He revealed it when he used the colors and was invited to express what they suggested to him. His images express a disturbed personality. The marine background is very serene and calm, but the white sails are still; there is no wind, no hull, and no people. . . .
>
> (Bortino et al., 1987, p. 70)

In Edith's typical simple and dry manner, she showed us the immense solitude of Carlo's inner life and explained that, "Thanks to his creativity, he managed to externalize it, making it artistically visible and tangible" (Bortino et al., 1987, p. 70).

The fundamental issue expressed by Edith had been assimilated by Carlo to his advantage. Another important teaching for the group came with the revelation that the properties of color, like those of any art material, are extremely effective in evoking the inner image and helping to define it as a form.

Case Vignette: Barbara

Finally, let us focus on one of the most beloved and surprising art materials: clay! We will see how it represented a great leap forward for the participant in the group whom we called Barbara. Barbara, after a very expressive but somewhat disturbed group experience in which she displayed considerable anger, used the clay to produce a human couple that referred back to the group's original choice of subject, that of motherhood.

In her first attempt, she shaped a mother with a baby in her arms holding a bottle of milk, but they were too small. So she changed everything (with clay you can do and undo whatever you want!) and put the child in a sitting position next to the mother who was also sitting. It was a long and tormented process. Should the child remain in contact with the mother or not . . . near or far? She raised the same problem that presented itself to the group on the first day and, through some very significant changes, came to a positive solution: The baby and the mother, while physically detached, looked at each other and were therefore united. Barbara created the figurative solution to a union in separation.

Barbara's success was very important to her, because she came from a family situation with a violent father, but she had come out quite healthy, and during this group work, she was the one who found a good, positive expression of what happens when human development follows a positive course. With her

Figure 9.3 Barbara's clay sculpture depicting a mother and her child

art, she made a contribution to all participants in the group who felt touched and united in the discovery of the evolutionary, cognitive, and, ultimately, ecological power of art as therapy.

The Evolution of the School

This group experience with Edith Kramer enriched the program of the Community Il Porto. Thanks to the interest it attracted, not only in Turin, it was followed by many contributions that stemmed from contact with the New York University Art Therapy Program. Of significance was the relation between the two schools, which further intensified to the point that a joint course was launched – Il Porto-ADEG (Association for Youth in Existential Distress) – with New York University. Applications poured in from new students, and other American teachers came to share their teachings in many annual and summer courses. After expanding significantly, the school moved to Milan, Italy, and took on the name Lyceum, becoming one of the most respected art therapy training institutions at the national level. Today, major courses are also taught by New York University faculty, a fact that has earned the institution a solid reputation and that further consolidates the concept of *art as clinical therapy*, its main course of study.

References

Bortino, R., Cipriani, W., Gamna, G., & Gilardi, A. (Eds.). (1987). *Arte terapia. Esperienze di un corso di formazione* [Art therapy. Experiences of course-forming]. Milan: Franco Angeli.

Kramer, E. (1977). *Arte come terapia nell'infanzia* [Art as therapy in childhood] (G. Noferi & V. Silvi, Trans.). Florence: La Nuova Italia.

Kramer, E. (1987). Corso teorico–pratico [Theory–practice course]. In R. Bortino, W. Cipriani, G. Gamna, & A. Gilardi (Eds.), *Arte terapia. Esperienze di un corso di formazione* [Art therapy. Experiences of course-forming] (pp. 61–71). Milan: Franco Angeli.

Artist Identity

10 Edith Kramer's Artistic Legacy
Beyond the Studio

Geoffrey A. Thompson

Introduction

This chapter presents my reflections on organizing the 2009 exhibition *Process and Product: The Art of Edith Kramer,* which took place at the Norwood Flynn Gallery in Dallas, Texas, during the American Art Therapy Annual Conference. I invite the reader to accompany me on this journey, as I reflect upon the numerous visits I made to Edith Kramer's New York City loft and studio and the ultimate selection of works for the exhibition. Through this process, an introspective window into the life of Edith Kramer, the artist, emerges with implications on the lasting impact her artistic legacy exerts on the field of art therapy. This chapter focuses on Edith Kramer the artist, and includes extracts from the original exhibition catalogue.

In the spring of 2009, I was visiting David Henley in Edith Kramer's loft on Vandam Street in Manhattan, and as we talked, the constant presence of Edith could be felt, through her artwork and the milieu of her studio. This presence of Edith pervaded the evening. It was strange to feel Edith's presence in her studio knowing she had recently left the United States for Austria permanently and was unlikely to return. As David and I talked about art therapy, the idea first came to me about organizing an exhibition of her art. This would be a perfect fit for my next conference project as the chair of the Art Committee. David agreed, and the process was underway!

Kramer did not return to the United States and died in 2014, and I now revisit this time on the occasion of this book project to recognize and honor her legacy. I had met Kramer only in passing during several art therapy conferences, and we had exchanged only a few words, but I was obviously aware of her writings and her standing within the field. Edith was a diminutive figure but formidable, and in my experience during conferences, many people approached her with caution. I was familiar with her persona and quickly wondered how an exhibition could be situated that could reflect honesty, respect, and a neutral stance, in relation to her art. I asked myself, could this be achieved? What works should be included and how to decide? This project was both exciting and somewhat daunting after the initial excitement had subsided.

Edith's Loft

Once I made the decision to go ahead with the show I returned to Edith's loft countless times. The first essential action I needed to do was to begin the process of familiarizing myself with her artwork and the ambience of the studio. This required several visits and each time I simply pondered the space, the architecture, any artwork that was readily visible (there was a lot!), as well as objects Edith had collected over the years (see Figure 10.1). I absorbed the loft's studio and living space with its energy. I paid attention to my own emerging self in response to the increased awareness I was developing from these intimate visits. The loft felt open and inviting with different nooks and crannies, comfortable sofas, large windows providing good light, and above all a stillness and quiet that was quite surprising in Manhattan. Every space was full of Edith's artwork, shelves filled with sketchbooks and books, flat files filled with drawings and prints, and an intricate array of objects. Several of her sculptures were visible. David was in the process of archiving her work, which eased access to the vast storehouse. There was a well-worn and loved feeling to the physical and metaphorical space and contents.

I confess that I was relatively unaware of her personal artwork, but I was aware of some of her strong opinions about art in general and contemporary art in particular. I did not agree with all of her views and worked to bracket this in order to remain open to her work. I was also curious about her artwork based on this knowledge, and eager to see what discoveries might lie ahead.

Figure 10.1 Treasured objects in Edith Kramer's loft

Edith the Artist

Edith was continually informed by her artist identity, through which she intrinsically understood the haunting beauty and the precarious potential of art to transform and sustain the artist and the viewer. This was her path and for Edith there could be no other way. Edith committed to a sustained relationship to making art throughout her entire life, and this took precedence over everything else. She fiercely defended her practice and insistence for all art therapists to be practicing artists first and foremost. Practice as an art therapist without this intense personal commitment would devalue the therapeutic and artistic enterprise. Edith searched for the expression of an essential humanity and humility, and this had a powerful effect on her identity as an art therapist. These experiences helped to shape her theoretical orientation and informed the very particular method of art therapy that Kramer practiced clinically: *art as therapy*. This poetic integration was felt in Edith's loft, where the harmony between her different voices could be experienced firsthand; the importance she placed on her own artist identity shone through loud and clear. Anni Bergman (as cited in Thompson, 2014) contributed a personal reflection on Edith for the original exhibition catalog (expanded in this book) where she eloquently described Edith's relationship to art: "The need to create seems to be a part of her. It is not something she tries to accomplish, but rather it seems to be a need and ability to turn her perceptions of the world into works of art" (p. 183).

Edith insisted on authentic art-making, which for her included maintaining respect for each given subject, reconciling conflict, working to ease repressive defenses, and responding truthfully and consistently with one's own essential self. There were multiple realities and enduring narratives visible in her work, and I reflected upon the search for beauty and harmony, which at times interacted with resonant imperfection. Edith sought not only to reconcile, but also to perceptually grasp through making art, inner and outer realities and conflicts. Imperfection often appeared as a companion to perfection, which frequently took the form of transient time, perceptual truth, and the preciousness and delicate beauty of the natural world. It is common knowledge that Kramer would rail against certain aspects of the modern – of potent despoiling industrialism, toxic wastelands, and the deadening effect derived from the omnipresent bombardment of runaway commercialism. Perhaps the psychoanalytic imperative of integration drove her to explore the dichotomy of these polarities by actively attuning to them as worthy adversaries through which she might visually tame them, embodied in an aesthetic form with the potential of reaching internal harmony and homeostasis.

86   Geoffrey A. Thompson

Edith grappled with the harsh realities of life, such as the growing turmoil in 1930s Europe, with the rise of Nazi Germany, which ultimately led her to flee her native Austria and travel as a refugee to the United States. I found many drawings and pen and ink sketches from this early period that possess a haunting beauty. Newly arrived in the United States, Edith grappled with the grim reality of working in a factory during World War II. She found subjects wherever she was, such as the subterranean depths of the New York City subway system, or the depictions of the sublime beauty of the industrial wasteland of northern New Jersey. David Henley (personal communication, May 7, 2009) recalled the times he drove Edith around the New Jersey Turnpike as she scoped out possible sites to paint, until she discovered a suitable site, whereupon he would have to stop the car to let her out!

She dealt with both pleasant and unpleasant realities through her reflexivity as an artist. Even in the unpleasant she could find a poetic solution. Edith wrote: "no plants can grow on soil poisoned by industrial waste, yet the huge cylindrical bodies of chemical tanks, exposed to wind and weather, take on formal dignity that can stand up against the beauty of the wilderness they have invaded" (Kramer & Gerity, 2000, p. 15). Many of Kramer's paintings on this subject explored a formalist response to architecture, which came closest of anything she did to resembling abstraction. Amidst the wastelands, there was always the presence of the resilient evidence of beauty in the form of wild plants or weeds to provide a measure of comfort afforded by the power of the natural world to offer hope.

Edith's Art

I recall the great enjoyment I felt at undertaking the task of selecting works for the exhibition. There were precious moments, as I respectfully viewed a lifetime of Edith's artwork. I loved the task and always felt eager each time I left the loft to make the next visit. As the visits continued, I became more familiar with her artwork and remember feeling excited to facilitate the opportunity for others to experience the wonder of her art and her world. How many people in the art therapy community were also naïve about Edith the artist? I knew the exhibition would provide this opportunity, and I was confident that it might come as a surprise to some, who like myself, primarily know Edith from her art therapy writings.

Edith's artwork contained many of the key theoretical concepts she endorsed as an art therapist. These included the integration of process and product; the struggle for formed expression; quality in art; truth and authenticity; the efficacy of the *third hand*; the transformative process of loosening defenses; and the primacy of art as an essential undiluted poetic form that can defy adverse psychological interpretation. Although she was not always successful in reconciling these dynamics in her art, Edith modeled a tolerance for both success and failure, a fitting artistic metaphor for life. Kramer stated: "The essence of art and psychotherapy is flexibility and openness. It also implies

Edith Kramer's Artistic Legacy 87

tolerance for periods of disorganization and turmoil as ingrained habits of defense lose their hold and new organization is only in the making" (Kramer & Gerity, 2000, p. 23).

That the search for the authentic self involves loosening rigid defenses was an evident thread within Edith's oeuvre, as she persevered as an artist and as an art therapist to permit the essence of the creative act to exist and be nurtured. Perhaps this is best illustrated by many self-portraits she made. The first two works I knew I wanted in the exhibition were the pastel self-portrait drawing, circa 1937, and the circa 2006 oil painting, another self-portrait, which was one of the last works she completed before she returned to Austria. These self-portraits reveal a deep sensitivity, and an honest self-reflection imbued with hope, but they also communicate a sense of doubt and sadness, possibly regarding uncertainty and the unknowable future. Both works make visible unconscious process and intrapsychic dimensions, and both transcend technique, defenses, and repressive forces to project a freshness and honest autobiographical glimpse into Edith as a person. Some self-portrait studies in between these two works fall short of this accomplishment and pale in comparison. Edith believed artists, ". . . must battle to protect their creative efforts from the dominance of stifling mechanisms of defense" (Kramer & Wilson, 1979, p. 11). Overcoming defense mechanisms, which can distort an artist's perception of truth, requires ". . . considerable moral courage, and because it constitutes a profound moral victory such art has the power to move us deeply" (Kramer & Wilson, 1979, p. 10). Edith firmly believed that with a high degree of moral courage and effort, the struggle over conflict and defenses could be aesthetically won. The value Edith placed on these characteristics was reflected in these two paintings; both remain open as the works probe an aesthetic and psychological depth. The final self-portrait bears out her belief that art therapists should also be artists and respond to these callings with flexibility and an openness to change: ". . . I do not mean to imply that their style should remain static; throughout their lives they must establish and reestablish their self-perception and their perception of the world in their art" (Kramer & Wilson, 1979, p. 275).

There were many other works that successfully combined openness, subtlety, a clarified sense of aesthetic perception, and the working through to achieve a powerful artistic statement. The painting in Figure 10.2, *Still Life with Etching Plates*, demonstrates these qualities. Many of the objects Edith collected figured prominently in a series of still life paintings framed with gold leaf paint and visible in Figure 10.1. This painting has an evocative power, with an idiosyncratic sense of space. It is both flexible and resolved, and emits a calm meditative feeling. Her depictions of still life, which employ gold leaf paint, reflect the intimacy of her studio as the treasured and humble objects resonate with an emotional significance gained through her artistic and emotional investment. Edith's best works contain a degree of attention and curiosity, with care and respect for a given subject matter. Each was fueled by an innate drive to create and transform her perceptions of the world around her into art, as a natural consequence of her receptivity to the aesthetic dimension.

Figure 10.2 Gold still life with etching plates. Circa 2001. Oil, gold leaf, and egg tempera on canvas by Edith Kramer

Surrounded by her art and immersed in the phenomenology of her studio environment, I was struck by the modernist dictum, which informed her intentionality and the reliance on authentic self-expression and honest depiction of the world around her. Ironically there were counter currents to this visible in her work, namely in her reliance on a representational paradigm, which quickly dissipated in modern art, as the range of subjects related to inner and outer realities became embedded in abstraction. The absence of abstraction appeared to me to lend her work the quality of a quirky phenomenological time warp. This quality helped to guide me to the selections I ultimately made, which would reveal one of the strengths of her best work; namely, works capable of communicating Edith's sense of humanity, which in turn could activate empathic responses from the viewer.

Edith's wide range of subjects illustrated her visual responses as an artist, which served to document her physicality together with her symbolic presence. I pored over countless drawings and mostly small watercolor paintings made in Europe before she arrived in the United States in 1938. From Vienna and Prague to Paris, from humble street scenes, landscapes, figure studies, plants and sketches made in museums, the humanity embedded in these works was

Figure 10.3 Landscape: The Alps, circa 1935. Watercolor painting by Edith Kramer

haunting, delicate, and deeply moving. The watercolor *Landscape: The Alps*, circa 1935 (Figure 10.3), is a humble but beautiful example that was strewn in a flat file, torn from a sketchbook, and communicates the magnificence of nature and the fragility of life. I pondered this work and considered Edith's state of mind as she rapidly painted this beloved scene of her home, on the eve of the Nazi annexation of Austria.

Another work that I am fortunate to own is the deceptively simple 1966 painting titled *Spring Branches*. This painting exudes a haunting sense of beauty and perfection, and the deftest brushstrokes are economic, considered, and reflective, while the overall impression of the work still retains a spontaneous feeling and freshness. Having lived with this work for several years I can reaffirm these qualities and enjoy its presence, which always appears fresh and innocent in its aesthetic simplicity.

Reflections

The exhibition revealed Kramer's heightened relationship to an "aesthetic dimension" (Scharfstein, 2009) and an "artistic sensibility" (Thompson, 2015).

90 *Geoffrey A. Thompson*

Within the reflective space of her art, a deeper aesthetic empathy of Kramer could be felt, or "grasped" (Scharfstein, 2009), which was consistent with her own sense of self as an artist.

The Norwood Flynn Gallery in Dallas, Texas, graciously hosted the exhibition, which included 20 paintings, drawings, and sculptures. Kramer's position on authenticity, giving up defenses and surviving the struggle towards actualization, applied to my own process in realizing this project. For example, this highly personal and intimate aspect of the two-sided paintings demanded my attention and posed a practical difficulty. I encountered the strangest system in the gallery of a space to hang freestanding artwork, allowing the viewer access to both sides of the canvas. The dialectic relationship between the chosen image (the front) and the reverse could be experienced in the gallery. Unfortunately, Edith was permanently living in Austria and did not see the exhibition. However, David Henley informed me that she reviewed the catalog and project favorably. The majority of the works on exhibit sold, and the gallery waived commission, and David transferred the proceeds directly to her.

Edith Kramer the artist and private person shines through in the selections of the exhibition. Her work reveals her deep humanity, as she honed her perceptions to accomplish empathic depictions of people, places, and things. One of my intentions for the exhibition was to share the discoveries I made of Edith's intimate world of art with the art therapy community and beyond. I wanted to widen the visual context of her work, in order to suggest that, contained within these gaps, there exists meaning in her work and her life that has often been overlooked or excluded.

References

Kramer, E., & Gerity, L. A. (2000). *Art as therapy: Collected papers*. London: Jessica Kingsley.

Kramer, E., & Wilson, L. (1979). *Childhood and art therapy: Notes on theory and application*. New York, NY: Schocken Books.

Scharfstein, B-A. (2009). *Art without borders: A philosophical exploration of art and humanity*. Chicago, IL: University of Chicago Press.

Thompson, G. (2014). Process and product: The art of Edith Kramer. *Art therapy: Journal of the American Art Therapy Association, 31*(4), 183–190.

Thompson, G. (2015). *Aesthetic action and self-construction of an artist identity: The impact of art and art therapy on subjectivity and mental illness in qualitative research* (Unpublished doctoral dissertation). Saybrook University. Retrieved from: www.academia.edu/11818866/Aesthetic_Action_and_Self-Construction_of_an_Artist_Identity_The_impact_of_Art_and_Art_Therapy_on_Subjectivity_and_Mental_Illness_in_Qualitative_Research Accessed 18 September 2017.

11 Remembering Edith Kramer

Karl Pallauf[1,2]
(Translator, Martha Haeseler)

In an essay published in 1917, entitled "What is Painting?" the well-known American artist and art critic Kenyon Cox (1856–1919) seemed to suggest painting can show us things that we have never seen for ourselves in nature.

These words seem to describe Edith Kramer's comprehensive collection of works precisely. Much has already been written about her life and her work as one of the most recognized art therapists; however, this exhibition deals exclusively with her artistic work.

Kramer's images are mosaics of life – in them, you can read where the painter holds herself back, what she surrounded herself with, and what she was occupied with.

Edith Kramer was born on August 26, 1916 in Vienna. Already by her fifth year, she received her first drawing lessons from Trude Hammerschlag (1899–1930), a student of Franz Cizek (1865–1946), a pioneer of art education.

In 1929, she was a student of the Schwarzwald School, founded in 1901 by Eugenie Schwarzwald. It was a place where artists and liberati regularly met and also taught. At this time, Trude Hammerschlag taught Kramer, as did, most importantly, the Bauhaus artist and art teacher Friedl Dicker (1898–1944), who was recognizably as influential on Kramer's later work as an art therapist as she was on her painting.

After graduation from high school, Kramer followed the fleeing Friedl Dicker to Prague. From there, she also commuted to Vienna to study sculpture from Fritz Wotruba (1907–1975). From 1935, Kramer began to grapple with a different subject – art education. In 1938, Edith Kramer emigrated by ship from Gdansk to New York.

Edith soon found a job as a crafts teacher in the Little Red School House in Greenwich Village, and continued her psychoanalytic studies with Annie Reich, whom she already knew from Europe. In the time between 1943 and the end of the World War, she worked as a machinist for the defense industry.

After the war, Edith Kramer devoted herself to both her passions – painting and art therapy. Subsequently, she wrote numerous books such as *Art Therapy in a Children's Community*, and *Art as Therapy with Children*, taught at a large university, and organized exhibitions of her paintings.

92 *Karl Pallauf*

Edith Kramer spent the summer months for many decades in Grundlsee in Austria, a place of numerous childhood memories. From there, she would go and spend weeks in a shepherd's hut at 1700 meters high.

Edith Kramer told me some time ago in her New York studio – at the time I was sitting for my portrait – that after three workdays, there were four days in which she devoted herself exclusively to painting. I have learned very much in my numerous talks with Edith Kramer. Neither bitterness nor hate was stuck in her. Her openness toward the world and her pure joy of living were both factors which drove her, even in her later years, to paint. When I once asked her if she regretted not having children, she looked at me, totally astonished, with her big and always loving eyes, "The paintings are my children! It would not be fair for me to bring children into the world, when I know that art would always take first place for me." At that time, I was very impressed with those words. And as a result, they were fundamentally responsible for my determination to make Edith Kramer's artworks known in Europe.

Notes

1 This essay was originally submitted in German. Translation provided by Martha Haeseler.
2 A version of this essay was included in the catalogue for a show of Edith Kramer's work at Günter Pallauf's art gallery in Vienna (Gallery Pallauf) on the occasion of her 90th birthday.

Center Figure 1 Herschel J. Stroyman – Edith Kramer at Wiltwyck School for Boys art show

Center Figure 2 Herschel J. Stroyman – Edith Kramer and Eleanor Roosevelt at Wiltwyck School for Boys art show

Center Figure 3 Herschel J. Stroyman – Edith Kramer

Center Figure 4 Herschel J. Stroyman – Edith Kramer's painting of "urban renewal"

Center Figure 5 Herschel J. Stroyman – Edith painting Herschel's children

Center Figure 6 Herschel J. Stroyman – Herschel's children supervising Edith

Center Figure 7 Herschel J. Stroyman – *Working in Stillness*

Center Figure 8 Herschel J. Stroyman – *The Loft 1*

Center Figure 9 Herschel J. Stroyman – Edith Kramer

Center Figure 10 Herschel J. Stroyman – *The Loft 2*

Center Figure 11 Herschel J. Stroyman – Edith Kramer with bas-relief subway study

Center Figure 12 Herschel J. Stroyman – Edith Kramer teaching at NYU

Center Figure 13 Herschel J. Stroyman – Edith Kramer studying drawings made with Friedl Dicker's techniques

Center Figure 14 Herschel J. Stroyman – *Objects in Window*

Center Figure 15 Herschel J. Stroyman – *Devil Puppet Obscured*

Center Figure 16 Herschel J. Stroyman – Edith Kramer

Center Figure 17 Herschel J. Stroyman – *Ladies and Bathtubs 1*

Center Figure 18 Herschel J. Stroyman – *Ladies and Bathtubs 2*

Center Figure 19 Herschel J. Stroyman – Edith and friends

Center Figure 20 Edith Kramer and Herschel J. Stroyman

Center Figure 21 Karin Dannecker – *Grundlsee*

Center Figure 22 Edith Kramer – *Child in Prague* (from Lani Gerity)

Center Figure 23 Edith Kramer – *Machinist during World War II* (from Lani Gerity)

Center Figure 24 Edith Kramer – *London after the Blitz* (from Martha Haeseler)

Center Figure 25 Edith Kramer – *Kostia Bergman* (from Lani Gerity)

Center Figure 26 Edith Kramer – *New York Subway* (from Kathryn Bard)

Center Figure 27 Edith Kramer – *Herschel J. Stroyman and Family* (from Herschel J. Stroyman)

Center Figure 28 Edith Kramer – *Still Life 1* (from Herschel J. Stroyman)

Center Figure 29 Edith Kramer – *Aunt Liesl* (from Kathryn Bard)

Center Figure 30 Edith Kramer – *Still Life 2* (from Herschel J. Stroyman)

Center Figure 31 Edith Kramer – *Juniper Tree* (from Susan Anand)

Center Figure 32 Edith Kramer – *Landscape* (from David Henley)

Center Figure 33 Edith Kramer – *Mountains* (from Martha Haeseler)

Center Figure 34 Edith Kramer – *New York Roof Top* (from Kathryn Bard)

Center Figure 35 Edith Kramer – *Still Life 3* (from Martha Haeseler)

Center Figure 36 Edith Kramer – *Vegetable Still Life* (from Martha Haeseler)

Center Figure 37 Edith Kramer – *Still Life in Window* (from Kathryn Bard)

Center Figure 38 Edith Kramer – *Potted Plants* (from Vinod Anand)

Center Figure 39 Edith Kramer – *Hay Stacks* (from Karin Dannecker)

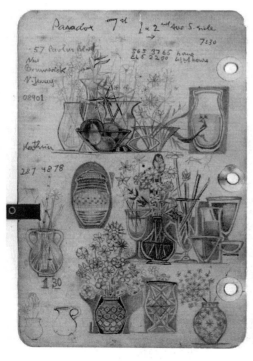

Center Figure 40 Edith Kramer – *Telephone Book Page 1* (from Herschel J. Stroyman)

Center Figure 41 Edith Kramer – *Telephone Book Page 2* (from Herschel J. Stroyman)

12 An Edith Collage

Katherine Williams

In 1992, my husband and I were walking toward Edith's studio to see her subway mural in progress when he had a heart attack and died. On her next trip to lecture at the Art Therapy Program at George Washington University, she brought me a beautiful egg, painted in Russian style with a brush that must have had only a few hairs, and using dyes that she created from beets and onions. I have always wondered how she could rip and mutilate bread to mold it into temporary sculpture, could bang around in her studio, hike the Austrian mountains, tramp through the subway, and yet manage to paint the most intricate of lines on a blown-out egg and carry it to DC without breaking it. This surely reflects the toughness and delicacy that Edith needed to live her life fully as an artist.

One spring day a few years ago, coming up out of the Spring Street Station with my daughter Rachel and her little girls, we came upon the final version of Edith's mosaic depicting the passengers waiting in the curved track section of the Union Square Station. We were en route to the children's art center, and Rachel and I hadn't seen the image since it was temporarily installed at the Atlantic Avenue stop some years before. Before that, we had viewed its predecessor, a large collage of the image, in the show that the New York Transit Museum had mounted of Edith's artwork inspired by the subway. And even before that, I spent a night on the cot in the studio near the work in process, created from sketches and watercolors done in preparation for the collage that became the mural. So on this lucid afternoon, confronting the piece amid the bustle of humanity at the subway station was like coming upon an old friend and it brought tears to my eyes. Perhaps because Rachel and I were so moved, but also because the mural was large and vital and we knew the artist, my granddaughters seemed entranced as they viewed the mosaic.

Edith and my granddaughters would have liked each other, since they share a passion for art and use language in interesting and idiosyncratic ways. Charlotte and Lila were intrigued when I told them about Edith's studio – a place where the art materials were always waiting and never needed to be cleaned up, and where she could even sleep over if she didn't want to stop drawing until bedtime. They were delighted to hear that, in the midst of the profusion of art materials, Edith had once cooked me a goose egg. It tasted ambrosial – just the enormous egg, boiled in a battered pan on a hot plate, served in a

Figure 12.1 Katherine Williams' granddaughters with the Edith Kramer subway mosaic at the Spring Street Station, New York City

cracked cup. Yet the woman who warmed me with an egg and tea on a cold day could be fierce. And this fortitude and resilience were surely part of the reason she was able to lead our field in exploration, in staking out new territory, and building a "cabin" of art therapy in the wilderness of mental health treatment for poor children at that time. To try to convey some of this to my granddaughters, I have searched for stories to show how inimitable Edith was.

I think of Edith arriving at Union Station in DC, for instance. She would plant her orthopedic shoes firmly and stride at a good pace, balancing the backpack in which she carried not only the clothing she needed for the weekend but also the slides and books for her classes. The crowds would part, as younger people, walking more slowly and burdened by multiple suitcases, would turn and stare at her. I'd gather her up and drive her near GW where we would have dinner before a Friday night class. As we ate, I could count on a diatribe against American food. Then she would set herself up, unpacking her slides, and settle in to frighten and entrance the students before her. She never remembered a name but could recognize the artwork of nearly anyone she had taught, no matter how many years before. Those end-of-the-week classes exhausted me but Edith seemed to gain energy as the evening progressed. Afterwards, she would come home with me, put on her flannel nightgown, and pad around my house, as though she were at home. Did she ever have a shoulder injury?

An Edith Collage 95

I remember brushing and braiding her hair a few times, and so wondering if she had come to teach even though she was having some sort of physical trouble.

It would be a rare injury or incapacity that would keep her from her teaching duties, even when she was in her eighties and having considerable physical problems. She was made of stern stuff. One year not too long before she retired, GW responded to large protests around the IMF or World Bank by announcing that it would be closed for the whole weekend, canceling all classes and blocking the campus off against any entry. I called Edith to tell her of the problem and to plan a future date for the class. She was astonished I would think of canceling and said, matter-of-factly, that there was no reason why the students, and she and I, couldn't just get to Building L before the campus was closed off, and simply stay there all weekend, sleeping on sleeping bags in the two old rooms that comprised the art therapy program. My decision not to try this was probably less about reluctance to brook the university administration and more about not wanting to tell the young, able-bodied students that they would have to be sequestered and sleep on the floor for two nights with the terrifying Edith Kramer.

One of my granddaughters recently ran into the room to show me a huge castle she had drawn, which she had started when she began third grade. She was excited to have drawn the last brick and finally colored in the flag. It had taken her all year to complete. On the plane back to DC, I realized that Charlotte is now ready to hear details about the progression of Edith's mural – how she started with a sketch, moved into watercolor, and after that, collage over some years. How the work later spoke to her and said, "mosaic." How, at 77, she found a teacher to help her learn this ancient art, how a pattern of each tiny line and shadow was created and mounted on slabs of plywood, then cracked out of stone and painstakingly glued. How delicate and how huge this all was. How she had to find grants to fund the project and ways to transport the heavy piece. She commented that people marveled at her patience, but she saw it as passion that carried her through all the vicissitudes of the project.

When Edith had an exhibit at the Austrian Embassy in Washington, DC, my faculty members asked me which painting I most loved. When they surprised me by buying it for me, Edith was pleased at my selection. "You know that kid, Katherine," she said of the sweet, moody boy slouched against the side of the subway seat. Many visitors in my house are surprised that I find this image beautiful. But it is Edith's genius that she could depict the boy's nuanced expression of sadness, fatigue, vulnerability, and wisdom so fully that it is uplifting to me. Her uncomplicated embrace of the complicated human experience and her belief that art, its making, and its viewing can enliven and transform this experience – this is what I would like to be able to convey to the little girls who never met Edith but who, on that spring day, saw the shattered stones she formed into a story that continues to speak to busy people each day of their lives.

13 The Mosaic[1]

Edith Kramer

In 1992, my long-standing interest in the New York subway led me to study one of its oldest, most complex stations, the IRT section of Union Square Station. I made a number of drawings and watercolors on site. Then I set out to compose a representational collage made entirely of paper, which was based on my sketches, measuring 38"x58". It was exhibited in 1994 at the New York Transit Museum Gallery.

The collage insistently suggested transposition into a mosaic. I could not resist its bidding. Evidently, I had to make the transposition myself. No professional mosaic artist, however skilled, could be expected to translate collage into mosaic.

Therefore, I who had never made any mosaic before, set out at age 77 to learn about mosaic making. I consulted Simon Verity, sculptor and creator of a large mosaic depicting the city of New York, which is presently installed at Bellevue Hospital. Mr Verity gave me much valuable information. He also introduced me to his best assistant, Kirsten Westphal, sculptor and mosaic artist, who became my teacher and technical director for the project.

I spent one year acquiring the technical skills of mosaic making, obtaining the necessary machinery: water-saw, grinder, diamond-belt saw, tumbler, as well as Italian glass, and the marble, granite, slate, brick, and ceramic tile needed for the job.

In April of 1994, I obtained approval from Creative Stations of Metropolitan Transportation Authority (MTA) for the temporary installation of a mosaic mural capturing the life of the Union Square Subway Station. However, Union Square Station, being scheduled for extensive renewal, was not available for any temporary installation at that time. Instead, the mosaic was installed at the Atlantic Avenue Station in Brooklyn, at the passageway between the D, Q, N, and R lines. I secured the sponsorship of Art Initiatives and Art Information Center.

The mosaic was produced at my loft at 95 Vandam Street, New York, NY, 10013. It measured 5'6"x8'8". It was made in seven sections, fitting together like a jigsaw puzzle, the joints following the lines of the architectural structures. The stones were mounted on perforated aluminum. They were secured by PC11, a white epoxy. This is an elastic substance, which could be expected to withstand the vibrations of the subway environment. A silicone impregnator was used to protect the stone. Thus, the mosaic could be easily transported and installed, and has a good chance to survive in the exposed environment of a New York subway station. Throughout the making of the mosaic I had the invaluable advice of the mosaic artist Laura Bradley, who was at that time engaged in making two abstract mosaic images for the MTA. She generously shared her technical knowledge with me.

The translation of paper into stone entailed extensive experimentation; I had to be able to shift the size around, change tesserae, shape, and placement. It was impossible to proceed in the classical manner, laying out a mirror image into a water-soluble adhesive surface to be flipped over onto the mosaic's permanent bed. Instead, each section was first laid out upon plywood, cut into shapes that corresponded to the sections planned for the completed mosaic. The resulting image was then covered with gauze, saturated in a solution of methyl cellulose dissolved in water. The dry gauze was stiff and transparent. It could be cut into smaller sections. Sections of the aluminum, which had been cut to corresponding sections of the mosaic held in shape by the gauze, were then quickly placed upon the prepared surface. The epoxy's setting time allowed an hour for repair and changes. Finally, the gauze was removed and the finished section allowed to set. Thus it was not necessary for me to learn to work with mirror images.

Creating the mosaic was a year's work. It was completed in January 1995. Beyond the MTA's financial contribution, I obtained partial financial assistance from the Austrian Cultural Institute. Combined, these contributions covered less than half my expenses for materials and labor.

Figure 13.1 Subway mosaic at Spring Street Subway Station. Photo by Herschel J. Stroyman

98 *Edith Kramer*

Individuals who observed me working on the mosaic often admired my "patience" in shaping and assembling innumerable little stones. I never felt that the work demanded patience. I was motivated by *passion* for the infinite possibilities that the various materials offered; for the sculptural and painterly imagination the work stimulated. I expect that my year of mosaic making will heighten my perception of color and texture and bear fruit in my work as a painter.

Before all, I hope and trust that my image will make people aware of their environment. It will offer interest and pleasure in an area where people are usually pressured, impatient, and bored. In this manner, I will fulfill my function as an artist.

Edith Kramer
January 26, 1995

Note

1 This description of the Spring Street Station mosaic was found in the *Edith Kramer Papers* at the New York University Archives. The original is handwritten by Edith Kramer and titled "The Mosaic."

14 Create Your Own
Kramer's Criteria for Quality as Central to Art Therapy

Jordan S. Potash

In this essay, I briefly describe Edith Kramer's definition of quality in art therapy, its influence on my practice, and its centrality to the profession.

Quality in Art: An Art Therapy Aesthetic

I remember the exact moment that Edith Kramer left a lasting impression on me. It was during a plenary at the American Art Therapy Association conference (Kramer, Anand, & Gerity, 2001) when I first heard her describe her criteria for quality in art therapy as "inner consistency, economy of artistic means, and evocative power" (Kramer, 1975, p. 54). Inner consistency guaranteed that the art accurately matched the client's experience in terms of depicted imagery. Economy of means pushed the artist-clients to work to the best of their abilities so that the art truly came from their own efforts. Evocative power made sure that the art was derived from a significant personal experience.

In my professional work with clients, these ideas helped me to see how particular attention to the image could guide clients motivated to complete expressive art. When art conveyed its meaning, it could function as symbolic communication and perhaps promote catharsis. Being challenged to exhaust one's artistic aptitudes and extend beyond perceived limits could provide new skills and a metaphor for encountering new situations. Through attention to these characteristics, art therapists "are attempting to free them [clients] from the constraints of artificial standards so that they can find their own expressive style" (Kramer, 2002, p. 219).

In learning this definition of quality, much of what concerned me about art therapy's lack of focus on the art itself became clear. Too often I heard art therapy described as placing emphasis on the process with little attention on the product in order to help clients feel more comfortable. In other words, the non-judgmental attitude of traditional aesthetics accidentally translated into an expectation of no aesthetics. Kramer's description offered an alternative in which both process and product mattered. More so, it provided an affirmative definition that gave me a language to confidently say what art therapy is and how it uniquely contributes to one's health.

Create Your Own

The remainder of this essay is an adaptation of a presentation titled "Create Your Own" that I delivered at TEDxNYU: Color Party on April 15, 2016 as a representative of the American Art Therapy Association (Potash, 2016). This forum was intended to present various perspectives on coloring and its relation to health and wellness. I share it as an example of how I describe Kramer's teachings on quality as a defining feature of art therapy. A recording of the talk is available at http://jordanpotash.com/art/podcasts/ and https://vimeo.com/164510921.

My sister is an athlete. Not a sit-on-your-couch-at-home-yelling-at-the-ref-through-the-screen kind of athlete – she's more like a real athlete. Much of her free time is given over to exercise and coaching and working out. So, when she called me one day and told me she made a painting, I was pretty surprised. Because in my family, I'm the one who's been doing art since I was a kid, I'm the one who dual majored in psychology and studio arts in college, and I'm the one who still makes art to this day. But, my sister and her friends went to a painting studio one night. In that painting studio, they were each given a canvas, a palette of colors, and a glass of wine. An instructor told them which colors to mix and where to place them on the canvas in order to create a tree-lined landscape complete with a lakeside view. And my sister had a great time. And she was proud of herself – proud enough to tell me about it and give me

Figure 14.1 My sister's painting

her painting. She hasn't made any art since that night, but for one night, she thought of herself as an artist.

"No-fail" Art

Currently, adults have a lot of choices when it comes to being creative. We have these painting studios (and wine) and we have adult coloring books. There are pottery studios you can go to and glaze pre-made ceramics and there are the equivalent studios that will let you make mosaics. If you come to the neighborhood where I work, there is a truck that drives around, parks, sets up a table, and invites passers-by to create crafts in ten minutes or less. All of these activities are billed as leisure or as alternatives for a night out to, you know, "paint the town red."

Although we see this as a new phenomenon, it's not that new. It's actually based in the 1950s paint-by-number movement (Smithsonian Institution, n.d.). And in 2001 when the Smithsonian Institution's Museum of American History (Bird, 2001) mounted an exhibit, they focused on how paint by number democratized art making. It introduced ordinary non-artists to the simple joys of using art materials and the fun that can come out of it. Mostly, what they found was that paint by number gave adults an opportunity to be creative without the fear of failure.

We see a lot of this kind of opportunity today, with our creative arts activities for adults, particularly in coloring books. And there are some other aspects added, as well. There are people who find that it promotes escapism and distraction from the world. There are those who find that when you narrowly focus on coloring, it frees up a whole other part of your mind to unconsciously work out problems. And there are those who find choosing images and coloring them in soothing. There are a lot of great benefits to coloring and all of the other "success guaranteed" art activities.

However, there are times when life's challenges require our attention, not our distraction. What that means is that we need to shift how we see art. We need to shift from seeing it as recreation to seeing it as being able to re-create how we see ourselves, our relationships, and our communities. However, what that also means is we need to let go of the predetermined lines, and shapes, and images to free up the lines, and shapes, and images of our imagination. Now if it sounds scary to create art without instruction, trust me, under the right circumstances, anyone can do it. I know, because I'm an art therapist. And I have seen people make amazing pieces of art with little more than a willingness to try, combined with a supportive studio, and an attentive facilitator.

Defining Art Therapy

When it comes to coloring books, the phrase "art therapy" is thrown around a lot, and it's often used as shorthand for relaxation or happiness. But that's not actually what art therapy is. Let's set the record straight.

102 *Jordan S. Potash*

According to the American Art Therapy Association (2016), art therapy is "an integrative mental health profession that . . . use[s] art media, and often the verbal processing of produced imagery, to help people resolve conflicts and problems, develop interpersonal skills, manage behavior, reduce stress, increase self-esteem and self-awareness, and achieve insight" (para. 1).

Principles of Art Made in Art Therapy

When I tell people I'm an art therapist, some of the immediate reactions I get include, "Well, that's not for me! I'm not creative! I'm not artistic! I can't even draw a stick figure!" You may be thinking that now. And that's the beauty of the coloring page, isn't it? The remedy for the blank page, the fear of uncertainty, and the unknown. Here's something to know. Art therapists work with everybody. We have a special way of helping people create art, and we do that by honoring the principles and teachings of one of the founders of art therapy in the United States, Edith Kramer (1975).

First, we help you to create art based on you – your thoughts, your feelings, your memories, your dreams, your ideas. Because when you base art in your experiences, it gives it an emotionally evocative quality that will help you find it special and help those who you share it with find it special.

Secondly, we want you to find an image that matches that experience. You don't need to have the whole idea formed out in your head ahead of time. Not even seasoned artists can successfully translate their mental images onto a canvas. What we want is for you to have a start or what I describe as "the seed of an art" that you put down on paper to begin, and you add to. That way, it ensures that the image you are creating as it evolves has a consistency with the experience you want to convey.

Thirdly, we want you to work with the abilities that you have. We are not interested in the skills that you do not have – they are uninteresting. We believe that everybody has the ability to make a mark on a page that's meaningful, make a stroke on a canvas that's meaningful, and an indent in a ball of clay that's meaningful. We will work with you with the skills you have, and then we'll help you to expand them when needed.

When art is made in these three ways – is emotionally evocative, has that inner consistency, and is made according to your ability – we call that beautiful. We call it whole and we call it complete. From there, we'll get you in conversation to help make meaning of your art, because we don't interpret art. We're not tealeaf readers or palm readers. Our job is to get you into dialog so that you can discover the messages of your art for you. Here are the three types of lessons that we think your art can teach you.

Learning About Self

The first is that art making in art therapy can help you learn something about yourself. Art making can promote expression, communication, and contemplation to give you a new perspective on an idea or situation.

A young man who was struggling a lot with anger and being impulsive created a drawing. He created a black sketchy ring on the outside, which represented the irritation he felt when dealing with other people. Then he created red as an intense reaction to the irritation. And after he drew this, he was really interested in that space where the red met the black. Because there he noticed that possibly other people experienced him the way he experienced them – and even worse, because his reaction was so much more intense. But more than that, he was very curious about the center, which he described as filled with light and having a calm core. After a few minutes of silence, he said, "I didn't even know I had this part of me. And probably all of my ways of reacting prevented anyone else from seeing that as well." For this young man, making art in art therapy allowed him to gain awareness of himself.

Learning About Others

Creating art in art therapy can also help us learn about others. When we focus on relationships, our art can promote a sense of familiarity and empathy.

On many occasions, I had the opportunity to bring medical students into the art therapy studio for the purpose of using art to change their perspective on their patients and how they saw illness. A young doctor in training created a drawing, and described how doing so allowed her to see through her patient's physical pain to appreciate her patient's emotional suffering. To convey this idea, she wrote a poem to accompany this piece.

> The clock was ticking, the Lady sighed
> Her world was grey. She shook her head
> Feeling distressed and confused, anxious, and sad
> She had a sense of guilt and ongoing pain
> Perhaps all she needed was a tender touch
> To rescue her from the world of helplessness.

For that medical student, creating art in art therapy helped her gain awareness of others.

Learning About World

Creating art in art therapy can also help people gain awareness of the world. When we focus our attention on social issues like poverty, and discrimination, and violence, we get a glimpse as to what it is like to live with that as one's reality. And it can even motivate us to social action.

My colleagues and I had an opportunity to work with adults living with mental illness who were interested in creating an exhibit in order to help challenge perceptions of mental health and to break a stigma. And viewers that came to the exhibit had the opportunity to make art in response to their feelings about pieces in the exhibit. One of the viewers was really focused on a very colorful piece with very little story attached; she didn't know what it meant. And the longer she sat with it, and as she made art about it, in her mind, she started to untangle the confusing colors in order to discern a ray of hope. In her reflection afterwards, she noted that she no longer viewed this person as "just someone living with mental illness," but she saw them in a more holistic way, as somebody with strengths, and hopes, and abilities, as well. For that gallery attendee, creating art in art therapy helped her learn more about the world.

So, coloring and all of our success-oriented art activities are great. They promote relaxation. They promote distraction. They may even give you some joy. But if you start to find that these activities lose their joy, and they become stifling, or if you start to become a bit more curious about your art, then it's possibly time to try something else. Find an art therapist. Use your creative energies and activity to learn something about yourself, about your relationships, and about your world. Sometimes the answer isn't to fit into somebody else's lines, shapes, and images, but to create your own.

References

American Art Therapy Association. (2016). *What is art therapy?* Retrieved April 1, 2016 from: http://arttherapy.org/aata-aboutus

Bird, W. L. (2001). *Paint by number: The how-to craze that swept the nation.* New York: Princeton Architectural Press.

Kramer, E. (1975). The problem of quality in art. In E. Ulman & P. Dachinger (Eds.), *Art therapy in theory and practice* (pp. 43–59). Chicago, IL: Magnolia Street.

Kramer, E. (2002). On quality in art and art therapy. *American Journal of Art Therapy, 40*(4), 218–222.

Kramer, E., Anand, S. A., & Gerity, L. A. (2001, July). *Quality and inner satisfaction: Revisiting the importance of quality in art and art therapy.* Panel presented at the Annual Conference of the American Art Therapy Association, Albuquerque, NM.

Potash, J. S. (2016, May 4). Color Party: TEDx NYU. *Art Therapy Today.* Retrieved from: http://multibriefs.com/briefs/aata/aata050416.php Accessed 20 September 2017.

Smithsonian Institution. (n.d.). Paint by number. Retrieved from: http://american history.si.edu/paint/picturePlace.html Accessed 20 September 2017.

Edith Kramer's
Theoretical Concepts

15 Edith Kramer's Notion of "Quality"

Elizabeth Stone

For forty years, Edith's teachings have been integral to my work and thinking, so much a part of the art therapist I became, that only upon losing her in February 2014 have I been able to think more clearly than ever about what Edith as person, teacher, supervisor, and friend meant to me.

Edith became my mentor in 1973 when I enrolled in her art therapy course at New York University (NYU). This course preceded the official opening of the master's degree program in 1976.

I was already a graduate student in NYU's Interrelated Arts Program (no longer extant), but trying to figure out how to become an art therapist myself after having taken a course with Edith's great friend Vera Zilzer at the Turtle Bay Music School. After I became Edith's student, she invited me to apprentice with her on Jacobi Hospital's Children's Psychiatric Ward. Most happily, I agreed. Upon her retirement from clinical practice two years later, Edith turned the position over to me and then succeeded in convincing NYU's administration to open the art therapy master's level program. Upon its inception, once again, Edith tapped me to supervise and teach. So new was I that I was sure she had overvalued my skills. How could I supervise students when I was only two steps ahead of the them? The confidence she had in me inspired me to try to live up to her trust and to remain "on the side of the angels," as Edith would say. While this phrase has a rather black-and-white ring to it, she really meant that a person should be primarily a positive force in life, in spite of human frailty and foibles. She was too much the realist to expect more than what was humanly possible.

Fundamental to any understanding of Edith – the art therapist, the teacher, the artist, and the person – is the notion of quality, which she vociferously espoused both vocally and in writing. I shall focus primarily on how she imparted it to me, but will also note other aspects of the broader debate on quality in which Edith was involved as its epicenter.

Edith as Mentor and Co-Therapist

What was it like to practice side by side with Edith? From the very beginning, what amazed me was how she treated me as an equal, giving me free rein.

108   *Elizabeth Stone*

Though I had prior experience working with children and art, I had none as an art therapist. Nevertheless, without the need for much discussion, we somehow divided up the small latency-aged group; she gravitated toward some children, I toward others. Such a complementary way of working was part of Edith's uncontrived simplicity and expertise.

In her own inimitable and natural way, Edith showed me that offering only the most basic media such as paint, drawing materials, and clay permitted the widest range of personal and artistic expression. She suggested using the highest quality materials one's budget allowed because better quality materials would facilitate a richer expression and were easier to handle. Such basic media enticed these emotionally fragile children into relying upon their own fledgling internal resources, and in doing so, strengthened their ability to express their inner worlds. A believer in free choice of subject matter, medium, and means of expression, Edith understood that each child would gravitate toward the medium that he or she most needed on any given day. A passionate and formidable guide, she knew that the sensuous qualities of the media would draw them in naturally and become their allies. However, exceptions were provided for the severely affectively or cognitively disorganized children who needed guidance toward a more structured medium to avert harmful regression.

Implementing a Sense of Quality in Art, Life, and Language

Careful attention to quality ran throughout every aspect of Edith's approach to art and life. Her conviction about what constitutes art was frank and sometimes fearsome. Edith decried the "anything goes" attitude toward art, at its height in the 60s and 70s, for she knew that the children with whom she worked could not be nourished with haphazard or wild approaches. Having experienced severe trauma and loss, they needed reliability, structure, a positive affective climate, and respect. An "anything goes" approach would not rescue their elusive creativity and build ego structure.

Edith's devotion to quality went far beyond art and clinical work. Well-known for her advocacy of the correct formulation and expressive use of the English language, Edith was emphatic about not short-changing her acquired tongue (Agell, Howie, Kramer, Williams, & Wilson, 1993). She taught art therapists to think without pretense about the meanings they convey rather than use facile technical or clinical terms in place of more graphic lay language. By attending more assiduously to the authenticity of one's thoughts and observations, meaning could emerge in a more colorful, communicative, and humane way. For example, Edith believed that calling a boy a male, rather than a boy, stripped him of his humanity (Agell et al., 1993). She endeavored to evoke the fullest possible picture of any child presented rather than to focus upon symptoms or pathology. In doing so, she promulgated the notion that a sense of professionalism need not dehumanize a patient; on the contrary, a well-explicated clinical vignette evokes a more comprehensive human story.

Edith Kramer's Notion of "Quality" 109

Edith railed often against the misuse of the English language, but why was she so offended? Above all, she valued clarity, not muddiness, not approximation, not "almosts." While I never had the discussion with her that I shall articulate now, I think that her vehemence about and veneration of language must have been rooted in early happy memories of being surrounded by an entourage of stimulating intellectuals. In her beloved homeland, Austria, she received a progressive education and learned to revere the life of the mind. Her insistence on precision and the values embodied by these people must have formed the bulwark of an intellectual blueprint that she carried within her upon arrival in New York. Her sense of rigor must have been a reliable source of integrity and ethics that could befriend her in this potentially lonely new world.

Just as she populated her paintings with nuance, color, and unremitting exactitude, she graced her expressions in English with thoughtful and simple beauty through attention to the clearest of observations. She wrote with a forcefulness that was all the more significant because she continually delineated the true from the false. I think that Edith's entire relationship to life hinged upon adhering to what was real and repudiating what she considered "fake." Certain forms of art expression reeked of intolerable falseness for her, usually due to sloppiness, inaccuracy, or kitsch. For example, she was known to voice reproach about logos for the American Art Therapy Association's Annual Conference when they appeared contrived or clumsily conceived artistically. Hearing Edith's outspoken criticism at conferences against the aesthetics of logo choices often caused me to cringe, wondering how their creators must have felt as the object of her rage. Nothing stopped her when she felt she was in the right with "truth" on her side. Not only was the public side of Edith's plea for quality endemic to whom Edith was, but her sense of quality permeated her clinical point of view as well.

Among the many clinical essentials Edith taught us, her notion of quality cuts across theoretical approaches and remains as provocative as ever. This is because quality has often been relegated to the subject of aesthetics and conflated with strivings for beauty. To tie quality to aesthetics exclusively only reduces it to an oversimplification. Quality also refers to the way in which we address standards of competence, ethics, craftsmanship, training, supervision, and more.

Fostering optimal conditions for a healing experience in art therapy also means adhering to certain artistic rudiments in Edith's teachings. If the art therapist accords sufficient time and space for a session and offers good quality art materials, this will have a profound impact on the resulting artwork as well as the aesthetic outcome. How the art therapist cares for the art products will influence the patient's therapeutic experience. Edith knew this. If we offer short sessions, how can patients even begin to explore their creativity freely? The possibility of creative or therapeutic transformation, whether or not we call it sublimation, is virtually amputated when a patient is not given ample time to think, feel, and to become, not to mention, to allow the creative process to flow.

The Position of the Art in Art Therapy

The term *art as therapy*, coined by Edith, positions the art as the central force within the therapeutic relationship. The substructure for the art therapist's professional identity is derived from both her sensibility as an artist and commitment to practicing this art. While less emphasis has been placed upon the centrality of the art therapist-as-artist in many graduate programs in recent decades, the attainment of competence with art materials remains an indisputable prerequisite of an art therapist's training. Edith's insistence was not for naught. We know how hard it can be to stay with the art when working with patients for whom talking or moving into another modality might seem so much easier. Edith felt that unless one is an artist steeped in love of the art materials, it is too easy to veer away from art as the primary vehicle of expression in therapy. I think she was probably right. Only when art is truly our language of communication can we infuse our sessions in such a way that art becomes our patients' language too. Of course if we are not artists, art can remain a useful therapeutic tool, but that is not what Edith was about. Art created as a secondary therapeutic tool would not look or feel the same to Edith. Her love affair had been with art, and it was this love affair that she believed had healing power. I think that she saw the art relationship as tantamount to a kind of object relationship, a bridge between the sensuous world of physicality and the internal psychic world.

The notion of art-making as strengthening, when employed by a trained professional with a firm grasp of psychodynamics, underscored Edith's concept of art as therapy. This concept was so sustaining for her because art had saved her at crucial times in her childhood, adolescence, and adulthood. She, therefore, promoted the belief that art could save others when offered by an empathically attuned art therapist.

Although art therapists have sought to differentiate their competencies from those of art teachers, I think that Edith would agree that the best art therapists have in their armamentarium (an Edith word!) a capacity for and love of teaching. The ability to engage another human being in an attempt to draw – someone who was previously too timid or uninterested – often depends partially upon enlisting teaching skills, but those that become infused with empathy. This uncontrived form of involvement fostered by Edith offers access to an individual's inner world in a state of maximum personal freedom. Engaging a "resistant" client or patient in an open-ended way, using the imagery that emerges from that individual's psyche, can be recognized as a very different approach from the kind of facile themes or directives that are frequently considered to be the protocol by many art therapists today.

Attention to Craft in Art Therapy

While her notion of the well-made object may seem quaint to some, along with her belief that not anything goes, she believed in equipping children with the technical means to produce a solid product, whether in clay, paint,

Edith Kramer's Notion of "Quality" 111

or even wood. To help a child pour his or her heart and soul into the making of a clay sculpture, only to allow it to fall apart eventually because the art therapist did not want to interfere, or instruct, or cast judgment on how the object was made, was considered by Edith as not only counter-therapeutic but actually inhumane. She did not see the teaching of correct use of materials to be extra-therapeutic. She felt that our job is to help patients, not to permit gratuitous failures.

Therefore, ensuring that two pieces of clay are put together with sufficient "scratches," well saturated with slip between them, then worked back and forth with a tool (a split tongue depressor worked perfectly for Edith) until the two pieces of clay became one, enabled a piece of sculpture to survive and for the child to know his effort was valued. Edith helped the child to understand that the effort to attend to each and every crack in order to prevent breakage later during the drying or firing was well worth the frustration and time spent on these mechanics. If a child was developmentally unable to conceptualize the reason for eliminating cracks or physically or psychologically too impaired to handle the task, Edith would take time after the session to examine the sculpture of each patient and make sure every crack was carefully sealed, not altering a hair of the child's own style.

What is an Aesthetic Attitude in Art Therapy?

While she believed in a non-judgmental attitude toward artwork in art therapy, recognizing that aesthetics were secondary, they still were very important to her. "Art is characterized by economy in means, internal consistency, and evocative power" (Kramer, 1971, p. 50). Edith considered this formulation a guiding principle for art therapists who strive to help patients create meaningful artwork.

While we acknowledge the enduring value of this precept, we might wonder whether we should use our own artistic skills to help our patients make "better" artwork? Where does the art therapist's involvement in the quality of the patient's artwork begin and end? What gives us the authorization, as therapists, to enter into the patient's expressive world, and how do we determine when and how it is essential or appropriate to do so? Edith's theoretical concept of *the third hand* is not only relevant in helping an art therapist develop appropriate interventions, but it can also provide a vantage point from which to acknowledge our own thoughts and wishes about a patient's artwork. In other words, we need to think about how we enter our patients' artwork with our minds. Such reflection, incorporated into our countertransference protocol of self-scrutiny, will inform our perceptions so that the ensuing therapeutic relationship will benefit.

In recent years, we have seen the rise of artists without specific therapeutic training working in hospitals. Often these artists see their purpose as helping patients to create "art" or aesthetically striking work. Although Edith would have insisted that they have at least some basic training in psychodynamic

112   *Elizabeth Stone*

theory so as not to cause harm, she would have insisted that the art produced be personally relevant for the patient. Edith truly believed that art therapy training required supervision to ensure that the art-making experience would not be psychically destructive with fragile individuals.

The Principle of Clarity

If we reinterpret the role of aesthetics as a striving to attain clarity of expression, both affectively and cognitively, instead of purely aiming to achieve an aesthetically pleasing outcome, we offer a path toward reconciliation. I think Edith would agree that the principle of clarity embraces her central objectives and obviates domination by an aesthetic model. In my own experience, by helping a patient work toward clarity, an aesthetically richer result is often a striking result.

Here is a rudimentary example of how an art therapist encourages a process toward clarity in image making: When a child says that he wants to draw a tiger but doesn't know how to begin, I will ask, "Where shall your tiger be on your paper?" Then, "How big will your tiger be?" Or, "How much of your paper will be taken up by your tiger?" These questions help a child to visualize his tiger mentally. Then, by asking, "In what position do you want your tiger to be?" the child's emotional as well as conceptual internal image becomes identified and clarified. This ultimately translates onto paper with much more ego investment since he experiences the image to be more connected to himself and thus, his "own tiger." A pouncing or sleeping or growling tiger becomes affectively richer than a generic animal. Edith espoused this procedure wholeheartedly.

Another example of the relationship between clarity and aesthetics can be seen in helping a child to mix the exact color of his or her own skin. Often a child would begin painting an anonymous figure or a specific character without any particular notion of what skin color the person would have. When the time came to paint the skin, the child would often hesitate. Edith knew that this meant that the child was wondering what skin color to paint. She asked, "What shall be the color of skin for this person?" Edith understood that even if not intended as a self-portrait, the child's unconscious identification with the image would imply a self-portrait. Edith encouraged the child, using trial and error, to choose the colors to mix and to experiment with alternative shades until the exact skin tone the child wanted was achieved. Attaining such clarity enabled the child to recognize that the person she was painting was a lot like herself or even was herself! Such identification was important in strengthening the ego and building or re-building identity. The pleasure and satisfaction the child took in claiming his own skin color was a way to fortify the notion that he was valued as he was. To devote such unlimited time and painstaking attention to the search for the right color meant that the art therapist had to be patiently available and fully invested in the task. The result was a cognitive acquisition as well as an affective victory.

Edith Kramer's Notion of "Quality"

The following vignette illustrates how the effort toward clarity of expression functions in art therapy, whether the image is figurative or abstract.

Case Vignette: Louise

At sixty-one, Louise was diagnosed with advanced colon cancer. Her creative medium had always been dance. The opportunity to use art materials delighted her, though she was concerned about whether the visual arts could be her means of expression. Several months into our work that lasted for eight months, she learned that her cancer was incurable. The following images illustrate three different manifestations of the principle of aesthetic and affective clarity. In each, Louise sought to bring forth the mental representation of an image or affect that was in her mind, or that developed as she began to use materials.

She began by painting a beautiful mountain landscape, but her sadness covered it over. Unafraid to express exactly what she felt, for her this outcome was just right. The sitting clay figure surprised her as it emerged (Figure 15.1). At the last minute, Louise scratched a gash with the clay tool from the corner of the right side of the mouth to the chin. Though she wasn't sure why or what it was, she felt she just needed to do it. Perhaps it was a way to strike out and

Figure 15.1 Sitting clay figure

114 *Elizabeth Stone*

express her anger or the feeling of being damaged. After the sculpture was completed, she thought it was a boy, perhaps an adolescent. He wore a hat and carried a ball, as though he had just been actively participating in life. The position and shape of his legs reminded her of dancer's legs, like her own. She recognized the searching expression on the face that I thought was related to the experience of her illness – a beseeching look in the way he connects to us, we readily and unequivocally connect to him. While there appeared to be some tiredness in the figure's posture that caused him to sit down, there seemed to be plenty of vitality left to thoroughly engage us. Louise explored the clay to find an expression that felt real to her.

A third image, painted when she knew she was facing death, communicated ineffable emotion and required no actual words. The motif evokes, for me, a colon or anus or the experience of being in a vortex. Louise was not trying to "make art," rather, simply to speak in her new visual language that resonated well with how she felt.

Conclusion

To conclude, running throughout my musings about Edith's notion of quality is the singular thread of "clarity" – whether in language or creative expression, Edith transmitted an imperative to strive for clarity, no matter how complex the ideas or imagery. Her quest for clarity ran throughout many aspects of her creative and contemplative life, whether in theory building or art-making. She could paint intricate motifs from nature, twisted branches, or complicated subway steel girders and crossbeams, rendering them comprehensible for the viewer.

She believed that clear, unfettered communication valued the recipient as much as the transmitter (whether artist, clinician, writer, layman, or child) in spite of complex affect that may underlie any given art expression. Edith's pursuit of the "true" has been a mainstay to my own thinking and meanderings. Her work, her life, and her voice have emboldened many of us to achieve our truest expression and not accept an ersatz facsimile or meager substitute.

Acknowledgments

My gratitude to Judith Rubin, PhD, ATR-BC, HLM, and Beatrice Beebe, PhD for their help in editing this chapter down to fit the book's format.

References

Agell, G., Howie, P., Kramer, E., Williams, K., & Wilson, L. (1993). Quality in art therapy: A panel honoring Elinor Ulman. *American Journal of Art Therapy*, *32*(2), 34–45.

Kramer, E. (1971). *Art as therapy with children*. New York: Schocken Books.

16 On Edith Kramer's Seminal Concept of Sublimation in Art Therapy[1]

Elizabeth Stone

> Making art helps people to contemplate themselves to experiment with different ways of being. This sanctuary of art might help build internal structure. . . . Distancing oneself metaphorically is what happens, helping to build structure that is less amorphous, more healthy and able to remain under pressure.
>
> (Kramer, 1992–1994)

Edith Kramer's central contribution to art therapy theory, the concept of *sublimation,* continues to reverberate throughout many other approaches, not only the psychoanalytic where it started, in spite of the diverse evolution of art therapy approaches that could not have been imagined when Edith began to formulate her ideas. Her work on sublimation stands as a cornerstone in our literature, spanning the very roots of art therapy theory through contemporary practice. As my teacher, mentor, supervisor, and then friend, I had the privilege to hear her lectures on sublimation at New York University (NYU), and to witness how she put these ideas into practice with latency-aged children hospitalized on the Children's Psychiatric Unit of Jacobi Hospital, Bronx, New York, as her apprentice in the mid-1970s. This formative experience provided the theoretical and practical impetus to my future work with children.

Edith championed sublimation as the central underlying mechanism in her therapeutic approach (Kramer, 1971; Kramer & Wilson, 1979; Kramer, 2016). At that time (mid-20th century), this concept occupied a particularly elevated position among psychoanalysts as a positive psychical achievement. Initially introduced as one of the crown jewels in Freud's metapsychology, sublimation appeared in his earliest writings (Freud, 1892). Conceived as heir to the positive resolution of the Oedipus complex, sublimation was viewed as a neurotic defense and, therefore, thought impossible to attain by those with borderline and psychotic pathologies. In contrast, Edith's application of sublimation to psychotic and borderline personalities represented a decisive departure from the classical approach.

116   *Elizabeth Stone*

Here is an extract from Edith's sublimation description as borrowed from Freud:

> According to Freudian theory, *sublimation* designates processes whereby primitive urges, emanating from the id, are transformed by the ego into complex acts that do not serve direct instinctual gratification . . . primitive behavior, necessarily asocial, gives way to activities that are ego-syntonic and are as a rule *socially productive*, although they may not always be *socially acceptable*. . . .
> Sublimation is no simple mental act; it embraces a multitude of mechanisms. These include displacement, symbolization, neutralization of drive energy, identification, and integration. . . . Sublimation invariably implies some element of renunciation. . . . Inasmuch as it involves postponement of instinctual gratification and channeling of drive energy, we can perceive sublimation as one of the mechanisms of defense. . . . Implied in the concept of sublimation is the awareness that man's instincts are in disarray and can no longer be relied on to safely regulate behavior.
> (Kramer, 2016, p. 87)

Sublimation, an Evolving Concept

When Edith formed her ideas, sublimation was regarded as indispensable to ego psychology as an unconscious psychological survival strategy (Hartmann, 1958). Ernst Kris's conceptualization of regression in the service of the ego (Kris, 1952) buttressed Edith's stance that dipping into unconscious psychic content, known as *primary process*, was necessary for art to emerge. After Anna Freud's emphasis on ego defenses (Freud, 1966), Heinz Hartmann and his collaborators paved the way for a major shift of focus in psychoanalysis from the id to the ego, and this fit perfectly with Edith's thinking.

Sublimation: Edith Kramer's Conceptualization

To date, in spite of controversies that have arisen within psychoanalysis (Fogel, 1991; Loewald, 1988; Schafer, 1975; Toulmin, 1978), Edith's description of sublimation remains our most coherent explanation of how exceptional artwork comes into being. No concept has ever adequately replaced its rigor. Edith demonstrated how individuals with fragile egos could muster sufficient inner organizational capacities to transcend their immediate conflicts and create aesthetically powerful art expressions infused with symbolism. She recognized "evocative power, inner consistency, and economy of means" in art that attained sublimation (Kramer, 1971, p. 67). Her theoretical views on sublimation were essential in helping art therapy gain recognition in the eyes of the psychoanalytic community as distinct from art education.

Edith's aim was to help a patient function on the highest possible level of ego development, a theoretical position consonant with that of experts in developmental ego psychology (Jacobson, 1964; Blanck & Blanck, 1972). In this approach, a fragile child was helped to mobilize fragments of ego organization to activate capacities that had been minimally available. Edith regarded the safety of the art therapy setting as a crucial therapeutic element in fostering developmental growth. That the art therapist was first and foremost an artist underpinned the therapeutic effort whereby affective expression was encouraged through the creation of art. In this approach, ego defenses became concomitantly strengthened. Edith understood that both the cognitive and affective dimensions of functioning had to work in tandem, bolstered by the therapeutic relationship that she considered the "benign" therapeutic climate. Edith conceived of the art therapist's role as carefully nurturing opportunities for sublimation to take root within the maelstrom of psychic disorganization. She provided sensitively timed therapeutic interventions to shield the sublimation process from untimely interference, and to protect emotional health.

To achieve sublimation, Edith encouraged a sense of ego mastery that marked the victory of the ego over id impulses. One overarching aim was to enable the artwork to "live," not be destroyed by aggressive forces. The child was helped to surmount the challenges inherent in the art materials, such as the regressive pull of paint or clay that threatened to thwart the flourishing of formed artwork. By fostering a modicum of pleasure through interaction with the sensuous art materials, she gently encouraged the often arduous effort toward completion.

In my own work with psychotic and borderline individuals, I recall thinking when working with a turbulent child or adult who managed to transform internal chaos and produce what Edith called a "miracle," that this could have only come about through sublimation. To bear witness to such powerful artistic expression makes a cogent case for putting this concept at the center of the artistic effort. By fostering an authentic sense of agency, the child came to experience being in charge of him or herself. Activating creativity as a new language to believe in helped the child to be inventive and feel competent.

Not All Artwork Achieves Sublimation

Edith taught us that not all art achieves the miracle of sublimation. Pictograms, stereotypic art, or art that embodied rigid ego defenses such as *intellectualization* or *isolation of affect* often blocked the freedom necessary for unfettered creative experimentation. When the components of sublimation (displacement, symbolization, neutralization of drive energy, identification, ego mastery, and integration) did not work in consort, the creative process fell short. Yet, Edith understood and respected that not all art expression was *meant* to achieve

118   *Elizabeth Stone*

sublimation. She recognized that pure discharge of affect could be extremely cathartic, even if the work did not reflect sublimation.

To illustrate an instance where artwork fell short of sublimation due to the defense of intellectualization, I recall an artist who came to our class and showed us a drawing of her hospitalized baby, intubated, amply monitored, all skillfully rendered. Edith later expressed consternation to me about this portrayal: the baby's little body so helplessly pinned down, and interlacing snake-like hospital equipment emerging everywhere. Edith wondered about the artist's empathy, notwithstanding acknowledging her to be a nice person who manifestly cared for her child. What Edith questioned was this mother's ability to sufficiently detach herself from the trauma of her baby's experience in order to sketch it. The mother needed to graphically represent the exposure to and affective acceptance of violence, but that she drew her own baby made this affectively different and more frightening than any other such drawing. This concrete expression failed to achieve sublimation because it did not undergo sufficient psychic transformation, and thus remained an illustration of the defense of intellectualization or isolation of affect. Edith's poignant explanation helped me understand the role of affect, or defense thereof, concerning rawness in personal artwork.

Preparing for this writing, I viewed archived videos of Edith's lectures (part of the *Edith Kramer Papers*) at the NYU Bobst Library. To paraphrase one of her lectures, Edith described feeling mesmerized in Vienna by the 15th century artist Michael Pacher's *Flagellation of Christ*, where the beauty in the way he painted Christ's droplets of blood made the horror of the flagellation okay for her. Reconciliation was possible because she saw his exquisite rendering as aiding sublimation (Kramer, 1992–1994). Edith's appreciation of this powerful transformation of monstrous iniquity into a bearable and beautiful image encapsulated how sublimation functioned.

Sublimation and the Role of Interpretation

Edith taught that successful sublimation obviates the need for verbalization. Even so, we can find instances where she saw the need to respond verbally. Evincing this side of her clinical work is important to portray her as fully as possible. In one example from the NYU Archives, she used verbalization after a girl had painted tall grasses that illustrated the place where she had been raped. Edith's ego-oriented, rather than id-based, verbal intervention helped this girl make sense of the image she had created. She said, "We can't undo what happened to you but we can become more able to contemplate what happened to yourself" (Kramer, 1992–1994).

Edith sought to protect the artwork from the kinds of intrusive probing that was often de rigueur in her day. In keeping with psychoanalytic thinking, Edith understood aspects of artwork as linked to id-based *drive derivatives,* often represented by symbolic omissions, as in castration themes. Edith made these interpretations to her students, but not to her patients. Eventually, analysts

Kramer's Sublimation in Art Therapy 119

directed interpretations away from uncovering the chaotic unconscious, particularly in borderline and psychotic patients. This shift in verbalization toward the ego would only take hold later in the late 1970s, after Edith had retired from clinical work.

Historical Arguments over the Meaning of Sublimation

Psychoanalytic theory is in constant evolution. Where does the concept of sublimation fit? By definition, the transformation of energy from the drives lies at the heart of sublimation. However, as psychoanalysts continued to expand upon and challenge Freudian concepts, they also questioned drive theory. In the 1970s, analysts debated whether concepts derived from physics, such as a transmission of energy from one intrasystemic part of the psyche to another, at the heart of drive theory, accurately described the way mental life actually worked (Toulmin, 1978; Schafer, 1975). Ricoeur (1978) argued that simple language could replace energy concepts in describing mental life. This would alter the basic definition of sublimation, since concepts such as neutralization were no longer appropriate. Gertrude and Rubin Blanck (1988) postulated a clarification of the drives, describing libido as the force that sought [object] connection, while the aggressive drive powered separation (p. 964).

Reconfiguring the drives demonstrated one way in which analysts searched to know how the mind really functioned. The drive controversy has bearing upon the way sublimation is interpreted. We no longer have to assume that the intent of sublimation is to transform sexual or aggressive strivings. If we use the term "sublimation," other affects, such as trauma and relational conflicts, could be at the heart of what is transformed. Widening the concept of sublimation has permitted a major expansion in our understanding and ability to apply this term within a contemporary theoretical framework.

Another development in psychoanalytic theory with implications for the concept of sublimation is the idea that a reciprocal, mutual regulation characterizes the therapy process. This idea was derived from infant observation, such as Winnicott's (1965) revolutionary statement that there is no such thing as a baby. A mother is inseparably part of an ongoing mutuality with her baby, a concept that Edith quoted. Current infant research of the last several decades has documented that both mother and baby reciprocally influence each other's affective states, a process described as self- and mutual regulation (Tronick, 1989; Sander, 1977). Beebe and Lachmann (1998, 2002) argue that the infant's experience of relatedness develops within the back and forth of a co-constructed relationship. From this point of view, sublimation could be construed as part of the self-regulation process, which is inextricably intertwined with the mutual regulation process (Beebe & Lachmann, 2013). That is, in art therapy, sublimation is also co-constructed.

Just as Edith turned to ethology to compare human behavior with our animal counterparts and found far-reaching resonance, I believe that she

120   *Elizabeth Stone*

would have been intrigued by the newer, groundbreaking observational infant research. Bowlby's integration of Konrad Lorenz's work on ethology with infant studies and psychoanalysis would have appealed to Edith. She was fascinated by Mahler, Pine, and Bergman's (1975) and Spitz's (1965) observational studies; Edith mentioned the work of Daniel Stern (1985) in her lectures in the 1990s. She would surely have incorporated the more recent research of Tronick (1989), Sander (1977), Beebe and Lachmann (1988), and others into her understanding of child development and the creative art-making process.

In 1988, Hans Loewald wrote an influential book on sublimation. Gerald Fogel (1991), in his review, pointed out the following:

> [Loewald] assumes that classic concepts which persist despite theoretical shifts that seem to render them outmoded or inexact, do so in part because the experiences signified remain important. . . . Theoretical concepts must be reexamined in the light of these [clinical] experiences, in effect, continually reinterpreted and revitalized. . . .
>
> (p. 251)

Loewald's insight underscores sublimation's ongoing relevance amidst theoretical shifts over time. Donald Kaplan, though a proponent of sublimation, pointed out that its inherent opacity escapes the rigor of the psychoanalytic process of inquiry. He meant that successful transformation of psychic content does not help us to penetrate the particular way in which the internal world was constructed (Kaplan, 1993, p. 558). According to Kaplan, sublimation had to be seen, therefore, as an inference, about a completed artwork.

Art Therapy Process and Sublimation

Yet, we as art therapists *do* have a special window into how the internal world is constructed, an aperture to which psychoanalysts are generally less privy. While the analyst reflects upon a patient's experiences or an artist's completed work, the art therapist is present throughout its creation. Even with minimal verbal communication, we register many implicit aspects of the patient's internal processes, such as quality of affect, personal investment in materials, expression, the interactive therapeutic alliance, and transference. Our receptivity informs us in a unique way. An example of how a window into the workings of sublimation briefly opened, allowing me a glimpse, is contained in the following vignettes from my adult practice.

Case Vignette: Emma

Emma, aged 57, felt guilty to leave her imperious, self-involved, hospitalized mother with a life-threatening illness in the care of relatives for a long-awaited weekend getaway with her husband to New York. Upon returning

Kramer's Sublimation in Art Therapy 121

home, Emma was eager to recapture her pleasure in walking across the Brooklyn Bridge. To do so, she copied Georgia O'Keeffe's *Brooklyn Bridge* in art therapy (Figure 16.1). Emma's deep absorption in meticulously filling in its thick blackness suggested to me that it contained potent meaning. Watching her paint, I suddenly sensed the blackness as linked to feelings about her mother's dramatic decline. The art-making *process* often informs art therapists about implicit meaning that escapes perception in the finished *product*. Had I been privy only to the finished work, I would not have had access to the camouflaged, more impenetrable meaning. Instead, my internal sensors permitted me such insight via the observational art-making process.

During the sharing time, Emma said that her painting had no meaning beyond the joy recalled by her trip. This implied successful sublimation, yet I pursued my hunch by wondering aloud whether the heavy blackness could have been connected with affect since her investment of time and care appeared more intense than her attention to the rest. I felt on safe ground exploring this openly since Emma was generally eager to ponder meaning in her artwork. When I suggested a link with the traumatic ordeal with her

Figure 16.1 Reproduction of O'Keeffe's *Brooklyn Bridge* as Emma copies it

mother and her guilt about leaving her, she agreed, smilingly. This insight enabled Emma to see that her painting also served as a mirror of this trauma, but did not detract from the triumphant joy she took in remembering the pleasure of her trip.

Peter Fonagy (2015) said, "Knowing what one is feeling aids self-regulation." For Emma, sublimation occurred as a transformation of affect via the relational unconscious into a symbolic representation. Yet, this transformation into artistic form did not rely upon sexual or aggressive drive energy, which was at the center of Freud's definition of sublimation.

Case Vignette: Emmanuelle

Sometimes verbal interpretation does not add positive therapeutic value when sublimation occurs. I argue that particularly when sublimation serves a reparative role involving bodily trauma, opening up unconscious meaning can break down self-cohesion. One instance of when bodily integrity would have been threatened had I offered a verbal interpretation of artwork that had achieved successful sublimation was with Emmanuelle.

One day, Emmanuelle, a post-mastectomy breast cancer survivor, was horrified that her prosthesis had malfunctioned, leaving her newly reconstructed breast deflated. Not sure what to paint, she reproduced a Georgia O'Keeffe flower on large paper. With time remaining in the session, she replicated the same flower on small paper. During the sharing time, we looked at the two paintings side by side (Figure 16.2). I saw them symbolically as the full "good" breast alongside its now deflated counterpart. When I asked Emmanuelle if she saw any meaning in the paintings, she replied that she did not. I was surprised

Figure 16.2 Large and small flowers, after Georgia O'Keeffe

since she too generally sought personal insight in her artwork. Never during the subsequent two years did she acknowledge these flowers as symbolizing breasts when we revisited these paintings. For her, the trauma was too deep; it needed to be worked through metaphorically, rather than directly in words. In this case, traumatic aggressive and sexual body-based drive components underpinned "flower" imagery, so interpretation via verbal uncovering was not prudent.

Case Vignette: Louise

Louise, whose work can be viewed in my chapter on "Quality" in this book, created four flat clay heads at the end of her unsuccessful battle with colon cancer (Figure 16.3). Lacking the strength to handle a three-dimensional volume of clay, she thought she could work with thin, flat pieces. She intended them to be viewed separately and together, her final gifts to her four children. Each head was imbued with a powerful sense of intimacy. Ambiguous emotion and anger prevailed in the first two, gradually giving way to an exquisite, yet painful solemnity in the last two. Taken together, these heads symbolized the relinquishing of life. The heads' evocative power, inner consistency, and economy of artistic means fulfilled Edith's conception of art that has achieved sublimation. Further, they embodied the notion of reconciliation, which Edith considered an underpinning of sublimation. To be able to transform the pain of impending death, its inevitability, and impart a sublime dignity that moves us emotionally in its composure could only have been accomplished through sublimation. The beauty of the heads embodied what I think was the truth/beauty equation that Edith sought in the highest level of art.

Louise's artwork helped mediate the horrific reality that she faced yet hoped to embrace with grace. Donald Kaplan, consistent with Edith's thinking, said, "This is why we think of optimal sublimation not as a muting of passion in deference to the reality principle but, on the contrary, as passion expressed, clarified, and as we shall see, comprehended" (Kaplan, 1993, p. 561).

Figure 16.3 Four flat clay heads

124   *Elizabeth Stone*

Some Further Thoughts

Edith often referred to Kohut's "gleam in the mother's eye" (1966, p. 252). We see this as a metaphor for the therapeutic relationship: the patient needs to feel in the gleam of the therapist's eye. Without it, sublimation would not stand a chance of gaining traction. Not only does the mother–infant relationship, and thus the therapeutic relationship, arise within the interactive context, but when we examine it closely, we find that sublimation in art therapy, especially with very fragile individuals, also arises interactively; this affirms its kinship with self- and mutual regulation. Edith would have probably agreed with this statement today.

Today I argue for the centrality of the therapeutic relationship in bringing about change and even sublimation itself in art therapy, particularly with very traumatized, fragile individuals. The art therapist *contains* and *fosters* a sense of safety whereby the patient can feel actively "held" psychically (Winnicott, 1965, 1971). This encourages authenticity and freedom of artistic expression. Edith, herself, said: ". . . we may be the first to provide the essential catalyst that had been missing in the patients' lives . . . encouraging ego functioning" (Kramer, 2016, p. 99).

Note

1 An earlier, abbreviated version of this chapter appeared as *Addendum-Sublimation* to Edith Kramer's chapter 5, entitled "Sublimation and Art Therapy," in J. A. Rubin (Ed.), *Approaches to Art Therapy: Technique and Theory*, (3rd ed.), 2016, pp. 101–105.

References

Beebe, B., & Lachmann, F. M. (1988). The contribution of mother–infant mutual influence to the origins of self- and object representation. *Psychoanalytic Psychology, 5*(4), 305–337.

Beebe, B., & Lachmann, F. M. (1998). Co-constructing inner and relational processes: Self and mutual regulation in infant research and adult treatment. *Psychoanalytic Psychology, 15*(4), 480–516.

Beebe, B., & Lachmann, F. M. (2002). *Infant research and adult treatment: Co-constructing interactions.* London: Analytic Press.

Beebe, B., & Lachmann, F. M. (2013). *The origins of attachment: Infant research and adult treatment.* New York: Routledge.

Blanck, G., & Blanck, R. (1972). *Ego psychology: Theory and practice.* New York: Columbia University Press.

Blanck, G., & Blanck, R. (1988). The contribution of ego psychology to understanding the process of termination in psychoanalysis and psychotherapy. *Journal of the American Psychoanalytic Association, 36*, 961–984.

Fogel, G. (1991). Book review of Loewald's sublimation: Inquiries into theoretical psychoanalysis. *Journal of the American Psychoanalytic Association, 39*, 250–257.

Fonagy, P. (2015, Feb 3). Attachment theory and psychoanalysis: The need for a new integration? Presentation from *Alumni Conference Twenty Years of*

Kramer's Sublimation in Art Therapy   125

Developmental Lines at Anna Freud Centre, June 2014. Retrieved April 22, 2015 from: https://www.youtube.com/watch?v=vYg92Zps1Dw

Freud, A. (1966). *The ego and the mechanisms of defence* (rev. ed.). London: Karnac Books.

Freud, S. (1892). Draft L 1 [Notes I] frp. extract from the Fliess Papers. *The Standard edition of the complete psychological works of Sigmund Freud.* London: The Hogarth Press.

Hartmann, H. (1958). *Ego psychology and the problem of adaptation.* New York: International Universities Press.

Jacobson, E. (1964). *The self and the object world.* London: The Hogarth Press.

Kaplan, D.M. (1993). What is sublimated in sublimation? *Journal of the American Psychoanalytic Association, 41,* 549–570.

Kohut, H. (1966). Forms and transformations of narcissism. *Journal of the American Psychoanalytic Association, 14,* 243–272.

Kramer, E. (1971). *Art as therapy with children.* New York: Schocken Books.

Kramer, E. (Speaker). (1992–1994). Psychodynamic processes in art; *Edith Kramer Papers;* MC 215; Box 9 (Cassette Recordings No. 4–13); New York University Archives, New York University Libraries.

Kramer, E. (2016). Sublimation and art therapy. In J.A. Rubin (Ed.), *Approaches to art therapy: Theory and technique* (3rd ed., 87–100). New York & London: Routledge.

Kramer, E., & Wilson, L. (1979). *Childhood and art therapy: Notes on theory and application.* New York: Schocken Books.

Kris, E. (1952). *Psychoanalytic explorations in art.* New York: Schocken Books.

Loewald, H.W. (1988). *Sublimation: Inquiries into theoretical psychoanalysis.* New Haven: Yale University Press.

Mahler, M., Pine, F., & Bergman, A. (1975). *The psychological birth of the human infant.* New York: Basic Books.

Ricoeur, P. (1978). Psychoanalysis, physics, and the mind–body problem. *Annual of Psychoanalysis, 6,* 336–342.

Sander, L. (1977). The regulation of exchange in the infant-caretaker system and some aspects of the context–content relationship. In M. Lewis & L. Rosenblum (Eds.), *Interaction, conversation and the development of language* (pp. 133–156). New York: Wiley.

Schafer, R. (1975). Psychoanalysis without psychodynamics. *International Journal of Psychoanalysis, 56,* 41–55.

Spitz, R. (1965). *The first year of life: A psychoanalytic study of normal and deviant development of object relations.* New York: International Universities Press.

Stern, D.N. (1985). *The interpersonal world of the Infant: A view from psychoanalysis and developmental psychology.* New York: Basic Books.

Toulmin, S. (1978). Psychoanalysis, physics, and the mind-body problem. *Annual of Psychoanalysis, 6,* 315–336.

Tronick, E.Z. (1989). Emotions and emotional communication in infants. *American Psychologist, 44*(2), 112–119.

Winnicott, D.W. (1965). *Maturational processes and the facilitating environment.* New York, NY: International Universities Press.

Winnicott, D.W. (1971). *Playing and reality.* London: Tavistock/Routledge.

17 Sublimation Then and Now

Laurie Wilson

When I was working with Edith Kramer at New York University between 1976 and 2000, her views on sublimation made perfect sense to me, particularly as I believed that I had seen it in action many times in the art therapy work I had done with children. How can you not believe in the transformation of drive energy when you see an angry or frightened child furiously pounding a piece of clay? And then watch that same child calm himself and gradually form the mashed clay into an image? I had seen so many different versions of this kind of transformation – of both sexual and aggressive energy – that I had no trouble conceptualizing the neutralization of energy, which then allowed for a tamed (sublimated) version to fuel a much more "civilized" expression of intense feeling via art. This was the ego-psychological explanation that Kramer espoused.

Initially, Freud presented his ideas about sublimation as the means by which instinctual drives could be deflected from their original aims and/or objects to more socially valuable purposes. So, a sexual voyeur might become a photographer (or an artist) or an excessively hostile person might become a surgeon.

Hans Loewald (1988), a well-respected psychoanalyst in New Haven, was writing a book called *Sublimation*, and in 1986 I happened to hear him give a talk on the subject as he was formulating his ideas. At the end of the lecture, I had a burning question to ask him, which he kindly answered: "Does sublimation last or is it a brief experience?"

Loewald explained that the sublimation of powerful aggressive or sexual emotions did not lead to a long-lasting quietus but had to occur repeatedly. I was disappointed with what he said but took from his response that perhaps the best we, as art therapists, could do for our patients who needed to tame the drives – most often, aggressive impulsive behavior – was to help them develop a new habit, a habit of transforming their rage and anger into something that is both pleasurable to look at and pleasurable to make. As I understood it, Loewald was essentially saying the same thing about sublimation that Kramer had written about ego functioning: When a behavior becomes familiar and pleasurable, a person is usually willing to repeat it – that is, the behavior can become a successful new habit.

Sublimation Then and Now   127

The next stage in my understanding of how to deal with the pesky drives came from reading Pinchas Noy's (1966, 1969, 1979) work on creativity. Noy was an Israeli analyst who wrote eloquently about primary and secondary process. He described *primary process* as an unconscious thought process marked by unorganized, illogical preverbal thinking, and a tendency to immediate discharge, characterized by condensation or displacement using symbols and metaphors. Primary process is manifest in dreaming, psychosis, and in the thought processes of young children. For our purposes, it is often visual. Noy described *secondary process* as the characteristic mode of thought of adulthood, and directly related to ego functioning and conscious mental activities. It is characterized by being logical and verbal; it obeys the laws of causality and is consistent with external reality.

For decades, psychoanalysts believed that primary process eventually led to the next developmental stage, secondary process, where logic and order supplanted illogic and disorder. This formulation led to the conviction that words are superior to images. This was a big problem for anyone like myself, and you, the reader, who know differently. Words and images are equally important – only different. According to Noy, these two modes of thought develop independently and remain serviceable throughout life. He noted that artists deal differently with primary process from ordinary people.

James Thurber's iconic cartoon of "It's raining cats and dogs" is a perfect example of a poet using primary process in a very sophisticated way. His image of cats and dogs falling from the sky immediately makes us laugh. Creative individuals like James Thurber are more comfortable with primary process and can maintain it by maturing it as they go along.

Noy disagreed with Ernst Kris's famous notion of "regression in the service of the ego" as characterizing the creative process, because Noy understood that both the primitive and mature ways of thinking were not opposites but were, in fact, intertwined with much flexibility and nuance. But are we not still dealing with two different modes of psychic functioning based upon ideas of psychic energy, which are differently organized? And have we moved away from the concept of sublimation? Do we still need sublimation? Sometimes yes, because it seems to explain what we see in the art therapy, sometimes no because it doesn't.

Since the time of Noy and Loewald, the concept of drives has become unpopular and is now often rejected by psychoanalysts. As a result, the description or explanation of sublimation has also changed – either it doesn't exist at all, or it has been entirely transformed. In 1990, in a book called *Psychoanalytic Terms and Concepts*, sublimation was defined: "The term sublimation, without energic or drive implications, may be applied descriptively to such changes in behavior leaving open the possibility of other explanations for the underlying mechanisms of change, such as learning, maturation, and interpenetration of motivational systems" (p. 188).

If that sounds a bit like gobbledy-gook to you, I agree. But what are we to do if the drives have been abandoned as a workable concept of how human

128 *Laurie Wilson*

beings are motivated? Could we now argue that sublimation can best be described as a transformation from one mental state into another, presumably higher or more refined mental state? Could we maintain this position even though the very idea of higher has been questioned if not outright rejected?

Rossela Valdre, an Italian psychoanalyst with a strong interest in the arts, has recently written *On Sublimation: A Path to the Destiny of Desire, Theory, and Treatment* (2014). She begins with the question: Has sublimation really disappeared or does it merely seem to have disappeared? She then argues that, though sublimation is rarely referred to today in the theory and practice of psychoanalysis, the concept of sublimation can be sensed as more alive than ever.

Valdre underscores Freud's original idea, which was based on aim-inhibited sexual and aggressive drives and has been reinterpreted. Some of the main reinterpretations include: Loewald's discussion of the reconciliatory quality of sublimation; Klein and her followers' understanding of reparation (that is, creative work results from an individual's need to repair the imagined damage he or she has done to internal objects); Bion's idea of cognitive transformation, which allows the passage from the somatic to the psychic; and Matte Blanco's art of formalization or construction of a formal system of signs that can overcome instinct and broaden the perceptive field of the unconscious. These transformations are not originally drive-driven. As a result, Freud's linking of sublimation to the drives is abandoned and substituted by something close but different – reconciliation, reparation, or transformation.

My current way of understanding sublimation contains some of the old idea as Kramer described and explained it. But I also see some new ways of explaining the phenomena we see in the art room and in the lives of artists. I find the idea of transformation helpful because it is more encompassing than the concept of sublimation, and it is more evocative of what I have learned about the lives of two very different 20th-century artists, Alberto Giacometti and Louise Nevelson, as well as the lives of the various artists with whom I have worked clinically in the past few decades. Let me give two examples from the life and work of Louise Nevelson (Wilson, 2016).

Louise Nevelson

Nevelson's need and ability to organize disparate objects and shapes can be seen as an example of an artist's increasingly mature way of organizing forms in space; a practice that began when she was very young and needed to exercise some control on the physical things around her – a chair, a table, a bed – as a displacement from her need to control the people around her.

The earliest drawing that we have by Nevelson shows a child sitting in a chair in a roomful of chairs. As a child, she developed her household task of cleaning into a habit of moving the furniture around in every room in her parents' house and imagining that she could do the same as she walked by the neighbors' houses. As she grew older and more accomplished artistically,

Sublimation Then and Now   129

that habit emerged as an exceptional gift for composition. The original need was most likely Nevelson's way of dealing with the confusing disorder around her. Her father was frequently drunk, and her mother was so depressed that she often kept to her bed, crying; leaving no one in the household in charge of making cohesive order. Nevelson would compulsively have to correct this situation all her life, even during the years in which she was often drunk and despairing. Her house was always kept neat and clean, and her art reflected her intense focus on careful composition.

The second example is a transformation of her family heritage into two divergent artistic styles – the elegant and the archaic – that she often merged but sometimes separated. Nevelson's father, Isaac Berliawsky, came from Pereyaslav, a medium-sized city in the Ukraine. His family was comfortably middle class, well educated, and enlightened, with some celebrated ancestors, including artists and architects who had worked for the czars. When he arrived as a poor immigrant in Rockland, Maine, he soon made his way from being a penniless peddler to a successful landowner and contractor, popular and comfortably assimilated in the Protestant coastal city where he had settled. He expected to be as successful as his family had been in the old country – and so he was.

Nevelson's mother Minna Smolerank Berliawsky was a farmer's daughter – a peasant really – from a small village called Shusnecky near the river Dnieper. It was not far from Pereyaslav geographically, but distant in every other way. Her family, like most in the village, comprised Orthodox Jews who embraced a tradition of Chassidic mysticism and superstition at the opposite end of the social spectrum from the enlightened Berliawskys. Though she was attractive and well dressed, she held onto the old ways and was unable to integrate herself into the small, Jewish community in Rockland, much less the larger Yankee world that surrounded the Berliawsky family.

One of the frequent stylistic choices Nevelson made as an artist was the remarkable combination of smooth and rough, sinuous and angular, sharp and soft. She called the rough, angular work "archaic." She once referred to the different styles as walking down either Broadway or 5th Avenue. She was very conscious that she was mixing the styles but probably did not think of it as transforming her parental heritage into an aesthetic merger.

Whether or not we are actually aware that artists' drives, instincts, or feelings are tamed when they make their art, some transformation is taking place. Symbolization is a necessary step on the road to sublimation no matter how you define it. One thing standing in for something else is the essence of symbolization. Linus's blanket, for example, which stands in for mother, is the symbolic equivalent, the re-presentation, of a missing object in a form that allows for both attachment and development. Winnicott made this concept universally understandable with his wonderful term "transitional object." However, symbolization does not quite get us to the concept of sublimation, which, of necessity, involves a more radical transformation – ice into water, water into ice.

Figure 17.1 Sky Presence I (detail). Photograph taken by Laurie Wilson

Within the context of safe transitional space, symbolic transformation is possible, but not necessarily sublimation. Maturing a mode of mental processing – thought perception – can lead to artistic transformation and may not require the concept of sublimation. Nevelson's ability to compose her collage elements as an adult sculptor is certainly a transformation of her childhood behavior. But can we call it sublimation? Since Freud, sublimation has traditionally implied change from something base into something better, higher, more pure, more beautiful.[1] It was easy to understand in the context of a psychological system based on instinctual drives – libidinal and aggressive.

When Valdre reconsidered the concept of sublimation, she kept one fundamental factor. In order for civilization to continue and for particular individual humans to develop into civilized adults, the direct satisfaction of drives or instincts has to give way to some kind of transformation, to some indirect form of satisfaction via knowledge, imagination, or creativity. That means some psychical work has to take place. At first, this occurs through an inhibition of the drive, or instinct, or urge, and then something must move in the direction of creating some new means of satisfying the wish.

Alberto Giacometti

Alberto Giacometti was a voyeur as a teenager and throughout his adult years. Rather than ask a young woman to dance with him during his adolescence, he would stare at her while she was dancing with someone else. Later, when living in Paris, he embarrassed many women by his incessant habit of staring at them in cafes. As an artist he could justify (and in fact transform) that urgent need to stare at women, using the need to create his portraits, many drawings, and sculptures of women. Kramer would probably call that sublimation, because a drive-driven urge became a triumphant mastery of making the object of his stare something visible and highly valuable.

Finally, one more way of addressing the question is through Freud's original use of the term *Nachtraeglichkeit* – variously translated as deferred action or retroactive revision. Essentially, it refers to the mental activity by which the present transforms the past, giving it new meaning.

I have applied the concept of Nachtraeglichkeit to Giacometti's transformational postwar work. When he was ten, he experienced a trauma of seeing his mother ghostly thin and comatose after a long bout with typhoid fever, which had killed some of her neighbors. Though he certainly loved her, he also experienced severe anxiety and phobias due to his longstanding unresolved guilt and rage about her unmaternal behavior during his childhood. Decades later, Giacometti's memories of his gaunt mother were transformed into images of skeletal human beings. Many who saw and admired these postwar filiform figures connected them with concentration-camp survivors – men and women who had just barely survived the Second World War. Giacometti, however, always denied the effect of the Holocaust on his work. I have argued that the actual sight of the camp survivors in his Paris neighborhood, along with having seen the grisly newsreel coverage of the camp's liberation, reawakened his memory of his almost-dying mother (Wilson, 2003, p. 199).

As an adult, Giacometti knew that he was not guilty of aggressive attacks on anyone, and that it was the Nazis who had done the evil deeds. With and through his art, he could take comfort in the fact of human survival. What had intervened between his childhood trauma and the potential retraumatization was his loving relationship with a young woman who had the same name as his mother, Annette Arm, who later became his wife. He also experienced one of his models, Colonel Rol-Tanguy – a heroic leader of the Resistance in France – as a completely supportive paternal presence. With these new experiences, he could transform his own fear, aggression, and guilt into remarkably iconic images. I argue that this complicated phenomenon was a form of sublimation. Giacometti's anxiety and guilty feelings never disappeared, but because he could transform them into masterworks of art, they did not paralyze him.

In this chapter, it may seem that I have not taken a firm stand on the subject of sublimation. Edith Kramer would never have given up the concept any more than she would deny the existence of the unconscious. Fortunately, psychoanalysts as well as art therapists are not about to abandon the unconscious, though

132 *Laurie Wilson*

many have given up the idea of drive energy. If we exchange the word "energy" for "affect" we may get closer to understanding what I am getting at. So that little boy angrily pounding the clay over time becomes less angry and more able to create. Likewise, we could shift from calling it "psychic energy" and try to use "physical energy." Finally, as art therapists, I don't think we have to take a rigid position on sublimation. Transformations happen no matter what we call them.

Note

1 The Surrealists like Andre Breton and Max Ernst, who were deeply involved with doing and understanding the creative process, fastened onto the term alchemy, which in its archaic meaning was about the transformation of lead into gold. When they wrote or thought about what they called philosophical alchemy they were describing the creative process: taking the raw materials of poetry (words) or visual art (paint, canvas, stone, etc.) and transforming them into a new, higher refined form – a work of art.

References

Loewald, H. (1988). *Sublimation: Inquiries into theoretical psychoanalysis.* New Haven and London: Yale University Press.

Moore, B. E., & Fine, B. D. (1990). *Psychoanalytic terms and concepts.* New Haven, CT: Yale University Press.

Noy, P. (1966). On the development of artistic talent. *The Israel Annals Psychiatry and Related Disciplines, 4,* 211–218.

Noy, P. (1969). A revision of the psychoanalytic theory of the primary process. *The International Journal of Psychoanalysis, 50,* 155–178.

Noy, P. (1979). Form creation in art: An ego-psychological approach to creativity. *The Psychoanalytic Quarterly, 47,* 229–256.

Valdre, R. (2014). *On Sublimation: A path to the destiny of desire, theory, and treatment.* London: Karnac Books.

Wilson, L. (2003). *Alberto Giacometti: Myth, magic, and the man.* New Haven and London: Yale University Press.

Wilson, L. (2016). *Louise Nevelson: Light and shadow.* London and New York: Thames and Hudson.

18 The Building of an Artist's Identity

Kevin Maxwell

The Marvin Lipkowitz Gallery at Maimonides Medical Center's Department of Psychiatry in Brooklyn, NY, opened to the first of six exhibitions in 2006. Art therapists Geoffrey Thompson and myself, with the administrative support of the head of the Department of Psychiatry, Dr Lipkowitz, created the gallery within a conference room. Clients who regularly participated in outpatient art therapy groups were offered the opportunity to exhibit. Those who agreed to participate in the exhibition chose artwork from their portfolio with the assistance of their art therapist. Again with assistance from the art therapist, the artists would write a statement to go along with their framed work that would also be included in the show's catalog. We succeeded in these exhibitions by building alliances with the administration of the Department of Psychiatry and the hospital's graphic department's director, David Wells. Each of the six exhibitions was billed as a major publicity event for the hospital, the Department of Psychiatry's outpatient programs, as well as for the individual patients, who were now viewed as exhibiting artists in their own right, and their friends and family who came to celebrate the artists at the opening reception gala event. At each catered opening reception, press attended and interviewed the participating artists and the art therapists.

Creating and maintaining an art room environment, which supports patients' growth and independence, was not a feat that happened quickly. The first step occurred more than 25 years ago, when I discovered Edith Kramer during a continuing education course on art therapy taught by Cathy Malchiodi at the University of Utah where I was an undergraduate art student. During the Edith Kramer segment, I felt that my artist self was spoken to directly. The strength I received from the art making process was a strengthening of my ego skills that served as therapy, in and of itself, and I realized this approach could be utilized as therapy for those in need of healing. Her classes at NYU were enriching, and they served as ample preparation for my upcoming career as an art therapist in adult psychiatry. They met my expectations as they built upon the solid theoretical foundations of ego psychology and enriched my understanding of how the art making process heals.

I found that there are unique challenges in working with adults using Edith Kramer's *art as therapy* theoretical approach, which are distinct from

134 *Kevin Maxwell*

the challenges of working with children. I also recognized that more preparation and foresight needed to be conducted to address those challenges as an extension of Kramer's ego psychology framework of art as therapy. One of the biggest challenges for adults in the art room is allowing themselves to play. Kramer frequently referenced the British child psychiatrist Donald W. Winnicott (1971), who said, "It is in playing and only in playing that the individual child or adult is able to be creative and to use the whole personality, and it is only in being creative that the individual discovers the self" (p. 54).

Art making was indeed a healing process for my patient Anita at Maimonides Medical Center. Anita arrived at my art therapy inpatient group bearing a diagnosis of bipolar manic depression, as her mood was elevated and her thoughts were disorganized.

Anita was a Latina woman, originally from Honduras, in her late 50s, and was initially resistant to the art making process; she was easily distracted by all the stimuli of the other patients in the group as well as the noises on the unit. Soon, however, she seemed quieted as she allowed herself to listen to the light jazz I generally have playing on my CD player. Anita entered the art group uttering what is characteristic of adults initially participating in an art as therapy group, "But I am *not* an artist," for they carry the assumption that they will immediately be expected to perform and then be judged accordingly. If the art therapist wants to keep adults engaged in the art as therapy group, first and foremost must be the goal of convincing them they can trust the art therapist to maintain the group as a safe space to play, explore, and experiment in the art making process.

I responded to her disclaimers that she wasn't an artist by reassuring her that the art room was indeed a place to have fun with the art materials and make discoveries about what images were important for her. I began with a series of multiple-choice questions that I routinely train my developing artists to ask themselves, such as, "Do you want to experiment with the art materials?" or "Do you want to search through the art cards I have to look for inspiration?" She decided that she wanted to look at the cards.

I offered her my standard litany of four categories of cards stored in plastic containers of which I had gathered from museums, galleries, and tourist counters, including flowers, landscapes, animals, and people. I have found that having a good variety of art cards available as a resource for visual reference is vital for guiding the developing artist through the anxiety that they commonly experience as they confront the empty white paper in front of them, as well as providing stimuli to prompt their imaginations. Thus, I strongly recommend they be included in all art as therapy groups.

I offered her reassurances that I repeat often, "The images are meant for your use as reference material, not to be copied but merely serve as inspiration for your imagination." I find I must quickly soothe anxieties that may arise from the expectation of being judged or criticized for lack of artistic skills – a natural reaction of adults when asked to work with art materials, in contrast to children, who eagerly jump into the art making process.

The Building of an Artist's Identity   135

Anita chose what would be a series of involved landscapes to work from and, later, landscapes with people interacting within the landscapes. As she began expressing frustration with the task of planning out her image on the 12" by 18" white sheet in front of her, I strove to be present wearing the three hats that Edith Kramer emphasized as so crucial for the art therapist to be prepared to fill – artist, art educator, and art therapist (Kramer & Gerity, 2000). Here, I continued the series of questions that I am training them to incorporate into their own thinking process as they develop their own identities as artists: "Which art materials would you like to work with – water-based tempera paint blocks, oil pastels, colored or graphite pencils, or clay?" These are the standard art materials I offer, but I am careful to offer only the materials suited to level of ego strength.[1]

As I wear my art therapist, artist, and art educator hats, I am on hand to anticipate their concerns and be responsive to their questions about how best to plan out the images they have decided on as important to create, how to utilize fully the array of art materials available, and how ultimately to share these personal expressions which are vital to their developing identities as artists. Inpatients have opportunities to share at the end of every session and when they enter outpatient art therapy they have exhibits on the bulletin boards, as well as in the hospital's art gallery. As each new member enters the art therapy group, they learn through didactic instruction and active role modeling of the basic rules they must adhere to involving respect for their and their fellow developing artists' creative processes.

As I worked with Anita to guide her through the art making process, I carefully utilized what Kramer refers to as the *third hand* – integral to the three hats of art therapist, artist, and art teacher. She said:

> Art therapists must also command a "Third Hand," a hand that helps the creative process along without being intrusive, without distorting meaning or imposing pictorial ideas or preferences alien to the client. The Third Hand must be capable of conducting pictorial dialogues that complement or replace verbal exchange.
>
> (Kramer & Gerity, 2000, p. 48)

Anita gradually took to the art making process and expressed pride in her ability to think through the process of planning out her landscape projects step by step. She learned how to look at her composition as a whole, and how to plan it out using both the big shapes that are intertwined and interlocking on the empty sheet and the details that follow. She learned how to modulate the paints, colors, values, tones, and textures. She shared her successes with the group informally as it was transpiring and formally as it was exhibited. She beamed with pride as she received validation for her work from her fellow artists. As she shared her developing projects, she would describe her narratives and seemed to enjoy this process immensely.

As Anita developed her identity of herself as an artist with regular members of my outpatient art therapy groups, she seemed to be managing her

136   *Kevin Maxwell*

fluctuations in mood more successfully. She seemed to be utilizing the ego skills she learned through the art making process to strengthen the ego skills she needed for navigating her life, such as reality orientation, decision making, autonomy, focusing on task, frustration tolerance, stress reduction, and many more; all are ego skills that my patients incorporate through the art making process.

As Anita's ego strengthened, she sought out her own resources to augment what she was receiving in the outpatient art therapy groups, such as YouTube art instruction clips, and fashioned in her home an art studio, which she used to create art to manage her symptoms between her groups. Steadily, she began arriving to art group proudly presenting paintings she had developed in her home studio.

Kramer charts the progression of artistic development that can be correlated with the level of the ego skills as:

1   Precursory activities: scribbling, smearing; exploration of physical proper-ties that do not lead to creation of symbolic configurations but are experienced as positive and ego syntonic.
2   Chaotic discharge: spilling, splashing, pounding; destructive behavior leading to loss of control.
3   Art in the service of defense: stereotyped repetition; copying, tracing, banal conventional production.
4   Pictographs: pictorial communications, which replace or supplement words. (Such communications occur often in psychotherapy or other intimate relationships. They usually remain unintelligible to the outsider. Pictographs are, as a rule, crudely executed and seldom attain the inte-gration and creative power of art.)
5   Formed expression, or art in the full sense of the word; the production of symbolic configurations that successfully serve both self-expression and communication. (Kramer, 1971, pp. 54–55)

Achieving *formed expression* is the goal I seek, as an art therapist wearing Edith Kramer's three hats, for each of my adult psychiatric patients' art. It is other-wise referred to as "sublimation," which Kramer clarifies as follows:

> We call sublimation any process in which a primitive social impulse is transformed into a socially productive act, so that the pleasure in the achievement of the social act replaces the pleasure which gratification of the original urge would have afforded.
>
> (Kramer & Gerity, 2000, p. 41)

Sublimation is described further as ". . . a process wherein drive energy is deflected from its original goal and displaced onto achievement, which is highly valued by the ego, and is, in most instances, socially productive" (Kramer, 1971, p. 68). Edith liked Heinz Hartmann's conception of sublimation as

The Building of an Artist's Identity 137

freeing up libidinal energies and creating a sense of pleasure in the new substitute activity. Sublimation is thus served in the production of various other creative arts, such as dance, literature, music, as well as visual arts, but its strength can always be seen in the degree to which it can be channeled and can neutralize aggressive and libidinal energy into socially productive achievements. As mentioned earlier, essential to this production of creative arts is the process of shared sublimated formed expressions with society at large. As this occurs, the artist can sense their expressions have been acknowledged, and a dialog can continue. This authentic acknowledgment is crucial for the healing process to occur. It is to this end that we strove to create at Maimonides Department of Psychiatry a gallery to showcase the work of our developing artists who regularly attended the art therapy groups.

Anita offered two contributions, one each for the 2014 and 2016 exhibitions. The first (Figure 18.1) was an adaptation of an art card from my collection of two women in the forest. She described the skillfully executed painting as depicting the drama of a broken oven in which the women aren't able to bake their bread. She laughed during the opening reception, as the guests were aghast at the plight of the women's stove. She responded with an answer that seemed to demonstrate her growing ego strength by acknowledging life's difficulties: "Sometimes life is like that." In response to the outcry over the plight of the women in her original painting, Anita painted another piece (Figure 18.2). This painting is done from her imagination and includes two women in a forest; this time she positioned them around a repaired stove. She expressed pride that she could fix the stove and feed her fans the bread they hungered for as she submitted it to the May 2016 art exhibition. She again dressed up for the opening reception and beamed proudly in front of her painting as her adoring fans offered their congratulations on her artistic journey. As she pulled me over to pose with her while photographs were taken in front of her painting of the successfully repaired stove in the forest, I also beamed with pride. As her "auxiliary ego," wearing Edith's three hats, I had the honor to enter into this artistic journey, watching Anita as she enjoyed the results of her developing ego strengths. She recognized and incorporated the ego-strengthening powers of the art making process to harness it into the formed expression involved in sublimated art.

In summary, I have learned over my 25-plus years as an art therapist working with diverse pathologies of both adult inpatients and outpatients, that adults possess their own unique set of challenges, which are distinct from challenges found when working with children, and in many ways much more challenging.

Children seem to be inherently drawn into the art making process, while adults often seem more cautious, having built deeply entrenched defenses against allowing themselves to experiment, play, and acknowledge their successes. All the art therapist's interventions should be geared toward building the adult's identity as a developing artist; this comes with nudging, cajoling, and guiding the art making into creative variations of sublimated formed

138 *Kevin Maxwell*

Figure 18.1 Broken Oven. Tempera on paper

expressions. Ultimately, task orientation, organizational skills, reality orientation skills, tolerance for ambiguity, concentration, and focusing skills, as well as increasing self-esteem, are fostered from the development of art making skills. All of this occurs as the art therapist, while always available as the patient's *auxiliary ego,* wearing the hats of artist and art educator, encourages the patients to make their own decisions about what ideas or images are important – how to express those ideas, what materials to use, and how best to implement and organize them to optimally express their developing concepts. Additionally, the art therapist asks, "What is the best way to maintain and organize your workspace and materials?" and "How or where can you search for new ideas?" As the vast array of decisions involved in art making are increasingly

Figure 18.2 Fixed Oven. Tempera on paper

internalized by the developing artist, a stronger sense of autonomy and identity as a creator develops. This, in turn, becomes a powerful metaphor for the developing sense of empowerment over their lives. Culmination of the adult's identity as a creative artist occurs as they discover these sublimated formed expressions that are validated by the art therapist, as well as by their fellow artists and their community at large.

Adults within art as therapy bring their inherent challenges and advantages, which are again informed and enriched significantly by the grounding principles provided by Kramer that she reiterated so well:

> At this point a fundamental cleavage in the interpretation of art therapy must be briefly stated: some art therapists practice it as a specialized form of psychotherapy, but here we are concerned mainly with art therapy that depends on *art* as its chief therapeutic agent. Art therapy is seen as distinct from psychotherapy. Its healing potentialities depend on the psychological processes that are activated in creative work.
>
> (Kramer, 1971, p. 25)

Note

1 The art materials that I offer to patients are excellent quality and optimal for art therapy. They address the needs of a depressed patient for practicing emoting with color and fluidity. The colored pencils and pastels address the specific needs for the control and reality orientation of the patient with psychosis or mania. I use Triarco Super Value Alphacolor Biggie Cakes with Palette #RAO8440, Crayola Portfolio Series Water-soluble Oil Pastel Sets of 24 per box, and Scholar Prismacolor Pencils: https://www.etriarco.com/.

For clay, go to the Laguna Clay website – lagunaclay.com – where you will find their distributers. They have four basic staples. I use Laguna's self-hardening Mexo-white WC-641.

References

Kramer, E. (1971). *Art as therapy with children*. New York: Schocken Books.

Kramer, E., & Gerity, L. A. (2000). *Art as therapy: Collected papers*. London: Jessica Kingsley Publishers.

Winnicott, D. W. (1971). *Playing and reality*. New York, NY: Tavistock Publications.

19 Edith Kramer's Third Hand
Intervention in Art Therapy

Karin Dannecker

My first encounter with Edith Kramer was in 1979 in Germany. A student at the time, I read her book *Art as Therapy with Children,* which had been translated into German. Not only was I fascinated about what she wrote, but also I realized that Edith Kramer was explaining the very things that I had experienced in teaching art to children who were then called "mentally or emotionally disturbed." She was describing phenomena that, until then, I had only somehow had a hunch about, or intuitively sensed. Here was someone who succeeded in describing profoundly and convincingly what I had been experiencing all along: the healing effects of the artistic process and of art. This book was the stepping-stone for me toward studying art therapy in the US, the only place where such courses were offered at the time.

I was fortunate to be awarded a scholarship to study art therapy in New York and wound up at none other than New York University, where the author of that same book, Edith Kramer, was living and teaching. Professor and artist Edith Kramer became my teacher, mentor, and later a friend. For many years thereafter, she traveled to Berlin to hold lectures for us at the Weissensee School of Art. She also presented her artwork at the Galerie Taube in Berlin and loved to visit the many wonderful museums in the city. In 1990, which was only months after the Berlin wall had fallen, we took trips to the Eastern part of the country. Edith spoke of her time as a young girl in a school in the countryside when her family had moved to Berlin for some time.

One of my first experiences with the power of art in the art therapy training was in Edith's seminar, Art for Art Therapists. This was a course for new students. We were instructed to draw from life models with charcoal on large sheets of paper. In several of my drawings, the feet were missing – they just did not fit on the page. After the drawings of all students had been hung up on the wall, Edith went from picture to picture, describing and pointing out various aspects of the images. When she came to my "footless" drawing she commented: ". . . and here is someone not grounded yet!" In a straightforward manner, she had recognized and named what my picture was reflecting: that I was in a big, foreign city, and entering a field in which I hadn't quite found my moorings, or my feet, so to speak.

Figure 19.1 Edith Kramer and Karin Dannecker, 1990, Exhibit in der Galerie Taube, Berlin

In the following, I want to reflect on a subject which is, in my experience, more than anything else a matter of concern to those working in art therapy as well as to those who are studying it. It is the core question: What makes a good art therapist? Edith explored this issue in many ways – in theory as well as in practice. In numerous publications and essays, she arrived at conclusions, and finally identified the answer to that question in what, to this day, stands among the key paradigms of art therapy. Therefore, I would like to outline some of her thoughts and basic theories. My hope is to encourage others to seek out Edith's original writings for themselves. No summary, no matter how good, can give an account of Edith's theoretical formulations, or her stories from her clinical practice.

According to its Greek etymological origins, the meaning of *therapist* is someone who places himself in the service of others, someone who is a companion. How then, can we as art therapists best serve our patients? In what way are we servants or companions? At the start of her book *Art as Therapy with Children*, which has meanwhile been translated into nine languages and is in its sixth printing in Germany, Edith explains:

Edith Kramer's Third Hand 143

Art therapy is conceived of primarily as a means of supporting the ego, fostering the development of a sense of identity, and promoting maturation in general. Its main function is seen in the power of art to contribute to the development of psychic organization that is able to function under pressure without breakdown or the need to resort to stultifying defensive measures.

(Kramer, 1971, p. xiii)

From this statement of purpose, some important questions arise as to its application: How does one harness the healing potential of art? How does one support the ego functions of other people? Edith writes that the single most important task of the art therapist is to create a setting conducive to creative work (Kramer, 2003). She draws on the work of the child psychoanalyst D. W. Winnicott, who uses the prototypical term of the "companionable solitude" as a state of being alone together such as the relaxed tension between a mother and her child. Winnicott regards this as a capacity a child is able to develop when the mother establishes an environment of safety and trust. In her caring but unintrusive presence, the child is able to play and to discover his inner world of fantasies. This creates a transitional space in which reality and illusion can intermingle and connect.

Edith describes the situation in art therapy in much the same terms: The therapist accompanies the patient in his or her creative process in a kind of *working alliance*, encouraging and supporting without imposing their own ideas or disturbing the patient. In this environment the patient can submerge into his own inner world, explore his fantasies and wishes, hopes and fears, while lending them expression through pictures and sculptures. This means that the art process enables new experiences: ". . . conflicts are re-enacted under more favorable circumstances, and this ultimately lessens the destructive influence of early childhood tragedies" (Kramer, 1971, p. 39).

To utilize the full potential of the art materials and those of individual expression, one often has to lend assistance at critical moments during the act of creating. Such an intervention, or "stepping in," requires special competencies on the part of the therapist. Any actions the therapist takes should revolve around supporting the creative process and the creating of a work of art. Herein lies the difference between the art therapist and the psychotherapist, whose procedure relies mostly on the use of words – on talking.

It is this particular skill for which Edith coined a metaphor. It describes the scope of her own work with patients and clients: What makes an art therapist exceptional is her ability to implement a *third hand*. ". . . 'Third Hand,' [is] a hand that helps the creative process along without being intrusive, without distorting meaning or imposing pictorial ideas or preferences alien to the client" (Kramer & Gerity, 2000, p. 48).

Following Theodor Reik, who wrote that a good psychoanalyst develops a "third ear" to listen between the lines – to what the patient is *not* saying, but still communicating – Edith wrote that the art therapist must develop a

144   *Karin Dannecker*

"third eye" in order to recognize the different messages in the visual work of a patient. But what takes far more effort is the refinement of a third hand in order to support the patient in his creative process. For this, all those experiences that she had as an artist herself, her knowledge of materials, technique, and the creative process, are fundamental.

Part of the third hand is creating the kind of environment in which patients' artistic productivity can unfold. Ideally, this is in a studio where qualitatively good and adequate art materials are available. This includes sufficient light, a safe storage area, plenty of work tables, and an environment in which patients can work without being disturbed. Another function of the art therapist's third hand is her empathy resonating with the hopes, doubts, surprises, and joys a patient may experience in the creative process. However, the most active use of the third hand is for artistic interventions. Edith calls these "services," which, for example, could be offering the right-sized paint brush or suggesting a certain color at the right moment. It could mean coming to the rescue when paint starts to drip down the page or helping to save a sculpture from falling apart. Assisting by drawing a line in the air, or if a patient is physically handicapped, physically drawing the line for him are also third hand interventions (Kramer, 2003, p. 255). Edith gives examples describing the creation of a work of art in step-by-step detail while she reflects on her own facilitating and enabling interventions in her work with children. She considered her own artistic contributions in the relationship to be of the utmost importance, because they enable the child to find more autonomous expression and personal form (Dannecker, 2017).

According to Edith, the art therapist needs to exercise strict self-awareness and self-discipline in her work, which means that she must consciously deal with her own subjective impulses and perceptions to avoid disruptive influences on the patient. Edith pointed out the mechanisms and dangers of countertransference that can develop between patient and therapist, thus referring to the therapist's traditional and self-reflecting responsibility in her role. By the same token, she freely admitted her own mistakes. In the 1987 film of Edith's lectures for the Hochschule der Künste Berlin, she described how, on one occasion, her understanding of her patient's artistic expression was at such variance with her own concept of art that, as a result, she made entirely inappropriate suggestions. After that, she self-critically said that she had been "narrow-minded and led by countertransference."

In my viewpoint, the concept of the third hand is the best possible descriptor for the special competences of an art therapist and, at the same time, it sets the course for successful intervention strategies in therapy. Edith's theoretical framework is firmly rooted in the psychoanalytical concepts of drive and ego psychology. Central to the art therapeutic approach is sublimation and the potential for ego development through art; accordingly, the third hand focuses on the transforming power of the artistic process. Interventions are viewed in regard to broadening the artistic expression, supporting the patient's capacity for sublimation, and reinforcing the ego functions. The art therapist's

Edith Kramer's Third Hand 145

empathic supporting presence facilitates and unburdens the patient's resurfacing feelings and experiences, and he is able to develop greater self-awareness.

Edith illustrated the use of the third hand with myriad examples of her clinical work and that of her colleagues. Every story she tells of her work with children clearly and convincingly illustrates that an art therapist's identity must be firmly anchored in the realms of both art and psychotherapy. Artistic intuition and experience must be coupled with a solid understanding of psychodynamically based psychotherapy. Only when both elements are integrated do they prove to be helpful and effective in art therapeutic intervention. It would be redundant to summarize the examples about the third hand, when her detailed and vivid wording can be read in the original literature.

In these final paragraphs, I will introduce an exercise that I have carried out with students and workshop participants on many occasions. Edith developed this exercise to deepen our empathic understanding, while also demonstrating the mechanisms of countertransference, and of the intersubjective processes in art therapy.

This three-part exercise makes us aware of how interventions in art therapy are always influenced by our personal viewpoints, our hopes, our unresolved problems, and conflicts. It illustrates visually that the third hand is also always a subjective one. The first task is to take a picture made by a patient and to create an exact copy, thus staying true to the format and materials of the original. The participants are not given any information about the patient's age, gender, diagnosis, or complaints, as this information could easily influence the perceptions of the one doing the copying.

Sometimes it seems already difficult for some participants to "feel into" the style and the way of painting or drawing of another person. The copied picture may reveal differences in the pictures of which even the copier is unaware. Upon reflection, participants say that painting or drawing in the style of the patient was almost "intolerable." They felt limited, confined, or that the artistic expression was simply alien to their own.

In the second part of the exercise, the participants are asked to imagine how the picture would change if the patient were to feel "somewhat" better. The emphasis is on "somewhat." In this exercise one is asked to develop an inner draft, elicited through the creation of the copy, preliminarily, on an unconscious level. It is at this stage, if not before, that every participant concretely and consciously examines his or her own fantasy. One needs to assume a detached, "eccentric" attitude toward whatever the patient's picture had aroused in his or her inner world in order to be able to assess it more objectively. While becoming more aware of these inner processes and images a new image takes shape on the paper, which is actually then a composite of the patient's and one's own images.

This exercise gives way to a variety of "answers" or solutions. Each participant of the group makes his or her own unique variation of the patient's picture. Each "new" picture, which was done "in answer" to the patient's picture, contains personality traits of the participant who drew it. Here it

146 *Karin Dannecker*

happens sometimes that a participant abandons the style of the patient and his or her own style pushes its way through. Some participants struggle to imagine what the patient's picture would have looked like if the patient had felt "somewhat" better. When this takes place, the participant's picture shows a more successful integration than that which would be possible if the patient were to feel only "somewhat" better. What it reveals is the participant's need to quickly overcome the frightening and tormented aspects, which he or she perceives in the patient's work. This need is often stronger than his or her capacity to withstand the patient's mental fragmentation and to accept it and to respond to it empathically.

In the third part of the exercise, each participant is asked to imagine how the patient's picture would look if he or she had made a complete recovery. After having immersed himself in the patient's picture while replicating it, followed by the second picture, in which he acknowledges what his personal components are and how they contribute to his understanding and change in the picture, a third image begins to take shape. This one shows what the participant fantasizes about what the patient would create if he were able to solve his problems and conflicts in an integrating way that suited him best. Because the exercise is conducted without the patient present, every participant can be free to use his imagination when creating this third image. As expected, there are as many variations of pictures as there are participants. Each person reacted differently to the patient's original picture and came up with his or her own solution, guided by their own fantasies and conscious or unconscious notions.

This exercise, which Edith never wrote about but used with students, anticipated what has now become a major theme in psychotherapeutic theory and practice: The notion of the therapeutic relationship as an intersubjective phenomenon based on a continuous dialog and agreement on "what can be accomplished together" (Stern et al., 2012). From this intersubjective relatedness, the "moments of meeting" which are crucial for changes can crystalize.

In therapy, these events are of a special quality and intensity. Edith calls them "miracles": when in art therapy something unexpected happens and new and evocative aspects appear in the artwork (Kramer, 2003, p. 46). Such moments when a patient moves beyond the usual are rare. One cannot compel them, but one can create conditions that are conductive to their happening: offering appropriate materials, space, and time, being prepared for the unexpected, respecting the child's symbols and shapes, showing understanding for the unwavering and extravagant nature of the creative process. Then miracles can take form in art therapy leading to unusually expressive artwork as well as to changes in the child's or adult's personality. Today we call such profound experiences with art the aesthetic moment. In art therapy it is most of all the third hand that brings about transformation. Edith made the third hand available to us and, for her contribution, we are deeply grateful.

References

Dannecker, K. (2017). Der Ästhetische Moment. Intersubjektivität und Veränderungsprozesse in der Kunsttherapie [The aesthetic moment. Intersubjectivity and processes of change in art therapy]. In F. von Spreti, P. Martius, & F. Steger (Eds.), *Kunsttherapie: Künstlerisches Handeln – Wirkung – Handwerk.* (pp. 339–348) Stuttgart: Schattauer.

Kramer, E. (1971). *Art as therapy with children.* New York: Schocken Books.

Kramer, E. (2003). *Kindheit und Kunsttherapie* [Childhood and art therapy]. Graz, Austria: Nausner & Nausner.

Kramer, E., & Gerity, L.A. (2000). *Art as therapy: Collected papers.* London: Jessica Kingsley Publishers.

Stern, D.N., et al. (The Boston Process of Change Study Group) (2012). *Veränderungsprozesse*, Frankfurt/M.: Brandes und Apsel.

20 Kramer's Sublimation
Creative Expansion or Limitation?

David Henley

Introduction

Under the therapeutic guidance of Edith Kramer, a blind youth, whose pseudonym was "Christopher," spent months struggling to sculpt with clay (Kramer, 1971; Kramer & Gerity, 2000). At twelve, he utilized the medium regressively, smacking and smearing, all the while verbally obsessing on birds, his preferred object of autistic perseveration. Eventually, the bird-themed forms evolved into the first works of eggs, nests, and little trees, which Kramer termed "crude" and "somewhat disjointed" (1971, p. 76). After years of art therapy, Christopher began to develop the skills and self-control to give gifted artistic form to the media. Even as he entered young adulthood and was technically no longer a patient, Kramer functioned as an auxiliary ego, implementing *third hand* interventions. This concept is defined as assisting the artist without distorting personal or cultural meaning or intruding upon their artistic vision (Kramer, 1986). Eventually, with her support, he created the most ambitious sculptures by any account. One is a realistic work of a near life-sized human figure. Standing 5' 5", the figure took an astounding three years of their mutual work to create. Figure 20.1, where the figure is shown in process, reveals how ambitious the engineering was in creating this large-scale work. Kramer made a mold and cast the piece in plaster, an exhausting, complex process. Such an extensive commitment to a former patient and lasting decades is rare in the annals of art therapy.

Christopher's *art as therapy* had reached its zenith, as he was now an artist of considerable skill and aesthetic sensitivity. However, regressions during therapy or in studio work were a constant threat, often sweeping in severity. This holds true for any temperamental artist, whether an impoverished, blind young man or a Jackson Pollock. One breaking point was the traumatic breakup with a girlfriend. Facing this abandonment, Christopher inexplicably turned on his finished work and destroyed it in a fit of rage, literally kicking it down the stairs. Thus, the nature of sublimation as a defense is fraught with fragility, as developing ego strength uneasily coexists with the pressures to act out under the unbridled id. Yet, despite the regression, fleeting moments of sublimation brought some stability and sensory enrichment to this young man.

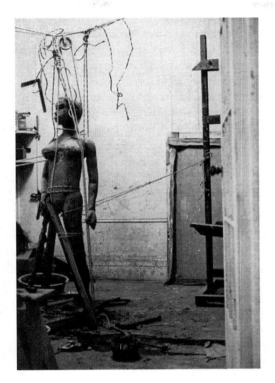

Figure 20.1 Clay sculpture (unfinished) by Christopher

Art provided a crucial outlet for giving form to his internal feeling states, while promoting maturation as a man and artist (Kramer & Gerity, 2000).

Sublimation

Kramer (1971) derived her work from Freud's late formulations on sublimation, most clearly described in *Civilization and its Discontents*. In this slim but seminal volume, Freud defined sublimation as the harnessing of the instinctual drives to avoid the suffering induced by the pressures of acting directly and destructively on libidinal and aggressive impulses (Freud, 1962, p. 26). Freud wrote that the aim of satisfying instinctual needs is not by any means to relinquish their expression – it is imperative that the drives seek and gain gratification – that, with the "shifting of instinctual aims," one may redirect primary process pressure while heightening the experience of pleasure. Freud viewed art making as ideal for giving fantasies bodily form, and that the artist's inner satisfactions seem "finer and higher" than releasing the instinctual impulses that "convulse our physical being" (Freud, 1962, pp. 26–27). Yet, like

150 David Henley

any defense, sublimation is "no impenetrable armour against the arrows of . . . suffering . . ." (Freud, 1962, p. 27), illustrated by a three-year sculpting process being destroyed in an instant. But for a time, in that sculpture, stood the enjoyments that come with experiencing "works of art . . . which, by the agency of the artist, is made accessible to those. . . . who are receptive to the influence of art . . ." (Freud, 1962, pp. 27–28). The sculpture was a mutually shared experience, a dialog between creator and audience, and despite its demise, was personally and "socially productive." Indeed, art has functioned in this capacity for the whole of civilization since time immemorial.

Kramer's Artist's Credo

How then does Kramer's work with children translate into her own oeuvre and the work of fellow artists? This question was raised on two memorable occasions when both she and I had artwork published on the cover of *Art Therapy: Journal of the American Art Therapy Association*. Both of us had contributed a work that stimulated questions about the artist's "intent," one of many topics we explored around the table in her SoHo studio in New York City. Discussing art with Edith did not entail "small talk"; discussions of an artist's work were a serious affair, historical, analytical and critical, and often generating heated but enjoyable exchanges.

Though Kramer was empathetic toward patients or children, for adult artists, art criticism could be a cutting affair. This is perhaps due to her own mentorship with the renowned Friedl Dicker, whom the impressionable Kramer studied under from her early teens in Vienna and Prague. Dicker was part of the Bauhaus movement, along with other luminaries such as Gropius and Klee. She was by all accounts a larger-than-life persona, a committed communist and radical, an artist and teacher of distinction, and then most famously, the art teacher/savior when interned at the Nazi camp, Terezin. There she made art with the beleaguered children, whose art has become a beacon of hope after the horrors of the Holocaust. She perished in Auschwitz, but her mark was left indelibly on Kramer's artist's credo.

Kramer believed that her job as an artist was to celebrate that which is perishable and endangered. She believed she should capture all the contradictions – beauty, as well as the horrors of the world – so that the repellent becomes comprehensible. She believed it was important to render the world faithfully, in unflinching terms, and to take a hard look at the mundane and unremarkable and transform it visually into poetry (Kramer & Gerity, 2000).

The Cover Art: Henley

With this stoic credo in mind, we return to the two cover images published in the journal, *Art Therapy: Journal of the American Art Therapy Association*. To illustrate our differences and similarities and to set the stage for our mutual criticisms, first I will introduce my own cover art. Drawn in graphite, it consists of a montage of detailed elements that are organic, erotic, and perhaps morbid. It is entitled *Upon Leaving Chicago*; in my artist's statement I wrote: "I know very little about my work and am not overly concerned with metaphor or symbolism." Having seen the work upon my return as a professor in Chicago, Edith pointed out that this statement was "disingenuous." The drawing's dark imagery obviously was permeated with rich symbolism in what she affectionately termed was my "grotesque brand of realism."

There ensued a lively and frank critique. Edith's closest colleague at NYU, Laurie Wilson, has written, "Edith does not mince words, suffer fools gladly, or lie when the truth is needed but not necessarily wanted" (1997, p. 102). This was indeed the case. She questioned whether this work was so intensely personal and emotionally loaded, and if it was suitable for publication.

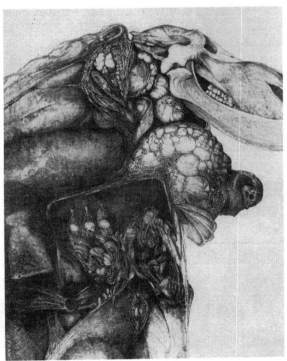

Figure 20.2 Upon Leaving Chicago. Graphite drawing by David Henley (1995)

152 *David Henley*

I can fully recollect Edith's critique like it was yesterday. The work rested on her easel, ready to be exhibited at the annual faculty show at Long Island University, where I now taught. She first pointed out that my title was obvious; my "leaving Chicago" referred to being denied tenure at the Art Institute of Chicago a year earlier. This to her mind amounted to a lack of "inner consistency," which Kramer defined as the artist being untrue to his- or herself and thus deceiving the viewer (Kramer, 1971). After going through the ordeal of being denied tenure, leaving the school and my home of seven years, I was now "acting out" through my art. Edith first pointed out the "three grisly hanging skulls" – hadn't I discussed with her over the years being at odds with my elder three faculty members who ultimately voted me out of the job? And the raw vaginal forms – clearly they suggest sexual encounters, quite a graphic, even gratuitous reference for a distinguished professor. Edith often digressed, having begun complaining about a recent show of Georgia O'Keeffe's closely cropped flowers, "Equally obscene," she exclaimed! Then, the faux dinosaur skull – she lectured – it too was loaded. Though it was partly within my usual style of scientific illustration, it had now morphed into a monster, having departed from any known species; might these be the "dinosaurs" I had referred to years earlier?

Edith proclaimed the work a "private picture" and not appropriate for public display. Far from sublimation, she remarked that it was another of my provocations. She admonished, "To overcome the injustices endemic to academia, one must be capable of renouncing infantile feelings of rejection" and instead find symbolic equivalents of what I had learned from the experience, depicting my strengths and wisdom, not bitterness. Ouch! Sitting amidst the lengthening shadows of late-afternoon tea, I recall sitting back and "taking in" these comments, at times nodding weakly, without even a withering defense. She delivered her comments with the same off-handed, dispassionate manner used to describe her own painting. I was not being personally attacked, nor was there any therapeutic tone or "psychologizing," a practice that we both detested. Edith used the plainest of words, and had simply pointed out the obvious – as an experienced therapist and professor – that these issues should have been self-evident! It was an example of Laurie's Wilson's description of Edith's "way," par excellence.

I felt relieved when I finally shuttled that piece out of the loft, and into the university gallery where the work was seemingly well received. Since the title and its context remained obscure, it was stripped of her informed analysis and taken at face value; a well-crafted, interesting work that garnered a modicum of attention. Did my current artist colleagues, sophisticated New Yorkers no less, know how the work had been slaughtered seemingly for the very reasons it was now accepted? Several viewers at the exhibition deemed the very elements that had disturbed Edith, to be powerful.

Edith's Cover Piece

During one of our many conversations at the studio, the topic turned to Edith's propensity for plein air painting and the crucial need to work from life. Known internationally for her paintings done on-site – whether her alpine mountain landscapes painted in Austria, or a monumental composition inside a NYC power plant, or the tiny works done from her VW Beetle while painting in the rain – for Edith, there was no substitute for real life. Her subway art is perhaps most prominent, as she often worked along the gritty tracks, set up in her paint be-splattered sweaters. It was not uncommon for a passer-by to drop coins in her tin cup, as she fully looked the part of an old lady in need. She prolifically sketched her preparatory drawings, never from photographs that were absolutely "verboten." The subway, she remarked, had all the elements of urban life – architectural scale and geometrics, the frenetic movement of trains and crowds, and an eerie, dingy atmosphere. Her only complaint was that the subway required using a difficult color, phthalo green, to capture the lurid light. Yet, all this held her allure.

The discussions over the need for life studies led to some remarks about her cover piece submitted to the journal. In an oil painting on sheet metal, titled *Uneasy Sleep*, Edith painted a derelict looking African-American man, obviously unconscious from exhaustion or being high.

He is shown with his head rolled back, clad in disheveled clothes, his body position contorted. I recall casually asking Edith whether, when sketching, she ever felt like she was intruding upon someone's personal boundaries. Had her subjects ever objected to her studying and rendering them? Presumably, this homeless man had no choice in the matter, but he could have awakened from his unconscious haze and become belligerent. The thought had never occurred to her, she said; in fact, "the usually abrasive nature of New Yorkers often softens upon seeing this elderly working artist, toiling in obviously challenging settings . . . they were often curious and even appreciative." But I continued my point about invading one's personal space, and how subjects such as those pictured in "street photography" sometimes strenuously object to or even demand payment for their services as "subject matter." I brought up Diane Arbus' gift at gaining access to many unusual characters, often taking photos in Washington Square Park, one of Edith's favorite haunts to paint and draw where colorful subjects were almost guaranteed. Annoyed at being compared to a photographer, Edith stated Arbus sought out "freaks," whereas her intent was to find dignity, even nobility in the most downtrodden figures. I wondered aloud if he would have agreed. I wondered too whether the picture was not so much social commentary but about capturing his formal qualities – a difficult pose, his ragged clothes yielding interesting color tones and texture, his twisted body framed against the hard-edged molded plastic seating. She said, of course, to capture her interest the figure must have some allure, but there was also an inherent social component, again "to transform the visual into poetry." I interjected that her stance seemed more a fascinated observer than social commentator. Could singling out an African-American man as drug-addled and homeless epitomize contemporary stereotypes? This comment caught her attention, as I felt Edith's eyes staring directly into mine, a sign that she was being challenged. I quickly added the disclaimer that, "Of course, you are among the most egalitarian of people, certainly not prejudiced

154 *David Henley*

Figure 20.3 Uneasy Sleep. Oil on sheet metal by Edith Kramer (1992)

in any capacity." Then I added, brazenly, "Might not others, such as the thousand art therapists who had received the issue with this image, possibly misperceive your intentions?" Edith put down her teacup and sank back into her venerable chair, clasped her hands, and looked distantly out over the Hudson River. After what seemed an eternity, she responded as if by reciting from her aforementioned artist's credo. I pressed her further, a rare moment in our thirty-five year relationship, "But what led you to choose this particular work to represent your oeuvre for the journal's cover?" The question was shrugged off as her artist statement read, "it was just another in a long series of subway paintings." It should be obvious to the reader by now that I had her critique of my own submission on my mind. However, I avoided heating up the conversation further out of deference to my mentor. Yet, my own intent in pressing her

Kramer's Sublimation 155

was purely as devil's advocate, as I considered the work strong and truthful, regardless of stereotyping or taboos that came with playing on themes of the homeless. Hers was the strongest sublimation of the lot!

Discussion

Sublimation is by nature a paradoxical defense of transformative power and yet also great fragility. Its premise is ambitious – to tap into the id, which is "a source of mortal danger to man" (Kramer, 1971, p. 67), without damaging the ego. Sublimation entails a "dipping into" the instinctual drives to harness those creative energies latent within. Yet, it was Edith's theoretical assertion that in sublimation this shifting of psychic energy from id to ego must neutralize the drives. It is this premise that has always seemed to be the theory's weakest link when it comes to the analysis of art. What of artists who crazily veer away from formal beauty, whose works are variously hideous, bizarre, or raw and profane, or have no formal qualities at all? Are works such as these to be dismissed from the pantheon of art for the sake of sublimation? Thus, my work, with its mindless outpouring of grotesquery, theoretically did not qualify as sublimation. Edith designated it a work of "displacement" rather than sublimation – more akin to "venting" than transformation. I had no argument with this analysis, since it is true that I have never exhibited that drawing again. So the work showed how raw discharge impacts the appreciation, longevity, and viability of the work. Again, Christopher's sublimations ended with his kicking a precious sculpture down the stairs after three years of work. Clearly, libido and aggression gained the upper hand in both our cases. Yet, the question was begged, did their lack of "neutrality" diminish the art as being fully realized?

In Edith's works, traces of aggressive or libidinal energy were almost always neutralized, many to the point of boredom. As executor of her oeuvre, I cataloged each remaining work, and dealt with hundreds of her pieces that included countless weak and mundane portraits, clumsily rendered figures, and seemingly endless, mild-mannered landscapes . . . each blade of grass faithfully painted in place. But in returning to *Uneasy Sleep*, I consider it actually one of her most dynamic and "edgy" works, an opinion borne out by the fact that it was one of the few to sell well at auction. The art market needs some roughing up of current taboos and the art therapy community benefited from a dose of political incorrectness, to confront a black man as emblematic of a subway derelict. She shook that figure up with both power and poignancy!

Edith's credo to render "exactly what was there" perhaps created an artificial ceiling, which may have limited the full scope of her artistic potential. While she took some workshops with the great Hans Hoffman and produced some abstractions under his influence, she never applied his teachings and expanded on them. Perhaps it was Friedl who had left her mark, stultifying in her austerity and discipline. In her devotion to Friedl, artistic license was to be sacrificed for realism. If Edith's notoriously bohemian attitudes were given a free rein

156   *David Henley*

in her art, who knows what unrestrained works would have come into being, necessitating a revision of sublimation!

In the end, Edith Kramer was a larger-than-life figure above reproach. Despite our closeness, I never lost sight that I was dealing with an icon. To me these analytical matters, while fascinating topics of table talk, served more as a deepening of our relationship than engaging in just stimulating debate. Edith's life experiences, of living through two world wars, a traumatic immigration, then hard-won success as a career woman and artist, were of historic proportions. Her work and knowledge base, with its breadth and verve, was far-reaching. Along with her great predecessor, Margaret Naumburg, two strong women pioneered a new and dynamic field in the US that was no small feat in that conservative era.

I will always be indebted and honored to have been given a seat at her table, to have assisted her as studio assistant, and near the end of her tenure in New York, cared for her affairs. Since her passing, I have worked to preserve her archives to help ensure her legacy. She was a little giant of a lady . . . even if she could freeze you with a single glance. She will be missed.

References

Freud, S. (1962). *Civilization and its discontents.* New York: W.W. Norton.
Henley, D. (1995). Cover art: Upon leaving Chicago. *Art Therapy: The Journal of the American Art Therapy Association, 12*(3).
Kramer, E. (1971). *Art as therapy with children.* New York: Schocken Books.
Kramer, E. (1986). The art therapist's third hand: Reflections on art, art therapy, and society at large. *The American Journal of Art Therapy, 24*(3), 71–86.
Kramer, E. (1992). Cover art: Uneasy sleep. *Art Therapy: Journal of the American Art Therapy Association, 9*(4).
Kramer, E., & Gerity, L. A. (2000). *Art as therapy: Collected papers.* London: Jessica Kingsley Publishers.
Wilson, L. (1997). Edith Kramer honored at AATA conference. *American Journal of Art Therapy, 35*(4), 102–105.

Memories

21 Panel Remarks
Edith Kramer[1]

David Henley

My relationship with Edith has now spanned some twenty years, but it began inauspiciously – as a young graduate student in the '70s, I attended one of her admission workshops where I recall the group was analyzing our art works. I was faltering terribly, since I was temperamental about drawing "on command" and felt intruded upon to open myself up for what I correctly assumed was a mechanism to see if I was mentally unstable. I felt it easier to save some time and just tell Professor Kramer that, yes, I was a crazy artist and thus, perhaps, unsuitable to become an art therapist. When it was my turn to speak about my art, I continued in this resistant tone: "Art is ineffable and thus cannot be interpreted – the image must stand on its own." Intrigued by this remark, Edith referred to the great art historian Ernst Gombrich, stating, "Perhaps . . . but we must be able to understand those forces which bring art into being." From that remark, I felt I could become her student – that perhaps I could somehow fit into this field – and thus was launched a twenty-year career in research and practice in child art therapy.

My earliest research interest was on the origins of art or the idea of *original artistic impulse*. Edith's flagship course, Psychodynamic Processes in Art Therapy, teased apart the psychodynamics of drive discharge as it pertained to creative expression, culminating in sublimation. Working with autistic and mentally retarded children at that time, I also drew heavily on the early work of Laurie Wilson and Judy Rubin, my thesis on symbiotic psychosis, the seminal work of Mahler, and of course, Anni Bergman. Upon trying to break into publishing in professional journals, Gladys Agell was a helpful mentor and editor who, early on, nursed my manuscripts into print.

Edith's readings of the animal behaviorist Konrad Lorenz led me to explore the whole of the developmental continuum, both as a child art therapist and as a researcher. After years of practice, I could finally work with different zoo mammals that were variously traumatized by their captivity. During this inquiry about the origins of art, Edith accompanied me on one occasion to interview a particularly famous and unfortunately disturbed gorilla named Koko near San Francisco. As we began our visit, Koko, who seemed incredibly to possess language, signed explicitly to Edith, "Want, see, lady's sex parts now!" Koko signed and pointed toward Edith's breasts in a kind of repetitive obsessive way;

160 David Henley

Edith's Freudian sensibility seemed to awaken, and some serious psychosexual analysis was undertaken while trying to accommodate Koko without becoming obscene in the process. In later years when Edith visited me at the Art Institute of Chicago where I was then professor, we observed chimps and elephants painting and making marks – all of these developmental experiences became the centerpiece of my own research to this day.

As I gathered case material over the years on the children and other art-making creatures, I began to work on a book. When I finally gathered the courage to tell Edith that I, myself, was writing a book, she studied me for a moment and flatly responded, "But you can't write." With that measure of encouragement, I went on to publish my first text.

Edith said little about it until the AATA conference in Las Vegas where she gave tribute to her dear friend and fellow art therapy pioneer, Elinor Ulman, in front of 800 people. Edith began by describing how Elinor abhorred those who butchered the English language. She then cited as a prime example this book that I had published with the "horrible title" of: *Exceptional Children Exceptional Art: Teaching Art to Special Needs.* "You can't possibly teach to a special need" she railed . . . its nonsensical; Elinor would cringe! And this word Henley uses everywhere: "adaptive . . ." (a word borrowed from my background in special education). She yelled, "I am not adaptive; I shall never adapt to anything," and so on. As she used my book as a punching bag, she also added, "Writing problems aside, the case material and art productions in this book were some of the most important work to date on disturbed children." So, the Edith we came to honor is iconoclastic, irreverent, fist-poundingly truthful, incisively critical, and astute in her every observation.

I recall her relationship with artist and art therapist Vera Zilzer, a vibrant part of the New York University's art therapy community. Vera was deemed chief critic of Edith's art. I observed them in this fascinating battle of titans. Despite Vera's often outlandish eccentricity, Edith considered her artistic eye unerring, and her heated passions would prevail upon Edith to rework here, touch up there.

In their own way, both of these artist therapists represent art therapy at its best – they didn't settle. Edith waged her battles with penetrating and incisive criticism; one of Edith's last letters to the editor of the AATA Newsletter blasted the banality and emptiness of the logo used on the cover of our most recent conference program. No one else mounted the courage to make this call.

She was most vocal in her social criticisms. I heard them so many nights, when she put down her brush for the day, sat in the afternoon shadows over tea and good Lithuanian bread, peered over *The New Yorker*, and denounced the current political regime and its vile corruption that was wrecking our country, mourning the spoiling of the environment, the bankrupting of our country's wealth, and the killing of America's children at this very moment . . .

Yet, as angry as she got, it seemed always, in a way, that all was hopeful and redeemable; it was the benign mother figure – who had founded our field – one

Panel Remarks: Edith Kramer   161

whose passions were invested, and available, though in a dispassionate, thought-ful, even-keeled way.

As founding leader of our field, we will forever keep what she has given us in our minds, and as Anni Bergman said about Edith: "It becomes a kind of object constancy – we accept that she might be elsewhere, but we are reassured by knowing she'll always be with us."

Note

1 A version of this chapter was presented as part of a panel at New York University at a symposium for Edith Kramer.

22 Gleaning the Pearls
Reflections of a Student

Kathryn E. Bard

I will never forget the first night of class and meeting Edith Kramer at New York University. She began by saying that she knew many of us were new to the big city and *all* that it entailed: strong unpleasant smells, ugly filthy sights, loud confusing noises at all hours. Instead of trying to ignore these experiences, she cautioned us not to shut down our sensations as foreign, unwanted, and unworthy, but rather to embrace them for what they were. She urged that as students of art therapy, we would need to expand, rather than filter out, our repertoire of experiences to become highly sensitive, keenly aware of our environment, and truly sensory in order to understand people whom we met and to empathize with their situations.

As a young graduate student of Edith Kramer's, I remember being in awe of the profound material that Edith brought with her to class each evening. She often arrived with what seemed like reams of 18" x 24" paintings carefully preserved between sheets of newspaper as if for that very night, for that one teachable moment with us. Each piece was soaked with layers of tempera for us to plumb the depths and discover the subtle meanings. Each painting gave us clues to the child's level of development, areas of strength and challenge, defense mechanisms, and process of healing in *art as therapy*. While we recognized some images from her early books, to see them, touch them, and examine them first-hand provided such a close relationship. Later, when we were in internship supervision, Edith insisted that we bring the client's original artwork. If, for some reason, this was not available, we had to recreate a copy to the best of our ability. Not only did this act have empathic value, it highlighted opportunities for response art or a discussion on countertransference – so many layers to unfold!

Although some of my colleagues were quite competent and confident writers upon entering graduate school, this was not my forte. I was unspeakably fascinated by the other ream of paper she brought with her to every class. This one was A4, lined, and scrawled with large cursive handwriting, mostly in paragraph form – Edith's bountiful notes written particularly for the evening.

In the beginning, her rather thick Austrian accent was a challenge for those of us whose ear and brain channels were not yet attuned. Voilà! This

Gleaning the Pearls   163

vicarious immersion experience became part of our foundational learning in multicultural competence. Her hesitations, her smiles, her hand gestures, as well as her carefully chosen words and sumptuous vocabulary, gave us both verbal and nonverbal clues to understanding the subtleties of art as therapy as well as where art therapy had its roots. How the pieces of Edith Kramer's life were put together was partially told and partially left a mystery. One thing was inevitably clear – the marriage of art making and psychoanalytic theory took place in the life and work of Edith Kramer. Travail and joy were bound together and had a dignified place and meaning in reconciliation toward healing and peace. There were passion and intensity in her endeavors!

I wondered whether Edith Kramer thought of herself as a perpetual student of sorts: gathering information from the children with whom she worked, teaching and presenting, learning together in supervision, studying psychoanalysis and psychoanalytic theory, making art using a wide variety of media, writing articles and books to clarify her theories, as well as living actively in the world. Having witnessed her multilevel involvement at the 1979 American Art Therapy Association Annual Conference, I was keenly aware of her significance in forging the discipline of art therapy.

In class one evening, at some point in our discovery process, she declared with a twinkle in her eye, "It is our job to glean the pearls." My eyes left the artwork to gawk at this relatively short, older woman with a long, gray, wispy braid and baggy pants, and it seemed as if my jaw had dropped to the floor. She repeated, "Glean the pearls," very precisely, and then added, "to discern and gather wisdom." She clearly included herself in this ongoing task. "It is our job . . ." she purported. Perhaps this is where some of the mysterious, miraculous seedlings of art therapy may be found. With these quiet words of wisdom, she was taking us where we had never been before. What exactly does "glean the pearls" mean?

While I realize Edith Kramer did not originate this phrase, she borrowed it insightfully for her art therapy students, and it fit brilliantly. The process of gleaning was a method of social welfare in Biblical times. After the crop was officially harvested, the disadvantaged citizens were allowed onto the farm to glean the leftover bits for their own consumption and storage. Oysters, which accidentally get a piece of gritty sand in their homes, make precious pearls naturally; something beautiful and valuable is made from something that might be considered a mistake. No doubt Edith understood the concepts of *gleaning* and *pearls* intimately.

To clarify, it is our job as art therapy students (and lifelong learners) to discern and gather the nuggets of value (truth) worth saving. This might apply to us being able to see the value in a person who may be considered an outsider or worthless, or helping a client to pick up the pieces through a difficult time of development or after trauma. As art therapists, we must be there to witness and reflect the growth and resilience born through *mistakes* as well as intention. By experiencing stress and challenge we can cultivate areas of strength and beauty, like oysters creating pearls.

164   *Kathryn E. Bard*

I believe Edith was also referring to discerning the truths among art therapy theories. It is our job to think wisely through theoretical concepts and decide what is relevant in understanding behavior and fostering the healing process. She frequently reminded us that the practice of art therapy is not a cookbook of techniques that work for each situation, but rather a sensitive process, including developing a therapeutic relationship, setting and resetting goals, applying theory, and offering materials, methods, and assistance at the appropriate time. She taught that the discovery of truths is not a given that is seen in a particular symbol or style, but rather a process.

After I took the thesis seminar course, I still had not settled on a topic. Later, I found out that Edith would be my thesis advisor. It took me a long time to get up the nerve to submit my first draft. I was already working full time at this point and found it difficult to carve out the time over the weekend to compile a meaningful thesis. To my surprise, when I went to pick up the draft, Edith said it was fine as it was, that nothing else was needed. In her engaged and attentive way, she had written two pages of reaction to the areas that she had found of particular interest. Nothing could have thrilled me more!

Semi-annually, we had the treat of an invitation to the studio of Edith Kramer, initially on Delancey Street, but later on Vandam Street. Now considered a chic area of NYC, in those days it was dark, dirty, and nearly abandoned in the evening except for those people looking for a discreet corner to create a cardboard cot or conduct an illicit transaction. Traditionally, we had a holiday and summer celebration. Her large, spacious studio was a loft on the fifth floor of a walk-up building. Lined with enormous eastern, southern – and one western – exposure windows, there was ample natural light. Paintings were hung on every wall and column and stacked in every corner. Sculpture figurines placed on wooden boards adorned tables of all sorts and sizes. A quietly composed still life was neatly arranged on a bed of drapery. As I recall, this was seasonal and now reminds me of the small shrines one sees throughout Europe. We each brought something "Edible, not Oedipal, and potable, not smokeable" to share in the feast. Students, graduates, and professors had a chance to become better acquainted. By opening her studio and home to us, she provided a platform for hospitality and comradery. She was preparing the way for the future. In her rituals of daily discipline, joy, and perseverance, she showed us that *we* were the future.

If this essay seems overly sentimental, let me assure you that I was not one of the students who knew her personally, nor succeeded highest. Suffice to say, some 30 years later, the foundation that pioneer Edith Kramer, along with Laurie Wilson, built is still strong. Little did I know then that I would be relocating to Europe and spending most of my adult life living in the German-speaking part of Switzerland. My current multicultural experiences have given me even greater appreciation for Edith Kramer. I still can't speak German fluently, let alone write books. My English-speaking clients are from literally all over the world. And, having never been interested in landscapes, I am now surrounded

Figure 22.1 Alpine Wonders. Oil on canvas by Kathryn E. Bard

by natural beauty and find great tranquility in painting plein air, as Edith did each summer, and at the end of her life in Grundlsee, Austria.

Shortly after her death in 2014, I attended a retrospective of Edith Kramer's artwork in Vienna where I noticed that many of her paintings show as much attention to the background as to the subject. Perhaps this portrays the same respect, care, and diligence that she advised us on that first day of class: don't dismiss the unpleasant, the unfamiliar, the seemingly unimportant aspects, but rather pay attention to the details, since each contributes to the telling and the perceiving of the complete story. Each piece of the story is unique and worthy of compassion.

We, as Edith Kramer's students moving forward, have learned and will continue to learn from her multicultural life and steady, joyful, hard work as she paved the way for the discipline of art therapy. From a young woman who faced many, many personal challenges, she resiliently survived, gleaning the pearls of art making and psychoanalytic theory for each of us to hold onto and bestow upon others in the future.

23 Tales of Edith

Patti Greenberg

I was not the only first-year graduate student at NYU in 1979 who had a bit of fear and trepidation before meeting Edith. Her reputation for being exacting, brilliant, and blunt strode out ahead of her. After all, she was a founding mother! She "wrote the book" on art therapy.

All students were required to take Art for Art Therapists, a course Edith taught. I resented this required art course because I feared exposing my poor drawing skills. Sure enough, newsprint paper and charcoal were passed out. After the large gestural warm up Edith always did, we were expected to draw. Rather defensively, I scribbled something abstract, not much different from the warm up, and hoped that was adequate. Edith asked us to put our pictures on the wall, traveled around to each one, and told us what she could see. When she came to mine, she declared, "This person is bored and annoyed." I was stunned that she could see my feelings so perfectly! You could not hide or pretend with Edith. You couldn't fake anything. There was nothing false, no pretense about Edith. And she expected the same honesty and clarity in return.

Art for Art Therapists was not an art class. It was a fascinating look into what the art revealed, a glimpse into the reality of the artist. Her phrase, "What is professed (by the artist) is not what's expressed (by the work)," described how she interpreted the art. The therapist's interpretation was always yoked with whatever the artist might express verbally about the artwork. That, along with the artist's history or reason for entering therapy were the tools Edith used to help the individual. She was uncanny at this, a master, and she was teaching us to do it. This was an exciting, eye-opening class, and a cornerstone for art therapists.

When it came time to attend the first art therapy conference, held in Washington, DC that year, my husband came with me. He had heard about Edith but never met her. When he saw her from a distance, his first impression was that she looked like Mao Tse Tung's wife. This was greeted with laughter by other art therapists, but actually it was an apt description. She was a compact older woman sporting a dark-blue Chinese quilted jacket. Her eyes looked deceptively merry, twinkling, and she had perpetually rosy cheeks. Her graying hair was gathered in a single braid down her back. I never saw her wear her hair any other way except she would occasionally wrap the braid up around

Tales of Edith 167

her head. This trademark braid became thinner, and thinner, and more silver over the years. Finally, it was the width of a #2 pencil.

In another class, Edith asked each student to have a friend complete the House–Tree–Person test and then write it up as a class assignment. I asked a friend who was a landscape architect to make these drawings. He could draw very well. He'd also experienced some hardship in his life, early loss of parents, and his own divorce. However, he had a great sense of humor and survival, and his drawings reflected this. His tree was scruffy and stunted but hanging to a wind-swept cliff by strong roots. His house was equally precarious. These seemed to reveal strong, resilient character in the face of hardship. His person drawing exposed his optimistic and accepting take on his world. He drew a Buddhist monk on a skateboard with his eyes closed, calmly headed down a steep hill. Somehow he had an abiding faith in the universe that, despite life's risks, everything would work out well enough.

Edith, a survivor herself, enjoyed this paper, gave me an A, and I'm sure expected similar work in the future. I was not always able to do this! Later, when I asked for yet another extension on a paper, a frustrated Edith, her merry eyes piercing now, poked my forehead with a finger saying, "There was a little girl, who had a little curl, right in the middle of her forehead. When she was good, she was very, very good. And when she was bad, she was horrid!" Our relationship was close and honest, in good times and in difficulties.

After I married and left the program, I posed several times for Edith's paintings and sculptures. The first was a sculpture after I became pregnant. I sat for her, remaining as still as possible. One day, she remarked that it was possible to be too patient. I took that as a metaphoric life lesson. After all, an excess of patience at a certain time in Edith's young life in Austria could be taken as appeasement, or agreement, or lead some to dire consequences.

Next came a family sculpture. Edith came to our apartment in the evening. I sat in a rocking chair nursing the baby while my husband stood close by watching over us. It was a very cozy time and Edith often stayed for dinner after our sessions. She was great company with a wonderful sense of humor. She could be especially irrepressible. When she first met my baby, she exclaimed, "Oh, she has those funny ears that stick out!" She also loved a double entendre, especially taken in a Freudian sense, and in mixed company. She did seem to love the company of men! Once, as she tried to use a drill, my husband Larry said, "Just shoot it in." Edith loved this, chuckled and repeated several times, "Yes, you love to shoot!"

When our first child, Anna, reached about four years old, she sat on the windowsill of our small apartment downtown and posed for Edith on her own, the twin towers of the World Trade Center jutting up in the background. Anna sat enthralled and very still as Edith painted because Edith told her a nonstop stream of children's stories, all the Brothers Grimm, French, and Russian fairy tales, and many folk tales. Edith knew these tales by heart, so well that she could easily focus on mixing colors and painting while she spoke. For older children, she would recite the *Iliad* and the *Odyssey*. She was surprised

168 *Patti Greenberg*

that Anna enjoyed the cruel and bloody tales the most, but suggested that the severe retribution, the evildoers getting their just punishments, was satisfying to a child. As long as the good characters were rewarded and the evil ones punished in the end, the tale was acceptable, even comforting to a vulnerable and powerless child. The tales from the Brothers Grimm especially presented this justice and order to the child's world. Edith suggested that, for children, fairy tales are precursors of myths, legends, and tragedies that are part of the adult world, and do not always end so justly or neatly. She loved the Grimms' but disdained Hans Christian Andersen's stories; his were tales of redemption or resurrection through personal sacrifice, rather moralizing and religious in tone. These stories did not meet the true nature or requirements of a fairy tale, and she felt should not be categorized as such.

Sometimes we each spoke of our childhoods. One statement that stood out was that Edith felt her own mother was sad. She said her mother used to watch the other young adults going out and having fun, and as she watched them, Edith felt her mother could have been yearning for freedom and happiness. This was Edith's perception, and perhaps played a part in her choice to stay single and become an artist. She considered her paintings to be her children.

Edith had a yearly Christmas party for friends and colleagues. Though she was Jewish, she was quite secular and this must have been a treasured Austrian tradition for her. She held it in her studio, where we could look at paintings and sculpture. It was a lovely event, especially for families and children. Edith dressed in a long skirt and crisp white blouse for the occasion. Everyone brought food and drink to share and small presents for Edith and the children. The highlight of the evening was lighting the tree. She always had a small, potted, live tree covered with paper, wax, and glass ornaments, and beautiful eggs she'd blown dry and dyed with a wax batik method the previous spring. The crowning moment came when she lit candles; yes, real candles attached to the tree (we always had a bucket of water close by). Then it was time to sing Christmas carols as the candles burned down. This was a beautiful, magical celebration, memorable for being on a natural and human scale, rather than the usual, over-the-top holiday extravaganza. She invited children of friends to dye eggs with her every spring as well (see Figure 23.1).

Edith was anchored in the beauty and rhythms of nature, the changing seasons, and the timeless traditions marking this. Every summer she happily returned to the mountains of her childhood to paint the landscape. These paintings are some of her most powerful and peaceful. She had fashioned a lightweight portable easel and paint box as part of a backpack, which she called a "rucksack," that she could carry on her hikes in the mountains. She stayed in a shepherd's hut at a fairly high altitude. People from her town looked in on her and helped with supplies. She said she felt like a little pony, trekking across the mountains. Edith took pleasure in her physical well-being, remaining active and exercising until the end of her life.

Though Edith was an exceptional diagnostician and therapist, and a major theorist and creator of art therapy, she identified as an artist. She never stopped working on her art and craved recognition for that. She chose an artist's life deliberately, and embraced her notion of what that meant as a lifestyle. Her material trappings were simple and spare. She had a studio in TriBeCa that became more valuable over time, but lived on the Lower East Side on Delancey Street in a small flat that somehow had the bathtub in the kitchen. She lived frugally, requiring nothing too expensive. Edith proudly shared a humorous story about a child dropping coins into her coffee cup, mistaking her for a homeless person.

My husband Larry, also a painter, a born and bred New Yorker, knew many stark and unusual spots for landscape painting. He invited Edith to paint in some industrial landscapes. Together, with their portable easels and paints, off they went, year round. They approached their work very seriously, so there were long periods of quiet. In one conversation, she asked him how he could give all this, meaning painting all the time, up. How could he tie himself down to a family and go to work daily to support his dependents? He took a moment, smiled, and said that he did it for love. She simply smiled back at him.

We sat for what turned out to be the last family portrait that Edith painted of us, in an old house in Brooklyn. We had recently moved in. The previous

Figure 23.1 Edith and Christmas tree. Photo from David Henley (no date)

occupants had renovated in the '60s, removing the floor of one room to create a dramatic cathedral ceiling, the height of two floors. Most people seeing it for the first time reacted in a positive way. As blunt as ever, Edith entered the house and declared quite disapprovingly, "Oh, this is so grandiose . . . Just awful!" She had a point. The change created more visual space which was pleasing, but did not provide any more practical, usable space. My daughter Anna, now six, and the new baby, Sonya, and I posed for her in Larry's painting studio. Edith managed to include him in the painting, though he wasn't physically present, by copying a small self-portrait he'd drawn, onto the wall behind us.

Before concluding, I just want to share a story from fellow art therapist Ellis Eisner. She took her husband to one of Edith's Christmas parties, with the real tree, real candles, and real handmade Ukrainian-style eggs for ornaments. Ellis's husband was very impressed with these beautiful eggs and asked how old her ornaments were. With a twinkle in her eye, and without missing a beat, Edith told him a gentleman should never ask the age of a lady's ornaments (the quintessential Edith moment!).

In one of Edith's classes, Psychodynamic Processes, she gave a personal example of perceiving the passage of time, and how this changes with age. She explained how difficult it was for a young child to wait. For a child to wait an hour would feel like an excruciatingly long year, but for her, in her early sixties, the repeating years seemed to fly by like hours. As I was thirty at that time, I hadn't really experienced this. Now, at the age she was then, I know and feel exactly what she meant. I miss her.

24 Formed Expression

David Henley

> Art is characterized by economy of means, inner consistency, and evocative power. Beyond such very general description, art defies definition.
>
> (Edith Kramer, 1971, p. 50)

Studying Under: On Mu Ch'i

At the end of my first semester at NYU, Professor Kramer asked to see me afterwards to discuss my request for an incomplete for the course, Psychodynamic Theory. Such an invitation did not bode well. Up in the university penthouse in the art therapy studio above Washington Square, I waited outside on the rooftop deck inhaling the early winter chill until the last of the students filed out. She began by stating, without formality or small talk, that after reading my draft, she found my topic overly ambitious and my request for an incomplete was granted. (An audible sigh.) However, she remarked that most students were writing on their first client observations, while I was taking on the art of an obscure 13th-century Buddhist Zen monk. The Ch'an (Zen in Japanese) Buddhist abbot Mu Ch'i painted only a few attributed monochromatic ink paintings but they are still revered after some 700 years, for these paintings are believed to reflect the artist's state of "sudden awakening." I struggled to bridge the concepts of self-awakening to sublimation using the sparse existing literature of the period. I cited Alan Watts (1975), who wrote how the process of meditation and Zen-inspired states of consciousness leads to a "dissolution of the ego," an idea, Kramer stated, that obviously did not square with ego psychology and drive theory. "One cannot lose the ego," she intoned – let alone attain the highest state of spiritual being – "without becoming autistic or psychotic."

The paintings of Mu Ch'i utilized rapid flourishes of calligraphic brushwork whose forms fade off into an expanse of a white void. The painting *Six Persimmons*, examined in my paper, is a striking work hailed as an icon by Ch'an monks, while outraging the literati of the time who dismissed his six fruits as eccentric and crude. Academic style in the Southern Song period was predominated by vistas of precisely painted villages, figures, grand mountains, misty

172 *David Henley*

rivers, and towering forests. As the Zen "Broken Ink" style was heretical to the Chinese academy, the work was spirited off to Japan in the 17th century. It remains hidden today in a sanctuary within the Daitoku-ji temple in Kyoto, considered too sacred to be seen by anyone but Zen abbots.

Deceptively simple in form and content, the painting depicts six circular forms tranquilly floating on a mottled ground, its tonal values varying from veiled transparency to a blue–black wash. The darkest center fruit seems to boldly confront the viewer, while the others trail off. I explained to Professor Kramer how the painting reflected the study of the Ch'an state of "no-mind," requiring the artist to wield the brush with minimal deliberation, and deceptive effortlessness. "Ya, ya . . .," Professor Kramer agreed somewhat impatiently, but to create such a work "implies an arduous building of ego structure . . . demanding years of intense discipline to achieve a rare state of reconciliation

Figure 24.1 Six Persimmons. Ink on paper by Mu Ch'i Fa-Ch'ang

between the drives." An avid painter of fruits and vegetables herself, she was intrigued with its economy as the artist could bring these fruits "fully alive." She mused that the degree of sublimation was so complete (she seemed to be speaking to herself now) "that all traces of libido and aggression were. . . ." Here, she reached for a word and I suggested meekly, "Transcended?" "No, in harmony. It was integration of the drives that resulted in the balance of tensions," she said emphatically. "However, it is possible the Eastern ego was perhaps more elastic in such a time and culture, permitting . . . then again," she paused, and I volunteered, "regression in the service of the ego?" Finishing the sentences of Professor Kramer was decidedly not the place of a first-year graduate student. Yet, far from losing patience, she seemed to retreat into her own thoughts, and we stood together, leaning upon the roof door left ajar – what Winnicott (1965) would term "alone in the presence of the other." She then turned and said "enough"; it was late. She would read on, and we would discuss my paper further at her studio.

While visiting the SoHo loft, Professor Kramer continued to comb through my revisions, which of course entailed waiting around long enough that, after several sessions, I noticed building and repair projects requiring attention. Painting racks were under construction and the bathroom vanity was unfinished, so I asked tentatively whether she'd like some help on the carpentry. Nonplussed, she nodded "sure," and so I began working. For the entire winter break, I sweated over this paper, while re-visiting the loft time and again. I continued to do the kind of studio carpentry she preferred: using recycled "street wood," found hardware, etc. I would also be invited to take breaks and to sit with her over tea. During these respites from the daily work routine, she would hold forth on any number of topics, depending upon what she was working on or reading. I brought up her ideas on the quality of art and *formed expression*, to which she responded, "Ah, art in the truest sense of the word."

Using *Six Persimmons* (Henley, 1980) as an example, she suggested how my descriptions reflected her definition quite adeptly: how six simple ink-washed fruits, their graduated values contrasting to their blue–black stems drawn sharply in a few decisive calligraphic strokes, were boldly "evocative." Their power was deeply moving, aesthetically and spiritually. This clearly "arose from and conveyed different feeling states," which I had struggled to put into words. Then there was the painting's strongest element, *economy of means*. I had written about how the work's vastness and strength were balanced by simplicity and restraint. Nothing more could be added to the work, she pronounced, "Yet, it would suffer if a single element was taken away." We agreed the six fruits were full of life, yet they were also fleetingly ephemeral, a problem for any still life painter, as organic subject matter goes by in the endless cycles of life. I had also written how Mu Ch'i's Zen style was contrary to the conventions of his academic contemporaries of the Southern Song Dynasty. "All this spoke to the monk's *inner consistency*," she said. I had written about how the literati rejected his spontaneous style, but he remained true to himself and his unique enlightened vision. With this dialog in hand, I felt I could revise once

174   *David Henley*

again, using the three criteria of formed expression to give needed structure to my jumbled ideas.

After the winter break, Professor Kramer had re-read and graded the paper. She wrote extensively, sharing thoughts, ideas, and criticisms, seemingly at times carrying on an inner dialog with herself as she explored this unfamiliar art form (see Figure 24.1). She wrote: "This is a very thoughtful paper," the highest praise I could imagine, and that she had learned much herself, an astonishing admission. Her critique required remarkable patience and fortitude. Through it all, she gave me a structure by which to frame my ideas on the analysis of art. It eased my overwrought writing style that suffers on to this day, offering greater organization and clarity.

Many more editing sessions were to come eventually when writing my master's thesis. Even after three years of study, there were seemingly endless revisions necessary, though I enjoyed frequenting the loft for editing, work, and tea. I refer to these sessions as "sitting beside," a term used by British art therapists to denote a kind of attuned presence. For sitting at her table was an experience in itself. This was no suburban dining table but more a "tableau": A collection of found objects – shells, skulls, sketches, letters from around the world, always blooms of flowers, the innumerable books, manuscripts in-progress, various ancient looking tools, loaves of Lithuanian bread from the Lower East Side. And, of course, there was her iconic tea set, replete with an oozing honey-pot that seemed to encase everything around it in solid amber. It was to become a ritual enjoyed by me as well as so many others through the years. The studio was a kind of salon where visitors from around the world would come to exchange ideas. Into her late eighties she remained a creative powerhouse where her own prolific works of art and letters flourished.

It was also a place of long silences. While she was working, nobody spoke. To become part of that atmosphere was an honor. For years, I continued to make myself useful by building and doing the rough studio carpentry that always seemed to be needed. Being with her, in that space, added a profound dimension to my life for, unbeknownst to me, this "sitting beside" would define our relationship for decades to come.

Museum Visits: On Velazquez

As I matured into the field in the late 1980s, I began to write more extensively for publication. Still tethered to her as my editor, she referred to me as a "terrible writer with great material." By then, I was Chair of Art Therapy/ Art Education at the Art Institute of Chicago, but as far as she was concerned, I was still her student. That was fine with me, and I would spend a good part of winter and spring breaks in NYC visiting "Edith" at the loft regularly. One of our rituals was to go to the Metropolitan Museum of Art for their extended-hours Friday-night program. In 1988, there was an important exhibition of Diego Velazquez, whose works had not been seen outside of the Prado, and Edith was excited to revel in the collection of 17 rare works. Visiting an art

Formed Expression   175

museum with Edith was not a casual affair. There was no breezing through the gallery, pausing at occasional works, and then lingering in the gift shop. It didn't matter if Edith had a companion, she would become lost in time, spending seemingly forever standing and analyzing, sketching, and speaking to herself about the paintings. More than once she drew a crowd around her to listen. For me, it was an endurance test; with a fatiguing mobility handicap, standing over the works for hours was not so easy – albeit, I did it countless times, as had many other friends and colleagues over the years, and it was always rewarding.

She seized upon one painting in particular, a portrait of one of the "court dwarves" of Philip IV, in the *Portrait of Sebastián de Morra* (1645). As with every other work in the collection, this painting possessed dazzling technical virtuosity. It consists of the dwarf, de Morra, sitting and eyeing the viewer, which I found particularly unsettling. It held a fascination for her, however, and lecturing to no one in particular, she started in on how dwarves were coveted "pets" of the palace court. But, she marveled at de Morra's countenance, an imposingly miniature presence, and despite being deformed, he was portrayed with dignity. In order to truly "know an artwork, one had to draw it," Edith would always say, and she practiced this as her hundreds of sketchbooks at the New York University Bobst Library Archives bear out. Students who studied under her will also attest that she'd have us copy client art as a means of intensifying our empathy and understanding for the artist.

Edith worked on two drawings from the painting, which technically was not permitted in special exhibitions because of the large crowds but, being a Friday night, no one bothered this elderly little lady with her sketchbook.

She worked with an unerasable gold, Prismacolor pencil, capturing every nuance of this powerful psychological portrait. Over tea the following morning I questioned her about Velazquez's portraying a single dwarf, which eagerly set Edith into analytical motion: "Though it is problematic to guess at one's intent," she began, Velazquez was perhaps making a statement that "de Morra was not as subjugated as others would believe." Although commonly considered a jester or demeaned as a sexual plaything within the court, Velazquez had imbued him with a fierceness and intelligence that would rival any courtier in the palace. His countenance conveyed the degree of leverage which he wielded over others in the court, given their secret intrigues and perversities. His quality of eye contact with the viewer – which was always a big deal with Edith both in art therapy training and in the art world at-large – seemed to directly challenge the viewer's assumptions of his position within the world. Perhaps this was "subterfuge," Edith suggested, since the King permitted such portraits in order to emphasize his own perfection compared to his subjects. However, Velazquez's portrayal could have been construed as challenging the King's superiority. But, Velazquez's painting at face value affirmed the King's greatness and devoutness. In musing over her two studies (See Figure 24.2), I wondered how her aesthetic of formed expression applied in this example.

176 *David Henley*

Figure 24.2 Drawings by Edith Kramer (no date). Copy of oil painting by Velazquez. *Portrait of Sebastián de Morra* (1645).

Velazquez's portrait was of uncommon choosing: A misshapen figure of ridicule transformed, via the artist's vision, into someone heroic that evoked a sense of respect, not sympathy. Despite being patronized, he rose to a position of social power and influence. The painting's economy of means closely follows its evocative power. Despite the depiction of fine clothing befitting the court, few other embellishments or props are present. It suffices that de Morra's direct outward gaze demands our attention. Lastly, Velazquez achieves inner consistency – given the thin line he treads as one who paints at the pleasure of the King. Philip required that his portraits be painted in the most favorable light. Yet Velazquez's genius lay in his ability to both placate and perhaps satirize his dull-witted patron, by injecting his own social commentary, all without violating the rules of his engagement. Velazquez has de Morra rise above the role of lowly court jester, and instead connects the viewer with a wider truth, a deeply felt empathy serving as a "symbolic equivalent" of hope for the whole of humanity. This, Edith said, was his monumental achievement – remaining

Formed Expression 177

true to himself and fully realizing his artistic vision, while taking personal and artistic risks.

After our discussion, I left for Chicago with a newfound sense of how one must "take the time of sitting beside the image" with deep probing and rigorous study. These were not the superficial and reductive pictorial interpretations I was witnessing being taught throughout the field of art therapy. Instead, images slowly yielded their meaning to those who delved and pondered. Formed expression, once again, served as a systematic means of unearthing the complexity and wonder of artistic truths, whatever form they may take.

Riefenstahl: Images over Ideas

By the early 1990s, I was back in New York appointed to a new position at Long Island University. Not long after, I was asked to open the AATA conference with a plenary session consisting of a video montage accompanied by a narrative prose poem (Henley, 1999). It was an honor for me, and I devoted a year to editing footage and writing the 30-minute segment. By this time, I was living part-time at the loft, from which I would commute to the university for my three-day commitment. Edith had ample time to observe my process if she chose, and she was well aware of how I was overworking the piece. It must have been an act of great restraint not to say anything negative, as any criticism could have shut down my already strained efforts.

The video poem was a dynamic mix of both the contemporary and historical, high and low art, and its intent was to push the limits of art expression: A soundtrack by Philip Glass, video of Margaret Mahler reciting from *The Psychological Birth of the Human Infant*, autistic clients painting to Stravinsky, elephants drawing in charcoal, Jackson Pollock dripping to the strains of Charlie Parker, and in the finale, a vintage cartoon of Donald Duck having a melt-down tantrum over opening a stuck window. Included was also a segment of my deaf students hip-hopping to the Beastie Boys, which of course they could not actually *hear*.

Imagine Edith having to sit through Glass, whose droning sounds irritated her to no end, as well as the thrumming Beasties. Everything was fair game, which of course ran counter to the formed expression doctrine, as my excesses rolled over economy of means by any measure.

At some point, I entertained the idea of including footage from Leni Riefenstahl's film *Triumph of the Will* (1935), a documentary of the Nazi Party Congress. Exploring material by Hitler's "favorite filmmaker" of course touched a nerve in Edith, for she was an Austrian Jewish schoolgirl in 1935 when the film was popular in theaters across Europe. In seeing how they glorified the children participating in the rally, I thought there might be some interesting material there. Edith lamented, "Yet another provocation."

Riefenstahl was considered to be a modern genius of filmmaking throughout Europe. The film won the gold medal at the prestigious Venice Biennale,

178 *David Henley*

thus affirming the art world's acceptance of the piece as high art. While viewing footage of the immense rally involving 150,000 participants marching by torchlight in Nazi regalia, we found it disturbing but also morbidly fascinating. I brought out an essay by Susan Sontag (1975) whose withering criticism of the film as "fascinating fascism" struck a chord; in Edith fashion, she read and then re-read Sontag's piece. It was amazing how Edith remained so dispassionate about this obviously emotionally charged material. To temper the horrific Nazi content we both focused on its formal elements – how Riefenstahl documented the rally with innovative camera angles, using helium balloons for aerial shots, and integrated audio with strains of Wagner, tolling church bells, all innovations in the art of documentary filmmaking. She even had the power to requisition every anti-aircraft light in Germany, crisscrossing the beams into the night sky, creating a "cathedral of light" for the Fuhrer to emerge from as if by way of heaven. The Reich had an artist that could turn a political spectacle into a pageant of messianic fervor with original formalistic brilliance.

As for formed expression, Edith and I marveled at its technical innovations, but Sontag's contention that it placed imagery over ideas relegated it to dressed-up propaganda. Edith stated that propaganda, whatever the agenda, is disqualified from being fully formed art because, at heart, it is disingenuous. As always, I played devil's advocate, posing the question, whether Velazquez was purely detached in his painting, or whether he was also advancing his own political and social agenda. Had he not made veiled references about the absurdity of court life masked by his technical virtuosity? She brooded over this example. What about political artists, the darlings of the political left? Is their intent not far from being propaganda? Edith stuck to the aesthetic criteria and said indeed, that even left-leaning political artists were also not exempt.

For the next 60 years, Riefenstahl never wavered in defending her work. Her intent was to create a work of "beauty and harmony." She had ignited the passions of an entire nation who, not long ago, were mired in dire poverty and political chaos. The film evoked newfound civic pride, emotional fervor, self-dedication, and sheer joy in countless millions. Yet, in the end, Riefenstahl had to know she was using and being used by the Nazis to gain a horrifying result . . . much greater than perhaps any artist in history. We were both in agreement with Sontag: Despite Riefenstahl's intention to create something inspiring and beautiful, the work was not art, not any more so than China's opulent opening to the Olympics in 2008. As Edith put it, "it may be artful, but spectacle is not art." Despite it being a seductive, powerful stimulus, its end result, the eventual genocide of millions, was enough for me to drop the film footage from the plenary session . . . probably to the relief of Edith.

An Adolescent Artist: The French Revolution

In 2007, both Edith and I were on the verge of retirement. She was nearly deaf and becoming more fragile. After a decade of being with and sharing the space

Formed Expression 179

around this remarkable woman, it was time for her to return to her ancestral home in Austria. Understandably, we began to go through her archives where she came upon a folder containing a series of 30 or so of her earliest surviving drawings: A series of illustrations about the French Revolution completed while a young teen. As a child, she was fascinated with this era – the Enlightenment was beginning to overlap with Romanticism, and science, poetry, art, and revolution were in the air, both in America and in France. This led to an unforgettable cast of characters including the decadent yet tragic Austrian child bride Marie Antoinette, Robespierre, and either hero of the revolution or maniacal murderer, the Marquis de Lafayette, prince of the Continental Army and confidant to General Washington.

As is the case with our aging elders, the image led her back to early life, reminiscing about the joys and sorrow that came with being a free-spirited child. She suffered in an authoritarian German boarding school, but was indefatigable in her lifelong passion for art. The great depression followed WWI, which further impoverished her already threadbare extended family, all of whom seemed to be actors, analysts, or artists. Her father, himself a Communist, had left the family to travel to Russia to witness this failed social experiment. This bohemian group tried escaping the darkness enveloping Europe by retreating to their family home on a glacial lake in the Austrian Alps. Eventually, greater tumult overtook them: the annexation of Austria into Nazi Germany, the persecution of Jews, the arrest of her mentor Friedl Dicker, as well as the death of her beloved mother. Then, at age 23, there was Edith's immigration to an uncertain future in a foreign country, America. For a teenager, the French Revolution offered an escape, where her young imagination could take refuge, though its story mirrored the same grim and seismically violent story of the times. Edith sublimated these travails by re-creating the chilling story, as adolescents are apt to do, in romanticized, soap-opera fashion. It is a precious collection that is remarkably preserved in the NYU Library Archives.

To offer a form-and-content reading of one's venerable mentor is not so easy. It was with a sense of wonder that I studied this collection, choosing one picture in particular, because she had commented on it during our discussions. Edith described the image as a depiction of King Louis XVI and Marie Antoinette during the time they were secretly fleeing Paris at the height of the Revolution in 1791.

The King's plan was a disaster from the beginning given his indecisiveness, including Marie's unwillingness to leave her son behind, as well as many delays and other mishaps. Only 30 miles from the safety of their royalist stronghold in Montmédy, a lowly postman ousted the King, recognizing him from a simple coin. The rest is history.

The couple is sensitively yet confidently drawn in a loose array of pen and ink line work. The wavering lines are scribbly, maybe even agitated. The two figures stand closely together, perhaps caught in an anxious moment. Were they debating their dangerous plans or had they already fled? Disguised as travelers, it must have galled them both to be without their big hair and

Figure 24.3 Drawing by Edith Kramer (1930) of King Louis XVI and Marie Antoinette

extravagant finery. Nevertheless, the King seems to be appealing to her, consoling or reassuring. An equally anxious or angry Marie looks away; her hands clasped tensely over the coming or past ordeal. The King's imploring expression heightens the tension, as he gestures to Marie perhaps in apologia, for their predicament, one that would eventually result in their capture, arrest, and, ultimately, death by the guillotine.

This adolescent drawing already holds true to the tenets of formed expression, even in a rapidly drawn sketch meant only for her. The quality of eye contact, hand gestures, the proximal space between the two characters, are all evocatively convincing. Emotions run high and tensions mount, but their relatedness is intimate given the King's stance behind what seems to be a

Formed Expression 181

hand-wringing Queen. Whatever the affect, it is conveyed to the viewer with an economy of energetic line work, illustrating just enough information to evoke the intensity of the moment. It is spare, loose, and yet fully replete. The anxiety conveyed is inwardly consistent as perilous events of historic proportions are being played out in the world. It is perhaps another instance of symbolic equivalence, as Edith was living through similarly treacherous times. The sketch gives us just a glimpse of the child's thoughts and feelings, yet we are fulfilled; it is a vision fully formed. In later life, this unusual child would mature into the fascinating woman we would come to know, and touchingly, make her wisdom and humor generously available for so many in the years to come. She was the rarest of gifts.

References

Henley, D. (1980). *Mu Ch'i: Six persimmons.* Unpublished manuscript.

Henley, D. (1999, November). *Psychological birth: A video poem.* Plenary session presented at the American Art Therapy Association Annual Conference, Orlando, Florida.

Kramer, E. (1930). *Kramer childhood artwork: The French Revolution: A homemade storyboard* (within Series V: Artwork). New York University Archives, New York, NY.

Kramer, E. (1971). *Art as therapy with children.* New York, NY: Schocken Books.

Riefenstahl, L. (1935). *Triumph of the will.* Documentary Film.

Sontag, S. (1975). Fascinating fascism. *The New York Review of Books, 22*(1). (February 6, 1975).

Watts, A. (1975). *Psychotherapy east and west.* New York, NY: Vantage Books.

Winnicott, D.W. (1965). The maturational processes and the facilitating environment: Studies in the theory of emotional development. *The International Psycho-Analytical Library, 64:* 1–276. London: The Hogarth Press and the Institute of Psycho-Analysis.

Edith Kramer's Concepts Applied to Practice

25 Edith's Legacy as Artist and Art Therapist in the Art Room

Martha Haeseler

In 1972, I attended a workshop given by Edith Kramer. The experience was riveting, striking my life like lightning, transforming and affirming my perceptions as no other; nothing was ever the same. Soon I was taking her class: Art as Therapy with Children. Edith believed in me, encouraged me to write, and became my mentor and friend. Eventually, she asked me to teach in her new graduate program at New York University, and we roomed and presented together at numerous art therapy conferences. Her teachings have profoundly influenced my career of 43 years as an art therapist and educator. My intent in this paper is to identify some of Edith's concepts, which have been essential to my work in psychiatric settings – inpatient and outpatient – with children, adolescents, adults, and veterans. I include many quotes from Edith's writings so you can hear her own words.

Arriving for Edith's class, we students found large paintings ranged around the room. Edith said, "These are miracles." In the presence of the miraculous, thirsty, I studied long and deep. It was fascinating to learn about the child artists, and Edith's thoughts about the artwork, but what I appreciated most was her comment; it showed deep appreciation for this artwork, and for the children in her care.

When Edith died, I reread her books as part of my own mourning process. Time after time, I experienced "aha!" moments, as I encountered affirmation for my instincts and manner of working, found deeper understanding of current clients, and realized how influenced I have been by Edith. I recommend that all art therapists go back to the well, reread her works, and see an amazing mind struggle with ideas, experiences, perceptions, emotions, and instincts, to create roots for the field we are lucky to reap harvest from today. There are miracles within.

Edith as Artist

Edith was first and foremost an artist and sketched, painted, sculpted, and more, every chance she could get. Art therapy and teaching were important

186 *Martha Haeseler*

to her as well; she was always striving to understand her experiences working with disturbed children in the light of her life-long learning and psychoanalytic understanding, and sharing her insights with others. However, she considered writing a chore and did not enjoy it, and spent every summer painting in the Austrian Alps. Never without her sketchbook, she continually created. At a conference in Las Vegas, she set up her paints and easel in the casino, as well as in the desert.

Edith's subject was always the life that teemed around her, including men working on machines, sewage treatment plants, portraits, children at play, intimate family scenes, still lifes with secret devils, and alpine meadows.

In 1944, during WWII, Edith had her second exhibition of paintings in New York. At the exhibition, Berthold Viertel said, ". . . the highpoint of Edith Kramer's essence is her joy in truth, her courage toward reality . . . representationalism is a new achievement for Kramer, like the self-clarity and courageous cohesion needed in a disintegrating time" (Zwiauer, 1997, p. 69).

Art and Nature

> I really do feel that today we have a new task, to celebrate that which is perishable and endangered and nourish and cultivate our capacity for experiencing our lives in this world.
>
> (Kramer, Foreword, this volume)

Although Edith often painted machinery, many of her urban and industrial landscapes included nature. One of her paintings of bombed-out London showed flowers growing out of the rubble. Her NY loft was full of treasures from the natural world: Plants, cones, twigs, stones, dried flowers, and shells covered her windowsills, and were subjects of many paintings. When I brought her some allium seed heads from my garden they soon turned up in a painting.

She wrote (Kramer and Wilson, 1998) that Albert, 11, a reckless fire-setter, wanted to paint a beautiful picture. Edith suggested he go outside and paint a fall tree, a project he had previously abandoned. He sketched the tree and came back with a trunk cut off at the crown. She sent him back out ". . . to observe exactly how the trunk divided into several main branches" (p. 32). When he returned he was able to paint the tree. This painting became one of Edith's "collection of miracles" (p. 28). She wrote:

> The confluence of powerful impressions coming from the natural world and corresponding inner experiences leads to the creation of a painting . . . at once an image of the artist's personality and an inspired interpretation of nature. . . . We perceive the aggressive force that had driven Albert to fire-setting . . . neither extinguished nor imprisoned,

but channeled into constructive expression, so we can . . . speak of sublimation.

(p. 34)

Subways

Edith sketched and sculpted many subway scenes, culminating in a large mosaic of the 14th Street Subway Station. Many of the paintings were of solitary figures, often sleeping, possibly homeless; the small sculptures usually depicted groupings of people. In one sculpture (Kramer, circa 1985), the people remind me of refugees with somber faces, carrying burdens. The metal circles above them make me think of the gas chamber. Perhaps Edith's exploration of people in subways was a way of working through memories of trains headed for Auschwitz. A closer look at the mosaic shows a dizzying disregard for perspective in the tracks and glimpses of people almost hidden behind the poles.

Figure 25.1 Ceramic figures in subway. Clay and metal sculpture by Edith Kramer

188 *Martha Haeseler*

Edith's Artistic Influences

After high school, Edith left her family in Vienna and went to Prague to assist her art teacher Friedl Dicker (later Dicker-Brandeis), giving art classes to child war refugees. Dicker had studied in the Bauhaus, an art and design program, a ". . . philosophy, based on the aesthetics of empathy. Its students were encouraged . . . to seek the subject's essence, to see it both inside and out, to become one with their subject, to empathize with it" (Elsby, 2012, para. 3).

One of Dicker's Bauhaus teachers was Johannes Itten, a charismatic mystic who believed "If new ideas are to take the shape of art, it is necessary to prepare and coordinate physical, sensual, spiritual, and intellectual forces and abilities" (Skukair, 1987, p. 10). He instructed his students to do large physical movements, rhythmic breathing, meditation, and fasting to prepare themselves to make artwork.

Edith wrote (2006) that Friedl embraced Itten's teaching methods:

> She would beat out various rhythms, calling them out in increasing and decreasing volume. She would have her students draw as quickly as she called out – rhythmic images, such as how bamboo grows in bursts – quickly, up and up, until the new leaves unfold.
>
> (pp. 11–12)

She said that Dicker gave her ". . . an understanding of a thing's essence and the non-acceptance of lies and manneredness" (*Black and White is Full of Color*, 1994).

In the US, Edith admired the work of Florence Cane, a psychologically-minded art teacher. Cane also believed that before making art it was important to stimulate the mind, emotions, and body, which the resulting art-making could help integrate. In *The Artist in Each of Us*, Cane (1983) described the importance of rhythm and breath, and had children make large motions in the air with chalk, before they made movements and marks on paper. She also introduced the scribble technique. She wrote: "The teacher . . . seeks to release the essential nature of the child and to let that nature create its own forms of expression . . . The integrity of the child is thus preserved, and the art produced is genuine, primitive, and true" (p. 34).

Similarly, Edith rarely gave art directives. Instead, she worked hard to make the art room a place where the child felt safe to work spontaneously on whatever came to mind: "When material is given form without strict adherence to prescribed patterns it inevitably takes on the image of its maker" (1971, p. 29).

Edith readily shared incidents from which she learned while working with disturbed children. In one incident (1977, pp. 145–147), a boy who often provoked hostility came to the art room upset because another boy had hit him. Edith suggested he paint a big fist, which all the boys proceeded to do: "The art therapy session deteriorated into a sadistic orgy . . . The boys had

Edith's Legacy as Artist and Art Therapist 189

shared in an entirely conscious sadistic fantasy. . . . Instead of sublimation there had been regression" (p. 145).

Even today, one of the core concepts of art therapy is to honor and have empathy for and support whatever images originate with clients; if we give suggestions to clients, we do so in empathic ways that promote their safety, mastery, and self-discovery. If clients are angry, we might encourage them to use the art materials in whatever way they think is helpful at the moment – giving the clay a workout, or soothing themselves with colors, or taking a walk – until they are ready to work on those strong feelings in the art.

Teaching Techniques

Edith thought every art therapist should be an artist to help the child with technical matters, but also to have a personal understanding of the artistic process that the child was experiencing, and ". . . to curb the burnout that comes with exhausting clinical work, by restoring our zest and identity through the joys of creative work" (Kramer, 2006, p. 26). She felt that artists were also more likely to have a passion for art and ". . . the capacity to enjoy the art of the children in their care" (p. 26). "The mutual pleasure that grows up between adults who love their field and children who are inspired by and identify with their mentor's enthusiasm is . . . one of many different ways . . . adults strive to mobilize children's energies for constructive work" (Kramer & Wilson, 1979, p. 261).

Applicants for the NYU art therapy program had to participate in an art-making session. Edith was particularly interesting in learning whether they could draw figures that were grounded, and could convey that the figures were interacting with and looking at each other. In her class, Art for Art Therapists, she taught a variety of techniques and empathy exercises. She wrote (2006), ". . . the NYU Method . . . the idea that a productive art experience was itself inherently therapeutic – so long as the art therapist has long practiced as an artist, intensively and with joy" (p. 24).

Edith did not write about techniques she used as an educator, but gave workshops around the world encouraging participants to use big motions and rhythms on paper. In a video (Makarova & Kuchuk, 2012), Edith talks about the rhythms in a basket, and uses her whole body to show the movements – in and out, in and out – to prepare for drawing a basket. In the 1972 workshop, she asked us to feel twigs she had cut in early spring, and imagine how they were going to grow when the buds opened, and then had us make them grow up the wall on mural paper. She also had us close our eyes, feel our faces, and with our eyes still closed, create a face in clay. I was amazed at the emotional resonance of this; the face that emerged was that of my mother, critically ill at the time.

Of these, the technique I have used the most with clients has been making large motions in the air, then making them on large newsprint paper. I used it as part of the Ulman Personality Assessment Procedure (1992), and also as

190   *Martha Haeseler*

a loosening-up exercise with individual clients, adults, and teenagers in my private practice and psychiatric settings, particularly when I felt someone was blocked in art in some way. After we made the motions together, I held the newsprint pad and people would keep scribbling with the charcoal on fresh pages until they were done. It was an effective way to help people work more spontaneously, and to realize that they could use their whole bodies in art-making, not just their hands. One young man, leaving a psychiatric unit, gave me a picture and wrote: ". . . I want to thank you for . . . teaching me that my hand is part of my arm which is tied to the heart . . ."

Joy in Truth

In 2012 Edith said, "In art comes the truth, in a way that catches you immediately, not intellectually" (Makarova & Kuchuk, 2012). She wrote about art and truth many times:

> in order to produce valid art the adult's creative work must be beyond the reach of any defense mechanisms which would interfere with the perception of truth. This entails considerable moral courage . . . such art has the power to move us deeply.
>
> (Kramer & Wilson, 1979, p. 10)

Some early critics thought that Edith wanted clients to produce "good art," and that in art therapy the process, not the product, was important. Indeed, Edith (1971) wrote abundantly on the subject of ". . . the Problem of Quality in Art" (pp. 47–66), but she devotedly accepted whatever her clients produced, while conveying to them that they were capable of more. She felt that process craves a product, and they were intertwined. She hoped her clients would achieve artwork that would enable them to express and gain some mastery over the inner conflicts that were torturing them and interfering with their development. She wrote, ". . . the *miracle of art* . . . depends on the arduous creation of new objects whose sole function resides in their symbolic meaning" (Kramer & Wilson, 1979, p. 48). She felt that this ability to give symbolic voice to inner experiences promoted maturation in general. She called (1971) such artistic miracles "formed expressions" that possessed the qualities of "economy of means, inner consistency and evocative power" (p. 50).

I have observed that when clients are given plenty of time, a safe space, and art materials of quality, they will find ever-increasing abilities to make art that has coherence and resonates with their inner experiences.

Relating to Clients in the Art Room

Edith's teachings that have influenced me the most have to do with the relationship between art therapist and client. Edith would go all out to help the children in her care in any way needed. She wrote (1971), ". . . the art therapist

Edith's Legacy as Artist and Art Therapist 191

may have to bring his whole creative imagination and artistic experience to bear upon the problem of helping a child . . ." (p. 120). When working with one blind child she figured out how to help him make life-size figures with wire and foam rubber (1971, pp. 97–103), and to help another she first learned how to make armatures to support life-size clay figures and cast them (Kramer & Gerity, 2000, p. 145). Here (1971), she invites her reader to observe

> how the therapist speaks to the child in the language of the medium, respecting the specific problems that arise in the making of a piece of work, empathizing with the child's style, bearing with him until the work is completed.
>
> (p. 120)

Regarding the art therapist's approach, Edith (1971) wrote: "Nothing is more important than to observe the child's moods" (p. 147). She sought to develop therapeutic alliances with children, to become an auxiliary ego for them and support their strengths. In this, she hoped to minimize destructive transferences, and wrote "In art therapy . . . [transference] material should be expressed insofar as possible in the art work rather than in the relationship" (p. 40). She thought it was helpful when children identified with her as a potent art-maker, and borrowed her strengths.

Edith freely admitted to times when, after the fact, she realized she was acting on countertransference feelings. In one of these (1971), she angrily shook a child when he destroyed his caricatures of the school directors; he responded in a sexual manner (p. 41). She teases out the dove-tailing of his transference and her own countertransference feelings: "It is permissible, even essential, to draw upon one's childhood in order to better understand the child. However, an identification that is not consciously experienced may impede our understanding and open the door to irrational behavior" (p. 42). In a later book (Kramer & Wilson, 1979) she devotes a section to countertransference, and gives examples of when awareness of one's own countertransference feelings ". . . can sometimes yield valuable information about the meaning of a child's behavior" (p. 204). However, "To observe one's countertransference reaction can itself become a narcissistically invested preoccupation that constitutes yet another aspect of countertransference" (p. 206).

Throughout her writings and teachings, Edith taught us the importance of caring for and supporting children and their works unconditionally. Additionally, she emphasized the therapeutic power of relationships among the children in her group: "No adult's empathy or encouragement can engender quite the same mutual inspiration, understanding, and creative fervor that characterize such groups of children when they are functioning at their best" (Kramer & Wilson, 1979, p. 164). I would say that, in the art groups I have facilitated, the single most therapeutic factor has been the atmosphere of caring and mutual respect that develops between everyone present; this creates the safe space within which creativity and emotions can flow.

192 *Martha Haeseler*

Talking about Artwork

An early dichotomy in art therapy supposedly developed between those who felt the therapy occurred within the process of making the art – *art as therapy* – and those who felt that art-making was a springboard for gaining insight by talking – *art psychotherapy*. I believe this dichotomy is artificial, because art therapists encounter many clients who find talking about the artwork beneficial, and many who have difficulty talking about the art. Most traumatized people do not have easy access to traumatic material through words, and for some people words are shields against their inner experiences. In 2006, Edith wrote, "The difference between art as therapy and art psychotherapy perhaps has more to do with the age group and social environment of the individuals under our care" (p. 20).

Most art therapists will do whatever is most useful for the client. Edith's main point, the cornerstone of our work, is that whether or not people talk about their art work, the art-making itself is the therapy that can profoundly change lives.

There is a myth that Edith discouraged talking with children about their artwork. In fact, she talked quite a bit as children worked. However, when she "attempted to discuss their problems or their pictures, they would cry out 'Stop preaching, Mrs Kramer!'" (2006, p. 20). "Our comments can be integrated best when we offer them in response to a child who spontaneously talks to us about his work" (Kramer & Wilson, 1979, p. 253).

She cautions: ". . . the art therapist . . . will not, as a rule, directly interpret unconscious meaning, but he will use his knowledge to help the child produce art work that contains and expresses emotionally loaded material" (1971, p. 34). She urges art therapists to

> maintain a balance between ego support and respect for the child's need for unmolested introspection . . . only what emerges within an ambiance of supportive but nonintrusive contact can feel real to the person who brings it forth, for he has achieved it himself.
>
> (Kramer & Wilson, 1979, pp. 102–103)

In 1958, she wrote: "The art therapist's actions and attitudes . . . [conveyed] to the children the feeling that the unconscious meaning of their efforts was understood and accepted, without bringing more of the problem to consciousness than they could tolerate" (p. 71). She cautions: "Truth can be expressed in a manner that has intense reality and profoundly touches the core of the child's being and yet circumvents the stark finality of the spoken word . . . some truth must be kept at just the right distance . . ." (Kramer & Wilson, 1979, p. 157).

These concepts have been important in my work, especially with traumatized veterans. When a revelation comes, wait until the artist discovers it – sit on your wisdom. For example, a Vietnam veteran with PTSD did a series of rigid but more and more intensely colored drawings. Finally, he did a water-color with color flying all over the paper; it looked like an explosion. In the next session, he painted a beautiful pond scene, and under the water's surface, the wide-open mouth of a fish. He said it was a triggerfish, "the most vicious fish in the sea, with needle-sharp teeth; it pierces shells and sucks out their life. But it's its nature, it's not doing anything bad, it's doing what it's supposed to do." I wondered whether he was drawing an analogy, that things he did in Vietnam might have been vicious, but were not his fault, since he was supposed to do them. However, I kept these thoughts to myself. In the next session, he picked up a conch shell from the table, and started drawing it. He ended up with fragmented pieces of the shell drawn all over the paper. The next session, he did a portrait of the shell, whole. The next session, he drew the same beautiful pond scene, but without the fish, and painted across the bottom: "Tranquility." If I had asked him about the triggerfish at the time, we would have had a good talk, but I don't believe he would have spontaneously taken the opportunity to do the reparation that he needed to do, in breaking apart the shell and then making it whole again, to attain the tranquility.

Anticipating Current Therapies

Edith's work anticipates positive psychology. Have you noticed how many quotes from and about Edith refer to joy, pleasure, strengths? ". . . herein lies the power of art – all the children took great pleasure in making their work, whether or not its content was painful" (Kramer & Wilson, 1979, p. 15). She said that in art therapy "you very often find the strengths rather than the pathology" (Makarova & Kuchuk, 2012). Edith reminds us to maintain our own positive attitudes, "To work with dedication and spirit rather than under a cloud of depression . . ." (Kramer & Wilson, 1979, pp. 157–158).

Edith also anticipated cognitive therapies, as seen in this analysis (1971):

> Margaret must learn to distinguish between genuine hostility and benign controlling action that feels to her like an attack because it makes her angry. She must differentiate between angry responses which her aggressive behavior provokes and anger vented against her or reasons that originated in the aggressor. She must learn to modify her responses in accordance with these distinctions . . . Later she may attempt to tame the lion.
>
> (p. 168)

When she was nearly 90, Edith wrote (2006):

> My task remains to paint and sculpt the world around me with humility, vigor, and truthfulness: To depict both the horrors and the beauty of our world in a way that does poetic justice to the reality that surrounds me. If you live long enough, good things will come.
>
> (p. 28)

References

Black and White is Full of Color [Video file]. (1994). Israel: Argo-film. Retrieved from http://makarovainit.com/friedl/home.html Accessed 19 September 2017.

Cane, F. (1983). *The artist in each of us* (Rev. ed.). Craftsbury Common, Vermont: Art Therapy Publications.

Elsby, L. (2012, March). Coping through Art – Friedl Dicker-Brandeis and the children of Theresienstadt. *The International School for Holocaust Studies.* Retrieved from www.yadvashem.org/yv/en/education/newsletter/27/coping_art.asp Accessed 19 September 2017.

Kramer, E. (1958). *Art therapy in a children's community: A study of the function of art therapy in the treatment program of Wiltwyck School for Boys.* Springfield, IL: Thomas.

Kramer, E. (1971). *Art as therapy with children.* New York: Schocken Books.

Kramer, E. (1977). *Art therapy in a children's community: A study of the function of art therapy in the treatment program of Wiltwyck School for Boys.* New York: Schocken Books.

Kramer, E. (Circa 1985). [Ceramic]. Retrieved from www.edithkramer.com/ws01_s.html Accessed 19 September 2017.

Kramer, E. (2006). Edith Kramer, Art as Therapy. In M.B. Junge & H. Wadeson (Authors), *Architects of art therapy: Memoirs and life stories.* Springfield, IL: Charles C. Thomas.

Kramer, E., & Gerity, L.A. (2000). *Art as therapy: Collected papers.* London: Jessica Kingsley Publishers.

Kramer, E., & Wilson, L. (1979). *Childhood and art therapy: Notes on theory and application.* New York: Schocken Books.

Kramer, E., & Wilson, L. (1998). *Childhood and art therapy: Notes on theory and application* (2nd ed.). Chicago, IL: Magnolia Street.

Makarova, E., & Kuchuk, H. (Directors). (2012). *Edith Kramer, Art Tells the Truth.* [Video file]. Israel: LenFim Studio. Retrieved from https://vimeo.com/33476299 Accessed 19 September 2017.

Skukair, K. (1987). Johannes Itten: Master teacher and pioneer of holistic learning. *Marilyn Zurmuehlin Working Papers in Art Education, 6*(1), 84–94.

Ulman, E. (1992). A new use of art in psychiatric diagnosis. *American Journal of Art Therapy, 30*(3), 78–88.

Zwiauer, C. (1997). *Edith Kramer: Malerin und Kunsttherapeutin zwischen den Welten* [Edith Kramer: painter and art therapist between worlds]. Vienna: Picus Verlag.

26 Hector

A Case Study Illustrating Edith's Teachings

Martha Haeseler

> For every work of art holds within itself a secret story, matter concealed even from the awareness of the creator, which influences the choice and arrangement of pictorial symbols.
>
> (Kramer, 1993, p. 50)

Hector's secret story emerged in his artwork gradually over eight years, as I worked with him in the Giant Steps Program, a long-term outpatient psychiatry program in a VA Medical Center. Attending an art therapy group two mornings a week, and later a garden group as well, Hector did important work to discover and share his secrets, thereby ameliorating crippling symptoms caused by severe childhood trauma. I found that many of Edith's concepts applied to Hector's experiences with art-making, with the group, and with his relationship with me.

I was fortunate to have unlimited time to work with Hector. Edith often emphasized the importance of allowing clients to make their own self-discoveries, at their own pace, and not pushing for premature self-disclosure. Edith's discussion of "truth" seemed especially relevant:

> Truth can be expressed in a manner that has intense reality and profoundly touches the core of the child's being and yet circumvents the stark finality of the spoken word . . . some truth must be kept at just the right distance, close enough so that there will be no splitting of the personality into an acceptable part and another hidden, rejected one, yet sufficiently disguised, displaced, and distanced to prevent causing massive despair.
>
> (Kramer & Wilson, 1979, p. 157)

Before coming to the VA, Hector spent 34 years drinking and abusing drugs. When he was a child, despite growing up in an orphanage and experiencing sexual abuse, he played the trombone and guitar and liked to sketch. He did no creative activities during the decades of drinking.

In Giant Steps he revealed himself to be a man with many strengths. He learned to paint and sculpt, resumed playing the guitar, learned to play both classical and Native American flutes, and wrote prose and poetry. Consistently

196 *Martha Haeseler*

productive, he created artwork at home as well as in the group. He gave away and sold many paintings. He had a generous nature and went out of his way to be supportive of group members. At times, he found it hard to paint in the group but kept working at home. His problems came mostly at night, when his PTSD and schizoaffective disorder showed up in torturous nightmares and a voice that told him to do bad things, such as drink and hurt himself. Often he had racing thoughts, and problems relaxing and comforting himself. He appeared younger than his age (50s).

Hector and I presented his artwork together at an American Art Therapy Association conference (Haeseler, 2011). In Giant Steps discussions, he spoke freely about his artwork, but reviewing his artwork prior to the presentation brought him additional insights.

Early Works

One of his first works was a drawing of a child blowing a bubble, entitled *Just Like a Kid, Be What You Are*. At first, knowing that Hector had suffered abuse as a child, the image had great poignancy for me. I thought he was creating what Edith described as a "symbolic equivalent for experience," creating a carefree childhood he never had. However, coming to know Hector better, I believe that as a child he had resilience and love of life despite the abuse. When he reviewed his artwork, he said, "While drawing this I was a kid for a moment. When I do artwork I am in the moment, away from my symptoms and disability."

His other early drawings were in colored pencil. One shows him holding a Bible. When reviewing this artwork, he said, "this picture was important to me. When you are early in recovery, you have to grasp at something, and I grasped hard at religion."

Other self-portraits seem related to establishing identity: Hector with his guitar; Hector as a tree. He was not allowed to speak Spanish in the orphanage, and felt deprived of his native tongue. In Spanish, his last name means, "tree." Here he is identifying with and deriving strength from the mighty oak. He said, "Trees are part of my spirituality. They do more than endure through the winter; they burst forth and have their own dance."

Hector learned to paint, and a striking early work shows boats at rest in a harbor at sunset. In another, *In Celebration of Earth Day*, Hector painted himself as a tree, playing the flute, and a wise man nearby was sending prayers to the spirits. He said it represented his connection to the beauty of the world and his Taino (Puerto Rican Native) roots. He said Taino believe in the importance of protecting Mother Earth, and that he was no longer Catholic, more interested in Taino spirituality. The concept of Mother Earth was to become important in later works.

Sublimation

Some years later, when Hector brought in a painting he had done at home when he was very angry at someone, I was reminded of Edith's words (1993),

Hector: A Case Study 197

"Art can absorb and contain more raw affect than most other equally complex and civilized endeavors" (pp. 185–186). Hector said, "I was in an absolute rage, but I didn't get in trouble; I used to get arrested and thrown in jail when I was angry. It is wonderful to get command of your anger and express it in a painting." The painting, entitled *War Path*, showed some Native Americans furious because someone had cannoned their canoe. He hung it by his bed and said that when he was angry he would look at the painting and be able to release some of the anger. When reviewing the art, he said he learned that controlled anger is powerful, a tool you can use, as Gandhi and Martin Luther King did. In this painting, Hector handled the paint in a very spontaneous, almost abstract way.

Edith defined "drives" as ". . . blind forces charged with undifferentiated libidinal and aggressive energy . . . [that] push toward immediate discharge . . . in nonrational actions that threaten to destroy the individual and his society" (Kramer & Wilson, 1979, pp. 77–78). Hector was learning that the intense anger that had driven him to harm himself and others over many years could be channeled into a painting that he would feel good about. Edith described this process as sublimation, which ". . . serves a specifically human need to find ways of postponing instinctive gratification and channeling drive energy . . . the pleasure generated in the new activity [is] exceptionally great" (ibid., p. 78).

Another interesting comment by Edith seems to apply here: "Affect welling up from within seems frequently to find expression at the bottom of pictures . . ." (ibid., p. 241). In the painting *War Path*, the broken canoe, which can be seen as phallic, is at the bottom of the picture.

He entitled a subsequent painting *Lighthouse Dawn*. The lighthouse, beaming light into a dark sky, sits high on rocky cliffs, and a close look at the rock formations seems to show a malevolent eye, also toward the bottom of the picture. There is a boat in the harbor, and another at sea. In reviewing this painting, Hector said he was on the boat foundering in the storm, and the lighthouse was Giant Steps, which would bring him safely home to shore. He said, "When I am feeling at sea, and it's cold and rough and dark, all I have to do is look for the lighthouse and follow its light. It reminds me that when I feel lost I am not, I am part of a community." These comments show the depth of his connection to the group. In this painting he portrays both light and dark, a problem and its solution. A theme has emerged, from boats safe in the harbor, to a canoe being destroyed, to a boat at risk that can see the way to safety. It is interesting that a Navy man would use boats to depict strong feelings.

Identification

Giant Steps included a garden group, which created and maintained many gardens at the VA. Hector started working in the gardens with me and eventually spent many hours a week caring for them. He said that in the garden he forgot his PTSD, and just wanted to nurture the plants. His pleasure in gardening was obvious. Additionally, I thought that his growing relationship with me and

198 *Martha Haeseler*

identification with my love of plants added another layer to this pleasure. I recalled that Edith wrote of the therapeutic importance of identification: "Identification with me supplanted demands for direct nurturance and love. Identification in turn stimulated maturational processes . . ." (Kramer & Wilson, 1979, p. 211).

Transference

Edith thought that transference should interfere with art-making as little as possible, and wrote (1993) that working through transference relationships was part of psychotherapy, but in art therapy transference could be worked through in the artwork (p. 40). Hector had a strong, mostly positive transference to me, as is shown in a round painting entitled *Aunt Martha's Autumn Heirloom*. It is an idealized harvest scene, with a purple house and baskets of flowers and pumpkins. He said autumn is his favorite season, and he imagined that my house would look like the painting; he hung it in his kitchen. On a closer look, the brightly colored fall trees have a fiery intensity, almost seeming to engulf the house. Much later, after a symptomatic episode, he revealed to his clinician and me that sometimes he was tortured by voices telling him to slit Martha's throat. I was never afraid of him. In painting my house, he combined images of idealized beauty and nurturance with those of fire and engulfment, so I could see he could channel the intensity of his ambivalent transference feelings into his artwork and contain them, as Edith recommends.

The Secret Story

Soon he painted another colorful fall scene, a landscape. I commented that he kept deepening the intensity of the colors; he said the painting reminded him of the Catholic Boy's Home where he grew up, which was in a beautiful countryside. They had horses and gardens there, but the beauty was misleading; there was darkness under the beauty. He entitled the painting, *A Not So Wholesome Place*. This painting, also contrasting beauty with something frightening, stands in contrast to the VA gardens, a very wholesome and conflict-free sphere for him.

In the next few pieces of artwork, Hector departed from his usual realistic style to create intensely personal pieces.

One day, he set up an easel by my desk, and started painting a wall. A face soon emerged from the wall. In discussing the work with the group, he said this was the face that came out of his wall every night and told him to hurt himself. He said he thought that if he painted it he would have some control over it, some power. He told it: "You can't hurt me." Waiting for the group to be over, I asked him if the face reminded him of anyone. He said yes, that it was the face of the priest who had sexually abused him from the ages of 7 to 12. He said the priest would give him wine, which was the beginning of his

Figure 26.1 He Preyed at Dusk and Prayed at Dawn. Painting by Hector

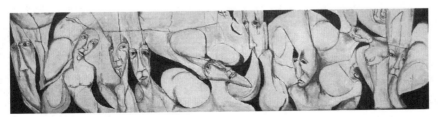

Figure 26.2 Priests and Nuns in Catholic Heaven. Painting by Hector

200   Martha Haeseler

substance abuse. He tried to tell the nuns, but they would not listen. He said that making this painting gave him power over the predator and he named it *He Preyed at Dusk and Prayed at Dawn*.

A week or so later he brought in a painting entitled *Priests and Nuns in Catholic Heaven*. He said the priests' mouths are missing because they said unspeakable things. The nuns' breasts are bared because they covered everything up. He said that when he was little the nuns told him he had to confess his sins to the priest. Hector said "I didn't do anything wrong." The nuns put him in a chest and closed the top, saying he could come out when he confessed his sins. So he learned to make up sins.

Hector told me that some years ago he bought himself a large cedar chest, but could not bring himself to use it for storage as he had planned. He put it in the closet for many months and would shake when he looked at it. One day, he decided to get into the chest, and lie there. After that, he brought it into his bedroom and started using it to store his sweaters. Taking the decisive action to enter the frightening territory enabled him to detoxify the fears. I believe he did the same with his paintings – entered frightening territory so he could move beyond it.

His next painting, *Spiritual Rape,* is a good example. There is a child-like naked homunculus suspended in the center of chaos. He said it was exactly how he felt when he was being sexually abused, as if he were an alien, his innocence strangled by his umbilical cord, ashamed and afraid. He said, "I used to think the abuse was my fault, because I came to enjoy the wine." I found it interesting that he described the umbilical cord as strangling him (in the painting it is floating in the air). I thought this might have something to do with his mother, and might explain the ambivalence in his transference toward me. Instead of asking him about it, I waited to see what would evolve in his artwork.

Six months later, Hector decided to enter his last three paintings as *Redemption Trilogy* in the VA National Arts Competition and wrote the following artist's statement:

> In writing this essay, I seem to have the same trembling of hand as I had when I started to paint on canvas my vision of my torturous childhood. To this day, I don't know what affected me most; loss of innocence; theft of my cultural heritage; or the sexual depravity. The physical aspect was very bad. To this day, I sometimes cringe when being touched. The emotional, mental, and spiritual aspects were far worse; I remember as a child feeling so alien when I left the rectory still smelling the fetid breath and alcohol of the predator. At night I relive the horror as if it happened yesterday. That is my PTSD.
>
> These three paintings represent a safe and nondestructive outlet for my anger and rage. The first is the face of the predator and it exhibits the hypocrisy of prayer in the mouth of one who preyed on the innocent. The second is the predators suffering in their own private hell. The priest has no mouth because he did the unspeakable; the nuns are uncovered because

they covered up the crimes. The third is about how alien I felt. Painting these has been a redemption for me.

Painting these, in some odd way, provides me with power and strength. It gives me a feeling that I am not alien but very human indeed and that it was not my fault and that I can regain my dignity if not my innocence and begin to heal in some small way. It gives me hope that maybe someday I will be well again and whole and complete, with peace and no more rage; and be able to be embraced and not cringe and not be haunted night after night by the monster that is PTSD. It seems painting and writing about it give me power and peace and a much needed outlet to express in a positive way deep-seated feelings that disturb me in a profound way.

He was interviewed by a newspaper reporter, and talked openly about his works and his abuse. He said it helped him get the secret out and feel less alone.

Next, Hector turned to sculpture, creating a large mummy head with chicken wire covered with clay. He wanted to be sure it looked as if the head were wrapped in cloth. It seemed to be an expression of how powerless he felt when trapped in the sexual abuse, and in the nun's box. When reviewing this piece, Hector said, "When I told the nuns 'Father is touching me,' they smacked me in the face and told me 'shut your mouth, you liar!' This mummy has no eyes, ears, nose or mouth, that is how I felt."

The next thing he created was a clay head, which he described as *A Proud African Man;* he has all his features and holds his head high. Perhaps making the mummy and identifying with an image of powerlessness enabled Hector to move on to identify with an image of wholeness, pride, and ethnic identity.

My Earth Mother

While reviewing his artwork for our presentation, Hector told me that he was taken to the Catholic Boy's Home when he was four, because his mother could not care for him and his father was not part of his life. His mother had asthma and was psychotic. Hector had no memory of the time before the Catholic home. The nuns said, "Now you belong to us," and would not let his mother visit because they deemed her unfit. His mother fought for years to be able to see her sons. The next time the brothers saw their mother, Hector was 11, and she seemed like a stranger. There was a point, after the Navy, when he lived with her, but he was angry with her most of the time. One day, when he returned to the apartment after buying drugs, he found she had died from an asthma attack. He said he had suffered unspeakable guilt since. I said that I thought his mother must have loved him, since he turned out to be such a resilient and caring person. Edith wrote something similar about a child, "We must assume that his mother had given him some measure of warmth and love . . . Without a foundation of positive real-life experiences Sidney could not have reintegrated so easily . . ." (Kramer & Wilson, 1979, p. 127).

202 *Martha Haeseler*

He went on to say that when he was 12, he was transferred to another boys' home. Before he left he was told by his abusers "Better not tell, or we'll put you in the delinquent home." He feels that was the seed of his PTSD. The new home was benign, but he started drinking regularly. When he was 18, he was discharged from the home and told never to return. He was given a job and an apartment but was devastated; he had never lived alone and was ill-equipped to cope with life and his symptoms. He felt so disenfranchised that he enrolled in the Navy. He liked it in the Navy, but continued to drink. After missing his boat three times, they told him they wanted to discharge him honorably, but if he chose to stay and continue drinking, he would be booted out with no benefits. He chose the honorable discharge and became eligible for VA treatment, which helped him decades later.

After talking about his mother, Hector made a small clay piece he entitled *Mother and Child*. The piece was stylized and somewhat chilling, with a garment shrouding a mother holding a baby, and holes where their heads would be. Hector was happy with it, however. He said making it helped him feel close to his mother and loved.

His next work was a clay head entitled *African Princess*. She had a face, but her eyes were closed. I thought of Edith's quote, "The substantial quality of clay . . . makes it a good medium for restoring what has been lost" (Kramer & Wilson, 1979, p. 254) and I thought that Hector might have been trying to recreate his lost mother's image. This quote of Edith's seemed to apply as well:

> His anger at her desertion, his confused and sadistic fantasies about the nature of her illness . . . his longing and grief all energized the act of making her image. . . . This helped him endure the separation . . . to keep her image whole. . . . We observe insatiable infantile demands transformed into protective tenderness.
>
> (ibid., p. 109)

After the four sculptures, Hector returned to painting. He started with a desert where a Native American woman is sitting by an empty bowl; we see her profile looking into the distance. He then painted the woman in the desert again, now standing, with the bowl on her head, and we see more of her face. He entitled it *In Celebration of my Earth Mother*. He said he missed his mother very much, but the painting helped him feel her presence.

His next painting was entitled *Mother and Child*. He said it was he, as a baby, being comforted in the sweep of his mother's embrace. He said he had tried out a new technique, sponge painting, and was pleased with the lightness he attained. A swirl of blue surrounds the warm embrace. Edith refers to blue as the ". . . color of heaven and of control . . ." (ibid., p. 107). His mother's Madonna-like robes, and the sun in the shape of a cross, might suggest some resolution of his spiritual conflicts. He said that for years he had felt guilt over his anger at his mother, especially before her death. He said that doing the series of three paintings restored his mother to him.

Figure 26.3 Mother and Child

Edith (1993) could have been describing Hector's work when she wrote:

> creating an image of infantile bliss led to a developmental spurt towards independence and masculinity. We see . . . art's power for symbolically restoring a lost object. I believe that such restitutions are usually possible if the child has somewhere in his life experienced some measure of gratification. . . . When these children later encountered other warm and understanding people and also received assistance in coming to terms with the emotional conflicts that centered around the original love objects, they could in their art create symbols of the positive aspects of these early experiences.
>
> (p. 219)

Within the supportive Giant Steps group and the positive therapeutic alliance with me, I believe that Hector found "warm and understanding people" and

204 *Martha Haeseler*

"assistance in coming to terms with the emotional conflicts that centered around the original love objects." Through his artwork and identification with an art therapist/gardener whom he perceived as caring and effective, he could work on ethnic and spiritual identity, deal with anger, identify and detoxify memories of sexual, physical, emotional, and spiritual abuse, and restore the lost inner representation of his loving mother. Hector stayed in Giant Steps for another two years, and continued to garden and paint. When I announced my retirement, Hector made plans to move to another city. He came back for my retirement party and said he had made a good connection with an art therapist and an artist's housing program in that city. Hector and I continue to engage in the arts and to thrive, inspired by Edith's supportive teachings and life lessons.

References

Haeseler, M. (2011, July). *Group art therapy with veterans with posttraumatic stress disorder (PTSD) and psychiatric challenges: A nondirective approach.* Paper presented at the 42nd Annual Conference of the American Art Therapy Association, Washington DC.

Kramer, E. (1993). *Art as therapy with children.* Chicago, IL: Magnolia Street.

Kramer, E. & Wilson, L. (1979). *Childhood and art therapy: Notes on theory and application.* New York: Schocken Books.

27 Understanding Lineage, Difference, and the Contemplative Dimensions of Edith Kramer's Art as Therapy Model

Michael A. Franklin

I will never forget the first time I met Edith Kramer. I was a young graduate student at The George Washington University (GWU) in 1979 in her Freudian theory of art therapy class. Between her modest attire, Austrian vocal tone and cadence, and reputation as an author and artist, I was thoroughly captivated by her presence. The class was rich in content and also a few jokes. For example, she surprised us all by nonchalantly talking about male anatomy, gender envy, and how boys can write their names in the snow while urinating. We all nervously laughed while squirming a bit; I know I did, unsure of how to read this pioneer in the field. This was my first lesson on how to listen to and study Edith's work. That is, her *art as therapy* model held significant theoretical ground, whereas her interpretations were often heteronormatively tethered to Freudian orthodoxy – more on this later.

After the end of the first day of class, by accident, Elinor Ulman bit her tongue while eating. Since she was on blood-thinners for her heart condition, her mouth was slowly pooling blood. They needed a driver, so off to the emergency room we went. While Elinor was seeing the doctor, I was sitting with Edith in the waiting room. Bolted on the wall was a color TV turned to some innocuous channel. Out of nowhere, Edith exclaimed in a surprisingly loud voice that the colors on the screen were a lie – green she said, does not look like that! While seriously critiquing the falsehood of the emerald, jade, and lime shades before us, Edith was showing me how to see the ingrained consensus reality of my perceptual habits. In this moment, she shared her unique way of seeing, revealing alternative ways of perceiving. Although slightly mortified by her outburst, I secretly liked the feeling of waking up from my acculturated, visual illiteracy. As a longtime student of Edith's work, I believe her observational skills were akin to *art and mindful awareness practice*. An unusually gifted experiencer–observer, artist–therapist, Edith was a keen, moral witness of the ecological and interpersonal fields around her and not just a witness. She also skillfully responded to her surrounds with exquisite artistic sensitivity. Sitting near her at a conference was a treat. I would marvel at her drawing ability as she quickly and accurately sketched the portraits of people in the immediate rows around her. Her enthusiastically active hands had to be holding some art

206　*Michael A. Franklin*

material while creating observant responses. This too hints at what I believe to be Edith's contemplative capacities of experiencer–observer–responder. Embedded in this triadic template of attentive action are further contemplative layers of ethical intention, attuned perceptual attention, and compassionate responsiveness.

Consideration of Edith Kramer's work from a contemplative perspective is the focus of this chapter. While there are many elements of her work to consider, I will focus on various mindfulness elements of art as therapy, particularly the *third hand*. For a review of artistic sublimation as it relates to the subject of karma, impulse, and action, see *Art as Contemplative Practice: Expressive Pathways to the Self* (Franklin, 2017).

Lineage, Interpretation, Theory, and Practice

Before beginning, a note about theory, practice, and lineage. A romantic yet applicable idea for this chapter, lineage in spiritual, educational, and artistic traditions is about transmission of living knowledge from the teacher or community to the seeker/student. Initiation into the sect occurs as the seeker absorbs the teachings of the lineage and extends to the next generations the wisdom of the line. When considering my own trajectory in the field, the art as therapy tradition has a unique, traceable throughput line from my studio education, to work in hospital communities as an art educator–therapist, to clinical and socially engaged work. I expect this is true for others who feel aligned with an art as therapy approach. Below is an example of this lineage arc that led me to the secure base of Edith's work.

Art as Oxygen

I always knew that art was oxygen for me, especially when practiced communally with groups. My mentor in undergraduate school at the University of South Florida (USF), where I studied studio art and art education, was Richard Loveless. A student of Viktor Lowenfeld, Richard was an experimental visionary. He successfully developed a community art studio in the late 1960s in Tampa's Ybor City called the "New Place," where he served disadvantaged youth by providing access to materials and new technologies. Similar to Edith's work at Wiltwyck School for Boys, Richard celebrated those who attended as able young artists and gifted performers. For me, Richard was a role model, applying Lowenfeld's art–education–therapy studio viewpoints to working in low-income communities.

A significant branch of the art school I attended at USF was the innovative Graphic Studio founded by Donald Saff in the late 1960s (Baro, 1978). Printmaker, researcher, and artist, Saff conceived of a professional printing facility staffed by master printers from Gemini G.E.L. and Tamarind Press. The goal was to bring studio art education together with notable artists like James Rosenquist and Robert Rauschenberg. As a lithography student, interaction

Edith Kramer's Art as Therapy Model   207

with some of these extraordinary people was intermittently commonplace as they worked on their print editions, spontaneously walked the halls of the school, and on occasion, visited classes. Witnessing the laboratory of Graphic Studio and the range of experimental work occurring modeled Edith's core ideas on art as reflecting inner consistency of expressive authenticity, evocative power of visual communication, and an adept use of materials that economically merges form with content (Kramer, 1971). Over the years Philip Pearlstein, Jim Dine, Chuck Close, Robert Mapplethorpe, Roy Lichtenstein, and others worked at the Graphic Studio.

At the same time, M.C. Richards visited my university and became my ceramics instructor. She too believed in contemplative, progressive education and working with communities through the arts (Richards, 1964, 1973). Her transpersonal influence as teacher and author was inspiring, especially in terms of contemplatively working with art materials and processes in a charged studio environment.

After college and before graduate school, by accident, while wandering the New York University bookstore in 1978, I found and read Edith's first two books (1971, 1977). I noticed that she held similar convictions to Lowenfeld's art–education–therapy, Richard's community-based work, and M.C.'s embrace of materials and processes. However, Edith added the important piece of clinical training, but not at the expense of art's primacy within an allied therapeutic relationship. Her art as therapy model confirmed what I felt as a nascent student, but could not fully articulate.

Elinor Ulman, mentor and friend, further accelerated my sense of lineage in the field. While spending several summers together on her Vermont farm, and with Bernie Levy living nearby feverishly painting every day, we all had many opportunities to talk about what I would refer to as the territory where art was therapeutic without being clinical in a traditional sense. Slowly, I galvanized my views on the therapeutic benefits of art to unfold and anchor psychological growth. Working with materials and processes while supported by a skillful artist–therapist relationship, the psyche, I believed, could be restored.

Knowing lineage is important, including questioning the inheritance of ideas. It would be disingenuous of me to exclude those moments as a graduate student when I was almost derailed from my studies. Early on, when reading Edith's and Elinor's work, I often felt split. Analytic, art-based theory fascinated me and almost always rang true. However, there were many moments when I was mystified and bothered by their interpretations of client art, often wondering how they arrived at their conclusions. The story of Lillian and her fearful response to a powerful thunderstorm represents one vivid example (Kramer, 1971). Rather than join the other children playfully rolling in the wet grass, nine-year-old Lillian fearfully remained inside where Kramer invited her to paint a picture of the still unfolding thunderstorm. This sensible art as therapy intervention allowed Lillian to find visual language for her frightened responses to the weather along with her apprehension to join the other children. Edith suggests that Lillian's painting did not depict the actual storm,

208   *Michael A. Franklin*

"but a much more destructive event." She surmised that "the symbolic shape of the tree, the position of its branches, the red flames that are densest in the crotch where the tree's crown divides in half – all strongly suggested a bloody, violent sexual fantasy" (p. 83). Following this comment, Edith then mentions that she does not know the meaning of the fantasy and is not interested to uncover this content.

I question if this painting even represents a fantasy let alone a sexually based one. Why is it not a response to the storm? Kramer does focus on the contextual fact of time and place and how the painting served Lillian during her moments of emotional upheaval. This example of debatable interpretation, which Kramer assuredly lets us know would never be repeated out loud to Lillian, allows the reader to observe Kramer's thinking regarding this example of artistic sublimation. I embrace her reasoning up until she arrives at her interpretation of the painting conveying a violent sexual fantasy. If I shift my clinical lens to an orthodox, conservative analytic interpretation, I can see Edith's point; I just fervently disagree.

Eventually, it occurred to me that I could criticize Edith's interpretations while embracing art as therapy theory. And this, I tell my students, is a helpful strategy for reading her work. I suggest to them that she formulated the most comprehensive, applicable theory of art therapy, yet her many interpretations of the art are debatable. Edith's three-legged stool metaphor (1994) of an art therapist's identity is helpful here. She suggested that we needed one leg representing effective teaching, another serving the therapeutic relationship and process, and the third standing for the importance of maintaining our artist identity. Without butchering the metaphor, the seat to which the three legs attach is also present and epitomizes intrepid, self-aware, inner observation – it is literally where we take our seat in order to do the work of therapy, teaching, and maintaining our artistic identities.

Art as Contemplative Practice: Taking Our Seat

The subject of *art as contemplative practice* has occupied my thinking for decades (Franklin, 2017). The word "as" in art as therapy or art as contemplative practice infers an important point in this discussion. It was no accident that Kramer chose this simple word, "as," to place between art and therapy. In this case, "as" denotes a comparison and a connecting emphasis between art and therapy. Simile also uses "as" to connect metaphoric relationships. Importantly, metaphor means seeing the similar in the dissimilar, and as we know, there are many in the behavioral sciences who do not understand the practical, metaphoric similarities between psychotherapy and art as a primary therapeutic intervention.

A great deal of therapy goes on at the level of using materials, processes, and responding to products. These three core aspects of any art experience, regardless of whether a therapist is in the room, can influence psychological growth. The ego is strengthened as inner self-structure fragments, regresses,

Edith Kramer's Art as Therapy Model 209

and enduringly reassembles in creative work. Ongoing lessons of personality reorganization are learned and relearned as mistakes are made, adaptable regressions are surmounted, and audiences attentively respond to our work. Children fortunate enough to have a quality art education learn that persistence always yields results.

Mindfulness and Art

During our graduate training at GWU, we were encouraged to enter counseling. Since so much of our learning was tethered to analytic traditions, I chose classical psychoanalysis. After participating in several interviews, I was accepted as an analysand at a training institute. For two and half years, three times per week, I reclined on a couch freely associating with my analyst sitting behind me. Making unconscious regressive and progressive transference neurosis patterns conscious became a vulnerable, yet eye-opening process. Exposed yet supported, I slowly uncovered the blueprints of my repetitive habits, thoughts, and emotions while increasing my capacity to witness myself.

Richard Sterba (1934), widely acknowledged as the one to advance the self-contemplative functions and capacities of the observing ego, noted the importance of these resources for assessing reality (Glickauf-Hughes, Wells, & Chance, 1996). With the help of my analyst reflecting my comments, and my artwork reflectively holding my visual speech, I slowly internalized the observing functions of each. Over time, as these discerning aspects of art and analysis merged together, my affection for the art as therapy model deepened.

I also had a concurrent yoga and meditation practice that was aided by my analytic work. However, it would be years later that I would crystallize my understanding of these connections during long meditation retreats. By far, the two most contemplative experiences in my life are analysis and meditation. Both taught me that waking up, emotionally and interpersonally, was predicated on setting aside time for reflective, nonjudgmental, moment-to-moment inner observation.

Roger Walsh and Shauna Shapiro (2006) defined meditation as "a family of self-regulation practices that focus on training attention and awareness in order to bring mental processes under greater voluntary control and thereby foster general mental well-being and development and/or specific capacities such as calm, clarity, and concentration" (pp. 228–229). Furthermore, mindfulness can be defined as relaxed, flexible attentiveness to the "reflective self," including nonjudgmental "moment-to-moment awareness" of emerging thoughts and sensations (Davis & Hayes, 2011, p. 198).

Contemplative practices like art and meditation, when joined together, cultivate inner observation of the reflective self. Relatedly, the ego Freud believed could listen to itself, treat itself, and sternly or benignly perceive itself (Glickauf-Hughes et al., 1996). Intentional, gentle self-reflection is both a function of the ego and a goal of meditation and art. We are at our healthiest, I believe, when we kindly and dispassionately observe our relational

210   *Michael A. Franklin*

patterns, interpersonal proclivities, and behavioral actions. Art slows down observation of these various schemas by making inner content felt, formed, and then seen by others. Although not a meditator, Edith knew and lived similar convictions.

While associations between art and meditation were not part of Edith's professional lexicon, she did model contemplative behavior. For example, on New Year's Eve, rather than go out, she would begin a painting and work through the night until it was finished. Purposeful intention, devotional attention, and mindful self-reflection were implicit in her choice to remain indoors and create her way through a New York New Year's Eve. Her response to the holiday frivolity was to embrace the solitude of the studio while honoring her consistent inner moral principles.

Elinor told another example of reflective astuteness to me. Edith, she said regularly, supported the ecological practices of organizations like Green Peace. From these conversations, I learned that Edith held strong conservational beliefs about protecting land, sea, and animals. Eventually, this made complete sense. While looking at the endless stacks of Edith's landscape paintings in Elinor's farmhouse attic, I realized her exquisite felt understanding of place and living systems. Environmental stewardship within a pervasive consumerist corporate culture has been eroding for some time. Edith saw this factual unraveling long before others made these connections. Another paper for an interested researcher would further address Edith's penchant for Green politics, ecological conservation, and landscape paintings.

Ethical Perception: Experiencing, Observing, and Responding

The compound word *contemplate* merges the Latin *con* and *templum* together. It means to observe with reverent attention in the sacred environment of a temple (Ayto, 1990). *Con* is to join something together. *Templum* originates from the work of an augur or religious official from ancient times who carefully observed and interpreted signs from the natural world. Sites were selected from this process for building *templum* or temples, which were sanctified spaces for observant attention and imaginal practice. The result of this insightful vision was the capacity to see "things as they really are" which is the meaning of *contemplari* (Mahony, 1998, p. 57).

Considering this etymology, the contemporary art therapy studio becomes a place for contemplative attention. We train to become keen observers, intentionally directing sustained awareness toward multiple, simultaneous events like the art process, art product, and the interpersonal field. Considering this brief explication, to me, Edith contemplatively approached her work within the studio *templum*. She emphatically insists that the main goal of the art therapist is to make available to those suffering, the "pleasures and satisfaction which creative work" can offer regarding personality integration (Kramer, 1977, p. 5). She notes further that the arts have continually served our species to reconcile

Edith Kramer's Art as Therapy Model 211

perpetual conflicts between individual instinctual urges and societal demands. If these premises are embraced, then the art therapist accepts "unbeautiful manifestations" of all kinds, including formless, impulsive, aggressive imagery (p. 6). Cultivating and then balancing discriminating awareness for variations in artistic quality with unconditional positive regard for chaotic discharge imagery is no easy feat. Yet, even if she did not always achieve this ideal, it is implicit in her art as therapy model. Considering these quotes, it becomes clear that Kramer is describing a desire to mitigate suffering through her encouragement of accessible, pleasurable art experiences.

Similar to mindfulness meditation, creating or observing artwork in a nonjudgmental manner is an exercise in noting the ebb and flow of thoughts as they take aesthetic shape. Avoiding or indulging self-deprecation does not result in an invitation of anything goes. Instead, mindful art fosters an attitude of inner kindness toward introjections of shame, guilt, or any other charged interiorized perceptions. Counterintuitively, we go toward what repels us. And as inner attitudes are turned outward toward the production of honest art, the process becomes an ethical exploration of authentic imagery, which is a value embraced by Edith's notion of inner consistency within a formed expression (Kramer, 1971, p. 50).

Qualities of art and quality in art create aesthetic questions for the art therapist. We support all expression, yet how do we differentiate between ways of using art materials and processes? Kramer's intimate familiarity with art media, pathology, and resiliency resulted in a deconstruction of the word art by considering similarities and differences between precursory activities, art in the service of defense, chaotic discharge, pictographs, and formed expression (Kramer, 1971, p. 48). These five ways of using art materials to manifest imagery begin to help us understand intentions behind artworks. Furthermore, they help us to join with our clients as they artistically present themselves in any given moment. In her seminal article on the third hand, Edith not only set the coordinates for how to practice from an art-based orientation, she further charted for us procedural assistance on how to prepare and move the therapeutic process forward (Kramer, 1986). Surprisingly, little follow up literature in our field has been devoted to her third hand theory.

The Third Hand, Mindfulness, and Interpersonal Jazz

Kramer defined the art therapist's use of a supportive, auxiliary third hand as a specific art-based, interpersonal intervention. A core skill-set in the art therapist's armamentaria, the third hand carries out responsive visual dialogs in the least intrusive way so as not to distort meaning or restructure the client's visual content. Adjusting and attuning artistic style to the client's visual "handwriting" and level of artistic development is essential for carrying out this form of effective visual empathy (Kramer, 1986). In session, attuned visual paraphrases from the art therapist or modified adaptive tools, supportively furthers the client's art process (Franklin, 2010). Because the intervention is guided by

212   Michael A. Franklin

awareness of developmental, cognitive, cultural, and psychosocial needs, the art therapist's artistic ability must be mindfully subordinated in order to reduce pressure on the client.

Sometimes people in art therapy need help finding unrecognized solutions to mounting frustrations threatening to derail their artistic process. Co-created visual dialogs, like a form of interpersonal visual jazz, help to regulate emotions within a relational context. Additionally, before art-based involvement is even offered, successful empathic attunement is considered from many angles, including intuitive forecasting of the intervention's extended results (Franklin, 2010). And this goes to the heart of how meditation, as an awareness practice, fits into the third hand equation. Since the art therapist is trying hard to avoid invasive countertransference intrusion, it is not enough to ask for awareness of unconscious blind spots. Wakefulness needs to be trained, and practices like meditation cultivate additional attentive layers of self–other dynamics. Between her personal analysis, ongoing artistic work, and environmental stewardship, Kramer conveyed hallmarks of an accomplished contemplative.

Conclusion

Although she did not claim interest in meditation, I do believe Edith's work conveys related contemplative overtones, particularly her guidance on third hand instruction and artistic sublimation. Empathy, empathic communication, and compassion for the suffering of others define the art therapist's desire to serve clients. These values are related to Buddhism's four immeasurables, which are loving kindness, compassion, joy, and equipoise (Wegela, 2009). Contemplatively-oriented art therapists work to develop these qualities while encouraging the same in their clients. We want consumers of our services, and through their own art, to discover versions of personal happiness, relief from distress, happiness for another, and to see themselves and others with equanimity.

When paired with a skillful artist–therapist relationship that embraces principles of the third hand or the four immeasurables, the psyche can achieve degrees of beneficial restoration. In my case, grasping the nuances of these convictions required that I look at my own lineage trajectory that guided me to this stimulating field. Decades later, Edith's work has taught me the most about my beliefs and also my doubts, and for this, I continue to thank her.

References

Ayto, J. (1990). *Bloomsbury dictionary of word origins.* London: Bloomsbury.

Baro, G. (1978). *Graphicstudio U.S.F: An experiment in art and education.* Brooklyn, New York: Brooklyn Museum.

Davis, D. M., & Hayes, J. A. (2011). What are the benefits of mindfulness? A practice review of psychotherapy-related research. *Psychotherapy, 48*(2), 198–208.

Edith Kramer's Art as Therapy Model 213

Franklin, M. (2010). Affect regulation, mirror neurons and the third hand: Formulating mindful empathic art interventions. *Art Therapy: The Journal of the American Art Therapy Association, 27*(4), 160–167.

Franklin, M. A. (2017). *Art as contemplative practice: Expressive pathways to the self.* Albany, New York: SUNY Press.

Glickauf-Hughes, C., Wells, M., & Chance, S. (1996). Techniques for strengthening clients' observing ego. *Psychotherapy, 33*(3), 431–440.

Kramer, E. (1971). *Art as therapy with children.* New York: Schocken Books.

Kramer, E. (1977). *Art therapy in a children's community: A study of the function of art therapy in the treatment program of Wiltwyck School for Boys.* New York: Schocken Books.

Kramer, E. (1986). The art therapist's third hand: Reflections on art, art therapy, and society at large. *The American Journal of Art Therapy, 24,* 71–86.

Kramer, E. (1994). *A portrait of artist/art therapist Edith Kramer.* Sacramento, CA: Chuck Conners Productions.

Mahony, W. K. (1998 – September). The artist as yogi, the yogi as artist. *Darshan: In the Company of Saints, 138,* 56–62.

Richards, M. C. (1964). *Centering in pottery, poetry, and the person.* Middletown, CT: Wesleyan University Press.

Richards, M. C. (1973). *The crossing point: Selected talks and writings.* Middleton, CT: Wesleyan University Press.

Sterba, R. (1934). The fate of the ego in analytic therapy. *International Journal of Psychoanalysis, 15,* 117–126.

Walsh, R., & Shapiro, S. L. (2006). The meeting of meditative disciplines and western psychology: A mutually enriching dialogue. *American Psychologist, 61*(3), 227–239.

Wegela, K. K. (2009). *The courage to be present: Buddhism, psychotherapy, and the awakening of natural wisdom.* Boston, MA: Shambhala.

28 Art and Cancer

Transference and Countertransference: Channeling Edith Kramer

Esther Dreifuss-Kattan

I remember a heated discussion at the famous private hospital Chestnut Lodge, in Rockville, Maryland in 1975. Many of the thirty-five psychiatrists at the monthly clinical meeting were critical of the art therapy session I was conducting with a violent manic depressive male patient. Gerry was creative, focused, and relaxed in our therapeutic encounters. Like other long-term patients, he was seen four times a week by his psychoanalyst. Often these regressed patients did not actually speak to their doctors, and thus art therapy became hugely important in understanding what was going on with them psychologically. The critical doctors accused me of ignoring the countertransference with my patient Gerry! I was a greenhorn art therapist and confused, as the patient did not show any anger in our sessions, nor was any sign of discontent or rage visible in his art. I did not think that I had done anything wrong.

Thus, I called up the famous Edith Kramer in New York to ask for a supervision session. I had never met Edith, but I was impressed by one of her early books when I lived in Zurich. In supervision, Edith fully agreed with me and told me that I should only address emotions or content that surfaced in the patient's art or in the relationship with me. This wonderful first meeting with Edith was the beginning of a thirty-year friendship. I visited Edith later from Switzerland, then with my little kids from Israel, enjoying her studio with her amazing sculpture and art, or strolling with her through the MET on Saturday nights. Edith stayed with me in Los Angeles on the occasion of her Museum of Tolerance talk for the exhibition of children's art created in Theresienstadt with the artist and teacher Friedl Dicker. Friedl, who was murdered during the Holocaust, was Edith's art teacher and mentor, both in Vienna and later in Prague before WWII. It was her work with Friedl that made Dr Kramer think of *art as therapy* with children.

I was so very fortunate to have Edith as one of my dissertation advisors for my eventual book *Cancer Stories: Creativity and Self Repair.* My introduction to understanding transference and countertransference started with psychiatric patients but then extended to my work with cancer patients. Edith's eye focused on the imagery as it related to the strong creative bond I experienced with my cancer patients.

Art and Cancer 215

This chapter focuses on using art and therapy with one cancer patient in the later, terminal stage of cancer. When cancer patients are confronted with their terminal illness and there are no longer any treatments available, multiple mourning processes are activated, forcing both the patient and his or her therapist to make tremendous inner changes. Art-making helps both the patient and her art therapist to reflect on death and separation.

In the course of art therapy with critically ill or dying cancer patients, an externalization of ego functions becomes necessary, as relationships keep changing and the patient becomes weaker and is much more self-focused. Consequently, no resolution of the mutual relationship or transference between patient and art therapist is possible and great fears can be activated in both. The death of a patient still strongly enmeshed in the transference with the art therapist can cause a partial "death" in the therapist that she has to mourn as well.

The Latin and Greek words for cancer present a paradox: While the Latin word for cancer is carcinoma, meaning tumor, the Greek word for cancer is neoplasm, translated as "forming of the new." The threat of destruction that this "new" cancerous tissue represents invariably evokes dread, but in many patients it also arouses new, formerly dormant, creative energy as the patients tap both physical and psychological resources to fight the illness (Dreifuss-Kattan, 1990). As a patient struggles to restore health and psychological balance after the trauma of a cancer diagnosis, a unique dialectic can emerge between illness and health and between despair and new hope.

A good example is the British singer and composer David Bowie, whose album and video, *Black Star* and *Lazarus,* were created when he became aware that he was dying of cancer. His last stark and powerful artistic expression illustrates that he contemplated his death, feeling an urgent need to work through his pending losses and leave a memorial for his family and for all of us. The work of mourning through creative expression engenders a wish to continue living in order to create something in the present and for the future.

A diagnosis of cancer evokes anxieties, fears, grief, physical suffering, dependency, and vulnerability. Cancer also allows the patient to focus on present experiences, and to transform her/his important interpersonal relationships, making reparation of inner objects and external relationships possible. From recent studies by Rodin and Zimmermann (2008) and from my own clinical experience, it is clear that hope and a will to live are preserved in most cancer patients despite advanced, metastatic, or terminal illness. Patients state that they want to continue living, in spite of more pain and suffering, and they do not want to hasten death, regardless of its imminence (Breitbart, 2000). Patients often experience the awareness of death simultaneously with a wish to survive. Rodin and Zimmermann call this phenomenon a "middle knowledge" or "double awareness . . . in which states of awareness and denial may alternate, fluctuate and coexist . . . evoking profound and contradictory emotions" (Rodin & Zimmermann, 2008, p. 186).

216   *Esther Dreifuss-Kattan*

The confrontation with cancer, a potentially terminal illness, forces the patient to undertake tremendous inner changes. On the narcissistic level, there is the mourning of the lost integrity of his or her own body, or body function, compounded by the aggressive assaults of invasive medical procedures, such as toxic chemotherapies, multiple surgeries, radiation treatments, and other more targeted therapies. As a result, the patient often feels that his body and memory are being attacked, painfully changing, or even disintegrating. If we remember that the earliest developments of the ego are closely connected with the image of an intact body ego, we can appreciate the threat to the feeling of self-worth, as well as feelings of shame and anger, that cancer can cause. The patient focuses more strongly on internal relationships and experiences from the past, as well as the reconstruction and interpretation of emotional and relational issues as they are accessed in the relationship with the art therapist in the present. Through this process, the patient in a terminal stage is able to withdraw the remaining good feelings and energy from his or her ailing body, thus allowing for a mourning process to unfold that can revitalize artistic potential.

Finding a new form of expression elicits pleasurable and satisfying feelings in spite of the life-altering situation of cancer and helps repair the narcissistic damage brought about by the illness and treatments. The art created can become a transformational object, a symbol that mediates between separation and togetherness, between death and immortality. Artistic expression helps cancer patients transform their experience of illness into a new creative form, an aesthetic moment, gaining psychological insight that helps them to work through life issues that they could not earlier.

This case vignette of an adult cancer patient named Henry illustrates the particular fears and concerns, both internal and external, that confronted him.

Case Vignette

I will first introduce you to Henry, a 69-year-old, married man. Henry projected to the art therapy group members and to me an adaptive denial, using excessive humor and sexual references to defend against his strong feelings of impotence in the face of his cancer. Henry's lymphoma was treated with chemotherapy and radiation that provided temporary relief, but a relapse eventually made stem cell transplantation necessary.

For three years, Henry was a member of two separate art/psychotherapy groups I facilitated for cancer patients of all ages and stages of illness at two different cancer centers. Because of our close bond, he developed a strong and positive transference relationship to me. With the help of Henry's pictures, I would like to give a short illustration of some of the psychological issues that arise when a patient is faced with serious illness and eventually, as in Henry's case, with death.

Art and Cancer 217

The powerful imagery of his work expresses the destructive process of cancer along with the restorative and reparative processes that are part of all artistic expressions. It satisfies the longing of the cancer patient for the transitional space between mother and infant, providing a supportive, playful, and creative space and a sense of expanding, infinite time that is part of this transitional space.

The title of Figure 28.1 describes the University of California Los Angeles–Santa Monica Hospital in which Henry was being treated. On one side, we see the monitor with its chemotherapy infusion bags, drawn in black and white, and on the other a pretty, blonde, sexy nurse with blue eyes and cute, perky pink breasts. The title suggests that when Henry focuses on the nurse's breasts, the scary, dehumanizing chemotherapy ride is not so bad. The nurse looks very similar to his wife Molly, upon whom he can depend, as she is a loving support to him. With her assistance and the distraction of his sexual fantasies, he manages to soldier on in this rather frightening journey.

This colorful scene in Figure 28.2 depicts three naked adults. In the middle we see a woman who looks like Henry's wife staring straight at us. On one side, we see our patient in a kind of self-portrait, wearing a white undershirt with his penis uncovered. On the other side we find a thin, vulnerable, completely naked bald

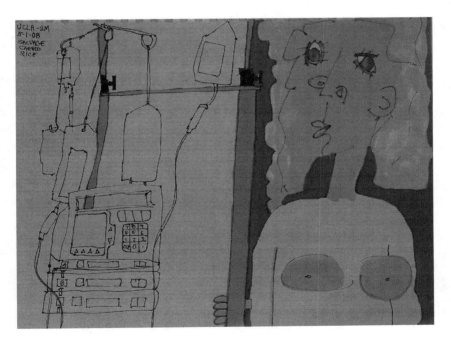

Figure 28.1 UCLA–SM, 2008, Salvage Chemo Ride. Pen and markers on paper

Figure 28.2 Untitled, 2008. Pen and markers on paper

man who looks down. The red fire hydrant looms in the background. Henry seems somewhat aware of his situation; he feels healthy and strong in one image, but vulnerable and sickly in the other. The two realities are surfacing unconsciously, but seeing them on the paper, he is confronted by his changing reality. The red fire hydrant speaks to his wish to receive help in order to extinguish the "cancer fire" that seems to be spreading.

In Figure 28.3, *Day After Chemo*, Henry portrays himself in the middle of a group of vulnerable, sick, naked adults. His use of a thin pen makes this feeling of vulnerability and helplessness very prominent. These people all seem very worried. Henry identifies with all the fellow cancer patients like the ones in the support groups he attends, who can understand and empathize with his challenging journey. It allows him to observe himself and others and acknowledge his sadness and fear of death and great physical and emotional defenselessness.

The hope he experienced at this time is well rendered in a colorful picture, *Basket of Blessings*, 2009, pen and marker on paper. The patient draws himself with a bald head due to chemotherapy and his wife/mother/therapist are contained in one basket that moves up into the sky. The basket is filled with "hope" and "wishes for good health." It also contains the "blessings" of his family and "art therapy" (the relationship with his art therapist) and "medication." These

Art and Cancer 219

Figure 28.3 Day after Chemo. Pen and marker on paper

things he draws or has written in his basket. Henry is not alone, his basket is full, and while his companion seems worried, she is also definitively present.

The picture *Knee Deep in Shit* or *The Grass is Greener on the Other Side*, 2009, is created in mixed media, markers, masking tape, and wood. Both titles explain Henry's situation very well. While he portrays himself in one corner with a woman, possibly his wife/therapist, he also holds open the coffin lid that he suggests is not for him, but for his ex-wife. She is the mother of his son, and he still projects onto her his dissatisfying relationship with her, as well as with his long-dead mother to whom he never really felt close. The street sign directs us to the cemetery, and a desperate Henry is standing on the brown surface of shit/dirt, while there still seems to be a potential escape to the greener grass on the other side, or out of the window toward the blue sky. The patient would like to shut the coffin on his bad internal objects – his aggressive father and unloving mother, who still fill him with rage. Time is running out, which he illustrates by drawing his legs already half inside the brown dirt, thus implying that he is being slowly buried. He becomes aware that the rage he projects toward his dead parents belongs partly to the destructive cancer that leaves him furious and impotent. He is sad that in spite of his very good and caring oncologist and caring wife and mother/art therapist, who all love him very much and admire his amazing artistic abilities and his humor, his cancer cannot be stopped.

220 *Esther Dreifuss-Kattan*

I asked the group members to make a self-portrait first and then another portrait of somebody who came to mind. After Henry painted his self-portrait, he explained that the second portrait was of me, his art therapist. I came to his mind, he mentioned, because he needed to talk to me. I did not know what he had planned to communicate to me, as after this Cancer and Creativity Group ended, Henry suddenly had to be admitted to the Intensive Care Unit in the University Hospital.

He was hooked up to many life-saving machines when I came to visit a day later, as he had requested. Henry was too weak to talk, but he carefully and slowly wrote out a dialog on his laptop telling me that he did not want to die; he wanted to live longer, as he was not done yet. He was sad, looking at me, wondering what I was thinking. I said that he must feel that death was close, but that he had not yet given up hope and neither had I, pointing out to him that he touched many people in his life and cancer journey, forged strong and loving ties to his oncologist/father, his close family, fellow patients, and with me. We all admired his courage and wit, particularly in view of his long struggle with cancer. He then asked me if he should go home to die, as his wife wished, but his doctors were trying to prevent. I believed he was reconciled to his fate and pointed out to him that he always hated being in the hospital for too long and that, if he felt more comfortable at home, I was certain that this would be a good option for him. When his wife returned after our session, they decided together to go home the next day. On his way out of his hospital bed the following morning, Henry passed away in the presence of his beloved wife.

After each group session and then after the ICU visit, I was deeply moved and emotionally overwhelmed. I had to take a few minutes outside his room to gather myself emotionally, as I mourned Henry while he was still alive and at the same time mourned my mother, who had died less than a year ago. Henry's pictures, like transitional objects, initially provided both of us with an acceptable defense against loss and allowed us to navigate our therapeutic encounter. Once he was hospitalized, no defense mechanism was available for Henry or for me. It was a great privilege to share Henry and his wife's journey to the end of his life.

Concluding comments

During psychodynamic psychotherapy/art therapy with seriously ill and dying cancer patients, an externalization of ego function slowly becomes necessary as personal relationships change and eventually come to be reduced. The closer the patient is to death, the more she is focused on herself, preserving psychic and somatic energies to survive (Dreifuss-Kattan, 2016). Consequently, a traditional resolution of transference cannot occur in many cases, provoking fear in both patient and therapist. When the patient dies while still strongly enmeshed in the relationship to the therapist, as we saw in Henry's death, the mourning therapist experiences a partial death within herself.

Art and Cancer 221

An idealized transference to the empathic art therapist can develop in a later stage of illness, as the patient wishes to regress to a very early condition of love, total security, and absolute trust. Handling the ambivalence that is inherent in any idealization can be a challenge. Often, while in the first phase of regression because of illness, patients imagine the art therapist as an idealized parental imago, or a punishing and neglecting one (Dreifuss-Kattan, 1990). The art therapist, due to her perceived good health and vitality, can quickly find herself in the role of the envied parent or sibling and thus rejected by the cancer patient based on related negative effects of anger, disillusionment, and envy. Rejecting the therapist often represents the only way for the very sick person to appease his or her harsh aspects of the judging superego. Thus, stopping treatment at a time when the patient needs the most support represents his attempt to ward off guilt feelings, a sense of shame, or a fear of being rejected or abandoned later on (Schaverien, 1999).

Spero (2004) movingly discusses a woman with breast cancer who, during psychoanalytic psychotherapy, spontaneously expressed a religious metaphor, revealing new layers of memory. The psychoanalyst, listening and recognizing his countertransference feelings even without verbalizing them, helped the patient to rediscover "a sacred healing breast," reconnecting her to religious experiences from her early childhood, allowing her to reactivate an early sense of expanding time that resulted in creative meaning and offered comfort.

In a later phase of treatment, as the cancer relapses or progresses, the therapist is often forced to take over more of the ego functions, as well as to try to balance a new therapeutic framework. Norton (1963) started to read to her patient with cancer when the patient became blind. A need might arise to see the patients in their homes, speak to them on the telephone, as they become too weak to come to the art studio or to the outpatient clinic. This new, more essential maternal connection can help the patient to perceive the therapist as more internally present, even when he/she is absent. Because of the greater dependency of the cancer patient on the art therapist, the mutual relationship can become particularly emotionally intense. In a fascinating case study, Schaverien (1999) discusses a patient with depression who was in analysis with her when he was diagnosed with inoperable lung cancer. Being faced with death, an even more intense, dependent transference developed that challenged boundary issues of the therapeutic encounter. During psychotherapeutic treatment, her patient could move from more defensive adult sexual Oedipal feelings to more pre-Oedipal ones, enabling an individuation process – despite his terminal illness – from dependency to self-reliance. He finally moved out of his parents' home, enabling him to die as a middle-aged man under the caring support of his adult sister. His newfound independence allowed his father to share with his dying son his great sorrow of losing him too soon.

One feature of transference/countertransference in a therapeutic partnership between art therapist and cancer patient as seen in Henry's case, is that the therapeutic relationship is always threatened by an impending loss and thus has to be preserved at all times. Hence, it has ambivalent characteristics. There is

222 *Esther Dreifuss-Kattan*

the wish to withdraw, to anticipate separation, and the opposing wish to cling, in order to avoid separation. Both these tendencies are true for both patient and therapist. This conflict has to be addressed verbally and/or artistically in order to keep this supporting relationship alive to the end of this difficult journey.

Edith Kramer's spirit lives on with me in her beautiful sculpture *The Pregnant Woman in the Bath Tub,* and the delicate painting of a baby bird done in gold leaf, both of which reside in my living room. Like Edith, my late friend and mentor, I married psychoanalysis with art-making and love to write about it.

References

Breitbart, W. (2000). Depression, hopelessness, and desire for hastened death in terminally ill patients with cancer. *Jama, 284*(22), 2907–2911.

Dreifuss-Kattan, E. (1990). *Cancer stories: Creativity and self-repair.* Hillsdale, NJ: Analytic Press.

Dreifuss-Kattan, E. (2016). *Art and mourning: The role of creativity in healing trauma and loss.* London: Routledge, Taylor and Francis Group.

Norton, J. (1963). Treatment of a dying patient. *Psychoanalytic Study of the Child, 18,* 541–560.

Rodin, G., & Zimmermann, C. (2008). Psychoanalytic reflections on mortality: A reconsideration. *The Journal of the American Academy of Psychoanalysis and Dynamic Psychiatry, 36*(1), 181–196.

Schaverien, J. (1999). The death of an analysand: Transference, countertransference and desire. *Journal of Analytical Psychology, 44*(1), 3–28.

Spero, M. H. (2004). Hearing the faith in time: Countertransference and religious metaphor in an oncology patient's psychotherapy. *The Psychoanalytic Quarterly, LXXIII*(4), 971–1021.

29 Edith Kramer's Influence on the Development of Medical Art Therapy

Irene Rosner David

Mentor to Mentor

When I began my art therapy training at New York University, I had already been working in a medical setting for several years. I implemented art activities for adults with physical illnesses and disabilities in my capacity as a recreation therapist, believing the patients would benefit. I read the few books that existed in the 1970s, among them Edith Kramer's. It was exciting to me to envision what I was doing as substantive, yet also baffling that there was no reference in the minimal literature to working with medically hospitalized adult patients. I knew I could continue working intuitively for so long, but even in my formal studies, there was nothing taught about what I thought of as *medical art therapy*.

In the art that was created by my patients, as well as in their responses and affect, there was apparent indication that something beneficial was occurring. Even after learning about the foundations of art therapy, I remained insecure in reading any meaning into processes or products. I was fortunate enough to have Edith as a mentor in clinical supervision, in addition to didactic classes. In presenting cases to her, it took merely a glance at the artworks to put a psychoanalytic spin on them – professing terms like "pre-conscious, symbolism, and sublimation." It all seems basic in retrospect, but as a loner in the medical community, Edith's perspective deepened my conviction that expressing oneself in the context of medical trauma was valid. Her ideas fortified my belief that this otherwise unexplored arena for art therapy made sense. It elevated the level of my work and placed it rightfully into the clinical milieu. I do not think I would have come as far as I did in subsequent decades, developing the specialization, writing and talking about it with confidence, if in the early days she had not been interested and encouraging.

Her way of understanding the artwork and of cultivating the therapeutic relationship was informative and enriched my approach. Reciprocally, she described being in a learner's role about medical art therapy, candidly saying she knew nothing about it. I found this aspect of her personality – that of taking pleasure in broadening her awareness and learning as much as possible – to be impressive. "You can enlighten us Irene; you're the expert." Her modest posture created an unexpected dynamic of me as a mentor for my mentor, and

224 *Irene Rosner David*

a famous one at that – daunting to be sure, but a powerful reinforcement for me to persevere with medical art therapy.

At one of Edith's festive holiday parties in her SoHo loft, I described a patient who had had a stroke with a resultant form of verbal aphasia referred to as apraxia. Edith was fascinated to learn that one could retrieve words, but not have sufficient mouth and jaw mobility to enunciate intelligible speech. Her own learning style was to simulate an experience, so she proceeded to undertake mouth and facial distortions with accompanying garbled sounds. This taught me the importance of empathizing as much as possible with a patient by having a taste of what the frustrations might be with such impairment. Hence, by understanding this impairment by "trying it on" versus reading about it, a therapist would become more empathic and provide relevant, manageable art experiences.

Medical Pictorial Analysis

Edith also said she learned there could be additional meanings of graphic features in the artworks of those physically ill and treated. For example, she came to realize that the use of red might be understood by its subliminal association with blood within a medical or surgical context, and not necessarily as an expression of anger and aggression. Similarly, a light brush stroke may have to do with hemiparesis, a physical weakening, versus a tenuous emotional state. This context of physical impairment made her aware of other dimensions to be considered in implementing and understanding art processes and products.

More important were Edith's contributions to expanding my understanding of artwork as reflective of patients' inner feelings and perceptions about medical conditions. I frequently saw patients pictorialize the part of the body injured or missing, the functional deterioration or particular medical treatment conveyed. However, I came to incorporate a "Kramerian" outlook, of course a psychoanalytic perspective, enabling a depth of insight and fuller scope. She guided me to embrace psychoanalytic tenets to glean hints as to where a patient might be in the process of confronting the reality of illness, disability, surgery, and changed body and self-image. In turn, I was better equipped to conceptualize clinical goals and implement artistic directives to support the patient toward the integration of change with a re-formed sense of self and well-being.

I had previously offered the creative process as a means of expressing emotions related to medical ordeals and instilling a sense of mastery when one is likely to feel victimized and out of control. Edith imparted a layer of understanding such that I could see patients' renderings for their symbols and themes suggesting psychological status and even personal meaning. This culminated in a multi-faceted scope of assessment and crystallized the value of art-making in the context of medical challenge.

Kramer's Influence on Medical Art Therapy   225

An example of this scope is a drawing we referred to as *Breast on Lawn* by a woman who had recently had a mastectomy. I worked with this patient in an oncology clinic while she awaited chemotherapy, and she readily created a landscape of her homeland. I observed pleasure in her manner as she drew the reminiscent scene, evoking a calm quality in her. However, I also noted the agitated quick lines, weeping willow tree, and cactus as indicators of her inner emotions as she embarked upon post-surgical treatment. Moreover, apparent was an image of two concentric circles – a wheel shape on its side, but also clearly breast-like. Seen as a breast, it was incongruous in the composition. When I invited her to talk about the drawing, she said it was from where she grew up and described several features such as the house, trees, and car then, upon coming to the vulnerable spot, pointed to "a decoration on the lawn, but you would not recognize it because they are only in my country." This glossing over of the shape was intriguing to me and signaled a reluctance to discuss this object.

Of course, I understood the avoidance, but it took Edith to glean deeper meaning and understand the benefits of drawing the symbolic breast. She proclaimed that this was a pre-conscious way of dealing with the removed part of her body, "indeed a decoration, as it used to be on her body before the mastectomy, a clear breast image misplaced . . . not quite unconscious anymore so maybe it will now move to consciousness after dealing with it in this way, it

Figure 29.1 Breast on Lawn. Drawing by cancer patient

226 Irene Rosner David

comes closer to the reality of it." I had learned about and understood psycho-analytic concepts, but it had not occurred to me to look at my patient's artwork through this lens. Doing so helped me to gain insight into where the patient was in her personal process of confronting and incorporating physical change, medical status, and related challenges. This framework better enabled me to conceptualize therapeutic goals and guide toward more effective adaptation with reality. This way of understanding patients' artwork became a cornerstone in my development of medical art therapy.

Several years later, a patient drew what Edith and I called *Dialysis House*, which I also understood via her lens. It was drawn while undergoing dialysis, a process whereby toxins are cleansed artificially in lieu of the patient's failing kidneys. The process takes many hours, often for several sessions per week, and is necessary to sustain life. The drawing of a house in a setting seemed to be an effective retreat from the highly clinical environment of the treatment room. The patient was pleased with his composition, which evoked an uplifting sensation and sense of artistic validation. Of note were the paths in and around the house as symbolic and representative of the equipment features of many tubes, lines, and vessels. The added Kramerian dimension was that it did not depict a direct rendering of the machinery, but in this case, was an entirely unconscious reflection of the treatment actively underway, as well as the dependency on it. This way of understanding the drawing provided insight on the level at which the patient could deal with all that hovered over him, literally and metaphorically. With Edith's help, I could support where he was psychologically comfortable, and guide toward movement to pre-conscious and even conscious levels. As she stated, "he could not draw the machines yet, but the many paths are like the tubes and connections . . . this was his way of dealing at this stage; the art-making helps him to face the reality slowly." Hence, such a rendering can be understood as part of a process toward ultimately coping more effectively.

Edith Kramer as a Medical Patient

Edith's station wagon was always full of art materials, so she would be equipped to paint wherever she went. One evening I had a call from colleague David Henley, who told me that Edith had been in an auto accident and was at New York University Medical Center, an affiliate of Bellevue Hospital where I worked. She was apparently driving near her loft in lower Manhattan, and as she put it, simply did not notice a car close to hers. Fortunately, she was not seriously hurt but had to be hospitalized for a week for wound care and physical therapy. The accident and hospital admission occurred on a Sunday evening and upon hearing the news, I bounded from my home nearby, went to my workplace for a bedside easel and supplies, and appeared at the bedside by 9:00 p.m. excited and anxious that I was to be Edith Kramer's art therapist! She welcomed me, "Hello my dear . . . what did you bring me? . . . Oh that's wonderful." Despite her pain, she was eager to paint immediately so

I positioned her and maneuvered materials so that she would have a comfortable setup. This took time and exploration of her physical range, capacity, and pain threshold to ensure a successful art-making arrangement. This finding of one's way was typical of my daily work, but it was certainly historic to be in this therapeutic dyad with my former professor and founder of the field. Moreover, the encounter was an example of something I had written about in my first publication, a paper she and Elinor Ulman edited, "to overcome the sense of loss and uselessness many medical patients experience it is essential that they produce personally satisfying works" and this sometimes requires adaptive measures – the cornerstone of medical art therapy (Rosner, 1982, p. 115). I left her happily engaged in the process, and a vivid visual memory remains for me to this day. She felt enabled instead of disabled, validated instead of victimized, and in a state of mastery, instead of passivity. This was the ultimate underscoring of the value of art as therapy in a medical setting.

I visited Edith daily until her discharge and replenished her art supplies as needed. I was impressed by her swift recovery, owing to her motivation in therapy, and the personal validation acquired by her creation of many watercolors of the view of the East River from her window. Her doctors were impressed by her physical resilience and, of course, her artistic skill. In fact, she gave many of the landscapes to caregivers as gifts upon discharge.

I savored Edith's comments about her newfound appreciation of art therapy with physical disability and hospitalization. She restated her respect for medical art therapy, for this time the experience was not a simulation as it was when she mimicked the apraxic patient. Now she herself was significantly impaired and subject to related psychological ramifications first hand, feeling suddenly dependent and constricted. She experienced the need to adapt – in outlook and in art-making – and allowed an art therapist to support her in doing so.

I will always be grateful to Edith Kramer for her depth and breadth of understanding, and for her folding of psychoanalytic elements into the psychological domain of disability and disease. Additionally, her openmindedness to embrace other ways of looking at patients and their artistic creations was memorable. By instilling confidence in me to carry on with the commitment that medical art therapy warranted further development and broader practice, she helped to ignite what had been a spark of an idea, transforming it into the flame of medical art therapy. Little did she realize that her interest in an unformed and underutilized area of our profession would influence the emergence of this special branch of our field now widely practiced in a range of health-care settings.

Reference

Rosner, I. (1982). Art therapy with two quadriplegic patients. *American Journal of Art Therapy*, 21(4): 115–120.

30 Experiences of Learning from Edith Kramer and Translating Her Book

Shyueying Chiang

Impressions of Edith

In 1994, people in Taiwan were not familiar with art therapy, and I was lucky to be accepted into the graduate program of art therapy at New York University (NYU) as the first Taiwanese student. I went to the United States to pursue my MA in art therapy and learn something new. I wasn't aware of any of the pioneers in the field such as Edith Kramer or Margaret Naumburg.

In the first semester, as a newcomer to New York, the city was interesting and fantastic, while at the same time, full of challenges. Learning to adjust to both the multicultural atmosphere of Manhattan and my studies at NYU was very difficult. I was unable to explore which instructor's research or which courses were more suitable for me; I could only follow all the basic requirements of the program.

I remember the first time I attended Edith Kramer's class. I heard little chatting sounds among my classmates, as if something big was about to happen. I was puzzled by their reaction before Edith walked into the classroom.

The Class of "Art for Art Therapists" Taught by Edith Kramer

Edith walked into the classroom in clothes completely covered in paint of all colors, a long silver braid, and a drawing board on her back. She started talking with a pronounced Austrian accent while every one of us listened with intense concentration. However, I could barely understand what she was saying at first.

Because the subject of the class was art for the art therapist, Edith would urge us to use art-making to express our feelings, and especially the vague feelings that are elicited when facing patients. In fact, the class had very little talking or lecturing and a lot of art-making and thinking about the art. As we thought about our own artwork and inner dynamics, we could see clearly that symbolic imagery in art expression implied so much more than words. Interestingly, the nonverbal nature of art-making allowed me to sail through the language barrier safely.

Once, Edith asked us to draw a tree. I did not understand her instructions, so I peeked at what my fellow students were doing and followed suit. Soon, I was

Learning from and Translating Edith Kramer 229

painting a huge tree using a Chinese brush, ink, and rice paper that I brought from Taiwan. Not only did I participate in the discussion afterward, but I also expressed my cultural identification with the Chinese materials I used.

Making a clay head sculpture was another nice memory about this class. Edith explained that we would be using red clay to mold a sculpture of our own head, and she then explained each and every step with intense concentration and as clearly as possible. First, every student was asked to pick one of the clay busts made by students in the previous year and break it into tiny pieces. Next, we were told to put these tiny, dried clay pieces into a very big bucket full of water and wait for the clay to soften. I was not familiar with the process of reconditioning dry clay, even though as an art teacher in high school in Taiwan, I taught sculpture with clay. When I taught sculpture, I always bought ready-made clay from art stores, and I gave each student a chunk of clay to work with. I had never prepared clay with my own hands before. Some of the clay chunks were very hard and in order to make them soft and workable we had to forcefully break them. Edith would come over and check to be sure the clay was small enough. This hand-made process was very challenging for me. The amazing thing is that Edith did not speak much during the process, and perhaps this is why a lot of my emotions were released when breaking the clay. I could sense that Edith really knew the materials and deeply understood what would happen dynamically. When students opened the bucket two weeks later, it was guaranteed that the clay we made would be in very good shape. It seemed that she only did a little, but actually she did a lot – during the process of preparing the clay materials she made us feel safe and secure.

Another delightful sculpting memory was with beeswax. One day, Edith brought in this strange material, beeswax, which I had never seen before. Edith asked us to put a slice of wax on our palms and slowly soften it with the warmth of our hands. We then sculpted the wax into interacting human forms. While we were at work, she demonstrated the technique by turning a little piece of wax into a small ball shape on her palms. It looked so simple yet it was actually quite frustrating when I tried to make a little ball in my hands. I was not very good at handling the hard wax or in making it into the shape I wanted. Edith, however, sculpted along with us and her magical hands quickly softened the beeswax chunks and made several children at play. Although the beeswax was just one color, the shapes of these children were so animated and fully expressive that we could easily see their movement and almost identify their facial expressions.

In all the various stages of this memorable class, whether we were handling familiar materials, or evoking nonverbal communication, Edith helped us experience the concept of *art as therapy* first-hand. She led us through these deceptively simple, yet thought-provoking art-making tasks.

Art as Therapy

Art as therapy emphasizes art-making and the therapeutic process inherent in making art. Edith once said in her class: "Everything an art therapist does

230 *Shyueying Chiang*

in the therapy room, everything said to the person you are working with, has to have therapeutic meaning." These words have stayed with me for 20 years now, reminding me always to respect the unique characteristics of each person I work with – to understand their needs, to think carefully about the meaning of each and every intervention, and to help each person as efficiently as possible in my clinical work.

During the process of art as therapy, art therapists encourage the people they work with to choose their method of art-making, to pick their own subject, materials and forms, or to develop a spontaneous drawing. If the individual encounters any difficulty, the art therapist can play the role of an auxiliary ego (Kramer, 1993), helping and encouraging them to develop enough self-esteem for art-making by themselves. The art therapist also provides the function of the *third hand* (Kramer, 1993), supporting the individual's efforts to bring what they want to create to completion. In other words, with the help of the art therapist and with their objective of the art in mind, they create their ideal artwork. The therapeutic achievements would be that the individual experiences nonverbal expression, finds relief in expressing difficult emotions, and reaches the therapeutic goal of increasing ego functions.

Lee (2006), a Taiwanese alumna of the Graduate Art Therapy Program of New York University and a student of Edith Kramer as well, once wrote about this concept in a short article, "Making Choices," which was published in *The Taiwan Art Therapy Journal*.[1] Lee described how the client needs to be the main character in the therapeutic process, and the art therapist should only help the client to make choices, which could be as simple as selecting the size of paper or the type of art material to use. This way the art therapist would provide the opportunity of developing better ego function. This creates an experience of warm support and encouragement for the client, of finding ways to autonomously fulfill wishes, and express and transform emotions constructively.

Misunderstanding of Art as Therapy

Therapeutic intention is very important for art therapists who align with the art as therapy orientation. However, it is easy to mistakenly think that the art therapist is merely a companion for art-making or to think that the session is merely teaching art, and disregard the theoretical underpinnings and wisdom of Edith Kramer's work.

While working with mild autism, Asperger Syndrome, and emotionally disturbed children in the resource or remedial classroom in an elementary school, one of the greatest challenges was to work with a limited school budget and materials. I tried my best to provide the children with as much choice as possible – the opportunity to choose from paper and materials – and allow them to develop their own subject matter. Different from their regular art class, the children were permitted to draw whatever they liked and encouraged

Learning from and Translating Edith Kramer 231

no matter how they performed with the art materials, which made them feel very happy. However, this kind of therapeutic group can face several obstacles, which may be due to cultural issues. First of all, parents usually find it hard to accept the fact that their children are participating in a "therapy" group. In Mandarin, there is a stronger connection between the word therapy and psychological illness than there is in English. Parents usually worry about their children being labeled and stigmatized after participating in a therapy group. Some parents even expect the therapists to analyze their children's artwork in order to understand them more easily. All the above factors actually create difficulties for art therapists.

To put the parents at ease, I typically invite them to join a meeting for parents before the class begins. During this meeting, I explain that the class is a special art class using the concepts of art therapy, instead of telling them it is a therapy group. The parent meetings are very effective, but can lead to more questions like, "Is there a big difference between art as therapy and art education?"

Art education has certain learning goals and course structures, while the goal of art as therapy is to help the participants express their inner world and feelings through art-making. The children in an art as therapy course are welcome to express what they want to express freely. As a result, some of the artwork of this "special art class" may not be acceptable by parent and teacher standards, as the artwork may contain violence, aggression, and chaos. Undoubtedly, the art therapist can accept and tolerate these expressions, and work with the children to transform emotions through the process. Chaos and ugliness may be exactly what the art therapist has to work with, but the parents may question the therapist: "What did you teach them?" or "Does it have to be so terrible?"

Professional art therapy training and knowledge becomes internalized and remains in the art therapist's mind. While an art therapist knows the objectives of art therapy very well, to the untrained eye, the interventions might be invisible. This can be difficult to understand. Children change emotionally and behaviorally through participation in these therapeutic groups. Some people might consider the therapeutic effects of art therapy as a mysterious force of magic, or they may think it is the analytical ability of the art therapist who brings forth the positive effects of the therapy.

Kramer (1993) never offered interpretations of the artwork during art therapy sessions. In order to gain deeper understanding of the children and the clinical process, she would consider their inner lives through the lens of psychodynamic theory, but only after the session was over. By taking the time to consider the inner life of the child, she could think about effective ways to intervene.

Besides the myth about art therapists analyzing art, art as therapy is somewhat confusing in Mandarin because the reader can easily ignore the theoretical content and mistakenly think that "as long as the client makes art, they can obtain therapeutic effects." This oversimplifies the concept of art as therapy and ignores the important foundation of psychological theories.

232 *Shyueying Chiang*

Chiang and Wu (2015) reviewed 162 graduate school theses about art therapy between 1987 and 2014 for the *10th Anniversary Special Issue for the Art Therapy Association in Taiwan*.[2] Most of the theses about art-making and self-growth were from the art as therapy perspective. There were two major types of researchers in the art as therapy camp. The larger group of researchers under this umbrella was from art programs in graduate schools. The researchers had not taken art therapy courses and merely wrote about their personal art-making experiences. Between 2005 and 2014, the number of these researchers grew resulting in a total of 29 theses. The second group of researchers was from art therapy programs in graduate schools with previous training in the helping professions. Their professional backgrounds included Jungian psychology, Gestalt psychology, narrative therapy . . . etc. These theses were about self-awareness and growth through art-making. They were finished between 2011 and 2014, with a total of ten theses of this kind. We are glad to see that the academy of Taiwan is showing interest in art as therapy, but it may not have an in-depth understanding of Edith Kramer's work.

Edith (1993) thought that art-making may happen because of psychological pressure that brings an almost magical energy of transformation to the mind. We assumed that this group of researchers must have been deeply affected by their art-making experiences because their theses were very moving. However, Edith's concept was from a therapeutic perspective. She suggested that the therapeutic process in art as therapy has art-making as the core, and it is more than just a personal experience for the artist. As Edith taught us long ago, "Everything the therapist says in the therapy room must be therapeutic." As a major orientation for both theoretical and clinical work of art therapy, art as therapy reminds us that we must think carefully and thoroughly to obtain the maximum benefit for the people we work with.

Translating *Art as Therapy with Children*

Books are important for transferring knowledge. Translation breaks language barriers and brings knowledge to even more people. As early as 1999, I planned to translate Edith Kramer's *Art as Therapy with Children* (1993) as the textbook I use for students, so I visited Edith in her studio in New York and asked for her permission. She was very happy that this book would have a Chinese version. However, we did not have a large group of art therapists in Taiwan at the time, so the publisher was very hesitant to publish a book that might not sell. After I finished translating the book, it was not published until 2004. Since then, this book has been a must-read for every art therapy student in Taiwan.

While translating, I began to realize that readers might not be totally aware of Edith's meaning of various terms, or even familiar with the field of art therapy. To make it easier for the readers to understand, I added some footnotes in the book to explain what Edith meant in certain places. These footnotes were highly praised by the readers, and written with several principles in mind.

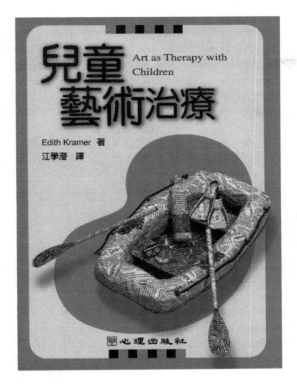

Figure 30.1 Cover of the Chinese version of *Art as Therapy with Children*

First, I provided simple explanations for psychoanalytic terms with regard to their meaning in the clinical work of art therapy. For instance, the original text only used "reality testing" to explain certain clinical phenomena, and I used the traditional Chinese edition of the *Dictionary of Psychology* (Chang, 1989, p. 44) to explain the meaning of reality testing in psychological theory in the footnote. Second, I provided further explanation for certain clinical processes that may be obvious and natural for art therapists but might be misunderstood by general readers. For instance, when Edith talked about "sublimation," she mentioned the process that Christopher took to transform fantasy to visual image. In this footnote, I explain further that art therapists can guide the child to move from fantasy to subjects related to real life (Kramer, 2004, p. 120). Third, I describe clearly the structural sequence in various processes that can be misunderstood due to cultural bias and differences. An example of this is Naumburg and Winnicott's scribble drawing (The Squiggle Game) that art therapists often lead clients to make in art therapy (Kramer, 2004, p. 12). The lay reader may easily misunderstand the process, thinking that coloring in the scribble would be the only thing the client could do in the scribble drawing. In the footnote, I spell out the various things that can be done with the scribble.

I really liked how Edith (1993) used the example of apple picking to explain cultural differences and how culture changes over time. She said that the children in the '70s were not familiar with picking apples from apple trees because most of the children got their apples from supermarkets; they probably didn't even know what an apple tree looked like. This situation is somewhat similar to Taiwan. Local children rarely have the chance to see apples growing on the trees because they usually see them either in the traditional food markets or in modern supermarkets. Moreover, apple trees only grow in the mountainous areas of Taiwan, since it is a subtropical island, and even if children do have a chance to visit a farm with apple trees, they look different from the North-American apple trees. As Edith said, this kind of subject matter does not connect to real-life experience, and we must remind ourselves that we need to consider cultural influences and real-life experience all the time.

Rich life experiences can bring us creative energy. Parents in Taiwan are keen to push children to learn. Beginning from nursery school, children have to learn English and other subjects. Art classes typically emphasize skills and do not provide opportunities for children to express themselves through art-making. The spontaneous art-making that Edith conducted relied on the concept that we can cultivate autonomous ability through creation. We need to have more communication with educators and parents to allow for the preservation of children's imagination and to allow them to discover and realize their hopes and dreams.

Edith also talked about how making crafts gave people the joy of holding and owning their own art. This brought to mind the rising popularity of

Figure 30.2 Edith with Shyueying Chiang

various do-it-yourself workshops in Taiwan. These simple workshops give the general public a great sense of fun and accomplishment. Although these craft-based activities are merely imitation and replication and hardly resemble real art-making, people still love them. As Edith said, even if the cup in our hand is not very beautiful, we still enjoy holding something we made ourselves.

As more and more art therapists finish their training in the US, Europe, and Australia, and return to Taiwan, the educational institutions in the universities under art or counseling psychology departments, and the Art Therapy Association in Taiwan are steadily providing more and more art therapy courses for continuing education. Therapeutic application of art therapy with a creative orientation is becoming more important in Taiwan. Art as therapy transcends cultural and temporal limitations. As long as we understand its essence, the therapeutic effect of art can happen anywhere, anytime.

Notes

1 For more information on the journal and The Taiwan Society for the Study of Art Therapy, please see their website at: www.arttherapy.org.tw/arttherapy.
2 *Ten years of art therapy, a hundred years of art healing: 10th Anniversary Special Issue for the Art Therapy Association in Taiwan* is freely available online here: www.arttherapy.org.tw/arttherapy/post/post/data/arttherapy/tw/10_anni versary_issue/

References

張春興 編著（1989）。張氏心理學辭典。台北：東華。 [Chang, C.X. (1989). *Chang's dictionary of psychology*]. Taipei: Dong-Hua Publisher.
江學澄、吳思華（2015）。研究論文整理。侯禎塘　主編：遊藝十年，療癒百年：台灣藝術治療學會十週年專刊：97–115。[Chiang, S.Y. & Wu, S.H. (2015). Theses of art therapy in Taiwan since 1987. In Z.T. Hou (Ed.), *Ten years of art therapy, a hundred years of art healing: 10th anniversary special issue for the Art Therapy Association in Taiwan* (97–115)]. Retrieved from www.arttherapy.org.tw/arttherapy/post/post/data/arttherapy/tw/10_anniversary_issue-8/
Kramer, E. (1993). *Art as therapy with children*. Chicago, IL: Magnolia Street Publishers.
Kramer, E.（2004）。兒童藝術治療。台北：心理出版社。 。兒童藝術治療（江學澄 譯）。台北：心理出版社。 [*Art as therapy with children*]. Taipei: Psychology Publisher.
李碧玲（2006）。做選擇。江學澄 主編：臺灣藝術治療會訊，4: 3–4。[Lee, P.L. (2006). Make choices. In S.Y. Chiang (Ed.), *Newsletter of Taiwan Art Therapy Association, 4*, pp. 3–4].

31 Edith, Puppets, and the Kindly Superego

Lani Gerity

I think Edith was a very subversive teacher. Not that she taught political revolution, but rather she taught a kind of personal emancipation. She valued freedom, freedom from oppression, and freedom of expression for the people we work with and for ourselves as well.

She had a way of drawing us into discussions with questions that opened our minds and changed our worldviews, and that process was subversive in the best possible way. She was a delightful storyteller, fascinated by folklore, the Brothers Grimm, and of course the series of stories she told the boys of Wiltwyck, *The Wonderful Adventures of Nils*, a hero's journey of sorts, by the Swedish author Selma Lagerlöf. Stories can be equally subversive; the characters can take up residence in our minds and move us to change our lives.

One of these discussions that was particularly life changing, was about the necessity for role models and ego ideals that are possible to grow into. Edith felt that in order for a child to succeed in life, there had to be some positive caretaking early in the child's life; there had to be a creation of a benign or kindly superego in the child, which would be internalized from benign or kindly adults in the child's early life. This kindly superego would be able to gently guide and support the individual even after the caretaker was long gone.

This made me wonder about the people I was working with at the time – a group of patients who were traumatized as children. Because of their experiences of physical, sexual, and psychological trauma when they were very young, a developmental rupture in their sense of self and body image led to symptoms, defensive strategies, and over time, a variety of diagnoses. As I worked with these patients in an art room, I repeatedly observed this rupture and defensive stance within the artistic expressions of self: art work depicting separation, dissociation, and aggression toward the self. At first, I saw very little evidence of anything kindly in their work or in the stories of their memories. I wondered if it was too late for them. Could they form a kindly superego?

What I noticed over time, though, particularly in the puppet-making group, was that the creative process was being used to repair disturbed body images, to bring together dissociated parts of the self, and to provide the artists with a sense of history, causality, and meaning. Over time, I observed a diminishment of feelings of alienation and estrangement, while the encouragement

Edith, Puppets, and the Kindly Superego 237

and growth of a stable community flourished; this by a population better known for instability and a dissociated sense of history. Repeatedly, I would watch amazing transformations; papier-mâché and cloth becoming magical, animated, little creatures, while a room in a dreary inner-city day treatment facility became a land filled with possibility, and the most difficult of patients were transformed into warm, generous human beings.[1]

Arthur Frank (1995), in a discussion on the wounded storyteller, described a process of "colonization," in which a patient hands over his or her body and life narrative to someone else, usually a "biomedical expert." I thought of the African-American Wiltwyck boys, and their need to draw and paint pictures of white men in positions of authority, and how with Edith's art as therapy approach a kind of decolonization began to take place.

The individuals I was working with in New York had, as children, been forced into a similar form of colonization by their abusers. As they became adults, they repeated this colonization in their various relationships, in peer and family relations, and in their relationships with the psychiatric community. However, in the process of making puppets with their attached stories, the dissociative patient could reclaim the authority to tell his or her own story, and construct a new life narrative from the "wreckage" of their early childhood trauma.

Frank described what he calls a quest narrative, in which illness or life challenges are seen as part of a spiritual journey, which took a certain amount of decolonization to be able to tell. This kind of narrative was beyond the experience of most of the dissociative patients until they began to work in the art room, until they began to develop a sense of agency in their own lives. While working on their puppets, they were able to express their problems in metaphor, which allowed for a creative distance between themselves and their problems. They would find artistic challenges, solve these, and see their resolutions in terms of their strengths and abilities. They could then anchor these strengths into the puppets they were working on. It seemed that as improvement could be found in their work and lives, the artists created little markers that could not be denied, and that, in fact, were often sought out like comforting touchstones.

In the group, there would be ongoing stories that developed organically, weaving together a tribal history. The hand puppets (very animated, three-dimensional, miniature beings) seemed to pull empathy from the hardest hearts with ease. Changes would be documented and remembered in the oral history of the group. Often the original trauma and misfortune could be retold in a more distanced way through the life and struggle of the puppet. This distancing gave them the opportunity to use a part of the mind which created hope, and dreams, and new possibilities, a part of the mind that could conceive of life as a spiritual journey. These hopes would then be anchored into the form of the puppet – some new clothing, new hair, or a new expression would mark the change.

Although each artist has his or her own amazing story of transformation, I'll tell you Jack's story and the story of his puppet Bogdan. I had often heard

238 *Lani Gerity*

Jack say "anything could happen in Puppetland," an optimistic statement about the world of imagination, the world of possibilities. He had not always been able to hold such an optimistic view, as a survivor of childhood trauma.

He told stories of rage and victimization for many years. He described his early life as being filled with seductive, unpredictable, often enraged adults – his mother and a series of shadowy, sometimes violent boyfriends. He first came to our center in late adolescence. He trusted no one, had little sense of object constancy, and struggled with his sexual identity, alcoholism, and agoraphobia.

During the ten years that followed, he developed a reputation as the worst, most hateful, frightening borderline patient one could work with. Psychiatrists dreaded their appointments with him. Jack had been asked to leave every verbal group he'd ever been a part of and every staff member lived in fear that he would be assigned to them. As a kind of therapeutic last ditch effort, it was suggested that Jack try art therapy.

Although the prospect of Jack coming to art groups was intimidating, I showed him where the materials were kept and told him whatever he did in the art room would be alright, as long as it was on the paper. He seemed to appreciate having this place where self-expression was really allowed, even encouraged. He gradually became a regular in many of the art groups during the week and after many, many pictures of guillotines, bombings, dismembered body parts, death, and destruction, he slowly allowed others within the art room to see a less hostile aspect of himself. At last, he could work quietly and expressively, but each piece seemed self-contained, each session seemed isolated and removed from the reality of his life, as if the art room were a sanctuary that needed to be kept protected from the danger of the real world, which was impinging on him.

When he asked if he could join puppet-making, I was delighted, even relieved. I saw from my work with others that this modality provided great potential for integration and a real way to anchor gains and growth. Indeed, it seemed the things Jack and the other group members learned in puppet-making could be integrated into their lives. Myths and a sense of history and context were woven around the puppets. Their stories grew or evolved from week to week, and the creators would carry the stories beyond the confines of the art room, musing over the meaning while riding the subway or cooking a meal. Jack used images well, expressing much of what had been inexpressible, but now, with the creation of puppets, he could make something else, new stories that could be reflected upon and linked to his real life, stories with possibilities.

Through participating in Puppetland adventures, Jack experimented with various parts of himself, with new ways of interacting. He could create a narrative to explain his puppet Bogdan's reactions to the world, and from the puppet's story his own suffering and motivations became clearer to him. He found it easier to talk about the puppet's fears and shame than his own, so he spoke in an empathic way for Bogdan, discovering that within his own imagination lay the magic of possibilities, generosity, and caring. It gradually dawned on

Edith, Puppets, and the Kindly Superego 239

him that Bogdan's difficulties were very like his own and that Jack actually felt a great deal better when he found solutions for Bogdan's difficulties.

Bogdan's story begins in the Ukraine, before the days of Stalin. Bogdan had experienced a happy childhood but then came the shadow and cold of the Siberian work camps, which were "unspeakable in their horror." While cutting down trees and suffering from the bitter cold, Bogdan vowed to himself that one day he would be free, that he would be warm and his stomach would be full. Jack was fond of saying that Bogdan had a hunter's fire in his heart.

He overcame the ice and oppression of Siberia and came to America. Bogdan often "blessed that day," because America was "a land of great opportunity, freedom, goodness, and safety." "You can make a real killing on Wall Street," he was fond of telling the other puppets.

The hunter's fire in his heart led him to acquire a sizable import–export business as well as an estate in an area where the boundaries of Long Island and Puppetland overlapped. However, these triumphs had not taken away the pain and regret from the memories of the work camps, so he tried to numb that pain and wall it off with the finest fire-water available, with very little success. Fate, being a capricious thing, had provided him with great suffering as well as the opportunities to learn and thrive, but he would have to be awake to act on these.

In Bogdan's personal story, Jack could describe the helplessness and misery of his adolescence. He placed Bogdan in a Siberian work camp where he was forced to suffer physically as well as emotionally. Bogdan's great excitement at finding freedom in America and on Wall Street paralleled Jack's gratitude at finding the art room and more specifically the puppet-making group. The freedom of expression that he found in that group was, for him, priceless and the ability to tell his own story with enough distance and through this small, animated hand puppet was humanizing.

But in all the most interesting stories I have heard, the hero is put to the test and the story of Puppetland was no different. Jack and Bogdan were about to be tested. This was the day that was later referred to as the day of the "Big Hunt." One of the puppeteers, an older woman, came into the session looking to create a situation with Jack. We, the group leaders, had been warned and were well prepared. I brought in a mysterious, female rod puppet (having one central, vertical rod) with long black hair and a body of blue fur. Du Rand (Du Rand & Gerity, 1996) decided that her puppet, Ungar, would take Bogdan on a hunt if he was willing, so that Jack would be able to experience his own rage with awareness, and containment, and then sublimate it into something that would be useful for the community. The awareness could occur because Jack knew Bogdan was a representation of himself – containment could occur in the enactment of a great hunt, and something positive could be created from the rage because "anything is possible in Puppetland."

Both interventions worked very well; the hunt was a great success, and Jack seemed genuinely delighted to find this female puppet, which he immediately picked up, and gave a voice. It seemed to provide him with an outlet for a

240 *Lani Gerity*

kinder aspect of himself that was something new and unexplored. So Jadwega, as he named it, and all she represented became a reason to stay, a reason to maintain the balance of the group, to avoid a battle "to the death," or the eviction from the group. The hunt provided an outlet for the rage, a socially acceptable one, which fed the tribe for months to come.

Puppetland was a perfect setting for the unfolding of quest narratives for puppets and puppeteers. These narratives truly belonged to the tellers. They were no longer a meaningless string of events and no longer about being colonized by their abusers or the psychiatric community. They could see their lives as their own unique narrative of an unfolding journey. Years after his Puppetland experiences, Jack attributed his feeling better to the reawakening of the ability to dream and hope that had occurred within Puppetland.

Another patient explained that the magic that she felt was a part of this puppet-making group in this way:

> When I think back to Puppetland, I think of bright colors, special music, playfulness, laughter, and freedom. And joy . . . and innocence . . . and trust. And all those things triumphed, in Puppetland, over the deep anguish, fear, and disillusionment that darkened the lives of its human inhabitants. Puppetland lives in my memory as . . . a bottomless "treasure box" filled to the brim with wonderful, mysterious, shiny things that you can explore to your heart's content . . . lovely little jewels, tiny dolls and figures, interesting pictures, fabulous fabrics. A huge toy store where everything you want is yours already. And Puppetland's celebrations live in my memory as . . . well . . . absolute joy. . . . There have never been any parties to rival Puppetland's celebrations.
>
> I know, in reality, Puppetland consisted of a handful of . . . emotionally disturbed adults making puppets and dolls with paper, paste, fabric, needle, and thread at long wooden tables in a big, somewhat run-down room on the second floor of a day program for mentally ill adults. But there were two Puppetlands – the external and the internal. And the internal Puppetland transcended everything.

As an art therapist, I saw the restorative value of the puppet-making and the connected stories as many layered. The first layer lies in the actual puppet-making, being on a deep pre-verbal level, a way for people to repair their body image, through *art as therapy*, through the creation of whole body image representations where they once only created representations of dismemberment and dissociation.

Another art as therapy aspect of this process was the ability and freedom the puppet-makers had to mark the learning and wisdom gained, metaphorically, through the changing appearance and embellishments of their puppets. One very clear example of this was an interaction between two finger puppets who each focused on experiencing the world in one way only. Mr Mad only saw the world with an angry heart. Wolfie was a very blue dog and only felt sadness. The puppeteers began to wonder about this. Was one right and one

Edith, Puppets, and the Kindly Superego 241

wrong? Or what if they had hearts that were of other colors? If Wolfie or Mr Mad had red hearts they might feel anger, and if they added a yellow heart (since anything was possible in Puppetland) they might feel joy, while a blue heart would allow for sadness. A blossoming of little felt hearts appeared on many puppets that day.

Often these stories seemed to effect change in a mysterious way. Sometimes the group members would put their puppets down and talk about the subversive qualities of the process, that they could feel things shift and change, but they couldn't figure it out. Also, it seemed that change could occur as they shared these stories, handing down the group narrative to newcomers as they sat around the metaphorical campfire.

There was a sense of community created as individuals shared history, stories, and their various quests, when they listened deeply, with empathy, to these stories. There was much healing and growth that occurred with this kind of listening. The empathic listening had a way of bringing out warm, generous feelings in the participants, and celebrations provided a vehicle for people to create gifts for each other. Puppetland was known for its celebrations. All transitions, leave takings, and special events were marked with music, food, gifts, and laughter.

On one of these occasions, a particularly beloved intern was leaving, so the puppeteers brought many gifts of food and artwork. The intern prepared a story of a wise old woman in the forest, who could be visited at any time for wisdom and comfort. The wise old woman had given the intern little beads to give the puppets that would be a kind of guide on their journeys. It seemed the intern had given us a wonderful group myth. Although we were losing her and her puppet, there was this reparative gift, this archetypal wise old woman who had come to life in story.

Some time went by, and it became clear that the group would benefit from the addition of this character, a nurturing and caring community elder, in tangible puppet form. Once the wise old woman was finished, the group as a whole brought her to life. Each member had a chance to hold her or work her, and to listen for something about who she was and what gift she had to give to the individual. We all listened carefully as the puppet was passed around, and in this way she developed a kind of group character.

We learned that she had gifts for each of us, that she was 104, and that she lived in an underground hogan or kiva. It was also discovered that she had knowledge of the earth, its herbs, seasons, and life in general. All the aspects of this puppet were warm and generous. All her gifts were good and simple. From the wise old woman's emergence, I learned about the importance of generosity. She was a wonderful character, possibly reminiscent of a kindly grandparent. I suspect she was internalized by many in the group.

At yet another gathering, at the end of another intern's time at our center, the puppeteers were sitting around the art room table. I asked if the puppets could make a list of things they felt they were holding on to and things they felt that they could let go of. A list of the puppets' concerns would be more accessible than individual concerns hidden under layers of resistance and denial.

Most of the lists of things being held on to included fears, emptiness, sadness, reality, and despair. Most of the lists of things that could be let go of were identical. I then asked everyone to turn the paper over and to write down a gift for their puppet, the thing they needed most. Some of the gifts were abstract things like happiness, friendship, and feeling whole, but many were concrete things that would bring the puppet (or puppeteer) happiness: art, maps, dance classes, a ride on the Central Park Carousel, a sapling, a peppermint stick, art supplies, and three wishes for friends.

When the writing was done, Jack asked if he could read the lists and the gifts to the group, without giving the name of the puppet. The group liked this suggestion, eager to hear what everyone else had written. When I picked up the pieces of paper after the group was over, I saw that Jack had added additional gifts to all the sheets of paper. He had not read these additions; he was not looking for acknowledgment of what he had done or for the generous feelings he was having toward the group members. They were simply his wishes for the puppet and the puppeteer, and in each case, they were strong, wise, and compassionate gifts.

Of all the kinds of groups I ran at this bleak inner-city mental health center, I never found such acts of generosity, such humanity as I found in this group.

Figure 31.1 Edith Kramer and puppet. Photo by Edward Glanville

Edith, Puppets, and the Kindly Superego 243

I suspected, at the end of this session, that all would be well, that we all had the tools or guides we needed to carry on within us.

As I look back over these narratives, remembering various puppets and puppeteers, I can see that they had indeed created ego ideals for themselves, characters that guided and supported them internally, even when they were not in the group. The puppeteers began to create decolonized life experiences for themselves through the puppets. The new experiences broadened their view of the world and allowed for freedom of expression. They animated this freedom in the unfolding narratives and in the art making aspect of creating and embellishing their puppets. They developed empathy for their own puppets and narratives, for their own personal stories and selves, which the puppets represented, and, most importantly, for each other.

If I could give you one thing from this experience of Puppetland, it would be that you have an adventurous heart, that if you come upon an opportunity to create puppets and quest narratives for these puppets, you take it, and see where the adventure leads you.

Note

1 At the time, these transformations appeared miraculous. Now, thanks to neuro-marketing research on how to create advertising that stimulates endorphins and other positive brain chemistry, there is a documented link between the physical attributes of small, animated creatures, like babies, puppies, and kittens, (to which I would add puppets and dolls) and these happy brain chemicals. For further reading about this subject, please see: Alley, 1981; Chuang, 2005; Garger, 2007; Glocker et al., 2009; Gould, 1992; and Lorenz, 1971.

References

Alley, T. R. (1981). Head shape and perception of cuteness. *Developmental Psychology, 17*(5), 650–654.

Chuang, T. (2005). The power of cuteness: Female infantilization in urban Taiwan. *Stanford Journal of East Asian Affairs, 5*(2), 21–28.

Du Rand, L., & Gerity, L. (1996). Puppetry: A collaboration between drama therapy and art therapy. *Dramascope: The National Association for Drama Therapy Newsletter, 16*(2), 9–10.

Frank, A. (1995). *The wounded storyteller: Body, illness, and ethics.* Chicago, IL: The University of Chicago Press.

Garger, I. (2007, March 1). Global psyche: One nation under cute. Retrieved from https://www.psychologytoday.com/articles/200703/global-psyche-one-nation-under-cute Accessed 19 September 2017.

Gerity, L.A., & Kramer, E. (1999). *Creativity and the dissociative patient; Puppets, narrative, and art in the treatment of survivors of childhood trauma.* London: Jessica Kingsley.

Glocker, M.L., Langleben, D.D., Ruparel, K., Loughead, J.W., Valdez, J.N., Griffin, M.D. . . . Gur, R.C. (2009). Baby schema modulates the brain reward

244 Lani Gerity

system in nulliparous women. *Proceedings of the National Academy of Sciences,* *106*(22), 9115–9119.

Gould, S. J. (1992). A biological homage to Mickey Mouse. In *The panda's thumb: More reflections in natural history.* New York: Norton.

Lorenz, K. (1971). Part and parcel in animal and human societies. In K. Lorenz, *Studies in Animal and Human Behavior* (Vol. 2, 115–195). Cambridge, MA: Harvard University Press.

Art, Art Therapy, and Culture

32 Quality and Inner Satisfaction

Re-Visiting the Importance of Quality in Art and Art Therapy[1]

Edith Kramer, Susan Ainlay Anand, and Lani Gerity

Introduction by Edith Kramer

During an American Art Therapy Association conference, a colleague approached me. She told me that she used my books with much success when teaching her students, but there was one issue where they had difficulties. This was the idea of *quality*. Had quality any place in our work? Did we not encourage our patients to forget all about making "good" pictures or sculptures? Did we not reassure them that we did not care what their work looked like, or that we would never be judgmental?

When we talk to our patients about drawing, painting, and sculpting we are often confronted with the patients feeling inadequate: "They can't draw a straight line." "They have not done any art since they were 6 years old." And so forth. And so we reassure them again and again that it doesn't matter how they draw. One reason why we must insist on this is the atrocious art that prevails in our western popular culture and in the media. We are fairly certain that any attempts to make a "pretty" or an "artistic" picture will yield either some revolting kitsch or an imitation of some of the worst examples of modern art.

Naturally, we must not hurt our patients' feelings by telling them that we expect their most serious attempts to paint a pretty picture would more often than not turn out to be something quite awful. And so we circumvent the issue and tell them that we do not care what their work looks like, that in art therapy, anything goes.

It seems that some of us have been taken in by our own propaganda and feel that we indeed do not care about the quality of our patient's art, while actually we are only attempting to free them from the constraints of artificial standards so that they can find their expressive style.

However, we see that our way of working is largely determined by the cultural environment in which we function. Suppose, for example, we were doing art therapy in an environment where folk art flourished. The request to draw or paint something would not appear outlandish to our patients, for folk artists and craftspeople are continuously embellishing their work with delightful additions that constitute a kind of overflow of their pleasure in the work

248 *Kramer, Anand, and Gerity*

of their hands. The prevailing pictorial standards of this hypothetical cultural environment would very likely be commensurable with the patient's faculties; our hypothetical patients would probably have tried their best without excessive distress. Their productions would have given evidence of the cultural environment, and everyone's artistic style, and emotional disturbance. I have discovered this kind of evidence in the artwork produced by some members of the Shaker communities. While their superb craft gives no evidence of psychic distress that caused some of these individuals to seek refuge in these communities, their artwork can reveal emotional disturbance or distress.

Folk art is never in bad taste, but it also rarely attains greatness, for this requires the total devotion which only the professional artist can give. However, whenever we encounter great art, we usually meet its shadow, great kitsch or other manifestations of anti-art. It would indeed be worthwhile to write the art history of kitsch that parallels the history of fine art.

Rather than provide the entire history of kitsch, I decided to investigate the nature of kitsch, by finding one small example tucked away in a corner of Paris that I could draw. One always learns more about the nature of a work when one draws it rather than when one just contemplates it. I found a charming Parisian park embellished by a fountain that featured three graces. The edifice consisted of three shell-like circular structures. Water sprang from the crest of the fountain and descended upon three devilish-horned heads, or were they meant to be fauns? Their mouths, distorted into angry expressions, spat streams of water upon a shell-shaped structure. From there the water descended in several distinct streams to the base of the fountain, so that a veil of descending water surrounded the three youthful women standing in the middle. Their ample but graceful bodies were partially draped, allowing seductive glimpses of nude breasts, thighs, and graceful necks and shoulders. The shell-like structure upon which they stood was adorned by faun-like heads spouting water with what seemed to me a discontented expression, upon another under shell-like basin that constituted the base of the fountain. The total effect of the fountain was charming. Even so, whenever I pursued any of the several elements of the composition with pencil and paper, I arrived at a dead end. The fauns or devils of the top structure spouted water with an angry expression. The heads beneath the shell that supported the three graces seemed to expel water with a disgruntled expression. Whenever I tried to follow the flow of the drapery that covered the graceful women's nudity, it somehow vanished to reappear surprisingly somewhere else, so that it remained elusive.

Within its overabundance of details, the composition lacked logic or consistency. The artist who designed the fountain seemed to have had no clear idea of what he wanted to convey. All he seemed to have known was that there should be much live water and feminine charms sharpened by the presence of masculine thrust in the three horned heads. The architect of the fountain could easily have added some more detail or omitted some elements without it making much difference. Using this fountain as an example, we have a description of the "quality of kitsch."

Quality and Inner Satisfaction 249

Figure 32.1 Photograph of fountain in Paris

How can we characterize its opposite, "good art," in general terms? Three elements seem essential: evocative power, inner consistency, and an economy of means, so that the quality of the work would be diminished if anything were added or omitted. Such work conveys an inner unity that gives great satisfaction.

Returning from our excursion into the realm of fine arts to our patients and the quality of their art, can we hope that some of their work would attain inner consistency? Should we indeed desire and support such a development

250 *Kramer, Anand, and Gerity*

or would this diminish the spirit of acceptance of all and anything the patient produces, which is essential in any therapeutic work? Both psychotherapy and art therapy imply a search for inner truth. Unlike psychotherapy where the transference relationship between patient and therapist is central, art therapy focuses on the patient's artwork. In our communications, we remain within the symbolic realm the patient has created. When our patients' artwork expresses inner truth, it invariably also attains formal consistency, and thus good formal quality. In this work, we are aided by the patient's desire to give form to their anxieties, preoccupations, and fantasies. We hope that giving form to such material will make it possible for them to contemplate their art and come to terms with what they see.

Not every kind of art therapy gives the emphasis to form that I have given it, however. Margaret Naumburg, who in the '40s tried to make art therapy acceptable to the psychoanalytic establishment, encouraged her patients to make quick sketches only, and next to free associate to their own productions. She also encouraged patients to make free scribbles, and find images in them, and elaborate on them. Such pictures are apt to bring forth much latent material and can be very helpful. But again, no high formal quality can be expected to emerge. We can understand that art therapists who apply such methods will have little opportunity to contemplate the phenomenon of quality in their practice.

To conclude, whenever a patient's creation – be it a drawing, a painting, or a sculpture – expresses some inner truth forcefully without being hindered by any unnecessary additions, the work will attain good formal quality. We see that inner truth and good form constitute two sides of the same coin.

In the cultural wasteland in which we function, it is surprising to encounter good quality in the work of artists, art therapists, and patients. It is not surprising that young art therapists should be puzzled by the concept of quality. I hope to have helped to make the concept more comprehensible.

Susan Ainlay Anand and Lani Gerity

In the following section, we will share what we learned from self-taught artists in Mississippi. We hope this material will speak to you as it did to us of the capacity for strength, dignity, and beauty that is inherent in all of us, whether we reside in the mainstream or margins of this culture. It is our intent to awaken the possibility of searching for, finding, or creating the stillness and space for experiences of quality, inner satisfaction, and wholeness. Our search for quality and the intuitive feeling of satisfaction took place in the Delta region of Mississippi, often called "the most southern place on earth."

Our best advice on how to approach the people of the Delta came from another outsider to the area, Sister Bertolli, a Catholic nun and self-taught artist from Oregon who had served her order as a community worker in Mississippi for many years. She found her way into the community through art. She began to create pictures while listening to the community elders' stories about how

Quality and Inner Satisfaction 251

life used to be. She found that by attending to the stories and the tellers, and embodying them with her materials, she developed a respect and love for them and all that they had been through, and she gained a feeling of compassion and esteem for herself, as well, for all she had been through. "Women have always been creative," she told us. "If the front door is locked, then we've always known to look around the back for another way in." Making art was her way in through the back door of the community.

Mrs L.V. Hull of Kosciusko was quite happy to talk about her satisfaction in her work in spite of being recently released from the hospital from gallbladder surgery. She shared with us her delightful wit and sense of humor: "I told those doctors just take out the gallbladder, don't go fishing around in there for anything else." About art making, she had this to say, "I get inspirations, and I just have to paint." Her house is filled with objects that she's covered with spots and phrases all in craft acrylic paints.

"People might think this is easy to do, just painting spots on things, but the colors are very important." She then explained her color theory, how some colors are dead or flat and some colors are living, vibrant, and placement is very important if you want a piece to come to life. When asked about her satisfaction in this work, she spoke of having been lost once, that she was on a "downward path," when she discovered her inspiration, a gift from God. It saved her life. "You see, the devil don't love a paintbrush," she explained. "And that is an inspiration. I'll have to paint those words somewhere." Phrases, little seeds of wisdom like that, come to her, and she paints them on an object. She had old TVs decorated with spots and phrases: "The straight and narrow path doesn't have any traffic problems." And "Do not try to understand me, just love me." "That's better than anything else you will see on TV," she explained. We could not argue.

She showed us a drawing a neighbor boy had made for her after she told him he was also an artist. "Kids need that, they need inspiration too." Then she showed us an assemblage dedicated to B.B. King, who she hoped would come and receive it one day. "Art is good," she said, "this inspiration is good, but what is really good is to share it, to think about it, to talk to folks about why it is important." She then said she didn't know why, but she was moved to sing. So she sang two spirituals, with a deep, rich, sure voice, while beating time slowly on her chest. Even though one of her "inspirations" suggested we should love her rather than understand her, we found her easy to understand and love.

We also talked with Reverend H.D. Dennis and Margaret Dennis of Margaret's Grocery in Vicksburg. For Preacher, as he called himself, and Margaret, art was about several things: First, a reverence for the written word, particularly words from the Bible; secondly, creating a gift for God and for Margaret; and, finally, it was about abundance and play.

Preacher asked Margaret to marry him one day, saying he would build a temple for the Lord and her if she said yes. She said yes. The inside of this structure was where we saw the abundance and play. It resembled an incredibly lavish Hindu temple, where everything was on wheels, turning, making "music," and lighting up.

When we asked about the playful nature of this artwork, these assemblages, Margaret explained that neither of them had toys nor the time to play as children. Life was much, much harder back then. She reminisced about Christmas, how every year her mother surprised 11 children by creating 11 Christmas boxes, one for each. And each box would contain a piece of pie, a slice of cake, two brazil nuts, eight or nine raisins, an orange, an apple, and a horn. Every year was the same, and every year it was a surprise and a delight. She never figured out how her mother did it. And she wasn't sure, but she thought maybe she and her siblings enjoyed those Christmas boxes as much as or perhaps even more than if they had had as many toys as children have today.

Preacher's story was about even poorer beginnings. He was born near Rolling Fork, Mississippi. He and his mother were isolated and lived alone at the time, and she died from complications during childbirth. The story was that they were undiscovered for five or six days, and the "smell alone would have killed a mule." But Preacher survived. His grandmother came to take him away, and the doctor tried to give her a pill to end the new baby's life. But she knew "The Man" (and Preacher pointed upwards as he told us this) and He would help her; she would show that doctor! She only knew two things, "The Man" and slavery, and she taught everything she knew. When she died, he went to live with his father, and eventually a white plantation owner took him in. The plantation owner and his sons taught Preacher to read, write, and do his

Figure 32.2 Margaret at her home, Margaret's Grocery in Vicksburg, Mississippi, 2001

Quality and Inner Satisfaction   253

numbers once the workday was finished. Because reading and writing were so very hard to come by (and at one time, illegal), and because they provided a way into a world of knowledge, words were very much cherished.

Initially, we heard in their stories of struggle only pain and deprivation. But then we noticed that there was grace beneath the pain – we were hearing about the importance of religion, family, and sense of place in Margaret and Preacher's lives.

Because of our northern, urban education, which was very much grounded in science and the material world, we were taught to see religion somewhat cynically. We were taught to stand outside of religious culture with knowledge that religion is created out of human need to return to the safety of mother and that with proper analysis this could be resolved. Such a jaundiced view separated us from Margaret and Preacher because religion was so thoroughly woven into every aspect of their lives and art. It became clear that to really understand them, or as Mrs Hull would suggest, in order to love them, we would have to set aside our views, as secure as they might make us feel.

Family therapist Melissa Elliott Griffith was of some assistance in this effort, reminding us that in Mississippi if people are speaking of the Lord, they are speaking of things that are very important, very close to their hearts. Thankfully, this caught our attention so that our training to listen to the things that are very important to a person outweighed our biases about religious belief. Griffith (1995a, 1995b) researched the role of religion in the south, collecting stories about life-changing experiences, moments in people's lives when they felt God was most present to them. When these people were asked if there was an individual in their lives that was in any way similar to the way they had described God, the answer usually turned out to be a parent or grandparent who was no longer alive.

What struck us about Griffith's research and both Preacher and Margaret's stories was the similarity between these descriptions of God and the rewarding inner voice that Edith Kramer has written about in *Art as Therapy: Collected Papers* (Kramer & Gerity, 2000). Edith explained how Europeans have an aspect of the self which is encouraging, which even says "I love you" when needed, but she found her peers in New York seemed quite vulnerable, always looking for external approval because they didn't have this internal support.

Had we stumbled on a place where this inner voice continues to reward people? Once we began to think about these southern ideas of God as being related to an internalized good object, we were freed from the walls we had created with our beliefs. We could talk more freely with Margaret and Preacher; we could listen more deeply.

This personal relationship to God provided Margaret and her family, and Preacher and his grandmother with a supportive inner voice. They now have a willingness to try new and different ideas, making toys out of discarded objects, wheels, lights, and Mardi Gras beads, without looking for approval from the dominant culture, or the local art gallery.

254 *Kramer, Anand, and Gerity*

Finally, we visited Mr George Berry in his studio or workshop behind his trailer in Pearl, Mississippi. Mr Berry began to whittle at age six, introduced to tools and wood by his father, a builder and worker on the railroads. In 1976, he represented Mississippi with two of his carvings in a Bicentennial celebration in Washington, DC. He was on the top of the world, and his workshop was everything to him – his identity and his escape from the world. It was an extension of the self somehow. One night there was a fire, and the workshop was destroyed. For him, this was a life-changing event; it woke him up. He used to lose himself in his work in a way he described as self-centered. However, when the fire destroyed this place that was an aspect of the self, his "self" was no longer the center.

He had very little left from before the fire, but a totem pole was one piece that survived. He kept it, reminding himself of how he used to be. "This was hard to explain," he said, "but it was as if the world cracked open, and I could now see. Things, people, it all feels closer somehow." He really delights in looking around at things. "Look at the way a leaf curls or the individual differences of leaves from the same tree. It's all so interesting. And then trying to make these things happen in wood, well, you can't beat it," he said with fervor.

He talked about working in schools, doing soap carving with children, introducing the tools to them, but encouraging them to do their best work, find their personal imagery, their own way in. "Watch me," he will say, "but then you have to do your own carving; you have to make it your own, you have to become self-taught." He was echoing what we had learned from other self-taught artists, like Mrs L.V. Hull, Preacher, and Margaret.

He also takes great delight in the way his work stimulates storytelling among total strangers. When he is in a craft show, people watch him whittle, and they just get to swapping stories. "I'm doing something I like to do," he said,

> and I do the best I can. People like to see this, and they start to talk to each other. They say things like watching a fellow whittle so happily, they get to remember something of themselves, something of their history, and their grandparents. They feel as though they had found something that was lost to them, something they didn't realize they had lost, something they didn't even realize they had been looking for . . .

As we watched him whittle, we could understand this feeling completely. As he worked, he embodied contentment, joy, generosity, and ease. He reminded us of what we had forgotten; the importance of doing something you really love, and doing it well.

Mr Berry told us that as time goes by he finds more and more of his parents in himself, and this gives him comfort. Giving credit to his mother, he said,

> She was a storyteller, she told her dreams so clearly, so vividly that you could see them. It was like poetry. It brought our imaginations to life. She was also the midwife in the area, and everyone would go to her if they

Quality and Inner Satisfaction 255

Figure 32.3 Mr George Berry in his home, Pearl, Mississippi, 2001

were having troubles. They would come into the house all down and full in their sorrows, and they would get to talking. I never could spot when it happened, but they would always leave feeling a whole lot better than when they came. I guess that is happening to me a little bit these days. Folks come in and talk about all their busy lives, all their pressures, and after they've been here a while, they seem kind of relaxed and cheerful. I must be doing something right.

Often he will whittle a little flower out of willow sticks as a gift. We imagine people come away from Pearl, Mississippi with a lot more than a little flower carved from willow.

We would like to end this chapter with a story quilt of Mrs Hystercine Rankin, a master quilter from Port Gibson. We feel her quilts embody the sense of healing, integration, and wholeness which can come from investment in one's art, from doing one's very best. Mrs Rankin's family story was a familiar one. Her father had been a man who wouldn't "cow" to white folks, and

256 *Kramer, Anand, and Gerity*

any time he found a "white man bothering a colored man" he had to stop it. White folks didn't like this. One day, he was shot down in the road by a white neighbor. Everyone knew who did it, because the man bragged about it.

She relayed this story to photographer and folklorist Roland Freeman (1996), who suggested she could create a story quilt about the incident. He described the process to her because she had never made a story quilt before. As she began working on it, Freeman called on her. He asked what it was like to work on this alone and she responded:

> To me it was joy, knowing after all these years, something I had kept inside of me, I mean just how that hurting feeling was, it was now coming out in the open. Wasn't nothing ever done about my daddy getting killed. . . . That white man robbed me of my daddy. The joy was doing that quilt. Daddy came to me in a dream and I said to him, now everybody will know how you got killed, and it seemed after all those years a burden was being lifted off of me and put into that quilt.
>
> (p. 98)

Perhaps she might have gained some relief in creating a drawing of the incident, but it became clear to us that the depth of healing and integration comes from time and effort put into creating these beautiful story quilts, putting as much investment into them as possible.

Roland Freeman (1996) said:

> The world of quilting by African Americans provides us a profound example of how from scraps barely enough for survival, we created beauty, and then engaged the knowledge and aesthetic we found around us, sharing what we knew and incorporating what we learned . . . continuing our distinct expressive culture. Our quilting is our history and as a quilter said to me, "it comes from our hearts and souls."
>
> (p. 379)

The folk artists of Mississippi moved us, touched us to the core, and taught us much that was useful to us, specifically as art therapists. They reminded us about the power of the paintbrush to bring light into dark places, and that loving others may be more important than simply understanding them. They taught us not to judge people so quickly; and that generosity of spirit is very much alive.

They also reminded us that part of their satisfaction in their work was that they had made it their own. No one gave it to them. They had to look at the world, really study their tools and materials; they had to be willing to make mistakes, to experiment. They had learned that in this way, they could teach themselves, if they remained open and sensitive.

We saw in their work the formal aspects of quality that Edith described: evocative power, inner consistency, and an economy of means. But we also saw

Quality and Inner Satisfaction 257

the strength that creation and quality can provide. We saw the embodiment of Greenacre's (1971) concept of "the artist's love affair with the world," that each of these artists had developed a sensitivity and empathy for the world around them, for their community. They expressed a sense of being a part of a greater tapestry, something much larger than just their own lives. And because they were part of this whole, they felt compelled to make a gift of their best work and to weave that gift into the tapestry around them.

This chapter began with a question from Edith's colleague, about how to present the idea of quality to students. We believe that the self-taught artists of Mississippi provide an excellent model for understanding how quality is essential to the process of self-esteem, self-actualization, and autonomy. There is no way for us to express the gratitude we feel for what we learned from our teachers in Mississippi.

Note

1 This chapter is based on a presentation given at the 2001 American Art Therapy Association Annual Conference (Kramer, Anand, & Gerity, 2001).

References

Freeman, R. L. (1996). *A Communion of the spirits: African-American quilters, preservers, and their stories.* Nashville, TN: Rutledge Hill.

Greenacre, P. (1971). *Emotional growth: Psychoanalytic studies of the gifted and a great variety of other individuals.* New York: International Universities.

Griffith, M. E. (1995a). Opening therapy to conversations with a personal God. *Journal of Feminist Family Therapy, 7*(1–2), 123–139.

Griffith, M. E. (1995b). Stories of the South, stories of suffering, stories of God. *Family Systems Medicine, 13*(1), 3–9.

Kramer E., & Gerity, L. (2000). *Art as therapy: Collected papers.* London: Jessica Kingsley.

Kramer, E., Anand, S. A., & Gerity, L. (2001). *Quality and inner satisfaction: Re-visiting the importance of quality in art and art therapy.* Plenary session presented at the Annual Conference of the American Art Therapy Association, Albuquerque, NM.

33 Cultural Gifts of Wisdom, Hope, and Beauty[1]

*Edith Kramer, Lani Gerity, and
Susan Ainlay Anand*

Introduction – Lani Gerity

We would like to begin this chapter on cultural gifts from an inclusive place – a position that acknowledges our diversity, our differences in privilege, belief, customs, gender, ethnicity, and even art therapy training. We believe that our understanding of differences needs to move from fear and denial to a place where we can cherish, protect, and make use of the rich currents of wisdom and imagery that can be found in cultural diversity. We believe now, more than ever, this is critical. But how do we get to a place where we can truly practice this deep listening that cultural humility and empathy can provide? How can we provide an art room that is safe, a common ground that mirrors each artist no matter their differences?

In order to think outside our cultural boxes, I would like to introduce the ideas of Jeannette Armstrong. Jeannette is a member of Okanagan reserve in British Columbia – a writer, educator, poet, and the director of the Okanagan Cultural Center. In "Keepers of the Earth" (1995), she describes an early memory of sitting on the hillside of a reservation with her father and grandmother looking down into the town in the valley below, listening to the sounds of traffic and machinery. As they looked down, she remembers her grandmother saying in Okanagan, "The people down there are all very dangerous. They are all insane." Her father agreed by saying, "It's because they are wild and scatter everywhere." Jeannette explains that her translation of their words doesn't really explain the words they are actually using. The Okanagan language is one that uses syllables to animate descriptions of activities. These syllables are combined to develop meanings that are close to meanings in English, but it is a much livelier, much more subtle, and context-dependent language – a language of connections. And this can't be communicated when you translate the words into English (a language of separation).

On top of linguistic differences, there are differences in self-perception. In order to understand the Okanagan meaning of "insane," you would have to understand the concept of the self that is functioning well. Jeannette explains that when Okanagan speak of the self, they are referring to a whole made up of four main capacities that operate together. These include the body, the ground of our being; the heart, through which we have the capacity to bond and form

Cultural Gifts of Wisdom, Hope, and Beauty 259

attachments; intellect, that dangerous part of the self that must never be separated from the heart; and, spirit, that part of us which is connected to all beings.

In the Okanagan language, a person can refer to being in relationship to others by a word that means "our one skin." This belief means that we share a physical tie that is uniquely human. We have a bond with our community and family. Jeannette says, "Without community and family, we are truly not human." As I read Jeannette's words, it felt like I was receiving this amazing gift. It felt as though she'd opened the door in my mind. While I was busy trying to understand *how* we speak is different, the realization slipped in this open door that the way we *think, speak,* and *perceive* is all connected. We think and perceive based on the way we speak, or the way we speak is based on the way we think and perceive. There's a connection. I hadn't thought about it before.

If my language is a language of separation, I will be more likely to think and perceive in a compartmentalized way. If my language is one of connection, I will see or perceive in an inclusive and connecting way. I wanted to know more – to see if I could add to the way I think and perceive; to add more colors to my palette.

In addition to the ideas of Armstrong, we also considered Greenacre's studies (1957) of the artist. She believed that artists have more libidinal mobility. They are more flexible than most people. She regarded creativity as a gift, and suggested that we as artists use these gifts to carry on our love affairs with the world; providing gifts to the world rather than simply seeking direct narcissistic gratification. Perhaps we need to remind ourselves that we are artists, and that we too can have a love affair with the world and that this world is actually a wonderfully diverse place in which to exchange these gifts. As you read our unfolding stories, you will notice a resonance between them and the ideas of Greenacre and Armstrong.

Edith Kramer will examine ego development from a variety of cultural perspectives, comparing her multicultural experiences with the writings of Swiss psychoanalyst and ethnologist, Paul Parin. Parin has suggested that we move away from the tendency to see ego development in other cultures in our individual hierarchical terms; move from our cultural ethnocentrism to a broader view, which necessitates developing "cultural-ethno-humility." When encountering a new culture, values may seem exotic, language may be different, even the sense of self might be unfamiliar. However, with a broader perspective, these things will become a part of our artists' palette.

In the last section of this chapter, Susan Anand and I will be sharing what we have learned from ethnographic art therapy research gathered while exploring the cultural margins of Mississippi.

Edith Kramer

Lani described how language forms our thinking and feeling reflecting the personality structure of different peoples, and in return forming personality

260 *Kramer, Gerity, and Anand*

through the language that individuals use. I want to examine personality structure in several different cultures.

This difference in personality structure first came to my attention when, at 22 years of age, I arrived from Central Europe in 1938. At this time in the US, the work ethic still was intact; people seemed to believe in hard work, duty, thrift, self-discipline, and social responsibility. I found that, like the European superego, the American superego was demanding. It demanded hard work, and good behavior, and it punished transgressions with guilt feelings. But, my superego and the superegos of Europeans that I knew could also be loving – if demands were fulfilled, it rewarded the individual with inner satisfaction.

When I first arrived, I was living in Greenwich Village, in a bohemian environment quite similar to the environment I came from in Europe. Although there was much similarity, the American superego was demanding and punishing without giving much loving approval. Approval had to come from the outside – good grades, popularity among peers, high income, etc. If you could show that you were good with these external rewards, you were fine. My colleagues seemed to be insecure and in need of reassurance, vulnerable, and unable to stand up against much criticism. I had to be cautious in order not to hurt their feelings. The mentors of my youth were much rougher with us, confident of our resilience.

Today, the work ethic has lost much of its power. People are driven to working hard in order to obtain material goods, so as to be admired and envied, rather than for intrinsic rewards. Even so, much remains the same. The difference between the American and European character structure may be caused by different social circumstances. In Europe's densely populated and stratified society, success could only be limited. A good cook could be known in some town or village, but it would not be possible for her to establish a nationwide franchise for her specialty. The difference in ego and superego structure in such similar cultures and in European and American individuals makes us expect enormous differences in more divergent societies.

I will give two examples found in Paul Parin's (1975) descriptions of two West-African tribes observed in the '70s. Parin made an intensive study of the Dogon. At the time of Parin's research, the Dogon lived in an arid, mountainous environment. Only very hard work could provide subsistence. They cultivated millet and onions. Onion bulbs were sold on the market and provided the money for clothes and things that they couldn't supply for themselves. Millet provided the main nourishment, but it was also used to brew beer to drink during the frequent tribal festivals and dances. Beyond onions and millet, the main riches were children. The Dogon mother carried her infant continuously on her back, nursed it on demand, and slept with it. There was no toilet training. At three or four years of age, the child was handed over to his playmates of three to twelve years of age, who socialized the little child. His playmates became his companions in communal work. The individual remained embedded within this or another group. There was no harsh superego. Bad behavior made the elders sad, it was said. There was a need to be at peace with others. Even when there were quarrels, there was

Cultural Gifts of Wisdom, Hope, and Beauty 261

no murder. In addition, a member of the Dogon would not be ostracized. A group ego developed, assuring stability. The infant Dogon lived in a conflict-free unity with their mothers, and that lasted for three or four years. The mother fed them, nursed them, and didn't have other children because the nursing usually prevented new pregnancies. After such a long blissful time, the young child was handed over to other children and socialized by them, also not harshly.

This early experience gave the Dogon a lifelong feeling of being held securely by their society. They felt secure even when life became hard or strenuous, because they felt held by their society. The Dogon could not be ostracized unless one was lazy; lazy people were really on the fringe of things. Because hard work was necessary for survival, laziness wasn't tolerated. It was only at that point that kindness and acceptance stopped, but nowhere else.

The Agni, another West-African tribe, lived in a much more fertile part of West Africa. Just like the Dogon mothers, the Agni mother carried the baby on her back, nursed on demand, and fulfilled all needs. However, this blissful state was cruelly terminated at age one and a half to two years, when a new infant replaced the child, which now had to fend for itself in a rather hostile environment. Also, mothers administered daily enemas of pepper pods soaked in water. These produced severe abdominal cramps and elimination would be enforced. (You can't hold back once you get this thing inside yourself.) The Agni people become addicted to this procedure, creating a kind of identification with the aggressor.

The Agni experienced the mother as powerful – she could persecute, she could turn into a witch. Nevertheless, the blissful experience of early infancy made the later hardship bearable. The Agni lived in a state of mild paranoia. They needed the administration of healers, exorcists, and holy shrines for protection. Although they were hardworking, they couldn't hold on to their possessions, they couldn't accumulate capital. Body contents that were forcibly expelled couldn't be retained, and that made them unable to hold on to other kinds of things as well, so it seems. Cooperation between men easily fell apart and there were quarrels. Women, however, were more able to cooperate. Women provided stability and their gardening provided nourishment. The relationships in both sexes remained precarious – one could easily be given up. Indeed, they were proud of the fact that they could drop a relationship immediately – it would seem that it all had to do with those pepper pod enemas. (In the original audio recording of this talk, Edith laughed heartily at this point.)

Even so, the Agni developed a group ego that remained a lasting source of resilience despite the paranoid inclinations. The sense of self was menaced, but the culture provided means of reparation that gave sufficient security to maintain the Agni tribe intact and functioning.

Lani Gerity and Susan Ainlay Anand

Traveling along the back roads of Mississippi and interviewing self-taught artists has enriched our practice of art therapy and taught us a great deal about

262 Kramer, Gerity, and Anand

being artists. We suspect we may also have learned to feel at home wherever we find ourselves. It is our hope that we can communicate a small fraction of what we have learned with as much authenticity and heart as these teachings were given to us. We learned new ways of seeing, looking, listening, and appreciating. We were reminded to pay attention to what is essential and to keep the doors to curiosity and wonder open. We learned about creating – out of a sense of devotion or a sense of the sacred – art that helps the maker create and give a gift to the world.

There is a feeling of spaciousness in Mississippi, of having enough time to sit and share a story. There's a very real warm heartedness in the give and take of story, of what art making means, how essential it is to us, how much joy is found in these creative acts. When we took the time to listen and exchange stories there was such a feeling of transparency and honesty, which led to a feeling the Okanagan describe as "sharing one skin." It was an inclusive feeling. We were exchanging ideas about what was most important to us, and in that exchange, there was a feeling of wholeness, of being a part of a bigger picture. We had to wonder why we would want to live in any other way, and we began to look for ways to integrate these teachings into our work and into our interactions with others.

One thing we discussed with the artists was the kinds of satisfaction they get from their work. Most talked about intrinsic rewards – a kind of deep satisfaction that was felt to come either from within or from that part of the self which is connected to something larger, making the satisfaction feel like a gift from the Divine. One artist though, W. Earl Robinson, spoke of his conflict and desire for external rewards. He told us how he used to paint freehand, that this gave him great pleasure, but the faces would come out "ugly," and the paintings wouldn't sell. He learned to paint what the galleries wanted him to paint; he learned to paint what would sell. He learned to use a projector to paint beautiful faces so everything would sell. He talked about a void within, which could only be filled with the Lord, and that one day, when his conflicts were over, he would go to heaven where he would be able to paint in three dimensions.

In contrast, we found the work of Arthur Green to be conflict free. He was delighted to talk about making art, about why he does it, why it is important, and how it gives his life meaning. Sometimes he would paint for eight hours without even noticing the time going by. "How do you look so relaxed?" people would ask him. "I do this," was his answer. "As long as I can hold a brush, it is the reason I get up in the morning. I like to do what I do. I do it for myself. I have to do it," he said. A friend asked him if he'd ever thought of sharing his work, so he thought why not, and took it to the gallery. "If folks like it, then that's okay. It isn't the dollar. It's the good, relaxing feeling. It's all fun. Keep it fun. Keep it fun," he said. He liked to paint from his past, the way things used to be, "so as not to forget where we have been." He showed us a painting of his great, great-grandmother, Jane Anderson, who had been a slave. She was holding a baby, his grandmother, and through a window the fields

Cultural Gifts of Wisdom, Hope, and Beauty 263

of the plantation in Lexington, Mississippi were visible. From Arthur's "keep it fun," we felt the embodiment of Maslow and Csikszentmihalyi's subversive ideas about freedom in finding deep inner pleasure and intrinsic rewards.

Carolyn Norris was an inspiration, a vital, emancipated woman who happily held us captive for hours in the heat of the Delta in July. Carolyn *adored* the Delta, with the work and sweat that were required to live there. She had come there following a young man, but she stayed for the Delta. She talked about finding her life's purpose there, finding painting (Shawhan, Norris, Black, Rankin, & Rushing, 2011). Her husband was a house painter, and she spilled some of his paint. "It got under my skin," she said, and she hadn't stopped painting since. "You don't know your purpose in life until you find it." She certainly found it. She painted exactly the things she wanted to paint and in just the way she wanted; she wasn't in the least interested in doing what a gallery wanted. "Isn't it great to be in charge of your life?" "Yes! Umm-hmmm," she exclaimed. We agreed wholeheartedly.

Carolyn told us about teaching the neighborhood kids in her garage/studio. She said you had to "teach them that the joy is in the doing, and then let them go wild. It's all inside them. Point this out to them and let them loose. And let them be themselves. But you have to also teach them to be responsible for their spot."

She explained the difference between really being yourself and being on stage; "stage play," she called it. She said, "when you go out, you are on stage and when you are on your own, then you are really you." She was concerned about people being too busy with work now, that most folks were letting the TV raise their children. "Children then think it's all stage play, they can't tell the difference between what's real and what's stage, they don't have time on their own to know who they really are. We need to tell children the truth as best as we can. We need to share what we know by communicating it and we need to let children know that good times will carry you through the bad times." We left her studio feeling completely refreshed, excited, joyful, and satisfied.

We went back to visit one of the artists we wrote about in the chapter, "Quality and Inner Satisfaction: Re-Visiting the Importance of Quality in Art and Art Therapy" – Mrs L. V. Hull. We found her in a reflective mood. She said she'd been a little lonely lately; her neighbors seemed a little resentful of her fame and all of her visitors and yet most visitors just came in, took her picture, and left without stopping to find out how she was doing. She talked about loss, how her only child had died at age four, and how sometimes the memory of it makes her sad; it's painting that helps her. She also described how she'd never paint certain natural objects, treasures of bone, shell, or rocks, because just sitting studying them can give her thoughts and inspiration. L. V. allowed us to watch her paint, and even asked how to spell a word. She seemed very interested in our note taking process; so we gave her a list of her own phrases, which she was delighted with, admitting she sometimes has trouble remembering what she had said, and sometimes spelling was

Figure 33.1 L.V. Hull in her home in Kosciusko, Mississippi, 2001

troublesome. From L.V. Hull, we learn the importance of reciprocity, and how sharing time is important; stopping a while to find out how a person is doing can make all the difference.

We went to Cultural Crossroads, the quilter's cooperative in Port Gibson, hoping to find and talk with Mrs Hystercine Rankin, the master quilter whose healing narrative quilt about her father was discussed in the previous chapter. We talked with master quilters Gustina Atlas and Geraldine Nash and with the young quilters who were just learning their stitches (see Figure 33.2). The feeling at the cooperative was of real community of all ages, all generations. We remarked how happy the young quilters seemed, and Gustina said, "Yes, they like what they are doing, and you'll do a good job when you like what you are doing." They showed us a gift they'd made for Mrs Rankin, based on her design. It was to be a gift for her, now. She and her husband were not well, and she'd had some eye surgery. In fact, we were told, her kids wouldn't let her quilt.

Then we went to Mrs Rankin's house. She was delighted to talk with us about the healing aspects of quilting, about joy, and love. She told us that there's the joy of making quilts to hand down to her children and grandchildren, and in the love and value that the children show these quilts. There's joy in seeing the young ones making their stitches or when they tell you that they are going to keep working on it when they get home – there's deep joy in that. It's also important to make a quilt for yourself before you start making

Figure 33.2 Young women being taught how to quilt at Cultural Crossroads, Port Gibson, Mississippi

them for others. There's joy in knowing how to do it, and there's a joy in putting your memories into the quilts. She also told us that she could quilt for 12 hours and never notice the time going by.

Mrs Rankin also talked about spiritual matters, the importance of providing a good foundation for her family. She said, "You never feel alone if the good Lord is always with you," and Mrs Rankin and her husband tried to teach this to their family. They have been poor, but they had pride and a good life. They provided the roots and foundation for their family, and taught them to keep their key, "Keep God with you." Her grandfather was that foundation for her, teaching her that you can be whatever you want to be, but you have to work for it. She let her children work for it. She didn't just give them things. She let them find the reward and pride of hard work. "The more you put of yourself into something, a quilt or your studies, or your family, the more you get back," she said.

We met with blind wood-carver A.J. Muhammad, an imposing man. He wasn't always blind, he told us. As a child, he and his brother would draw their own comic books and sell their drawings for five or ten cents. He used to be a painter, and had tried a little carving. When he lost his sight, he thought it was the end of everything, but it was just the beginning. It was his faith in the good Lord that saw him through this time. He didn't like to depend on anyone, but that had to change. After moping around for two years, he decided

266 Kramer, Gerity, and Anand

to teach himself to carve again. He cut himself quite a lot at first, but gradually he learned not to keep the knife so sharp. He also figured out how to keep the wood from splitting, using the twists in the wood instead of fighting with them. "I try to put messages in my work," he said. "Messages are about how to live better, how to live right. To help people get through . . . their problems" (Goekjian & Peacock, 1998, p. 80).

We visited with Mr George Berry again, in the art studio of the Craftsman's Guild. He had just got a grant to support two apprentice wood-carvers and was eager to talk about teaching. With carving, he told us, you taught them what you were doing, why you did it, how you did it, and even maybe where you did it, which was anywhere you could carry your pocket knife. He helped his students build up the strength in their hands, helped them use their tools and handle the materials, helped them start to listen to themselves, to listen to what makes them feel good, for what gives them satisfaction. That is the most important thing, to learn about enjoying it, to learn about the good feeling you get from doing what you do. And then there is how he makes others happy, making connections with other people through his work. He would still carve if he didn't meet other people, but there's a deep joy that comes from sharing and making other people feel good by what he does. It's a "gift" that he has. He saw it as God's gift to him; that in teaching others, he can pass this gift along.

We learned so much from these artists, and perhaps the primary lesson was to be willing to learn from others, others who are outside of our culture of origin, and familiar belief systems – to listen deeply and accept their gifts. (For more on the self-taught artists, please see *Souls Grown Deep: African-American Vernacular Art*, Arnett & Arnett, 2001; *Self-Made Worlds: Visionary Folk Art Environments*, Manley & Sloan, 1997.) We learned that collaborative work with its unconditional reciprocity could be filled with joy. We observed this with the quilters and even experienced it ourselves in collaborating for this chapter and the book as a whole. This joy is deeply healing to the self and to the community with whom we "share our skin," according to Jeannette Armstrong. We learned the importance of using everything we have, of being fully present with our whole selves, doing our best work, and loving it. We saw how segregation and dismissive, reductionist attitudes diminish us all, but that by taking seriously what is deeply meaningful to others, gifts are given, gifts are received, and all are enriched.

Conclusion

In conclusion, we hope that this chapter has opened some doors for you, added some ideas about thinking and perceiving, and some new colors to your palette. There was a man in Jackson, Mississippi who asked us, "How do you explain the sweetness of a thing if someone has never tasted sugar?" How do you explain the beauty to be found in creating an image or carving wood if someone has never tried these things? How do you explain the

Cultural Gifts of Wisdom, Hope, and Beauty 267

gifts of wisdom you find talking to folks about what matters most to them? Well, you can do your best and then you can urge your readers to go and try these things for themselves, engaging in and creating culture through the arts, whether they live in the mainstream or in the margins: most of all, "keep it fun."

And, if you can't "keep it fun," if times are too dark and fearful, we found something in our explorations that we would love to share with you, and this is the bottle trees that we saw throughout Mississippi (for more information about bottle trees, please see *Bottle Trees – and the Whimsical Art of Garden Glass* by F. Rushing, 2013). The use of the bottle tree dates back to ninth-century Africa, according to Bill Steber, where hand-blown glass was hung on huts and trees as protection against evil. The bare, upward pointing branches of a cedar tree are usually covered with colorful medicine bottles. These bottles attract evil spirits (or what is destructive in us) during the night. Like a genie caught in a lamp, these spirits get trapped inside the glass bottles and are transformed in the beauty and sparkle of the morning light, and in the sounds made in the play of the wind in the tree. We liked the idea of beauty and light transforming the darkness and negativity. We were delighted by the fact that this tradition had such a rich, far-reaching history. We think, during dark times, it may be most important to create many bottle trees to bring more light and sweet sounds into the world.

Figure 33.3 Bottle Tree photo taken in Mississippi by photographer Eyd Kazery

Note

1 A version of this chapter was given as a panel presentation, *Cultural Humility: Recognizing Wisdom, Hope, and Beauty in the Cultural Fringes*, in 2002 at the 33rd Annual Conference of the American Art Therapy Association in Washington, DC.

References

Armstrong, J. (1995). Keepers of the earth. In T. Roszak, M. Comes, & A. Kanner (Eds.), *Ecopsychology: Restoring the earth, healing the mind*. Sierra Club Books, 316–324.

Arnett, W., & Arnett, P. (2001). *Souls grown deep: African-American vernacular art*. Place of publication not identified: Tinwood.

Goekjian, K., & Peacock, R. (1998). *Light of the spirit: Portraits of southern outsider artists*. Jackson, MS: University Press of Mississippi.

Greenacre, P. (1957). The childhood of the artist – Libidinal phase development and giftedness. *Psychoanalytic Study of the Child, 12,* 47–72.

Manley, R., & Sloan, M. (1997). *Self-made worlds: Visionary folk art environments*. New York: Aperture.

Parin, P. (1975). Is psychoanalysis a social science? With discussion by Robert A. LeVine and Lawrence Friedman in the Chicago Institute for Psychoanalysis (Ed.). *The Annual of Psychoanalysis, Vol. 3* (pp. 371–393). New York: International Universities Press.

Rushing, F. (2013). *Bottle trees – and the whimsical art of garden glass*. Pittsburgh, PA: St. Lynn's Press.

Shawhan, D., Norris, C., Black, P.C., Rankin, T., & Rushing, K. (2011). *Spirit of the Delta: The art of Carolyn Norris*. Jackson, MS: University Press of Mississippi.

34 Religion and Cultural Humility
Lessons Learned in Conversation and Practice[1]

Susan Ainlay Anand

> From the dawn of man's imagination, place has enshrined the spirit; as soon as man stopped wandering and stood still and looked around him, he found a god in that place. . . . Indeed as soon as the least of us stands still, that is the moment something extraordinary is seen to be going on in the world.
>
> (Welty, 2002, pp. 47–48)

Edith Kramer could observe the extraordinary going on in the world around her. She taught us to do the same as artists and as art therapists – to find truth through the interpretation of "the subject with respectful comprehension" (Kramer, 1998, p. 102). Edith also stressed the importance of being aware of and appreciating a person's culture, and from this knowledge, helping individuals find their inner strengths, develop ego ideals, and strengthen a sense of place. One of the gifts I received from Edith Kramer and her approach to art and life was learning how to look and listen deeply while "standing still" with another person in their "place." Her teachings, my collaborative work with Lani Gerity, and life experiences have helped me develop a better understanding and respect for the cultures and lives I encounter.

Some of the most poignant experiences I have had since living in Mississippi have been conversations with self-taught artists. Similar in some ways to folk artists, the self-taught tend to blend what they know with what they learn by creating from materials on hand or by using a preferred medium. They also appear to have fewer rules allowing more freedom for personal expression (or could it be my Midwest cultural perspective that forms this perception of fewer rules?). According to Edith, folk art provides us with examples of objects made by hand and demonstrates the "overflow of pride and joy" that the artist experiences. Once the folk artist fashions an object, they then add details or "embellishments" derived from the "imaginative and spiritual storehouse of their culture." This, in turn, helps the artist link "everyday life with the enduring and transcendent values of the culture . . . confirming the existence of the everyday world and . . . place in it . . . lending reassurance and stability to life" (Kramer & Gerity, 2000, p. 58).

The self-taught artists whom Lani and I met in Mississippi reminded us of Edith's thoughts on folk art and when we told her about our visits with these

270 Susan Ainlay Anand

artists, she encouraged us to go back and learn more – talk with the artists about the inner satisfaction they gain through making art, and how their cultural values help them stay rooted in the world. She thought that the lessons we might learn from these artists could be useful in the art room and in our work as art therapists.

We followed Edith's advice and what we discovered was truly wonderful and magical. We were deeply moved by the lives, stories, and art of the self-taught artists, and while talking with them, we were able to deepen our understanding of this place called Mississippi. We also developed ideas and inspiration for ways to enrich our work with people in art therapy and when teaching others.

An outgrowth of the conversations with the self-taught artists and my work in Mississippi has been a heightened curiosity about religion in culture, and how this influences creative expression and the making of meaning. On religion, Edith Kramer said, "Paired with the powerful laws of morality, religion supports social stability by providing structure both for the libidinal and the aggressive elements within the human psyche" (Kramer & Gerity, 2000, p. 221). For many of the people I have met in Mississippi, matters related to God and faith seem to be important and provide them with an inner structure and a way to understand their world.

As Lani and I traveled through the Mississippi Delta, we found murals on buildings, "stained windows" in country churches, yard art, and assemblages. According to historian Lisa Howorth (1993), "Like blues music, this art is quintessentially Southern: a potent blend of tradition, history, environment, religion, and individual expression" (p. 16). These creations testify to the shared experiences that cut across artificial boundaries drawn by race or geography. Much of this art is considered sacred and is conceived of through personal religious convictions or visions. Researcher Joyce Ann Miller (1992) believes that these works also illustrate the pervasiveness of the evangelical religion that influences not only Southern life but private life and creativity as well.

While many religious faiths and denominations exist in Mississippi, the region is strongly embedded in the evangelical Protestant tradition – Baptist, Methodist, and Pentecostal denominations have especially large memberships. Churches tend to be racially segregated with pronounced differences in styles of worship. However, the dominant forms of religion in the region have a biracial tradition with common characteristics, including beliefs that rely heavily on the authority of the Bible, personal conversion through divine revelation, a strict moral code, and informal worship (Wilson, 1995). One of the identifying traits of the evangelical Protestant religion appears to be its expressiveness; people talk openly about faith and spreading "the Word."

In our conversations with the self-taught artists, Lani and I found that most of them made a connection between creative work and their religious faith. For L. V. Hull, her beliefs came as "inspirations" that she spelled out in words tucked into patterns of colorful dots of paint – she said she had a special connection to God, and everything had a meaning. George Berry described how

Religion and Cultural Humility 271

the Lord worked through him when he carved a bird or animal for the first time: "The first piece, the good Lord just gives to me . . . the next pieces you have to think about. We can't just take it as a gift and have God do it. No, we have to do it." When discussing what is important in her life, master quilter Hystercine Rankin said, "You've got to keep the key [faith], that's God's gift." During a phone conversation with Mrs Rankin, she talked about starting a quilt top for a grandchild after months of letting her eyes rest following surgery: "When I thread the needle, that's joy. Thank you Jesus!" Carolyn Norris described a "power" greater than herself as she talked about the day she found a spilled can of paint, and "it [the power] just entered my body, and I began to paint." The Reverend Dennis said he built Margaret's Grocery in Vicksburg for his wife and as a "temple to God" and "God done it through these hands."

In the South, some talk of the Lord nearly always comes up when conversing with another Southerner who is experiencing illness or pain: "It's in the Lord's hands," "It's part of God's plan," or "God will surely show me the way." In psychiatric settings, when a patient quotes the Gospel or talks of Satan, family members are questioned to determine if this behavior is typical for the family's belief system or methods of practicing their faith. It is not uncommon in art therapy groups for adult patients to refer to their relationship with a personal god. This has been particularly true in my experience working with cancer patients and groups of women in treatment for addiction.

A few years ago, I provided weekly art therapy groups in a residential treatment program for addicted women who were pregnant or had young children. Often these women were taking care of their children for the first time in their lives. In art therapy, many women created art as gifts for their unborn children or other family members. This process seemed to help them build their sense of identity as mother, and make connections with others. As one woman said,

> When you do art as a gift, you are doing it for your pleasure, and the pleasure of the other person. When it is just for you, flaws are not as important; when you are making a gift for someone, you think about the person you are doing it for; their likes and dislikes – you try to make it come out nice.

Another woman added,

> We've had the experience of making things ugly. In art therapy, you have the chance to make something beautiful. In art, you can put a face to a mental picture, and your ideas become concrete. It's almost like a miracle – like when you feel that you know God's there and then when something happens, like in art or in life, he seems more real. God allows you to create something.

I have been facilitating weekly art therapy groups for patients recovering from cancer since 2002. Jane was in her mid-forties when she received a diagnosis of stomach cancer and decided to try art therapy. Treatment included removal of her stomach, chemotherapy, and radiation. Jane regularly talked about her illness, and God's miracles performed in her life. For her, a Southern Baptist, God was "constant love," and most like her grandmother who lived in the country in an "old shanty." Beneath the trees in her grandmother's yard and on a porch swing, she felt safe, and she used these memories as a source of strength throughout her illness. After attending two group sessions, Jane started to paint at home.

Following a week of puppet making and storytelling with Lani and teachers in the Delta, I offered the idea of making puppets to the group. Over a period of four weeks, the patients made hand puppets, developed a group story, and made a book. The puppet Jane created was named "Lucifer" and she used her puppet to describe for the first time the horrible, the unspeakable consequences of her illness. Through this character, Jane was able to talk about how cancer affected not only her life, but also the lives of the people she loved. She found the group story was a place for her to describe the inner "chaos," without harmful repercussions including feelings of guilt. She recognized that Lucifer could be "tamed" through relationships with others in a community that created beauty out of the chaos. For Jane, talking about the negative in

Figure 34.1 Jane's puppet, "Lucifer"

Religion and Cultural Humility 273

her life was not in her nature, perhaps due in part to her religious upbringing, but the puppet making, storytelling process allowed her to gain access to the aggressive forces within that needed release in a safe and constructive manner.

Group members have always challenged each other to develop their creative interests. As a result, Barbara, who was in her seventies, often drew trees or painted them on cardboard or paper. She was a 13-year survivor of lung cancer. She told us that she found a connection between her drawings of trees and the memories of her childhood. One tree was described as having "strong roots" and grew in her grandmother's front yard. She talked about her relationship with her grandmother who raised her by saying, "This was the relationship that taught me love." For her, grandmother's house was a sanctuary of freedom. Barbara recalled that she was seven or eight years old when her mother told her to "receive God," the typical age for girls in her small rural town. "Every time you turned around, you were in the door of the church. I always asked a lot of questions and couldn't take the Bible literally. Momma didn't like that." Raised in a Baptist church, Barbara said she became agnostic as an adult.

Exploring the nature of Southern religion as culture through research and clinical work, has helped me to listen with more sensitivity to stories different from my own – stories of religion that are woven into the cultural fabric of the South, affecting interactions with people and creative work. Raised in the Midwest and married to a Hindu, I now realize the importance of questioning myself when I think I *know* someone's experience with God. I have learned that we need to examine our biases and underlying assumptions about religions and cultures that are a part of place in people's lives. According to family therapist Melissa Elliott Griffith (1995), we must "open these certainties to the refreshing breezes of curiosity and wonder, in which multiple realities can co-exist and relationships can evolve" (p. 127). By doing so, we make space in the art room for a community of shared cultures, and for possibility and surprise in our encounters.

Edith's directive to go back to the self-taught artists and learn more was indeed a good piece of advice. As a result, I learned to be more open, less certain, and rethink some of my original ideas. I had initially thought that the self-taught had fewer rules, and that this was the reason for their freedom of expression. Perhaps their rules came from a deeper place. The artwork of the self-taught, and sometimes people in my groups, seems to grow out of a desire to stay connected to the world by taking time to try to understand it – by looking closely at things, as Edith did when she painted in place. This artwork feels authentic and radiates a kind of pride and integrity suggesting communal culture and freedom. The artists we met who seemed most happy would not submit to the conventions of galleries or shops in order to please customers. They made art for themselves, occasionally for others, and often as a way to communicate their belief in "a power" that gives them strength, and as Edith suggests, social stability. Rather than living in a world of artificial stimulation, these artists find happiness in creating art which remains true

274   *Susan Ainlay Anand*

to their belief that God does it through them, and that this along with their cultural values can be restorative during times of struggle or even joy. Instead of being cultural outsiders, these artists appear to be "insiders," and as Edith told us, we have much to learn from them.

Note

1 A version of this essay was presented as part of a panel presentation, *Cultural Humility: Recognizing Wisdom, Hope, and Beauty in the Cultural Fringes,* in 2002 at the 33rd Annual Conference of the American Art Therapy Association in Washington, DC.

References

Griffith, M. (1995). Opening therapy to conversations with a personal God. In K. Weingarten (Ed.), *Cultural resistance: Challenging beliefs about men, women, and therapy* (pp. 123–139). New York: Haworth Press.

Howorth, L. (1993). *The South: A treasury of art and literature.* Fairfield, CT: Hugh Lauter Levin Associates.

Kramer, E. (1998). New feature: Art therapists who are artists. *American Journal of Art Therapy, 36*(4), 100–106.

Kramer, E., & Gerity, L. A. (2000). *Art as therapy: Collected papers.* London: Jessica Kingsley Publishers.

Miller, J. A. (1992). *In the handiwork of their craft is their prayer: African-American religious folk art in the twentieth-century south.* (Unpublished master's thesis). University of Mississippi, Southern Studies Program, Oxford, Mississippi.

Welty, E. (2002). *On writing.* New York: The Modern Library.

Wilson, C. R. (1995). *Judgment and grace in Dixie: Southern faiths from Faulkner to Elvis.* Athens and London: Brown Thrasher Books.

35 Sense of Place
Edith Kramer's Wisdom for Times of Isolation and Dissociation

Susan Ainlay Anand

> "Place produces the whole world in which a person lives his life."
> – Eudora Welty

Edith Kramer carried her place within – her beloved home of Austria and the family and friends who were a part of that community – throughout her life. Her deep sense of belonging to Grundlsee, in particular, gave her a special "rootedness," shaped her identity, and kept her going back to Austria during the summers where she devoted her time to painting. She was also able to be in or create community wherever she went, and she demonstrated the importance of place through her approach to art making and art therapy, and the way she lived her life. As described in her books and taught in her classes, the *art as therapy* approach can help people restore a sense of place and bring healing through meaningful interactions with others and a feeling of belonging to community. Edith taught us that a person could touch "home" within and help others to do the same, and as a result, strengthen resilience and connection with others.

The place of a person's life goes beyond the physical environment. Place includes community, which embodies a sense of belonging, a sense that we matter, a shared faith that our needs will be met, and a commitment to be with others. We bring our cultural perceptions to the places where we live, shaping the way we respond, and in some ways, reshaping and helping us define place as well. Place can be an integral part of our personal history, and hence, influences all future places that become "home." The sense of place is an experience created by the setting where we find ourselves and is combined with what we bring to that place. In some ways, we create our own place (Cross, 2001).

Our sense of place can be disrupted when circumstances change. This feeling of being separated from place can be caused by something external, such as displacement from one's home, or by something internal, like learning of a diagnosis of medical illness. Many of the people I work with have described themselves as feeling lost, uprooted, and no longer connected to others or their place in the world. They have been referred to art therapy after being displaced

276 *Susan Ainlay Anand*

from their communities because of hurricanes and other natural disasters, being diagnosed with cancer, or in treatment for other serious medical illnesses.

For several years, I have provided group art therapy in an outpatient clinic that is a part of the University of Mississippi Medical Center (UMMC). Here, I work with adult patients referred to groups and teach residents in psychiatry about group therapy and art therapy. Patients come from a variety of socio-economic, racial, and ethnic backgrounds. Symptoms of depression and/or anxiety are common and often associated with a chronic medical condition, serious injury, and significant life change, such as job loss, divorce, or death of a loved one. Services provided in the clinic include medication management, counseling, and group art therapy.

Psychiatry residents in our program spend their third year of training in the clinic and during the year co-lead an art therapy group for six weeks. This group experience helps to fulfill requirements in psychiatry training of the Accreditation Council for Graduate Medical Education (ACGME). Approximately two thirds of our residents are graduates of foreign medical schools. These doctors are commonly referred to as International Medical Graduates (IMGs), but each in their home countries would simply be called "doctor."

The majority of our foreign-trained residents were born and raised in South Asia, while other doctors have traveled to the US for training from Middle Eastern countries, China, Canada, Nigeria, the Caribbean islands, and the Philippines. Residents who belong to minority ethnic groups may find themselves in marginalized positions of social space in the residency program, hospital, and/or communities where they live. They sometimes deal with issues such as feelings of loss, identity, acceptance, and in some cases, forms of discrimination. What I have found is that being uprooted for reasons described by our patients can be quite similar to the migrant doctor experience of uprooting from home and family, communal networks, and culture – all part of one's sense of place.

Residents from other countries have described how when they settle in the Deep South "not being from here" takes on an entirely new social meaning. If they lived in another part of the US prior to entering training in Mississippi, they explain that what they face in this new place are brand new systems of meaning, people, and worldviews. However, as we have found in the art therapy groups, the need to adjust once again to a new culture, a new place, can be viewed as an opportunity – to appreciate and work through previously unacknowledged feelings and issues of identity, which can strengthen integration of the culture of origin and the new culture.

Living in two cultures is a unique experience that can enrich medical treatment and promote successful health outcomes (Kissil, Niño, & Davey, 2013). Therefore, it only makes sense to support the development of this "cultural meta-perspective." Having this ability allows a person to look outside the "culture box," be more flexible and less biased when working with people (Cheng & Lo, 1991). Those who have this capacity are able to view culture from the outside and are aware of its relativity and fluidity. My experience with life in two cultures comes from my upbringing in the Midwest and graduate training in art therapy in New York City where I met my husband, who was raised Hindu in India. After completing medical school there, he immigrated to the US for residency training in New York and afterwards joined the faculty at UMMC in the early '80s. While the move to New York City from Indiana and India required a bit of transition, we both faced even greater challenges when we moved to Mississippi. Finding a sense of place took time, tolerance, and patience.

Edith could look outside the culture box, probably as a result of her upbringing and the influence of mentors like Friedl Dicker-Brandeis. In 1934, Friedl and Edith began working with children in Prague. These children, mainly offspring of political refugees, lived with their families in camps while awaiting immigration to other countries. From this experience with refugees, Edith learned how children could be helped through art making to deal with feelings of loss, sorrow, uncertainty, and fear. Edith further developed what she learned from Friedl when she worked as an art therapist with poor, oppressed, and minority children at the Wiltwyck School for Boys (Kramer, 1977). As our teacher, she taught us how being attuned to the gifts people give through their art and stories can help us honor and strengthen the circle of community, tradition, and multiple cultures that sustain and connect people.

In this chapter, I will describe the group art therapy experience in our clinic where residents co-led groups and created art along with patients. As a consequence, the groups allowed people from diverse backgrounds to come together in the art room where the relationship was not doctor-to-patient, but rather person-to-person, and artist-to-artist. All group members were provided a means of self-expression, which in turn allowed for deeper cultural awareness, insight, identification of strengths, and ultimately, a renewed sense of place in the world. The group provided a safe space for the sharing of realities between resident doctors and patients, and resulted in better understanding and empathy between patients, and among patients and doctors.

Medical Training in Art Therapy Groups

The ACGME encourages multicultural training in psychiatry programs to strengthen compassion, integrity, respect for others, and sensitivity and responsiveness to diversity in patients (ACGME, 2017). Training programs that use experiential and mentored learning seem to influence doctor behavior in a positive way by fostering a deeper understanding of race and culture (Reimann, Talavera, Salmon, Nuñez, & Velasquez, 2004). Finding ways to highlight the diverse experiences of medical residents can enrich this training and raise doctor awareness of their own and others' cultural identities (Smedley, Stith, & Nelson, 2003). The art therapy group that is a part of our training program provides our doctors with an experiential, mentored approach using cross-cultural learning to develop awareness of and appreciation for diversity.

278 *Susan Ainlay Anand*

Traditional approaches to teaching clinical skills in medical training have mainly involved a top-down method of instruction where clinicians learn by observing attending doctors or senior residents as they interact with patients. In this group experience, medical students, residents, and patients learn about each other in a less hierarchical manner as they create art, share stories, and reflect in a supportive group environment. This experience also allows residents to spend more time with patients where they learn about their lives. Often, details not spoken in brief medical encounters are more readily revealed through artwork and stories; what matters most to people is made real through the art and discussion. This also seems true for all trainees as they become comfortable with the art therapy process and sharing stories with others about their ethnic backgrounds and cultures of origin.

At the beginning of each academic year, third-year residents receive a full day of orientation to the adult outpatient clinic. During orientation, I introduce group art therapy to them through a brief art experiential followed by discussion. Residents often say that they learn new things about each other from this experience. For many of the doctors, this is the first time they have discussed home or family when together as a group. During orientation, trainees also learn about their group responsibilities, such as the role of co-leader, participation in the art making process, and documentation of patient involvement.

Third-year medical students spend two weeks in the clinic as part of their rotation in psychiatry. At the beginning of the rotation, they receive a brief orientation to the clinic and learn about group art therapy. Students are encouraged to attend a group session with their assigned resident and are asked to work with art materials as part of the group experience. Residents do not wear lab coats in the clinic and while medical students do, they remove them before entering the art room or at the beginning of group time. This practice has been encouraged so that students are not concerned about getting pastels, paint, or clay on their lab coats. Alternately, removing the white coat seems to lessen boundaries between students and patients, which allows for more personal connection. Some students have even found that being a part of the group enhances their interactions with patients. For example, one student described how he discovered more about the challenges patients face and what he could do to improve his interactions as a healthcare provider (see Figure 35.1).

Edith's art as therapy approach has been used to anchor the group art therapy experience in our clinic. Sessions are longer than is often allowed in an outpatient medical setting (one and a half hours), with the majority of time devoted to art making. A variety of plentiful and good quality art media is available for group members to use, including drawing materials, water-based paints, collage supplies, clay, and opportunities to work with three-dimensional media, such as masks and boxes. Patients and residents learn how to work with materials following instruction in their use.

During the first session of each group, members are requested to introduce themselves using the art materials and include a personal strength in their artwork. Other sessions have included themes such as safe place, life experiences,

Figure 35.1 Pastel drawing by a medical student showing him reaching out to a patient in distress

"otherness," home and family, religion, and cultural identity. Some group members who struggle with anxiety have found that breathing exercises and rhythmic drawing with chalk on large paper help them relax and be more mindful. Residents who have been trained in relaxation techniques are encouraged to teach the group about mindful breathing, and I guide them in drawing exercises as taught by Edith.[1]

During the six weeks of group art therapy, there is usually an art project that requires more than one session to complete, such as work with clay or masks. Sometimes, this has led to opportunities for residents to use their artwork to promote group goals. For example, using clay a resident made an "open oyster shell" with four pearls inside. When she shared what she made with the rest of the group, she said that the oyster depicted how we carry "pearls" or good things inside of us that others may not see. "These pearls are within all of us," she said, "and can be shared when we are more open."

I encourage the use of empathy, curiosity, respect, and humility during group interactions by modeling these behaviors in sessions. These attitudes, as taught and modeled by Edith, are so important in communicating with all patients and healthcare providers, whether from a similar or distinctly different cultural background. Through self-reflection, patients and residents are encouraged to listen deeply, pause, and consider personal assumptions, biases, and values. This practice helps to shift one's perspective of others, and opens up the potential to consider conditions that create misunderstanding, bias, and marginalization through better understanding and knowledge of a person's place in the world.

280 Susan Ainlay Anand

Patients often ask questions of the residents and students about their backgrounds and training and why they chose the medical profession as a career. Patients in turn talk about their lives, the effects of illness, and the challenges they face every day. This exchange of information is at times extremely beneficial to patients and trainees alike. For example, during one session, a medical student listened and responded to a patient's description of her artwork. The patient talked about her clay sculpture depicting her feeling of being "closed down" like the "four o'clock flowers that close after blooming each day." The medical student said she could relate to that feeling because she too had experienced something similar in her life. The student said her faith had been a source of strength that helped her in her struggles, and she learned that she didn't have to be perfect, compare herself to others, or think she was "less than." These comments seemed to resonate with this patient who had been struggling with pseudo-seizures (seizures that are emotional or stress-related in origin) and depression.

From Edith, I learned that the identification and development of strengths, through work with materials and art expression, helps people mobilize and strengthen empathy, ego strength, and effective sublimation, which in turn can build resilience. In these groups, a person's cultural roots and how these contribute to individual strengths are acknowledged along with social concerns, religious beliefs, race, and ethnicity. As a result, residents and patients often recognize the importance of home and place of origin for themselves and others. Both have talked about the value of identifying and using strengths from cultural and ethnic backgrounds for personal growth. Through this strengths-based approach, people have found a renewed sense of self, and at times, a reconnection to the inner places of strength that support resilience.

For many of the residents, clay has been particularly useful in reconnecting to cultural identity, traditions, and sense of place. Upon being introduced to the use of clay, a few doctors from India have spontaneously created a sculpture of Ganesh – the deity widely beloved and worshiped by Hindus as a "remover of obstacles." This elephant-headed God is invoked at the beginning of endeavors, and his worship is particularly auspicious during Ganesha Chaturthi, a celebration marking his rebirth. During this festival, families may purchase an unfired clay sculpture of Ganesh in the market or children can make one out of clay, frequently with a parent who shows them how to sculpt the image. This figure of Ganesh is often kept within the home temple until the last day of the festival when it is carried ceremoniously to a river or body of water and immersed to symbolize the return to his "heavenly abode."

Residents who made Ganesh have formed the image in a variety of styles – sitting, reclining, or standing on a leaf. During group, they have described how the use of clay brought back childhood memories of home and family. One resident, who had been particularly timid during group, made his Ganesh prior to Ganesha Chaturthi. He later shared with me, using photos on his

Figure 35.2 "Ganesha." Clay figure made by a resident raised in India

phone, how he took his Ganesh to the temple with his wife and children for the puja. Following this experience, he seemed more confident and became more active as a co-facilitator of the group. As Edith said, "The substantial quality of clay . . . makes it a good medium for restoring what has been lost. When the sense of self is endangered, clay may help . . . [a person] to restore his image" (Kramer & Wilson, 1998, p. 254).

Improvements had been noted in patients following group participation, including increased relatedness and decreased feelings of isolation, improved communication with others, increased assertiveness, reduced stress, appreciation for underlying themes of loss and hope, and development of healthy coping strategies (Chandraiah, Anand, & Avent, 2012). Patients have described the sheer enjoyment of working with art materials and a sense of mastery in completing artwork that has personal meaning. Many have purchased their own art materials, started creating art at home, and encouraged others to do the same.

Another benefit cited by patients and residents is that they realize they have experienced similar problems in life. For example, a resident, who was pregnant while co-leading group, created a butterfly puppet and book and used them

282 *Susan Ainlay Anand*

to talk about her experience with a stillbirth. She then discussed the fears she had for the health of her unborn child. This led to a group discussion about grief and loss, sources we can turn to for support and strength, and ways to strengthen resilience. Another resident included in his drawing a memory of his father's death from a car accident when he was a young boy. Patients then spoke of losses experienced during their lives with empathic understanding. Generally, the benefits of group art therapy are described at the end of the experience. As one resident said,

> I started with low expectations . . . what happened took me by surprise. Patients started talking about their hardships because they knew that they were not alone. One of my current patients said, "When I do things with my hands, I can put worry to rest."

Resident and patient benefits from group art therapy have exceeded my expectations. Many of the personal and professional gains for the residents were not anticipated, but became evident as they moved toward a deeper appreciation of their own and others' similarities and differences. Both patients and residents seemed to find art expression as a way to connect with sources of strength in their lives – family, community, religion, home, and creativity. For some, strength was found in reconnection to cultural identity. This exchange of information through artwork and stories has contributed to increased empathy and rapport between residents and patients, and even among the resident group. As a doctor from China said after completing a collage,

> My collage includes a picture of art from an impressionist artist, who portrayed life as a big illusion. After listening to my patients, I realize that there are so many different ways to perceive things. Our beliefs are affected by our own past experience and wishes. The impression we end up with is the product of our inner and outer world[s] influencing each other.

Conclusion

Cross-cultural education through art therapy groups offers promise as a way to improve medical students' and residents' abilities to provide quality care to diverse patient populations and to help reduce marginalization in the workplace among healthcare providers. As described throughout this chapter, it is important for doctors to look carefully at their own cultural backgrounds and those of others to develop the awareness necessary for curbing bias and increasing understanding for the role culture plays in the lives and health of patients and those with whom they work.

Like Talwar, Kapitan, Moon, & Timm-Bottos (2015), I have found that through the animating process of art making, all group participants could welcome the complexities of identity, culture, and unease while diminishing the negative effects of "power over," privilege, and oppression. The art as therapy approach is an example of a decolonizing model, which encourages an

Sense of Place 283

organic building of strength and community, communication, empowerment, and resilience. This way of working in art therapy welcomes pluralism in the art room, and allows for many diverse forms of expression, variety of experience, philosophy, faith, belief, and narrative.

Edith painted in place, lived in place, and recognized that one of the ways to help others realize their potential was by rediscovering their roots. Her own work emerged from a sense of place that framed how she taught and lived her life. This knowledge, that strength and resilience can be found in one's roots, has become a cornerstone for how I work as an art therapist and guided me in teaching psychiatry residents about group art therapy. It has also helped me to navigate the cultural divides in the Deep South where I live. Group art therapy in our medical clinic and the subsequent benefits for psychiatry residents, medical students, and their patients is part of the Edith Kramer legacy.

Edith taught us to be curious about the world, and discover what makes us similar as well as what makes us unique in the communities where we live and work. Her wisdom continues to guide me in creating opportunities for meaningful interactions in the art room that can lead to a deep sense of belonging, healing, and sense of place.

Note

1 More information on this Bauhaus method that Friedl Dicker-Brandeis taught Edith can be found in the following chapters in this book: "Edith Kramer on Friedl Dicker-Brandeis, Erna Furman, and Terezin" (from interviews with Elena Makarova) and "Edith's Legacy as Artist and Art Therapist in the Art Room" by Martha Haeseler.

References

Accreditation Council for Graduate Medical Education (ACGME) (2017). *ACGME program requirements for graduate medical education in psychiatry.* Retrieved from https://www.acgme.org/Portals/0/PFAssets/ProgramRequirements/400_ psychiatry_2017-07-01.pdf Accessed 17 September 2017.

Chandraiah, S., Anand, S. A., & Avent, L. C. (2012). Efficacy of group art therapy on depressive symptoms in adult heterogeneous psychiatric outpatients. *Art Therapy: Journal of the American Art Therapy Association, 29*(2), 80–86.

Cheng, L. Y., & Lo, H. (1991). On the advantages of cross-cultural psychotherapy: The minority therapists/mainstream patient dyad. *Psychiatry, 54,* 386–396.

Cross, J. (2001, November 2–4). *What is sense of place?* Speech prepared for 12th Headwaters Conference, Western State College.

Kissil, K., Niño, A., & Davey, M. (2013). Doing therapy in a foreign land: When the therapist is "Not from here." *The American Journal of Family Therapy, 41,* 134–147.

Kramer, E. (1977). *Art therapy in a children's community: A study of the function of art therapy in the treatment program of Wiltwyck School for Boys.* New York: Schocken Books.

284 *Susan Ainlay Anand*

Kramer, E., & Wilson, L. (1998). *Childhood and art therapy: Notes on theory and application* (2nd ed.). Chicago, IL: Magnolia Street.

Reimann, J.O., Talavera, G.A., Salmon, M., Nuñez, J.A., & Velasquez, R.J. (2004). Cultural competence among physicians treating Mexican Americans who have diabetes: A structural model. *Social Science and Medicine, 59,* 2195–2205.

Smedley, B.D., Stith, A.Y., & Nelson, A.R. (2003). *Unequal treatment: Confronting racial and ethnic disparities in healthcare.* Washington, DC: National Academy Press.

Talwar, S., Kapitan, L., Moon, C., & Timm-Bottos, J. (2015). *Decolonizing art therapy: Social justice and new paradigms of care.* Keynote panel presented at the 46th Annual Conference of the American Art Therapy Association, Minneapolis, MN.

Saying Goodbye

36 Do You Require Inspiration Just to Breathe?

Elena Makarova
(Translator, Tali Magidson)

Existence is singular, and likewise, there is only one book. Even considering the abundance of genres, here and there wandering heroes resurface.

An eternity has passed, and yet I'm still sitting with Edith on the veranda of her house in Grundlsee and am talking of the same thing as before. Why has art lost its place and definition? Everything that you like and don't like can be labeled with these words.

It's getting dark. In front of an enormous mountain with a sparkling white crown, Edith seems like a fairytale creature – she is wrapped up in a time-after-time refitted shirt of thick wool and only her nose peaks out from under her black, pre-war-style hat. But this particular fairytale creature reasons very realistically.

Art has exhausted its function in society. Rather than serving others, it hangs on via self-sustenance. Today, it is almost impossible to be a high-quality artist. Mannerisms are ruining everyone. Pretentiousness. There is a desire to create a new language without knowing the old. Art has stopped sensing itself.

But if art has stopped sensing itself, is it still possible to sense others with its help? While honing her proficiency in form and color, Edith Kramer sought a social use for art, not as art itself but as its potential for humanistic, healing functions. Precisely these searches led to the birth of her art therapy.

A Meeting with Edith Kramer

Living in the Soviet Union and teaching sculpting to young children, I felt that something interesting was going on, and interesting-ness that wanted to be shared! Who among my friends didn't I regale with my stories! I evidently annoyed one of my friends with stories of children and clay work to such an extent that he, an editor of a creditable paper, ordered me to present him an article in written form. I wrote it, and he published it word-for-word. Only my title, "To Free an Elephant," turned out to be too much for his solemnly titled collection "The Writer and Time," and he changed it to "Playing Seriously." I held onto the title for a future book.

Everything would probably have continued in this way (I would have continued working with children and describing my experiences), had a catalog

288 *Elena Makarova*

of children's artwork from the Terezin concentration camp not fallen into my hands and changed my life.

In January 1988, I managed to get to Prague to see thousands of original artworks in a Jewish museum and to acquaint myself with Friedl Dicker-Brandeis' biography and her article "A Child's Drawing." She had written it in Terezin, but many places in my books almost literally coincided with her text.

Without being able to find a similar-minded person in my real life, I had found a similar-minded woman who was obliterated in Auschwitz seven years before my birth. I needed to find out everything about her. Thus, all my paths, no matter how wayward, would have to lead me to her.

On my return to Moscow, I went to the Leningrad library to see what English literature exists on art lessons for youths. I was directed to a cataloged box with indexes. The first card read "Art as Therapy with Children," Edith Kramer, 1971. I ordered this book and received it soon thereafter. The top right corner of the title page displayed a dedication to Friedl. I decided that I'd lost my mind.

The book couldn't be checked out, and since I had forgotten all my English at that moment due to excitement, I left for home. The next morning – a letter from Prague. The curator of the Jewish museum relayed that he had gotten acquainted with a student of Friedl's – Edith Kramer – and that it was exactly this person whom I had to meet. He said that she lived in New York, and an address and telephone number accompanied the letter.

But how to get to New York? Because after a twenty-year travel ban, I had only recently been able to cross the border for the first time to go to Czecho-slovakia, a Socialist country, I wondered who would grant me a visa to America? Surprisingly soon, however, I received an invitation to give a liter-ary lecture at Cornell University, all expenses paid by the Soros Foundation. It was unbelievable, but on October 18, 1988, my birthday, I flew to New York. Truth be told though, this happened ten days later than expected due to bureaucratic pitfalls, and so there was no one there to greet me.

My luggage had been lost, and I didn't have a cent on me, but most impor-tantly, I had arrived and would soon see Edith. One charming black woman taught me how to use a payphone without paying. I called my friends in Bos-ton, and they sent someone who would take me to them by plane.

Having gathered some courage, I called Edith. What a voice! Deep, velvety, and calming. I said that I was flying to Boston, but that I'd be at her place tomorrow. "Boston isn't the other side of the street," she noted.

The morning of October 19, I boarded a bus in Boston and got to a hotel on Vandam Street by evening. So that the reader can relax, I'll say here that my luggage was eventually found, and the lecture did take place.

Edith – round faced and red-cheeked, of small stature, in a pair of stained overalls, with a side braid and a scraper in hand – stood in the doorway. Had this youthful woman actually studied under Friedl in Vienna, and later in

Inspiration Just to Breathe?   289

Prague? Of course, when looking closer, I noticed the wrinkles under the frame of her glasses, among other signs of age, but that first impression of youthfulness and purpose-filled motion has stayed with me forever.

While Edith made tea, I wandered around her studio. Her sculptures made the strongest impact on me: tired people in a subway station, holding onto the rails, and a homeless man, lying on a bench in the same station; factual and expressive clay work; an urban landscape and an outline of a subway station which would soon be transformed into a mosaic on Spring Street, the closest subway stop by her home.

Edith followed me with the corner of her eye. The brewed teapot already stood on the table, but she didn't rush me. She knew that I came to visit her due to Friedl – I had earlier explained this to her in a letter – but having noticed my interest in her work, she began pulling out paintings from wooden niches built into the wall, and arranging them along the perimeter of the studio. Among these new pieces, my favorites were especially those made on her windowsill. The window theme, peering at the brick wall across, captured the life of the shown objects with a Cezanne-like freedom, so I saw them where they happened to be, not where they were placed. I found I was really looking at the objects.

The tea was aromatic and very timely. I hadn't slept for several nights and so was horribly afraid of forgetting to ask something, of missing or misunderstanding some part of the conversation. What if I never happened to see her again? As kindling, I told Edith about my trip to the Leningrad library.

"So you don't have that book?" exclaimed Edith, her hands flying up, "I'll give it to you, right now!" And she immediately gave it to me. "Do you know who wrote a review on it?" she asked, and continued, "Erna Furman." I told her I didn't know who Erna Furman was. "A famous child psychoanalyst; she lives in Cleveland and studied under Friedl in Terezin; she has drawings from there. You decidedly must visit her."

Edith went somewhere and returned with an envelope. It was addressed from 2689 Colchester Road, Cleveland, Ohio, 44106. This was the letter inside:

Dear Miss Kramer,

I owe Dr Gardiner your address as well as the encouragement to write to you. It was she who thought you would be interested in the strange coincidence that made me write a review for your book. I am enclosing the review and here is the story:

Last May the *Psychoanalytic Quarterly* asked me to write a review of your book at the suggestion of Dr Shelley Orgel, whom I do not know personally but who probably knows of me professionally. I reluctantly agreed because I was busy but was tempted by the idea of art with children, and by the fact that Muriel Gardiner wrote the introduction. When I later received the book and got to read it, I felt deeply stirred

290 *Elena Makarova*

both by its beauty and truth and by an idea of, I know this. I finally realized that "I knew it" in the sense that it reminded me so much of Friedl Dicker-Brandeis and brought back so many memories of my times with her. Then I read on and came to the place where you describe your association with her, and I was overjoyed, and I must admit, rather overwhelmed.

Since the end of the war, I had never known anyone who knew Friedl, or knew of her work, or worked quite like her, and so I had never been able to tell anyone how much she had meant to me. In my teens, I spent almost three years in Terezin alone since all my family had been killed. I had always liked to draw and paint and was very glad when Friedl made it known that she would do some art work in a group. It was indeed in my living quarters (I worked as a Betreuerin or caregiver in a children's compound) that our drawing sessions started to take place, consisting of a number of other young people and some older ones. We met weekly for a long time, I think years. Each session was a wonderful experience and made life worthwhile. Friedl taught me much more than art though, she taught me a lot of that and it has remained a special treasure with me. But she also helped me to integrate, through art, some of the things that I lived through with myself and with my camp experiences, and she helped me by being a kind, and a thoughtful person, which made her very special in that environment. I do not know what happened to her. I know my pictures were among those exhibited after the war and some others I still have with me. It has always made me very sad that I have had no opportunity to tell her how much she meant to me and how important my contact with her and my identification with her in some respects has been to me, I do not say this lightly.

Thank you, especially for your book, both for itself, and for what it revived in me. Needless to say, when I agreed to write the review, I took on a much bigger emotional load than I bargained for, but it was worth it.

With best regards,
Yours,
Erna Furman
October 12, 1972

I got to meet with Erna Furman only in 2001, at the opening of Friedl's exhibit in Atlanta. The result of our acquaintance was a documentary film and an interview-based book.[1] Both were, unfortunately, finished only after her passing. But she had read and approved the entire text of the interviews.

Curiously, Erna's fate also included traces of Grundlsee, even if indirectly. After the war, she worked with children who survived Terezin in the Poemysl Pitter Children's Rehabilitation Center before moving to London; there she completed Anna Freud's therapeutic courses, graduated from the University

Inspiration Just to Breathe? 291

of London, and accepted Anny Katan's invitation in 1952 to work in The Hanna Perkins Center for Child Development as a child psychoanalyst. This was the same Anny Katan who was friends with Siegfried Bernfeld and who spent her summers visiting in Grundlsee.

I spent that night in the art studio. Edith left after pointing me to a cardboard box holding works made during lessons with Friedl. I pulled them out one after another – spirals, circles, dictations with a cliff and fox tail, baskets, spiral-like dancing figurines, tulips, bamboo, the infinity symbol.

It was a mystical night. New York, the enormous studio with tall windows, my physical exhaustion and yet clear mind – that state when you look and see everything, and everything ties together into one . . . I think that moment, that night, was when I first got the idea of tracing how the art system in Bauhaus was reflected in Terezin. These works were the missing link that I had searched for. I had seen examples of Friedl's studies from Bauhaus, I'd seen the girls' responses to her exercises in Terezin, and now here was someone who could tell me about these exercises. From Bauhaus to Terezin; through Edith, I could now find out more about what I saw as Bauhaus reflected in the art of the children of Terezin (see figures 36.1–36.4).

In the morning, when Edith briskly entered the studio with a sketchbook on her shoulder and a framer in hand, I asked her whether she could write commentaries to the stack of drawings that I had picked out.

"Breakfast first!" said Edith and revealed cheese, bread, and apples from her bag. She had already painted an oil study in the subway and had worked up her hunger.

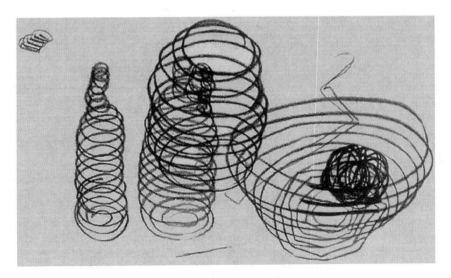

Figure 36.1 Edith Kramer's response to one of Friedl's exercises

Figure 36.2 Ruth Gutmann's response to Friedl's exercises in Terezin

Figure 36.3 Edith Kramer's response to one of Friedl's exercises

Figure 36.4 Charcoal study by Friedl Dicker-Brandeis from Bauhaus

Our first conversation about art commenced after breakfast, and it has continued to this day. Edith evidently felt my surprise at her inescapable realism, and said,

> I'm in a romance with the world and everything in it, immeasurably more beautiful in all its complexity that in any simpler version that could be recreated. There are rare artists, say, like Paul Klee. He can place squares on a canvas and call them a "blooming tree," and say something about this blooming tree that has never been said before.
>
> The same can be said of Brâncusi and of early Mondrian. Late Mondrian is boring. In general, abstract art repeats itself. Its styles, mannerisms . . . There is a popular demand for this today. Real artists give the world something never seen before, a wonderful gift; artists can create awe like nature can. I can generalize thoughts, but in art I succeed only then when I can really examine that which exists. I am truly intrigued by the world.

Edith believes that art, having gone through all possible branches of subjectivity, will return home one day and, like the prodigal son in Rembrandt's painting, will fall to its knees before reality.

294   *Elena Makarova*

> The latest painting is always the most important thing in the world. Since the world's sorrows and fears accompany any thoughts of the future, right? You can't run from the terror of this current reality, from the madness of individualism, which destroys our living Earth, from the war which looms. In this manner, all the wonderful things on this Earth become even more valuable, more precious, and one needs to paint them with a special reverence since tomorrow they may cease to exist. To paint them, because they are still here, but are not eternal. Do you know that feeling, when you find yourself in a forest and feel yourself there as if in eternity? Well, that moment no longer exists.

I listened silently, although I wanted to protest. How about photography and documentaries?

We can record this world, rushing toward the abyss, in these ways too. It was good that I hadn't said this. Later, Edith ranted about photography.

> It kills the living imagination, kills memory. For instance, the visage of a dear one lives in your consciousness in different ways, but one glance at a photograph and this same person becomes frozen into one pose, one static gaze. It's hard then to get rid of this. A painting freezes in our memory, too. But every time you perceive it differently; in the same painting, you see completely disparate things at different stages of life. A photograph – a historic document; a painting – an enigma with no age. It is no slave to time.

After breakfast, Edith sat down at a little table and annotated every drawing that I had picked out in a sweeping script. She gave her consent to display them at shows, if such an opportunity arose. It did. And not just one.

We met at openings of Friedl's exhibitions in Vienna, Berlin, Frankfurt, Paris, Stockholm, Atlanta, Los Angeles, and New York, and everywhere toured museums together. Once, we entered the Metropolitan at ten in the morning and left with the last stragglers. In Vienna, we spent half the day in Brueghel's gallery. We met in Holland, where I annually lectured in the University of Nijmegen. Edith had a dream to see Rembrandt's *The Jewish Bride*, and we fulfilled it. Ninety-year-old Edith sat silently in front of it with a small notepad and pencil stub in her hands.

Together, we also visited the summerhouse of a common friend in Hudiksvall, Switzerland. Once, Edith, hunting for lilac lupines, fell into a ditch, and my husband and I extracted her from there.

Often I was a guest in Grundlsee, during and after Aunt Liesl's life.

Obviously, we often discussed Bauhaus's tutelage, but also Itten, the problem of immigration, and, of course, Friedl. I got to be present at Edith's seminars at New York University, Austria, and Switzerland. In truth, it was completely irrelevant what assignments were given. Edith was important, coexisting with her in one space, and working under her gaze and care was enough. Art therapy isn't the

Inspiration Just to Breathe? 295

possession of a number of scholastic methods, but rather a calling. Edith inherited it directly from Friedl, and I caught it from both Friedl and Edith.

Eyes

June 2011. The same house in Grundlsee, and still the same Edith, sitting in the kitchen with a book in her hands. Still the same roughly-woven shirt, the same braid grasped by a rubber band. It's just that Edith herself has become a miniature; only her ears have grown larger, like Buddha's, almost to the level of her chin.

Upon sighting me, she closed her hands into little fists and pumped them into the air. As if saying, "What a joy!"

With the help of a wheelchair, we moved from the kitchen to the veranda.

We drank out of the same thick ceramic mugs with white-green designs, looked out at the same view of the lake, the same boathouse . . .

Five years ago, Edith left New York and returned to her birthplace.

Edith barely hears anymore; you have to yell right in her ear. I asked in English whether she still draws. "No," she answered in German.

Her small but ever sparkling eyes are heavily lidded. Her gaze reaches you from the side, like a bird's.

"Bring paper and pencil."

The Nurse's hands flew up. "Two years I offer paper and pencil – no!"

In the studio upstairs there are neither paints nor fresh canvases; a large bed stands in the center of the room. A low table for instruments, previously laden with jars, scrapers, and stacks, dirty boxes of chalk, bedding, white crayons, towels, feathers, empty containers. I found paper and a pencil on a shelf over a small trestle-bed, where Edith sometimes took naps throughout the day.

I sat next to Edith, and she, locked onto me with her gaze, started drawing. Eyes, eyes, eyes . . .

They bumped into one another. Edith turned the page the other way and got the same result.

"Dynkle, morgen!" she exclaimed.

I can understand these German words: dark, morning.

The veranda is overflowing with sunlight, and yet she finds it dark. Based on the sketch, her vision filters out distinct details; she doesn't see the object as a whole. Maybe chalk is brighter than pencil?

The nurse brought chalk.

Edith focused searchingly on me with all her strength, asked me to move a little bit – still dark.

She tried drawing with chalk and failed.

We moved from the veranda to an open meadow. Again she picked up the pencil. She drew and drew – only eyes.

"Enough! Tomorrow there will be light."

296 *Elena Makarova*

I asked her for the drawings. She shrugged. She ordered me to find a book of her German articles in the studio, so that she could gift it to me. I ran to find the book. Edith autographed it. "Lena, Friedl . . ." she muttered and sighed. After a pause, she asked me about my daughter, how was she?

I yelled into her ear that she draws a lot, works hard . . .

"She's a talent; may she learn from the greats, and from nature – they won't let her down," said Edith in English, and then "Genug, shlafen" (Enough, sleep).

The nurse helped Edith to bed, brought a book, and turned on a lamp. What was she reading? Still the same book, about Van Gogh and his brother, Theo. Two years ago, she met Manny and me and talked about Theo and the fate of the genius's brother who devoted his entire life to Vincent, about insanity, which knows no mercy, and about brilliance, which forgives all.

Everyone reads his own book. Even if he can't see the letters.

Note

1 Book by Elena Makarova, *Erna Furman, Ways of Growing Up*, Rotterdam: Veenman Publishers, 2007; and also the film, *One Day with Erna Furman*: Part 1: https://drive.google.com/file/d/0BxZ2Freq0Qc1NHF3YTN5ekNLUGs/view?usp=sharing Part 2: https://drive.google.com/file/d/0BxZ2Freq0Qc1ajNvem1UOExmVWc/view?usp=sharing Accessed 21 September 2017.

37 Lyceum Art Therapy Training Program

Margherita Gandini
(Translator, Eleonora Marchesi)

Thanks to Dr Raffaella Bortino's commitment to the field, the first Italian training program in art therapy was created in the '80s in Turin, at the "Il Porto Adeg" Association, which dealt with the study of youth in distress. Dr Bortino, a psychoanalyst and art therapist, had been working as a pioneer within the field of art therapy for almost twenty years. After bringing art experiences into mental hospitals and primary schools, she decided to further her studies in art and psychology in the United States.

When Dr Bortino was at New York University, she had the opportunity to work with Edith Kramer and Laurie Wilson. Afterwards, she went back to Turin where she founded the training program in art therapy. For several years, this program worked in collaboration with the art therapy program at New York University (NYU). The first teachers who taught in the Italian program were from or suggested by NYU's program. Among those teachers were Ikuko Acosta, Catherine Free, Martha Haeseler, Cathy Malchiodi, Simone Alter-Muri, Elsa Pellier, Shirley Riley, Judith Rubin, Jill Scher Sacks, Elizabeth Stone, Katherine Williams, Laurie Wilson, and Vera Zilzer.

The Italian art therapy training experience was characterized by an atmosphere of research and experimentation, which gave birth to the first art therapy publications in Italy. Edith Kramer contributed to the didactic method of the training program. Within the books she wrote (1985, 1987), there are chapters that are fundamental for the focus used in the program that she defined as *art as therapy*. During this time, Elizabeth Stone played an important role as supervisor, and gradually the program's students became teachers – teaching and working according to Edith Kramer's method.

Since 2000, the program has faced some changes in management, but these have not affected its ideals and philosophy. For a certain period of time, the training program was managed by a group of art therapists who named their association "Edith Kramer." Starting with the name, this association declared its approach and an undeniable sense of identity with Edith Kramer's legacy. Shortly thereafter, the training program moved from Turin to Milan. Since 2007, the Association became a part of Lyceum from which it took the name, while maintaining its original method and didactic system. At the moment, Lyceum builds on the legacies of Edith Kramer and Friedl Dicker-Brandeis.

298 *Margherita Gandini*

The training program is dedicated to these pioneering figures and during the classes particular attention is given to their biographies.

Lyceum offers two different courses or programs: The Two-Year Training Program for Experts in Art and Expressive Laboratories – which, without any therapeutic pretensions, trains specialists in artistic expressive activities focused on childhood – and the Three-Year Training Program in Art Therapy with a clinical orientation. Both have been developed from Edith Kramer's experiences and methodology, and (albeit with different levels of depth) they use the method, art as therapy.

Two-year Training Program for Experts in Art and Expressive Laboratories

In 2008, Lyceum created the Program for Experts in Art and Expressive Laboratories. This two-year program incorporates the cultural and experiential legacy of Edith Kramer, who dedicated most of her research in the field of art therapy to children and their development. Through this program, Lyceum pays particular attention to how students can learn ways to motivate ideal functioning and create positive interventions in childhood. The methodological approach of the experiential laboratories for children fosters freedom and self-expression. It offers children a multifaceted experience, which weaves a subtle texture between the artistic experience and creativity, gesture and motion, voice and speech, and sound and breath, all in search of a more general harmony (Makarova, Dicker, & Miller, 2001).

The purpose of this program is for children to be involved in a holistic manner through physical and cognitive means, as well as affectively and emotionally, and in relationship, in order to develop their creativity and autonomy. They create art according to their own capabilities without following a specific model or method coming from someone else, and without depending on external judgment or approval, but with the gentle support of the art expert (Lowenfeld & Brittain, 1964).

What transpires in the program is not necessarily a therapeutic experience, but is absolutely connected to the art as therapy approach associated with Edith Kramer and Friedl Dicker-Brandeis. The playful dimension of this experience fosters the development of creativity, self-expression, art making, and relationship. This approach is typical of the training program, and also part of the experiences many students have encountered through their internships in several of the primary schools of Milan.

Besides the traditional internship, Lyceum has also organized some meaningful experiences called "On Holidays with Art," which were promoted through the support of UNICEF in some important public gardens of Milan and of Liguria. They provided an opportunity to experiment and create a methodology that has great artistic and pedagogic significance, along with cultural and historical importance. Through this experience (repeated throughout the program's two years) many students of the Lyceum Program for Experts in Art and Expressive Laboratories put themselves to the test by organizing open-air laboratories for hundreds of children. At the end of the activities, the public gardens, which had been used as backdrops for the art experience, were then turned into open-air museums.

In September 2015, Lyceum activated a project called E.Kr.A.M. (Edith Kramer Atelier Method) with the motto, "Art Lets You Grow" (see Figure 37.1). This project is proof that Edith Kramer is symbolically present in the training program. Some teachers and former students of the Lyceum two-year program are part of E.Kr.A.M., as they are very active in and around Milan with the aim of helping youth in distress through creative, artistic experiences.

E.Kr.A.M. has promoted many activities, and many are currently being planned. In addition to artistic laboratories, "Bike Art-tivity" has been a big success. Riding funny, colorful bicycles, experts go into the public gardens of Milan with paintbrushes, colored papers, and art media in their bike baskets. The materials are used to develop art activities for children who are playing in the gardens, and sometimes even their parents or grandparents

Figure 37.1 E.Kr.A.M. logo

300 *Margherita Gandini*

join in as well. Children wait eagerly for "artistic bikes" to arrive in order to "make art."

Edith Kramer's favorite exercises are proposed during these extemporaneous art activities. When engaged in these activities, the children and the art all become very animated, and Edith Kramer's thought, energy, and spirit can be felt. This shows how Edith Kramer's experiences and her legacy live on, and are being passed down to new generations of experts working with brand new groups of children.

Lyceum Three-year Training Program in Art Therapy with a Clinical Orientation

Lyceum offers a three-year training program in art therapy with a clinical orientation that is recognized and accredited by APIART (the Italian institution that verifies the didactic programs of Italian training programs in art therapy, and manages the membership registration of accredited art therapists).

From a methodological point of view, this three-year program is rooted in Edith Kramer's art as therapy method. Today, these roots are still alive and updated with research contributions from the fields of art, psychology, and neuroscience. What distinguishes both Lyceum training programs from others in Italy is the identification of precise methodological guidelines that recognize the centrality of the creative and artistic process in the therapeutic experience.

Art itself becomes the therapeutic end, as the technique does not aim to disclose and interpret the unconscious contents that can emerge through the art. Art as therapy is not based on verbal interventions, nor are the images created simply as a visual stimulus that needs to be understood and worked through verbally between patient and therapist (Kramer, 1977). Instead, this method offers a symbolic path through which fantasies, energies, abilities, and resources can be activated; one's way of functioning is pointed out, and autonomy and a sense of identity are fostered.

This methodology has several characteristic features but the crucial one, the one that is most vital and significant, has to do with the importance of the creative process and artistic expression. With an art therapist available, not only can the art itself activate personal resources, autonomy, and possibilities for resolution of challenges, but the art can also modify the emotional state of a subject, producing self-regulation without being perceived by the patient on a conscious level.

Edith Kramer's early intuitions have later been confirmed and described by the most up-to-date research in neuroscience, which shows how neural circuits and emotional mechanisms can deeply influence the subject without necessarily involving consciousness (Maffei & Fiorentini, 2008; Damasio, 2000). This helps us understand how Edith Kramer and her thinking were actually ahead of her time.

During the training program, students attend theoretical and methodological classes. They experience for themselves some art therapy sessions,

Lyceum Art Therapy Training Program   301

read art therapy books, and hold their own sessions through internships with different kinds of populations, including able-bodied children, as well as adults affected by various types of pathology.

Internships are organized in several areas. Besides the most common ones where art therapy has become well established, such as psychiatry and addictions, other settings for art therapy in Italy now include new experiences and types of populations. The new areas where art therapy is being used are oncology, hospice, centers for abused women, eating disorder centers, mother–child communities, migrant homeless shelters, and centers for terminally ill HIV patients. Special attention is also given to professional and family caregivers.

Internships have given art therapy greater visibility and have been added to the therapeutic offerings both in prevention and care fields. Lyceum students bring their unique contributions to these placements. As a result, students are part of the care process and treatment planning. Art therapy is now integrated into the traditional medical model, and is routinely a part of the preventive and rehabilitative goals that are established for populations of all ages.

Edith Kramer as an Ego Ideal

The Lyceum three-year program is fundamentally connected with Edith Kramer as a person, so much so that she becomes deeply and symbolically internalized by each student as they begin to construct their "therapeutic identities."

Internalization takes place at different levels – in a more concrete and methodological way through the internalization of art therapy methods and techniques, and also in a more symbolic way through the ethical and personal growth of the students, who are gradually learning to play an increasingly therapeutic role in their interactions. For art therapists who identify with the method of art as therapy, the memories of Edith Kramer have contributed to her becoming a sort of role model and "inner guru." As students become teachers, they more or less consciously transmit this role model to their students.

Teachers still read aloud from Edith Kramer's publications and let the students actively and critically reflect on the methodologies she suggested. Edith Kramer elaborated on several concepts such as the art therapist's use of the *third hand* and the *third eye*, and *quality* in art. She also described how "sublimation" is promoted by the art experience or the creative process and offers a rare moment in the therapeutic experience where personal limits and resources are tested. These are all relevant aspects that are embedded in the Lyceum methodology (Kramer, 1977).

According to Edith Kramer, special attention is paid to the art therapist's role. The art therapist must support and accept the patient, even becoming an extension of the patient's ego. They support the patient while keeping an empathic communication with the patient's creative imagination, almost

302 *Margherita Gandini*

Figure 37.2 Portrait of Edith Kramer by female student in art therapy

becoming able to predict the patient's ideas, intervening in an active way but without imposing their own style. The art therapist reflects back to the patient their intention, now clarified, but not changed, and fosters, as much as possible, his or her autonomy (Kramer, 1977).

Even though art therapists develop a certain competence in understanding symbolic communication and imagery, their task is to help the patient find their own understanding. This can be done with the art therapist's guidance, but it cannot be done for the patient (Stone, 2000, p. 114). The art therapist is described as a person who is in constant balance between the active intervention, and the neutral role that they are playing.

Some of Edith Kramer's unusual art activities are still fresh and create space for reflection. Among them is the "scribble" that provides a holistic experience by combining gesture, voice, and graphic line. There is also the possibility of encouraging free drawing without a topic or theme, where art media is offered as if on a banquet table with a large variety of both dry and wet materials.

Edith Kramer's distinct personality strongly influences Lyceum students, not only from a methodological point of view, but also from an ethical one.

Lyceum Art Therapy Training Program   303

Her particular experience, commitment to the Prague Ghetto, deep relationship with Friedl Dicker-Brandeis (who created the beginnings of art therapy with the children deported to Terezin internment camp), and her entire life intensely dedicated to art therapy and art, have a big impact on our students and their questions about ethics.

The Lyceum students naturally and intuitively internalize these ethical, moral, and philosophical values that are treasured and necessary to become art therapists. This is in sharp contrast to the "commercialization" of art therapy, the power dynamics that can invade even the field of social services and medicine, and the competition that can arise among different professionals. For our students, the feeling of walking with Edith Kramer, who cultivated art therapy through political difficulties and the Nazi oppression, leads them to develop and maintain durable ethics in order to support patients, even against any power dynamic.

It is quite clear that Edith Kramer's personality, even without real and direct contact, has a strong symbolic influence on students. She becomes an inner compass, a role model, and a valued ego ideal to emulate and internalize. The following examples are taken from the training program experience and illustrate this influence.

During the first year of the program, the students are asked to keep a journal in order to process their initial formative experiences. Many of them instinctively start their journal by using the classical diary mode and begin their entry with "Dear Edith . . ." Then they "tell" her their stories that are sometimes quite private and intimate, as if she were really leading them along their paths of professional and personal growth.

Another example of this influence is given by the last greeting placed on Edith Kramer's grave. When the news of Edith Kramer's death spread, a lot of students, art therapists (former students), and teachers contacted the Lyceum administration office and sent writings, drawings, and images dedicated to Edith. These were collected in booklets and given to Manja Makarova (a teacher at Lyceum), who took them to Edith Kramer's funeral on behalf of the Lyceum training program team. Those who observed these "collected papers" were moved, and it did not go unnoticed that many people who had not even had the chance to meet Edith Kramer had, nevertheless, written personal, intense dedications, telling her intimate fragments of their own lives.

Here you can find one of the many images gathered in a big cardboard container that Manja Makarova instinctively tossed on Edith Kramer's coffin before it was covered with soil (Figure 37.3).

All of us thought Edith Kramer would have been glad to know that her strength and determination lives on in the lives of students and art therapists, and that the dialog she started with art therapy continues in Italy. Good teachers, like Edith Kramer, exist inside their disciples' psyche as ideas or symbols. The teacher keeps on living and teaching inside of her disciples, and becomes a sort of internalized role model, firmly fixed in their minds as a protective guide.

Figure 37.3 "Thank you Edith." Collected papers placed on Edith Kramer's coffin

We believe that Edith Kramer will continue to lead many art therapists along the path of art therapy.

References

Damasio, A. (2000). *Emozione e coscienza* [Emotion and consciousness]. Milan: Adelphi.
Kramer, E. (1977). *Arte come terapia nell'infanzia* [Art as therapy with children]. Florence: La Nuova Italia. (Original work published 1971).
Kramer, E. (1985). Che cos'è l'arteterapia? [What is art therapy?]. In R. Bortino, G. Gamna, & A. Gilardi (Eds.), *Che cos'è l'arteterapia? Atti della Giornata di studio* [What is art therapy? Proceedings of the workshop]. Turin: AISCNV-ADEG.
Kramer, E. (1987). Corso teorico-pratico. In R. Bortino, W. Cipriani, G. Gamna, & A. Gilardi (Eds.), *Arte terapia. Esperienze di un corso di formazione* [Art therapy. Experiencies of course-forming] (pp. 61–71). Milan: Franco Angeli.
Lowenfeld, V., & Brittain, W.L. (1964). *Creative and mental growth* (4th ed.). New York: Macmillan Company. [*Creatività e Sviluppo Mentale*, 1967, Florence: Giunti Barbera].
Maffei, L., & Fiorentini, A. (2008). *Arte e cervello* [Art and the brain]. Bologna: Zanichelli.
Makarova, E., Dicker, F., & Miller, R.S. (2001). *Friedl Dicker-Brandeis: Vienna 1898–Auschwitz 1944: The artist who inspired the children's drawings of Terezin*. Los Angeles, CA: Tallfellow/Every Picture Press, in association with the Simon Wiesenthal Center/Museum of Tolerance.
Stone, E. (2000). Arte terapia nel rapporto individuale [Art therapy in the individual relationship]. In C. Palazzi Trivelli, & A. Teverna (Eds.), *Arti Terapie: I Fundamenti* [Art Therapy Fundamentals] (pp. 108–126). Turin, Italy: Stampatori.

38 On Leaving and Preserving

David Henley

After sixty years of being a fixture in Manhattan, it finally came time for Edith to decide to retire to her ancestral home in Austria. Many factors came into play when making the decision to leave New York. By this time in 2007, her hearing loss prohibited any further teaching, while her mobility and even creative energies began to wane. She painted less and spent days rereading her German sage poets, Schiller and Goethe. Her disgust with American politics after enduring years of the Bush White House seemed the final blow, easing the decision to rejoin her native homeland. Edith's plan was to split her time between Vienna, the city of Freud, and her alpine home on its glacier lake. Edith's cosmopolitan travel itinerary required the skill of her trusted travel agent who, for almost half a century, had coordinated Edith's complex arrangements as a matter of course. Used to multiple stops across Europe to teach and paint, Edith was now content to visit her dear old friends. A colleague from Iceland, Sigridur Bjornsdottir, had agreed to join her in Sweden where they planned to reunite with their analyst-friend Ingegerd Hansson. From the Nordic countries, she would travel on to Austria where her first stop was Salzburg, to see – of all people – her shoemaker. This ancient artisan kept a wooden mold of Edith's foot and would repair or hand-make another pair of hiking shoes from calfskin. From there she made her way to the family mountain redoubt in Grundlsee. Eventually, she would travel to her house in Vienna where she would check-in on "her" beloved Breugel collection at the Kunsthistorisches Museum. The pilgrimage to these galleries assured her that she was truly home.

A seasoned traveler, Edith packed with both precision and chaos all manner of media, objects, gifts, books, and a few corduroys and woolen jumpers that were spread throughout her studio. In actuality she carried surprisingly little in her paint splattered knapsack and beat-up suitcase.

A week later, after painting one last portrait of a neighbor, she was finally ready to leave the studio loft on Vandam Street. She showed no visible sentimentality, as she had made this trip every spring for fifty years. I followed her out to her JFK-bound town car, and for some reason, I glanced at her passport. I paused and silently shrieked: it was three days expired! This set into motion the most frantic ordeal ever packed into an hour's time. Edith

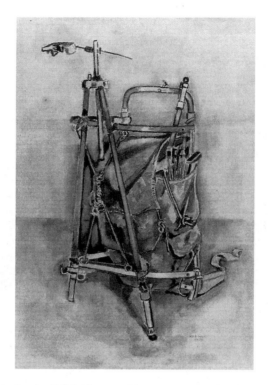

Figure 38.1 Painting by Edith Kramer. Photo courtesy of David Henley and New York University, Art Therapy Program

insisted that this complex trip could not be easily rescheduled, and *every* effort had to be made to make a flight that was only three hours until takeoff. In this one hour, I had to secure her renewed passport – a process that in most cases takes days if not weeks. Thus, I engaged the services of a professional "line sitter" – someone who stands in New York lines for a living. He promised that for an enormous sum, he could secure the document within the tight timeframe. With the town car idling by, I anxiously waited outside the federal building, which was thankfully nearby, and at the last moment, our shady character emerged with her renewed passport. I phoned the driver who wheeled round the corner. As he drove by, I handed off the passport to her, and trailing behind the limo I called out: "What about all your stuff?" With her cherubic head stuck out the window, Edith waved and said, "Oh you'll manage. I'll be back." It was not to be. I was to be the trustee of sixty years' worth of this person's *life*. After collapsing in relief and exhaustion, my eyes began to roam the racks of paintings that circled above; they now weighed down upon me in this empty, hallowed space.

On Leaving and Preserving 307

Eventually, a course of action to process Edith's belongings would be needed, especially in the likelihood she would not return. After several months, I felt her out, requesting a course of action. She wrote back, eventually, with her distinctive 3B pencil, that she was now happily settled in Europe. She directed me to take the necessary action to preserve, archive, and disseminate her life's work. In this endeavor I reached out to the director of New York University's Art Therapy Program, Dr Ikuko Acosta, who in turn enlisted NYU's Head Archivist, the late Nancy Cricco. The three of us began to chart a path to deal with this immense amount of material. The most important historical art, papers, and other memorabilia would go to New York University and become the *Edith Kramer Papers*. Ms Cricco, who has since tragically passed away, was a capable, no-nonsense professional who was undaunted by what she saw around her. Being a supportive, lovely person, she gave me ongoing advice to face this vast endeavor. With Professor Acosta's input, they ensured that not only would the co-founder of our field be given a place of honor; her material would be painstakingly archived. It would be preserved, catalogued, and digitally posted online for research purposes. Important art works as well as the fifty-year-old client paintings would receive badly needed restoration, as Edith was notorious for her "casual" approach to preservation and storage.

Further complicating this process was my own unexpected and premature retirement from university teaching and art therapy practice. In quitting the field and the City, my own feelings were naturally in turmoil. I would be permanently settling near Boulder, Colorado, which now meant I would have to accomplish this archival work from two thousand miles away. I shuttled back and forth from Colorado to the studio for the next three years. Fortunately, several former students and New York-based art therapists were enlisted to join me in this journey of sorting out the life possessions of Edith Kramer. This overwhelming and intimate task first fell to Shannon Pearce, who in the later years had been Edith's assistant and companion when I was not available. Pearce took on the challenge, despite her own exhaustive clinical practice, and began the daunting task of cleaning, sorting, and culling material. James Pruznick, who had been Edith's videographer since the late 1980s, took up residency in the loft, photographing and cataloging *every* painting in the racks. Jee Hyun Kim, another former student and now practicing art therapist, who computerized the endless lists of inventory, later assisted this process. Thankfully, Edith's confidant in Grundlsee, Elfie Klier, possessed email and English-language capability, so that Edith could now view her works digitally – despite her long aversion to computers. I sent Elfie and Edith files of works divided by rarity, stylistic period, quality, and medium/technique. Edith could decide which works would go to auction or be shipped back to Europe, while leaving a hundred other works as gifts for Edith's closest friends. Numerous meetings ensued with Edith's dealer Susan Teller, her Viennese representative from Galerie Pallauf, The New York Transit Museum, the Jewish Museum, and even the Austrian

308   *David Henley*

consulate – all wished bequests. At this time, I also began sorting through her personal effects.

As I sorted through her things, I was uneasy since Edith and I had always maintained strong boundaries despite my habitation at the loft for over a decade. Each flat file contained unexpected treasures: A fan letter from Elinor Ulman signed 1958; notices by Ernst Kris, Kurt Eissler, and Konrad Lorenz critiquing her first book. Her dear friend and Canadian art therapy pioneer Herschel J. Stroyman documented a photographic series from the late 1950s. Among his photographs was the opening of Edith's groundbreaking exhibit, "Art for the Troubled Child." One picture captures a prized moment of Edith lecturing alongside of an approving Eleanor Roosevelt. Albums of faded family pictures captured the carefree days before the coming of another world war, when Edith and her family gathered to summer together in the mountains. Imagine, coming upon our mentor cavorting and swimming nude in the freezing waters of that alpine lake! There were those of her beloved Aunt Liesl, her closest relative and a character actor of Hollywood repute, who was always mugging for the camera. Images of the young Edith herself, known affectionately among her family as "Mumi," seemed always a thoughtful, serious young teen, who quietly absorbed the influences of the characters of her tumultuous bohemian family. There were also some chilling effects such as letters pleading for sponsorship to escape the now Nazi-occupied Austria. Passports stamped with Nazi swastikas were a testament as to how late many family members waited to escape the continent. Edith's clinical charts and process notes made fascinating reading, especially those adorned with portraits and doodling in the margins. Anyone who knows Edith understands that sketching was the only means by which she could endure any form of a "meeting." Then there were her materials from her thirty years of teaching at NYU: syllabi, lecture notes, slides, even grade books where one could read her comments on everything from attendance, grades, and comments. Present leaders of the field would be humbled by what she wrote about their work! Eventually, this material was collated and divided, with most being placed at the NYU Archives. I became trustee of a small collection of especially prized works, which Edith hoped in the future might become a traveling exhibition for universities. I am still framing, matting, and building containers for this collection, which forms a condensed testament of her artistic legacy.

At the time of this writing, the *Edith Kramer Papers* archived at NYU is still an active ongoing project, with individuals adding material every year. Friends, colleagues, and former students have mined their own trove of memorabilia, and continue to present it to the archive. Students, researchers, and collectors inquire about this material from many countries around the world. It is meant to be a living, organic depository at her beloved New York University. It is there, just rooms away from her collection high above Washington

On Leaving and Preserving 309

Square, that a female red-tailed hawk has taken up residence on a window's ledge. Every time I spy that hawk, I am reminded that this is where Edith Kramer *belongs*. With a brood to feed, this magnificent raptor rarely rests. She circles the air with her raspy call, then sails through the park as yet another unique character plying this city. Her work, as was Edith's, is a thing of fierce beauty and a continual work in progress.

39 Creating a World of Possibility
Life Lessons from Edith Kramer

Lani Gerity

In thinking about all the things I have learned from Edith Kramer, I wonder what sorts of things art therapists might like to know more about, what sorts of things might be useful to know, that might make your lives easier. I wonder what I have learned from Edith that might be relevant in your lives today, or what might be relevant to the lives of your students or the people you work with.

I realized that one of the most amazing gifts that I have stumbled into is having the great honor of knowing Edith quite well. She was one of the grand-mothers of our profession, but more than that, she was a satisfied, inspired, curious, happy artist. When she was in her eighties, I started realizing that this was something I would hope to grow into as well. Isn't that something we all hope for, to be able to live a fulfilling, useful, happy life?

Our teachers often imagine they are teaching one thing, while we may actually be learning some other things as well. For example, while Edith was teaching psychoanalytic theory in art therapy, with a heavy emphasis on Freud, I suspect that while I took notes diligently, what I was learning that was most valuable was more to do with how Edith lived her life and how she worked.

A lot of this had to do with how to live a satisfying life, one filled with inner rewards, inner satisfaction rather than the trappings of our materialistic culture; a life filled with as much art as possible, great conversations with many friends over pots of tea and great bread; a contemplative life, a curious life, an artist's life. She called it a frugal life, but I believe it was actually a very generous life. I have a very deep sense of gratitude and debt for the many things that I learned from Edith. I'd like to share some of what I learned, so that you can have a happy artist's life as well.

I will start with the studio itself. It was a quiet place, a haven from the chaos of New York City. You could hear yourself think there. Edith emphasized the importance of stillness in her creative space. She wanted to be able to access what she called the "inner life."

When our art space is still, we can study our work and entertain the most amazing insights, flashes of creative thought, daydreams. When the studio is still, we can work with a clear and focused mind; our best work depends on

Creating a World of Possibility 311

our most creative state of mind. Stillness allows for these clear and focused states of mind, which allows for more creative work, which increases emotional well-being, reduces stress and anxiety, and provides a space for a happy artist's life.

Edith's studio was full of objects of interest and beauty. Edith believed in the importance of surrounding herself with beauty. And now, through research in neuroscience, Zeki (Kawabata & Zeki, 2004) and others are suggesting that surrounding ourselves with the things we consider to be beautiful is very good for our mental states. Edith's studio was a very beautiful place and very good for her and her visitors' well-being.

Lesson One: Make everything special. Embellish your life.

In *The Courage to Create*, Rollo May (1975/1994) said, in order for us to be open to creativity, we must be able to use solitude constructively. We must overcome our fear of being alone. This comfort with solitude was something Edith valued a great deal. If you ever had the opportunity to visit her while she worked in her loft, you could really understand the importance of quiet, undisturbed, creative time alone. Our culture seems to discourage us from being alone in so many ways, but actually solitude can be the key to producing our best work. For Edith, this had to do with giving herself the time and space for creative activity.

Csikszentmihalyi has written a lot about creativity, and how artists and others can get in the "zone," or into the flow state, allowing us to create at our highest level. In this state we transcend conscious thought to reach a state of effortless concentration and calmness. We become immune to any internal or external pressures and distractions that could hinder our performance. Time and the clock lose their importance. Csikszentmihalyi says we get into the flow state when we are doing something we enjoy, that we are good at, but that also provides a challenge. We find the thing we love, and we build up our skills, which results in the flow state. In Edith's studio, there was time enough, always.

Lesson Two: Whenever possible create a sense of stillness, beauty, "flow," and time enough to enjoy it.

Edith believed that our best work emerges when we follow intrinsic motivations or inner satisfaction. She observed from personal experience and from the children she worked with, that when we create from an internal prompting, we are rewarded through inner satisfaction rather than extrinsic reward. She described second wind phenomenon in the art room as occurring when we push through a wall of self-doubt, inner criticism, or even exhaustion, to find we are energized by the challenge of our work. This second wind is an intrinsic motivation, an inner satisfaction. We need stillness to find our "true passions" and our second wind.

Lesson Three: Follow your true passions. Find your second wind.

Seek out diversity of experience, which will definitely promote creativity. Edith would do this by travel, exploring new environments to paint, but also

312 Lani Gerity

by learning new ways of working. Constantly curious, constantly learning, Edith never found life monotonous or mundane. Her life was full of diversity of experiences. We can develop a habit of shaking things up. We can embrace diversity as well. If we have a drive to explore our world, both internal and external, if we have an intellectual curiosity, an openness to new experiences, an openness to emotions, and an openness to possibilities, we will be happy artists.

Edith was forced by historic events to leave her home, her limited perspective, and explore other ways of thinking and being. This was extremely helpful for her creative work, and conversely, her creative work was very helpful in adapting to life events. It allowed her to let go of old ways of doing things, and it also allowed her to imagine others' points of view. Understanding another perspective (especially the children she worked with) moved her toward more creative thinking and new solutions.

Lesson Four: Play more often, change perspectives, shake things up.

Wherever Edith went, she brought a sketchpad and pencils, a portable studio. Always. She sketched on the subway, when talking on the phone, in conferences, even in her own workshops. She observed everything and always took notes. She encouraged us to do the same. Our lives can be an adventure if we are actually paying attention. It's all an opportunity for self-expression. When we look at the world this way, our lives are full of all kinds of opportunities.

Lesson Five: View all of life as an opportunity for self-expression. Find something to love about where you are every day.

Of course, taking risks was something Edith was very good at from an early age – leaping into the unknown was exactly what she did all the time, her whole life. From following Friedl Dicker-Brandeis to Czechoslovakia, to her journey to the US, to working as a machinist, to traveling in Europe after the war; her life story reads like a series of risks. Every time Edith went to a new place to teach or speak, she was leaving the familiar behind. Every time she started a new painting or learned a new technique, she was taking a risk. We too can be brave and take risks. It's worth it!

Edith encouraged her own creativity by encouraging curiosity. She allowed herself to live an examined life in spite of or in defiance of the pressures of our culture. She saw no age limit to being curious about life. We don't need to either. We can look at the world around us and ask why things are the way they are, and how they might be otherwise. The world would be better off if we all did this a little more often. She was very fond of suggesting we should be maladapted to the culture if it asks us to stifle our creative thought.

Lesson Six: Take risks, question everything. If society asks us to stifle our independent thought, we can practice being "maladapted!"

Edith's resilience, flexibility, and creative success had everything to do with a daily art practice. She encouraged herself and us to work hard, creating a body of work so that even though we may not love every piece, if we create enough, there are sure to be a few pieces which we can appreciate. We can fail often but with a daily practice there is bound to be great satisfaction!

Lesson Seven: Look for good, interesting, curious things every day. Use them in your art. Make art every day.

We all know stories of pain and heartbreak. We may even spend a lot of effort avoiding this kind of experience. But Edith tended to use these stories to fuel her creativity, to explore, and grow. Like her mentor Friedl, Edith helped many turn hardships and trauma into personal growth, helping others to find appreciation for life, discover personal strength, and see new possibilities in life. We can do this too.

Edith painted a juniper tree when visiting the southwestern United States. This juniper tree is the perfect, inclusive Edith metaphor – grounded, rooted, and providing shelter and stillness for us all. This juniper tree was of great interest to Edith. When she saw the tree, she said it had a very strong "being" about it. The fellow who owned the property where the tree stood, told her it was hit by lightning at least twice and must be about 1000 years old. He remembered Edith's visit to the mesa and her tenacity as she marched across the field with this large painting strapped to her back. May we all be so tenacious and resilient!

Figure 39.1 Juniper tree print by Edith Kramer. Contributed by Elena Makarova

314   *Lani Gerity*

Lesson Eight: Turn life's obstacles around. Be generous. Look for what is good and strong in others. Be ready for experiences that will delight and surprise you.

In reviewing images of Edith's work, her home in Austria, and photos from her family, I realize that Edith valued history, and the idea of being a part of a lineage. We learned the things that Edith learned from Friedl Dicker-Brandeis, and of course we can pass these things on. Lineages are a very good thing to be a part of; we aren't as isolated and separate as we imagine. One of the best things I learned from Friedl through Edith was not to wait to do good things in the world. Friedl had told Edith that she thought that something was very wrong with her, that she needed a lot of psychoanalysis because she had never felt more alive than while she was imprisoned for her communist activities. Friedl thought this must be masochism, and so she should be analyzed right away. In actuality, her ability to remain fully alive under extreme adversity served her and the children she worked with in Terezin very well. This is comforting because I doubt that perfection is anything humans are going to achieve any time soon, and if Friedl could do good things without perfection and under such impossible conditions, then surely we could do some good, with whatever we have on hand.

Lesson Nine: Create beauty with what you have on hand. Don't wait for the perfect inspiration or the perfect materials.

Another aspect of appreciating history and of being a part of a lineage is the sense of community this engenders. I learned to appreciate that so much when visiting Edith in Austria. The sense of history going back generations and the sense of strong, living, supportive community was still very alive when I visited. Edith wasn't just Edith Kramer, artist/art therapist there. She was "our Kramer," in a way held by the community, as if they had created a supportive transitional space with this feeling of history and community. Just knowing such community and history is possible is more deeply satisfying and comforting than any material rewards could ever be.

Lesson Ten: Honor your history. Learn about your lineage.

One of the more useful things I learned was the idea of storytelling in the art room, and how appreciative the people we work with are when we can furnish their minds with inspiring, challenging, sometimes scary, and ultimately reassuring stories of resilience like *The Wonderful Adventures of Nils* by Selma Lagerlöf. Lagerlöf created the adventures as a way of teaching children about the natural history and geography of Sweden, but it was ultimately a hero's journey, and Nils discovered all kinds of treasure and compassion within.

Edith would tell these stories as she helped the Wiltwyck boys master paint and brush at the Wiltwyck School for Boys. They loved the stories of the little boy, Nils, and his struggles and adventures. They would beg for more when the art lesson was finished. I can certainly empathize with the boys' identification with Nils and all that he was learning from the wise, old, gray goose, Akka. I can certainly understand why they begged Edith to tell them more stories about Akka. Both Akka and Edith probably helped many children find their

Creating a World of Possibility 315

humanity. How satisfying it must have been for them to paint and listen to these stories.

Lesson Eleven: Play, teach, tell stories, and enjoy being with your descendants, as much as possible. They will inherit good things from you.

Finally I believe that Edith sparked in many of us the desire to search for things that provide inner satisfaction (more art, more puppets, more beauty, nature, and community) and to search for the part of the superego that is kindly and caretaking, the inner-Akka, or even, perhaps, the inner-Kramer. She set great store by her own kindly superego, and the importance of internalizing the wisdom and kindness of her mentors. For her there was without a doubt, an inner-Friedl.

The search for these things has been the best adventure of all. It must surely compare with Nils' adventures with Akka, and I have learned everything about being human from this adventure. Kathie Bard, another one of Edith's students, said, "Edith saw us as the future . . . she sought to inspire the artist, thinker, scientist, and writer in each of us . . . she wanted to open our senses and minds."

Lesson Twelve: Give some thought to the future. We, you, and I, and everyone we teach are the future.

Figure 39.2 Don't Give Up. Paper and digital collage by Lani Gerity

316 *Lani Gerity*

And for all of these things, and for so much more, I am extremely grateful to our teacher, Edith Kramer.

References

Kawabata, H., & and Zeki, S. (2004). Neural correlates of beauty. *Journal of Neurophysiology, 91*, 1699–1705. Retrieved from: http://jn.physiology.org/content/jn/91/4/1699.full.pdf Accessed 19 September 2017.

May, R. (1994). *The courage to create*. New York: W.W. Norton. (Original work published in 1975).

40 Conclusions

Is This the End or the Beginning?

Susan Ainlay Anand and Lani Gerity

In trying to find an appropriate ending to the experience of working on this book, what Laurie Wilson described in her chapter, "Sublimation Then and Now," as philosophical alchemy, we wanted to reflect a little on how much we have learned and what a creative experience it has been, working together with all the contributors. We thought we knew Edith Kramer fairly well, that we had a good understanding of her strengths, her generosity. We thought we had a developed an inner-Kramer, our own kindly superego. Although it was always fairly easy to call her to mind, now it all feels so much more real. Reading Edith's own narration of the importance of Mädi and Friedl in her life, we could see the importance of Edith in our lives, too, and we could sense the virtual company of Edith's caring net of amazing bohemian artists and thinkers.

We'd like to end this delightful collaboration by speaking about the New York University Archives, for two reasons. The first reason is that any future research could begin quite easily with this treasure trove of material. The second reason would be because this adventurous book began in the archives. Many of the contributors had participated in a memorial service which NYU had given for Edith Kramer on April 26, 2014. At the end of the service, some of us took a tour of the conservation area in the library where the restoration of the beloved paintings of the children Edith worked with was being done. We met Laura McCann, the conservation librarian, as well as archivist Janet Bunde. They gave us a taste of what was available in the *Edith Kramer Papers* and spoke with such enthusiasm that we were intrigued. Although these women had never met Edith, they seemed to know her very well; it was as if in some way they brought her back to us. We eagerly plotted our next visit.

First, we booked an appointment with Janet Bunde to explore what was available within the papers themselves. The papers reside in a very quiet, industrious reading room, with many assistants bringing out materials for the readers and then re-filing them when finished. No pens, food, or drink on the reading room tables were allowed, of course. The rules and hushed activity gave this room an otherworldly, almost sacred feel. We were not in the everyday, mundane world of Starbucks and chatter.

318 *Susan Ainlay Anand and Lani Gerity*

It was truly a surprising and wonderful experience to read some of Edith's own handwritten papers and notes in 3B pencil on recycled paper (in one case, on Lani's dissertation, which was a very humorous find). We enlisted Martha Haeseler's help to pore over the documents written in German. We felt, in a strange way, like we were coming home, finding these ideas and impressions from the past. However, at the same time, so much of Edith's writing seemed extremely relevant for today – the concern for marginalized populations, the work with refugees and their children, the need for social justice, and the desire to find a way to do the things that feed our inner life, that give our lives as a whole meaning. All of this is as important to us today as it was to Edith in her life.

We were provided access to videos of Edith teaching students and sound files of lectures and talks, which had to be taken to the AV department where we could secure equipment to view and listen to this material. Here, we got totally lost in cubicles, wearing headsets and taking notes. We listened to various lectures and talks with great enthusiasm, some of which you will find transcribed in this book.

Afterwards, we went down to the basement for our appointment to view the conservation of Edith's collection of children's artwork. Laura McCann gave us a fascinating tour of this area of the library and described with great enthusiasm the process of how she came to know and appreciate Edith through this collection. As she spoke, it became very clear that the work of a conservator goes far beyond an understanding of paper, bindings, glues, pH levels, and preservation. For Laura and the other conservators, the individuals behind the collections are at least as fascinating as the collections themselves.

Laura is responsible for preventive and treatment conservation programs at the NYU library, which includes Edith's 70 paintings on paper created by children during art therapy sessions from the 1950s through the 1970s. She found these paintings – ranging from kinetic abstractions to very detailed portraits – visually arresting works of art. Because Edith analyzed the works of art in published case studies and frequently brought the paintings into the classroom when teaching in NYU's art therapy program, Laura found that reading about the paintings helped her better grasp what she was working with. She read and enjoyed *Art as Therapy with Children* (Kramer, 1993) and *Art Therapy in a Children's Community* (Kramer, 1958). Of particular interest to her were discussions of the therapeutic use of "the third hand" and Edith's willingness to intervene in the child's artwork.

Laura explained to us that conservation of works of art produced during therapy raised significant ethical and legal considerations for her. Since the works produced by children in treatment are in a sense "medical records," they are protected under the confidentiality provision of the Health Insurance Portability and Accountability Act of 1996 (HIPAA). This posed a challenge for her in terms of documentation, as the child's name often appears on the verso of the painting. Additional complexity surfaced from the fact that in some cases Edith felt she needed to assist children by using small interventions in the execution of the works. Laura showed us evidence that she found in several paintings revealing Edith's third hand approach.

The conservation of these works was also challenging due to their composition and condition. The paintings were executed on poor quality paper with poster paint that was often unstable, vulnerable to cracking and flaking. Years after the paintings were created, Edith mounted the works onto boards, most likely to make them easier to transport and photograph. She attached the mounts with poor quality masking tape that subsequently damaged the paper and paint surface. Edith also repaired/restored approximately 20 paintings, sometimes using poor quality materials such as heavy tape that failed to stabilize the object. And, she also retouched about 20 paintings with mixed success. Unfortunately, she occasionally used media that over time was increasingly unsympathetic in tone and texture to the original paint.

As Laura learned about Edith's role in the creation of the art in the collection, she explained that her treatment protocol evolved from removing all evidence of retouching to preserving this evidence of Edith's interactions with the works.

Figure 40.1 Laura McCann with a child's painting of a wedding. Photo by Susan Anand

Laura felt it was imperative to preserve her interactions with the pieces whenever possible, since the paintings are a part of Edith's collection at the NYU Archives. Therefore, the treatment protocol included retaining her retouching, but removing failed mounts when they presented a current risk to the object. This protocol was successfully applied to 69 of the 70 paintings. However, the protocol was unsuitable in solving the problem of how to conserve the seventieth painting, a powerful but badly damaged 36" x 48" work titled, *Young Man with Switchblade*. As the work was in pieces, Laura concluded that standard treatment approaches to reassembling and visually integrating the painting would jeopardize Edith's retouching.

Consequently, Laura requested a sabbatical to conduct research on Edith's interaction with works of art created by her clients/patients, and on the interpretation, appreciation, and preservation of works created in therapeutic environments, as well as the specific ethical and legal obligations that the conservation of such works entails. In addition, she wants to research practical considerations (materials, treatment methodologies) for conserving *Young Man with Switchblade*.

And so the Edith Kramer research continues. We hope that the readers feel that the archives may be as accessible and welcoming as we felt they were. When Laura and Janet talked with us, we could almost feel Edith's presence.

Figure 40.2 Laura McCann with a child's painting, *Young Man with Switchblade*. Photo by Susan Anand

Conclusions 321

That is the main reason we wanted this experience to be at the end of the book, because it has always been our hope to encourage curiosity and the cultivation of possibility. Ironically, in the controlled air and unnatural lighting (two of Edith's pet peeves) of the depths of the Bobst Library, curiosity, possibility, and Edith's presence are very much alive.

Reluctantly, we need to draw this wonderful collaboration to a close. The whole experience of working with our contributors, going through the materials available for the book, reviewing Edith's theories and how people are putting them into practice, as well as Edith's amazingly resilient story has altogether created a truly life-changing, delightfully alchemical experience for us. We can now see clearly what we only vaguely realized years ago, that having a role model who valued creativity, strength, and integrity above everything was vital to living a meaningful life. Knowing about Edith's life and attitudes on how best to be of service helps us see and imagine possibilities. Knowing Edith had her caring net of bohemian artists and free thinkers for role models and mentors helping her create a meaningful art-filled life helps us see ourselves as a part of a legacy, part of something larger than ourselves. The historical context is also reassuring. Yes, we have been through very difficult times in the past. Yes, we will most likely go through some difficult times in the future, but we have our art supplies and our creative passion. We can be strong and persevere as Edith taught us.

We believe Edith sparked in many of us the desire to search for things that provide inner satisfaction (more art, more puppets, more beauty, nature, and community) and to search for the part of the superego that is kindly and caretaking: perhaps the inner-Kramer. The search for these things has been the best adventure of all, and we have learned everything about being human from this adventure. Thankfully, we were also reminded that as humans, we face adversity and often create good things from the experience.

Our hope is that you, the reader, give some thought to our inclusive, curious art therapy legacy. We, you (the reader), us (the contributors), and everyone we teach are all a part of this amazing history. We are the community, we are the net, and we are the legacy.

This is not the end, this is just the beginning.

References

Kramer, E. (1958). *Art therapy in a children's community*. Springfield, IL: Thomas.
Kramer, E. (1993). *Art as therapy with children*. Chicago, IL: Magnolia Street Press.

Index

Accreditation Council for Graduate
Medical Education (ACGME) 276,
277
Acosta, Ikuko *69*; teaching with Edith
69
aesthetic, art therapy 98
aesthetic attitude in art therapy
111–12
Agell, Gladys 11, 63, 159
aggression *see* anger; drives
Agni 261
alchemy, philosophical 132n1, 317
Alper, T. G. 49, 50
Alpine Wonders (Bard) *165*
Alschuler, R. 50
American Art Therapy Association
(AATA) 100, 102
American Art Therapy Association
(AATA) Annual Conferences 2,
53, 63, 83, 196; artwork done by
Edith while at 186, 205; Edith at
3, 51, 53, 56–57, 64, 83, 99, 160,
163, 166, 185, 247; journal of 150;
logos for 64, 109, 160; plenary
presentation devoted to Edith's life
at 1, 2
American Journal of Art Therapy 51,
53, 56; see also *Bulletin of Art
Therapy*
Amiens Cathedral xvii–xviii
Anand, Vinod 2
Andersen, Hans Christian 167–68
anger 160, 188–89, 214, 216, 219
"anything goes" attitude 108, 110,
211, 247
Arbus, Diane 153
Arm, Annette 131
Armstrong, Jeannette 258–59, 266

art: defining 171; lineage,
interpretation, theory, and practice
206; as oxygen 206–7; *see also
specific topics*
*Art as Contemplative Practice:
Expressive Pathways to the Self*
(Franklin) 206
Art as Therapy: Collected Papers
(Kramer & Gerity) 51–53, 253;
cover art for 10
"art as therapy," Edith's coining of the
term 110
art as therapy groups 134
art as therapy method 10, 20, 78, 85,
139, 148, 162, 163, 205–8, 211;
and art as contemplative practice
208; vs. art psychotherapy 192;
benefits of using 2, 78, 227, 235,
275; challenges in working with
adults using 133–34; concept of
110, 229, 231; core of 8; Edith as
epitomizing the meaning of 66;
Edith as role model for therapists
who identify with 301; Edith on
192, 232; Edith's development of
15, 20, 85, 110; Edith's writings
on 297, 318; ego-psychology
framework of 134; Friedl Dicker
and 8, 19, 214; goal of 231; in
Mandarin 231; misunderstanding
of 230–31; nature of 110, 229–32;
psychoanalysis and 8, 61, 209;
puppet-making and 240; research
and theses on 232; silence,
nonverbal communication, and
18; Taiwan and 232; therapeutic
intention and 230; training
programs rooted in 61, 298, 300;

324 *Index*

used to anchor the group art therapy experience 278

Art as Therapy with Children (class) 185

Art as Therapy with Children (Kramer) 11, 51, 71, 72, 91, 141–43, 288, 318; cover of Chinese version of *233*; Erna Furman and 38, 39, 289–90; Shyueying Chiang and 232–34; translations 141, 142, 232–34, *233*

art education 231; vs. art therapy 231

art exercises of Edith, examples of 68–70, 145

art experientials 68–69

Art for Art Therapists (course/ seminar) 67, 68, 141, 166, 189, 228–29

art-making as strengthening 10, 110, 133, 136, 137, 208, 280

art quality *see* quality

art therapist: most important task of 143; role of 117, 135–38; wearing multiple hats 135–38; *see also specific topics*

art therapist's identity, three-legged stool metaphor of 208

art therapy: attention to craft in 110–11; defining 101–2; functions and goals of 143; nature of 143, 282–83, 300; origin of the term 50; origins 33, 303 (*see also under* Dicker-Brandeis, Friedl); position of the art in 110; principles of art made in 102; *see also specific topics*

Art Therapy Association in Taiwan 232, 235, 235n2

art therapy group(s) 72–73, 134; beginning of group work 73–75; case vignettes 76–78; empathy in 191, 237, 238, 241, 243, 277, 279; medical training in 277–82; theoretical insights 75–76

Art Therapy in a Children's Community (Kramer) xix, 50, 51, 53–54, 91, 318

art therapy studios 206, 207, 210; *see also under* Kramer, Edith

Artist in Each of Us, The (Cane) 188

artistic ability 247; *see also* quality

artistic development, progression of 136

artistic impulse, original 159

artwork of Edith Kramer 86–89, 167, 205; chief critic of *see* Zilzer, Vera; etchings *21* (*see also specific works*); exhibition of see *Process and Product*; family portraits 169, 170; self-portraits 87; sketching in Toronto *34*; storage and preservation 307–9, 318–21; theoretical concepts in 86; *see also specific topics*

Atlas, Gustina 264

attachment theory 75–76

Auschwitz concentration camp 20, 187; *see also* Dicker-Brandeis, Friedl: death; Holocaust

Ausseerland region 26

Austria 16; Edith painting in 153, 186; Edith's departure from xvi-xvii, 16; Edith's home in countryside of 35, 314; Edith's retirement in 3, 87, 90, 165, 179, 305–7; Edith's visits/travels to xxi, 23, 35, 92, 186, 275, 305; Nazi-occupied xvi, 15, 20, 89, 179, 308; *see also* Grundlsee

Austrian Alps, family home in 179, 186

Austrian Embassy in Washington, DC, Edith's exhibit at 95

authenticity, expressive *see* inner consistency

auxiliary ego, therapist as 137, 138, 148, 191, 230; *see also* ego functions/ego functioning

Bad Aussee *see* Ausseerland region

Baruch, Dorothy 50

Bauhaus (German art school) xvi, 188, 291, *293*, 294

Bauhaus method 283n

Bauhaus movement 150

beauty 267; of art, qualities that determine 102 (*see also* quality); creating beauty with what you have on hand 314; *see also* cultural gifts of wisdom, hope, and beauty

Beebe, Beatrice 119

Beets and Onions (Kramer) 57

Bellmer, Hans 17

Bergman, Anni *36*, 85

Bergman, Kostia 33

Berliawsky, Isaac 129

Berliawsky, Minna Smolerank 129

Berlin, Edith in 16–17, 24, 26, 27, 141, *142*
Bernard, Viola Wertheim xix
Bernfeld, Siegfried (Brassi) xxii, 17, 23–26, *28*, 61, 291
Berry, George 254–55, *255*, 266, 270–71
Bertolli, Sister 250–51
Bjornsdottir, Sigridur 305
Blanck, Gertrude 119
Blanck, Rubin 119
blindness *see* cases: Christopher
Blitz, Edith painting after the xvii, xviii
boat at sea, painting of (Carlo) 76, *76*
Bobst Library Archives *see* New York University (NYU) Bobst Library Archives
body ego 216
body image: disturbed/distorted 39, 236; reparation and creation of whole 240
bohemian artists and free thinkers, Edith's caring network of 317, 321; *see also* bohemian environment
bohemian attitudes, Edith's 155–56
bohemian environment: in Greenwich Village 260; (in Vienna) in which Edith grew up xvi, xvii, 16, 23, 24, 179, 308 (*see also* bohemian artists and free thinkers); in Prague xvii
borderline personality disorder 115, 117, 119; *see also* cases: Jack
Bornstein, Steff 27
Bortino, Raffaella 71, 72, 297
bottle trees 267, *267*
Bowie, David 215
Bowlby, John 75–76, 120
Bradley, Laura 97
braid, Edith's 3, *5*, 67, 163, 166–67, 228, 288, 295
Brâncuşi, Constantin 293
Brassi *see* Bernfeld, Siegfried
Breast on Lawn (drawing by cancer patient) 225, *225*
Breton, Andre 132n1
Broken Oven (tempera on paper) 137, *138*
Brooklyn Bridge, reproduction of O'Keeffe's 121, *121*
Bulletin of Art Therapy 50, 51; see also *American Journal of Art Therapy*
Bunde, Janet 317, 320

cancer 215, 216
cancer diagnosis 215
cancer patients 214–16, 221, 271–73; case material 215–22; drawings 225, *225*; terminal 215, 220, 221 (*see also* cases: Henry; cases: Louise)
Cancer Stories: Creativity and Self Repair (Dreifuss-Kattan) 214
cancer survivors 273; *see also* cases: Emmanuelle
Cane, Florence 49, 50, 188
cards, art 134, 137, 288; *see also* Christmas cards
cases: Anita 134–37; Anna 72–74, 77; Barbara (22-year-old social worker) 72, 77–78, *78*; Barbara (elderly woman) 273; Carlo 72, 76, 76–77; Christopher 148, *149*, 155, 233; Emma 120–22; Emmanuelle 122–23; Gerry 214; Henry 216–22, *217–19*; Jack 237–40, 242; Jane 271–73; Laura 72, 74; Lillian 207–8; Louise 113–14, 123; Luisa 72, 73; *see also* Hector
charcoal 42, 76, 141, 166, 190, *293*
Chestnut Lodge 214
Child Art Therapy (Rubin) 53
Childhood and Art Therapy (Kramer) 51
Chinese, *Art as Therapy with Children* translated into 232–34, *233*
Christmas 252
Christmas cards *21*, 34, 313
Christmas parties and celebrations 34–35, 168, 170, 252
Christmas trees 34, 65, 168, *169*, 170
Churchill, Angiola 59–60
Cizek, Franz 91
clarity (of expression) 109, 114, 166; aesthetics and 112; affective 113; case material 112–14; in image making 112, 113; principle of 112–14
clay figure, sitting 113, *113*
clay head (art exercise) 68–70
clay heads, four flat 123, *123*
clay sculptures 148, *149*; depicting mother and child *78*
client-centered approach 230
cognitive therapies 193
collages xix–xx, 42, 93–95, 130, 282; Edith on xix–xx; Edith's xix–xx, 42,

326 *Index*

93, 95, 96; Gerity's 315; nature of xx, 42, 282
"colonization" 237
communism: Edith and 8, 24, 150; Edith's family and 16, 24, 179; Friedl Dicker and 18, 39, 150, 314
Community Il Porto. 72, 78
companionable solitude 143
compassion 22, 67, 165, 206, 212
concentration camps *see* Gulag; Nazi concentration camps
congruence *see* inner consistency
connection vs. separation 259
consistency *see* inner consistency
contemplation: art and 115, 207; Edith and 115, 118, 210, 212; etymology of the term 210
contemplative capacities of experiencer–observer–responder, Edith's 206
contemplative practice 209–10; art as 206, 208–10
Cook-Greuter, S. 17–18
countertransference 111, 145, 162, 212; awareness of 191; with cancer patients 214, 221–22; clinical material 214, 221–22; Edith on 144, 191; Edith's 191
Cox, Kenyon 91
creative practice, concrete 76
creativity 35, 49, 311, 312; *see also specific topics*
"Credo, as an Artist and an Art Therapist" (Kramer) 52; *see also under* Kramer, Edith
Cricco, Nancy 307
cross-cultural education through art therapy groups *see* medical student(s)
cross-sensory feelings (art exercise) 68
Csikszentmihalyi, Mihaly 263, 311
cultural-ethno-humility 259; *see also* religion
cultural gifts of wisdom, hope, and beauty 258–67
curiosity 283, 310, 312–13

Dannecker, Karin *142*
dark, artwork done in the 62, 68–69; *see also* cases: Christopher
David, Irene Rosner: as art therapist of Edith 226–27

de Morra, Sebastián 175–76, *176*
death 114; *see also* cancer patients: terminal
decolonizing art as therapy method 8
decolonizing model 282–83
decolonizing way of working, Edith's 2
defense mechanisms 117; overcoming 87; *see also specific defense mechanisms*
Delancey Street (Manhattan), Edith's residence on 169
Dennis, H. D. 251–53, 271
Dennis, Margaret 251–53, *252*
Dialysis House (drawing by patient) 226
Dicker-Brandeis, Friedl 19, 26, 38, 40–44, 303; arrests and detention 18, 19, 179; art as therapy and 8, 19, 214; art ethic 43; at Bauhaus xvi, 18, 91, 188; in Bauhaus movement 150; charcoal study *293*; children in Prague taught by 43; communism 18, 39, 150, 314; death 7, 19, 214; dictation 41; early meetings with 18, 24, 39; Edith and 15, 19, 54, 91, 214, 312; Edith on xvi, 8, 18, 38, 40–44; Edith's work with xvi, 18, 188, 303; education 188; Elena Makarova and 288, 290; Erna Furman and 38; as first art therapist 18, 303; general suggestions 42–43; influence on Edith 8, 18, 19, 91, 188, 277, 314; lessons 41–43; Lyceum and 297, 298; mentorship of Edith 18, 24, 25, 39–41, 54, 150, 277; personality and values 42, 43; in Prague 8, 18, 25, 39, 43, 91, 150, 188, 214, 277, 288–89; reportage and 42; responses to the exercises of *291–92*; teachers 91, 188; Theresienstadt (Terezin) and 8, 38, 39, 42–44, 54, 214, 289, 291, *292*, 303; using rhythm 41; wire figures 41–42
disabilities, teaching art to children with 160; *see also* cases: Christopher
Dogon people 260–61
Don't Give Up (paper and digital collage by Gerity) *315*
double awareness 215
drive derivatives 118

Index 327

drive theory, Freudian 119, 127, 132
drives: defined 197; Freud on 116, 122, 126, 128, 149; Hector's 197

economy of (artistic) means 207; case material 123, 173, 176, 256; as criterion for art quality 99, 102, 111, 171, 249, 256; formed expression and 177, 190; nature of 99, 102; sublimation and 116
Edith Kramer: Painter and Art Therapist Between Worlds (Zwiauer) 23–24
Edith Kramer Atelier Method (E.Kr.A.M.) 299, *299*
Edith Kramer Papers 307, 308, 317–18
egg tempera on canvas *88*
eggs 93–94; as ornaments 170; painted 93, 168
ego: body 216; contemplative practices and 209; dissolution of 171; Edith on 171–73, 192; group 261; individuals with a fragile 116; shift in focus from id to 116, 118, 119, 155 (*see also* ego mastery over id impulses)
ego defenses *see* defense mechanisms
ego development 216, 259; cross-cultural differences in 259, 260; *see also* ego; ego strengthening
ego functions/ego functioning: externalization of 215, 220, 221; progression of artistic development correlated with the level of ego skills 136; sublimation and 116–19, 124, 126, 127, 136–37, 144, 148, 155; supporting patient's 143 (*see also* ego strengthening); and therapist becoming extension of patient's ego 301; therapist taking over 215, 220, 221; *see also* auxiliary ego; ego strength
ego ideal(s): development of 10, 243, 269; Edith as an 11, 301–4; Edith on 31, 53; Edith's 31; kind/caring/caretaking part of 9, 11, 31, 53; necessity for 236
ego mastery over id impulses 117, 148
ego-psychological framework, Edith's 116, 117, 126, 133, 134, 144
ego psychology 116, 117, 127, 171

ego strength 135–37, 148, 280; *see also* ego functions/ego functioning
ego strengthening 10, 112, 117, 124, 135, 136, 143, 172–73, 208–9
Eisner, Ellis 170
Eissler, Kurt 61
E.Kr.A.M. (Edith Kramer Atelier Method) 299, *299*
Elmer Holmes Bobst Library *see* New York University (NYU) Bobst Library Archives
emotional evocativeness *see* evocative power
emotional self-regulation 119, 122, 124, 209, 212, 300
empathy 176, 188–89, 211, 212; art promoting 62, 88, 103, 282; of artists 257; Christine (Mädi) Olden and 30; of Edith 90, 150; Edith and 73, 110, 118, 144–45, 162, 175, 189, 224, 280, 301; in groups 191, 237, 238, 241, 243, 277, 279; puppets, puppet-making, and 237, 238, 241, 243; third hand and 144–46
empathy exercises 145, 162, 175, 189; *see also* dark, artwork done in the
English language, Edith and the 109, 160
Erikson, Erik H. 50, 53
Ernst, Max 132n1
evocative power (of visual communication) 207; of art based on personal experience 99, 102; case material 87, 123, 173, 176, 180, 256; as criterion for art quality 99, 102, 111, 249, 256; within a formed expression 190; nature of 99, 102; sublimation and 116
Exceptional Children Exceptional Art: Teaching Art to Special Needs (Henley) 160

fair in the rubble of urban renewal xx, *xx*
fairy tale (art exercise) 68
fairy tales 9; Edith on 168; Edith's use of 10, 33, 35; read by Edith 167–68, 236
fairytale creature, Edith compared with a 287
fascism 178; *see also* Nazi Germany

328 Index

Feitelberg, Sergei 26
Fenichel, Otto 26, 27
film stills *27, 28*
Fixed Oven (tempera on paper) 137,
   139
flexibility 41, 276; of art therapists 87;
   of artists 259; Edith on 2, 86–87;
   Edith's 2, 6, 41, 312; as the essence
   of art and of psychotherapy 6,
   86–87; *see also* mindfulness
flow state, getting into the 311
flowers 123; reproduction of
   O'Keeffe's 122, *122*
Fogel, Gerald 120
folk art 247–48, 256, 269
Fonagy, Peter 122
form 71
formed expression 177, 180; artistic
   development and 136; definition
   and nature of 136, 190; Edith and
   136, 137, 173, 175, 178; Edith
   on 190, 211; as ego skill 136; goal
   of achieving 136; quality of 173;
   struggle for, in Edith's artwork 86;
   sublimated 137–39; three criteria of
   174; *see also* "miracles of art"
formed expression doctrine 177
France 179–81
Frank, Arthur 237
Freeman, Roland 256
Freud, Anna 24, 26, 53, 116, 290
Freud, Sigmund 131; on art 149, 150;
   on drives 116, 122, 126, 128, 149;
   Edith and 7, 75, 116, 149, 310; on
   sublimation 115, 122, 126, 128,
   131, 149–50
Freudian theory of art therapy class,
   Edith's 205
fruit 171, 172, *172*, 173
Furman, Erna 38–40, 44, 289–91;
   Art as Therapy with Children
   (Kramer) and 38, 39, 289–90; letter
   to Edith 289–90; at Terezin 38–40,
   288–90
Furman, Lisa 1

Ganesha (Ganesh) 280–81, *281*
Gardiner, Muriel 289
George Washington University
   (GWU) Art Therapy Program 93,
   205, 209
German, *Art as Therapy with Children*
   translated into 141, 142

Giacometti, Alberto 128, 131
Giant Steps Program 195–97, 203–4
Glanville, Edward 2, *242*
Glass, Philip 177
"gleaning the pearls" (of art making)
   163, 165
Gombrich, Ernst 159
Graphic Studio 206, 207
Great Depression 179
Green, Arthur 262–63
Greenacre, Phyllis 257, 259
Greenberg, Anna 167–68, 170
Greenberg, Larry 167, 169–70
Greenwich Village xvii, 91, 260
Griffith, Melissa Elliott 253, 273
group ego 261
groups *see* art therapy group(s)
Grundlsee, Austria 24–27; Christine
   (Mädi) Olden in 23, 25, 29;
   description of 7; Edith's experiences
   in 7, 23, 24, 27–29, 92, 165, 305;
   Edith's residences in 287, 295, 305;
   influence on and importance to
   Edith 7, 275
Gulag (Siberian work camps) 239
Gutmann, Ruth *292*

Haaken, J. 20
Hammerschlag, Trude 91
Hansson, Ingegerd 305
Hartmann, Heinz 116, 136–37
Hattwick, L. W. 50
Hector, case of 195–96; early works
   196; identification 197–98; mother
   201–4; secret story 198, 200–201;
   sublimation 196–97; transference
   198
Heller, Peter 24
Henley, David 83–86, 90, 226; cover
   art 150–52, *151*; Edith and 24, 83,
   86, 90; Geoffrey Thompson and 83,
   86, 90
Hill, Adrian 51
Hinduism 280–81
Hitler, Adolf 17, 18, 25, 39
Hoffman, Hans 155
Holocaust 7, 19, 20, 25, 38, 45n2,
   131, 150, 179, 214; *see also*
   Dicker-Brandeis, Friedl: death;
   Theresienstadt concentration
   camp/Theresienstadt ghetto;
   World War II
House–Tree–Person test 167

Howorth, Lisa 270
Hull, L. V. 251, 253, 254, 263–64, *264*, 270
humility, cultural 258, 259

Il Porto ADEG (Association for Youth in Existential Distress) 297; evolution 78
independent thought 312
inner consistency (of expressive authenticity) 111, 181, 190, 207, 249–50; case material 123, 173, 176, 248, 256; as criterion for art quality 99, 102, 111, 171, 249, 256; of Edith's moral principles 210; and expression of inner truth 250; within a formed expression 190, 211; lack of 152, 248; nature of 99, 102, 152; sublimation and 116
inner life 4, 310; art as bringing out 4, 71, 73; Edith on 4, 71, 73, 76
intellectualization 117
internalization 301; *see also* ego ideal(s)
internships 61, 162, 298, 301
interpretation 166, 206; sublimation and the role of 118–19; *see also specific topics*
Irwin, Elisabeth xvii
isolation of affect 117
Italy *see* Lyceum; Turin
Itten, Johannes xvi, 40–41, 188, 294

juniper tree print (Kramer) 313, *313*

Kaplan, Donald 120, 123
Katan, Anna 291
Kazery, Eyd *267*
Kim, Jee Hyun 307
King, B. B. 251
King, Martin Luther, Jr. 11
Klee, Paul xxii, 150, 293
Klein, Melanie 128
Klier, Elfie 307
Kohut, Heinz 124
Koko (gorilla) 159–60
Kramer, Edith *75*; 2014 NYU Symposium honoring 23; aesthetic criticisms 64 (*see also* logos); anger 160; anticipating current therapies 193; on art 171; art criticism and 150, 160, 190; in art therapy 226–27; as artist 33, 85–86

(*see also* artwork of Edith Kramer); artistic influences 188–89; birth 7, 16; braid 3, *5*, 67, 163, 166–67, 228, 288, 295; central mission of her teaching 68; characterizations of 7, 11, 24, 37, 66, 67, 83, 150, 156, 163, 166, 168, 287, 310, 321; childhood 7, 16–20, 23–29, 91, 168; as co-therapist 107–8; collected papers placed on the coffin of 303, *304*; collection of children's artwork 318, *319*; contemplative capacities of experiencer–observer–responder 206; credo in art/artist's credo xxii, 52, 150, 154, 155; daily life 65, 86, 94–95, 169, 305, 310; death 93, 303, *304*; dress 65, 166, 288; early jobs and employment 9; education 24, 25, 91, 109; escape from Europe to New York 9, 19–20, 86; experience of being painted by 167; family background 16, 24–29; gestural warm up 166; health problems 95, 179, 305; hearing loss 70, 179; holiday observances 168; honors 11; identity as an artist 168–69; injuries 94, 95, 226; interpretations of art 166; Jewish background 56; legacy 1, 10–11, 44, 83, 283, 297, 298, 300, 308, 321; life history xvi–xxi, 91; life lessons 167, 310–16; as medical patient 226–27; memorials for 2, 317; as mentor 108; on mentors 8; nickname ("Mumi") 308; parties and other gatherings held by 164, 168; passion 34, 35, 91, 95, 98, 108, 161, 179, 311; people's first meetings with 29, 33, 59, 83, 162, 166, 185, 196, 205; people's internalizations of 317; personality 7, 8, 15, 21, 24, 34, 35, 37, 58, 65, 67, 92, 109, 144, 160–61, 166, 167, 170, 205 (*see also* flexibility; openness); philosophy of life 167; photographs of *3–5, 34, 64, 66, 69, 142, 169, 234, 242*; physical appearance 65, 67, 83, 163, 166, 288–89 (*see also* braid); portable studio 168, 312; portrait of, by art therapy student *302*; psychoanalysis with Annie Reich 8–9, 33, 35; psychoanalytic

330 *Index*

studies with Annie Reich 91; in the quietness of her studio *3*; relating to clients in art room 190–91; residences/homes 35, 37, 169 (*see also under* Austria; Grundlsee); retirement 67, 107, 119, 178–79 (*see also* Austria: Edith's retirement in); as role model 53, 303; settings in which she would draw 5, *312*; social criticisms 160; SoHo studio loft at 95 Vandam Street (*see* Vandam Street studio loft (Soho/ Tribeca, Manhattan)); storage and preservation of the work of 307–9, 318–21; studio on Delancey Street (Manhattan) 164; studios 93, 210, 214, 263; summerhouse in New Hampshire 33; teaching techniques 189–90; travels in Europe 305; types of art she disliked 67; values and aspirations 15, 18, 21–23, 67, 236; voice 162, 205, 228; willingness to create new points of view 6; writings 51 (*see also specific publications*); *see also specific topics*
Kramer, Richard (father) 16, 24, 26, 28, 63, 179
Kramer (Neumann), Josephine (Pepa) (mother) 16–18, 24–26, *27*, 28, 37; suicide 18–20
Kris, Ernst 116, 127, 308
Kuchuk, Haim Efim 20–21

Lachmann, Frank M. 119–120
Lagerlöf, Selma 314
Landscape: The Alps (Kramer) 89, *89*
landscape painting 169, 186, 198, 210, 225
language and terminology 109; psychoanalytic 233; *see also* English language
learning (in art therapy): about others 103; about self 102–3; about the world 103–4; *see also* mistakes
Lee, P. L. 230
Levy, Bernard (Bernie) 63, 207
libidinal mobility of artists 259
Liesl, Aunt *see* Neumann, Elisabeth
life's obstacles, turning around 314
Little Red School House xvii, 9
Loewald, Hans 120, 126–27
logos *299*; AATA conference 64, 109, 160

Lorenz, Konrad 120, 159
Louis XVI of France 179–81, *180*
Loveless, Richard 206
Lowenfeld, Viktor xvi, 43, 49, 50, 206, 207
Lyceum 297; Edith's influence on students at 302–3; Three-Year Training Program in Art Therapy with a Clinical Orientation 298, 300–301; Two-Year Training Program for Experts in Art and Expressive Laboratories 298–300

Mädi *see* Olden, Christine
Mahler, Margaret S. 120, 159, 177
Makarova, Elena 20
Makarova, Manja 303
"Making Choices" (Lee) 230
Malchiodi, Cathy 133, 297
Marie Antoinette 179–81, *180*
Marxism 24; *see also* communism
Maslow, Abraham 263
May, Rollo 311
Mayer, Fredi 26, 27
Mayer, Josi 26
McCann, Laura 317–19, *319*, 320, *320*
McFarland, Margaret 50
medical student(s): reaching out to patient in distress *279*; training in art therapy groups 276–82
meditation 171, 209–12; art and 68, 188, 209–12; defined 209
Metropolitan Transportation Authority (MTA) 96, 97
middle knowledge 215
Milan, Italy 78, 297–99; *see also* Lyceum
Miller, Joyce Ann 270
Miller, M. 17–18
Milner, Marion 50
mindful awareness practice 205
mindfulness: art and 209–10; defined 209
mindfulness meditation 211; *see also* meditation
"miracle of sublimation" 117; *see also* sublimation
"miracles" 146, 185
"miracles of art" 190; *see also* formed expression
Mississippi, self-taught artists in 250–57, 261–67, 269–70, 273

Index 331

mistakes: admitting 144; learning and growing from 163, 209; willingness to make 256
Mondrian, Piet 293
moods of child, observing 191
mosaic making 95, 96, 98
mosaic of 14th Street Subway Station. xxi, 187
mosaics of life, Edith's images as 91
mother and child: clay sculpture depicting (Barbara) *78*; Edith's painting of 74, *75*
Mother and Child (Hector) 202, *203*
mother–infant relationship 119, 124
mourning *see* cancer patients
Mu Ch'i Fa-Ch'ang 171–73, *172*
Muhammad, A. J. 265–66
"Mumi," Edith nicknamed 308
mutual regulation 119, 124, 212

Nachtraeglichkeit (deferred action/retroactive revision) 131
Nash, Geraldine 264
Naumburg, Margaret 15, 50–51, 59, 60, 156, 228, 233, 250
Nazi concentration camps 45n2, 54; *see also* Theresienstadt concentration camp/Theresienstadt ghetto
Nazi Germany 17–19, 25, 39, 86, 177, 178, 303, 308
Nazi-occupied Austria xvi, 15, 20, 89, 179, 308
Neumann, Elisabeth (Aunt Liesl) 17, 37; Edith and 9, 24, 37; Edith living with, in Berlin 16–17, 24; Edith on xxi, xxii, 25; in Grundlsee film 26; influence on Edith 17; interactions with Edith xxi, 9, 24, 26, *28*; overview and characterizations of 17, 24, 308; photographs of *27*, *28*, 308; portraits of 26; residences xxi, 16, 26; Siegfried Bernfeld and xxii, 17, 24–26
neuroscience, Edith's intuitions confirmed by 300
Nevelson, Louise 63, 128–30
New Hampshire 33
New York City 6; Edith's departure from (*see* Austria: Edith's retirement in); *see also specific topics*
New York City Subway *see* Spring Street Station; subway(s)

New York State Education Department 60
New York Transit Museum 93, 96, 307
New York University (NYU) 60, 107; 2014 Symposium honoring 23; memorial service for Edith 317
New York University (NYU) archives 29
New York University (NYU) Art and Art Education Department 59–60; Graduate Art Therapy Program started by Edith 59, 60, 67; NYU method 189
New York University (NYU) Bobst Library Archives 175, 179, 307, 308, 320
New York University (NYU) Graduate Art Therapy Program 60–61, 65, *66*, 78, 185, 189, 297, 307; Edith teaching at 2, 59–61, *64*, 107, 115, 116, 133, 141, 162, 171, 294, 308, 318; faculty 59–63, 65, *66*, *69*, 72, 78, 126, 151, 185, 297, 307; students 56, 59–61, 63, *64*, 65, *66*, 107, 141, 162, 166, 171, 223, 228, 230
New York University (NYU) libraries 318
"no-fail" art 101
Norris, Carolyn 263, 271
Norton, J. 221
Noy, Pinchas 127

oil paintings *165*; by Edith *xx*, *57*, 87, *88*, 153, *154*, 155, *176*, 291; Edith on xx
Okanagan 258–59, 262
O'Keeffe, Georgia 121, *121*, 122, *122*, 152
Olden, Christine (Mädi) 23, 26, *27*, 33; Edith on 29–31; Edith's relations with 23, 29–31, 33; in Grundlsee 23, 25, 29; importance on Edith's life 29–31, 317; lake house 23, 25–26, *27*, 29
openness 312; of art therapists 87; Edith's 6, 92; as the essence of art and of psychotherapy 6, 86–87
organic/inorganic (art exercise) 68
Orgel, Shelley 289
ovens 137, 138, *139*

332 Index

Pacher, Michael 118
Parin, Paul 259, 260
Paris xvii, xviii, 131, 248; fountain in 249
passion: Edith's 34, 35, 91, 95, 98, 108, 161, 179, 311; following your 311–12
patience 67, 95, 98, 167
Pearce, Shannon 307
pearls *see* "gleaning the pearls"
Pepa *see* Kramer-Neumann, Josephine
Perkins, Hana 291
Philip IV of Spain 175
photographs, paintings created from 34
photography, Edith on 5
Pittsburgh Child Guidance Center 51
place, sense of 253, 275, 277; art as therapy approach restoring 275; art room leading to a 283; clay's usefulness in reconnecting to 280; Edith and 269, 275, 283; life events disrupting 275–76; strengthening 269
play 25; art and 35, 252; in art therapy 25, 134; child 134, 137, 143; life lessons from Edith related to 312, 315; Margaret Dennis and 251–52; stage 263; Winnicott and 134, 143; work and 35
Polier, Justine Wise xix
Portrait of Sebastián de Morra (Velazquez) 175
positive psychology 193
posttraumatic stress disorder (PTSD) 192–93, 196, 197, 200–202; *see also* Hector
Potash, Jordan S.: painting by the sister of 100, *100*
Prague 288; bohemian environment xvii; Edith in 8, 18, 20, 27, 91, 150, 277, 288–89; Edith's family in 188; Elena Makarova in 39; Friedl Dicker in 8, 18, 25, 39, 43, 91, 150, 188, 214, 277, 288–89; work with children in 8, 9, 18, 39, 43, 188, 277
predation 198, *199*, 200
pregnancy 167, 261, 271, 281–82
Pregnant Woman in the Bath Tub, The (Kramer) 222
priest, sexual abuse by 198, *199*, 200

Priests and Nuns in Catholic Heaven (Hector) *199*, 200
primary process 116, 127, 149
Process and Product: The Art of Edith Kramer (2009 exhibition) 83, 85–87, 89–90
Pruznick, James 85, 307
psychiatry residents 276
psychoanalysis 61, 209, 214; Edith on art and xxi–xxii; Edith's study of 35, 91; as part of Edith's heritage 8–9; *see also* sublimation: psychoanalytic theory and the psychodynamics of
psychoanalytic terminology 233
Psychodynamic Processes in Art Therapy (course) 159, 170
Psychodynamic Theory (course) 171
Psychodynamically Oriented Art Therapy (course) 64
psychotic patients 115, 117, 119, 196
puppets and puppet-making 236–43, *242*, 272, *272*, 273; devil puppets *190*, 272, *272*

quality: in art 98, 190; criteria for 99; as a defining feature in art therapy 98–102; implementing a sense of quality in art, life, and language 108–9; importance in art and art therapy 247–57; and inner satisfaction 247–57
questioning everything 312
quilts 255, 256, 264–66, *265*, 271

Rambert, Madeleine 50
Rankin, Hystercine 255–56, 264–65, 271
Rauschenberg, Robert 206
reality testing 233
reconciliation and sublimation 118, 123, 128
reflections 89–90
regression in the service of the ego 116, 127, 173
Reich, Annie 8–9, 26, 27, 33, 35, 91
Reichmayr, Johannes 7, 23, 25–27
Reik, Theodor 143
religion 198, *199*, 200, 250–53, 270–74, 280–81
Rembrandt 293, 294
resilience 314
Richards, M. C. 207

Index 333

Ricoeur, Paul 119
Riefenstahl, Leni 177–78
risks, taking 312
Robinson, W. Earl 262
Rodin, G. 215
Rogers, Fred 50
Rol-Tanguy, Colonel 131
Roosevelt, Eleanor xix, 9, 308
Rosenquist, James 206
royalty 175, 179–81, *180*
Rubin, Judith (Judy) A. 11, 63, 159, 297

Saff, Donald 206
Schaverien, J. 221
Schehr, Jill 6, 65
Schwarzwald, Eugenie 91
sculptures: Edith's 167; family 167
secondary process 127
Selassie, Haile 10
selective incompetence, Edith's philosophy of 62
self, learning about 102–3
self-expression: viewing life as an opportunity for 312; *see also* inner consistency
self-image revealed through art 10
self-portrait(s) 112, 217, 220; creating a head self-portrait in the dark 68; disguised 10; of Edith 87; and establishing identity 196
self-regulation 119, 122, 124, 209, 212, 300
self-taught artists in Mississippi 250–57, 261–67, 269–70, 273
separation vs. connection 259
setting conducive to creative work, creating a 143
sexual abuse by priest 198, *199*, 200; *see also* Hector
Shapiro, Shauna 209
Siberian work camps (Gulag) 239
Singer, Franz 43
Six Persimmons (Mu Ch'i) 171, *172*, 173
Sobotka, Harry 26
social issues 85–86
Sontag, Susan 178
Soviet Union 287–96
special education, teaching art in 160
Spero, M. H. 221
Spitz, René A. 120

Spring Street Station (IRT Lexington Avenue Line) 289; mosaic at 93, *94*, 96–98, *97*, 289
stage play 263
Sterba, Richard 209
Stern, Daniel 120
Stern, F. 16
still life 164
Still Life with Etching Plates (Kramer) 87, *88*
stillness 3, 250; Edith and 269, 313; Edith on the importance of 4, 310–11; fostered by Edith 9–10
stills, film 23, *27*, *28*
Stone, Elizabeth 297
Stroyman, Herschel J. 2, *34*, 308
sublimated formed expressions 137–39; *see also* formed expression
sublimation 132, 155, 156, 159; as an evolving concept 116; art therapy process and 120; case material 120–23, 131, 137, 149, 155, 173, 187, 189, 208, 233, 239; components 117; conceptions of 21, 115, 116–17, 119, 127–30, 136–37; creative/therapeutic transformation and 109; definitions 116, 119, 122, 126, 127, 136, 149; development of Edith's theory of 17, 21; Edith and 30, 149; Edith on 115–18, 123, 126, 136–37, 155, 173, 187, 189, 196–97, 208, 233, 301; Edith's 155; Edith's clinical use of 17; Freud on 115, 122, 126, 128, 131, 149–50; Hans Loewald on 120, 126, 128; historical arguments over the meaning of 119; nature of 128, 149, 155; nonverbal communication and 118; not all artwork achieves 117–18; psychoanalytic theory and the psychodynamics of 115–19, 126–28, 136–37, 149–50, 155; reconciliation and 118, 123, 128; and resilience 280; and the role of interpretation 118–19; self-awakening and 171; strengthening 280; supporting the patient's capacity for 117, 144; symbolization and 129–30; therapeutic therapist, mother–infant relationship, and 124; transformation and 109, 116,

334 Index

118–20, 122, 123, 126–32, 136, 155, 233; writings on 120, 126, 128, 206

subway paintings xvi, 6, 93, *94*, *97*, 114, 153, 154, 187, 289; ceramic figures in subway 187, *187*

subway(s) 93, 96, 153, 187; Edith riding the 6, 86, 95, 187; Edith working on the 291, 312; exploration of people in 187; IRT section of Union Square Station 96–97; *see also* Spring Street Station

superego: American vs. European 53, 260; Edith on 31, 53, 236; Edith's 315; judging/punitive 221, 260; kindly/caretaking part of 31, 236, 260, 315, 317, 321

Taiwan, art therapy in 228–30, 232, 234, 235, 235n2

Talwar, S. 282

teapot, Edith's *4*

Teller, Susan 307

Terezin 150; *see also* Theresienstadt concentration camp/Theresienstadt ghetto

Terezin, Czechoslovakia 290

terminally ill patients *see* cancer patients: terminal; ego functions/ego functioning: therapist taking over

therapeutic alliance *see* working alliance

therapeutic relationship 124; *see also* *specific topics*

"therapist," etymology of the term 142

Theresienstadt concentration camp/Theresienstadt ghetto (Terezin, Czechoslovakia) 19, 38, 45n2; beginnings of art therapy with children in 303; children's artwork from 44, 214, 288, 291; Erna Furman at 38–40, 288–90; Friedl Dicker-Brandeis and 8, 38, 39, 42–44, 54, 214, 289, 291, *292*, 303; overview 38; work with child survivors of 290; work with children in 8, 38, 39, 42, 44, 150, 291, 314

"third eye" 143–44

third hand 146, 212, 318, 319; concept of 111, 144; defined 135, 143; Edith on 135, 143–45, 211, 301; efficacy of 86; empathy

and 144–46; functions of 144; meditation and 212; mindfulness, interpersonal jazz, and 211–12; nature of 135, 143, 145, 211, 230; and transformation 144, 146; use of 135, 144

third hand interventions 144, 148

third hand theory 211

Thurber, James 127

time, perception of the passage of 170

transference 198; *see also specific topics*

transformation 128, 216, 230–32, 237; sublimation and 109, 116, 118–20, 122, 123, 126–32, 136, 155, 233; third hand and 144, 146; of the visual into poetry 150, 153; *see also specific topics*

transitional objects 129, 220

transitional space 7, 130, 143, 217

trauma patients 118, 192–93; *see also* Hector

tree(s) xx, 167, 186, 208, 273; apple 234; blooming 293; bottle 267, *267*; Christmas 34, 65, 168, *169*, 170; Edith's instructions to draw 228–29; Edith's painting of juniper 313, *313*; Hector and 196; painting oneself as a 196

Triumph of the Will (Nazi documentary) 177–78

truth: art and 190; joy in 190; *see also* inner consistency

Turin, Italy 63, 71, 78, 297

Ulman, Elinor 6, 52, 56, 63, 64, 160; *Bulletin of Art Therapy* founded by 50; Edith and 51, 53, 160; Edith on 160; Edith's interactions with 53, 64, 65; Edith's tribute to 160; as editor 51, 56, 63, 160, 227; fan letter to Edith from 308; health problems 205; Michael Franklin and 207; talks 65

Ulman Personality Assessment Procedure 189

Uneasy Sleep (Kramer) 153, *154*, 155

University of California Los Angeles–Santa Monica Hospital (UCLA-SM) 217, *217*; *see also* cases: Henry

University of Mississippi Medical Center (UMMC) 276

University of South Florida (USF) 206–7

Upon Leaving Chicago (Henley) 151, *151*
urban lifestyle, harmful effects of 186
urban renewal xx, *xx*, xxi

Valdre, Rossela 128, 130
van Gogh, Theo 296
van Gogh, Vincent 296
Vandam Street studio loft (Soho/
  Tribeca, Manhattan), Edith's 3, 6,
  35, 57, 64–65, 73, 83–85, 87, 92,
  96, 150, 164, 168, 169, 173, 174,
  186, 289, 291, 295, 296, 305,
  307, 310, 311; Edith in *3*; studio
  assistants 85, 156; treasured objects
  in 84, *84*, 87
Velazquez, Diego 174–77, *176*, 178
Venture, L. 2
Verity, Simon 96
Vermont College, honorary doctorate
  from 11
Vienna *see under* bohemian
  environment
Viertel, Berthold 186

Walsh, Roger 209
war 16, 25; *see also* World War II
War Path (Kramer) 197
Watts, Alan 171
Wells, David 133
Welty, Eudora 269, 275
Westphal, Kirsten 96

Williams, Katherine: granddaughters
  with Edith Kramer subway mosaic
  at Spring Street Station *94*
Wilson, Laurie 6, 10, 15, 19, *66*, 151,
  159, 164, 297, 317; retirement
  party *66*
Wiltwyck School for Boys xix, 237,
  277; Edith at xix, 9, 50, 277, 314;
  Edith's program at 51; Edith's
  stories about 236, 314; Eleanor
  Roosevelt and xix, 9
Winnicott, Donald W. 52, 119, 124,
  129, 134, 143, 173, 233
wisdom, cultural gifts of 258, 266–67
Wonderful Adventures of Nils, The
  (Lagerlöf) 236, 314, 315
work ethic 260
working alliance 143
World War I (WWI) xvii, 7, 16, 24
World War II (WWII) xvii, 7, 9, 25,
  38, 45n2, 86, 91, 131, 186, 214,
  290
Wotruba, Fritz xvi, 24, 91
Wu, S. H. 232

Young Man with Switchblade (child's
  painting) 320, *320*

Zeki, S. 311
Zilzer, Vera 65, 107, 160, 297
Zimmermann, C. 215
"zone," getting into the 311